Studies in Eighteenth-Century Culture

VOLUME 4

Roy McKeen Wiles, 1903–1974

Studies in Eighteenth-Century Culture VOLUME 4

EDITED BY *Harold E. Pagliaro*
Swarthmore College

PUBLISHED for the
AMERICAN SOCIETY FOR EIGHTEENTH-CENTURY STUDIES
by THE UNIVERSITY OF WISCONSIN PRESS

Published 1975
The University of Wisconsin Press
Box 1379, Madison, Wisconsin 53701

The University of Wisconsin Press, Ltd
70 Great Russell Street, London

First printing

Printed in the United States of America

LC 74-25572
ISBN 0-299-06700-9

To the Memory of
Roy McKeen Wiles
1 9 0 3 - 1 9 7 4

Contents

Preface

The fourth annual meeting of the American Society for Eighteenth-Century Studies was held at McMaster University, Hamilton, Canada, from May 7th to 9th, 1973. David Williams, Chairman of the Program Committee, and his colleagues arranged for the presentation there of more than sixty papers on a very wide range of topics. With one exception,* the essays in this collection were chosen from those read at the meeting, the fields they represent including history of law, social history, philosophy, musicology, and art history, as well as English, French, German, and Spanish literary criticism, literary history, or history of ideas.

In collecting the essays for this volume, the Publications Committee of the Society has made no effort to present a special theme or subject examined from the vantage point of diverse specialists. Programs of past meetings of the Society have included a single symposium, whose subject provided both a theme for the meeting itself, and not quite incidentally, a title for the volume of the Proceedings that became at least a partial record of the occasion. But the program offered at McMaster University, much larger than those held earlier, did not give its chief attention to one theme. It comprised, instead of one symposium, several plenary sessions, at each of which a broad subject was discussed; in addition, it included numerous section meetings, held more or less simultaneously, on a great variety of topics. The Publications Committee has sought to represent this catholicity in the present volume, which though a limited record of the annual meeting, is a record nevertheless.

The question what use there can be in inter-disciplinary studies of the sort

---

*Homer O. Brown, "The Displaced Self in the Novels of Defoe," first appeared in *ELH*, 38 (1971); it was chosen by the Society for its annual award as the best scholarly article of the year in eighteenth-century studies.

represented by the Society's annual volume has many answers, no doubt. It is always valuable, of course, to gather information, to know more after reading a book or an article than one knew before. And it is useful, too, to have a sense for work in fields related to one's own. But such reasons for promulgating books like this one seem insufficient. At least it hardly seems rebuttable that fortuitous exceptions apart, every reader of essays outside his speciality will be in no position to do more than acquire an obvious level of information from them. However clear and persuasive the arguments, their implications for the specialist are likely to be beyond the non-specialist, a conclusion that supports a widely held view that inter-disciplinary studies are for the most part only superficially valuable. Such studies may not themselves be superficial, of course; still, only a small part of what they say is likely to be available to the general reader, as I have already suggested. But there seems to be a third way in which these essays may work on the mind. I take the clue from the stated or implied aims of several of the following papers themselves. These do not primarily stimulate the subtle modification of opinions already held by the reader—a response of the sympathetic specialist, presumably. Nor do they offer, primarily, a new body of information—information available to the specialist and the non-specialist alike. Instead, they aim at the conversion of the reader's way of seeing things. The essays by Henry E. Allison, Homer O. Brown, Ralph Cohen, Walter Grossmann, Kathryn Hunter, Martin Kallich, Eve Katz, and Carey McIntosh are among those that in one way or another urge the reader to a new perspective. They do not move him to see an old thing modified, so much as they expect him to view it as radically different from what it has generally been thought to be—which is to say they try to repudiate and replace an established and respected way of seeing.

Obviously almost any essay is likely, in some degree, to do all three things—provide information, modify existing opinion, and convert the vision of the reader. Nor is it necessary, obviously, that an essay be inter-disciplinary (or in an inter-disciplinary collection) in order for it to work primarily at the conversion of the reader's way of seeing. Nor is it true that inter-disciplinary essays invariably do so. But it seems likely that the growing sense, in recent years, that fields traditionally limited by period or genre or art medium have been fields to a great extent arbitrarily limited is a sense that originally developed out of the recognition that established ways of seeing often yield merely predictable and familiar results, which help to reinforce and perpetuate old perspectives. In short, the very auspices under which inter-disciplinary work began to flourish is likely to have pointed to the need for original ways of seeing. For the present occasion, I assume that whether an essay in an inter-disciplinary collection like this one draws on two or more of the traditional disciplines or draws on one alone is probably less important than whether it is written and read liberally, with an open mind—a matter about which I find it awkward to speculate, at the same time that I feel bound to do so.

What it means to read liberally or to see the world openly is a question that breeds diffidence, if not embarrassment, even when the terms involved can be defined. With rare exceptions, to regard the subject at all, experience indicates, is to regard it skeptically or naively. Given this context of extremes, one who steers clear of it may seem sensible, and one who steers into it, childish. But it may be that the very polarity of these choices is a comment on the subject. Maybe it is awkward or embarrassing to consider not because it is hopelessly difficult to cope with—though it may indeed be so—but because the mind has already dealt with the problem it represents, and dealt with it in a way crucial to its own sense of well-being, and at the same time in a way that is unsuitable for public display, and unsuitable for display to itself.

There is an obvious sense in which a fact is only a fact. But there is another in which the thing called "fact" is just as obviously the doubtfully informed identification of a something to be understood by the one who finds it within the limits of his scrutiny. A sunset, food, a number, a book, a person, the weather, are all of them both these things. For the present purpose, the real question is not what are they as *things,* but what does the mind *make those things out to be?* It is probably true that we seldom regard a "something to be understood" except with unconscious reference to past ways of seeing that something. We unconsciously identify what it "is," and instead of deciding *de novo* what it "means," we refer it to what we have customarily thought it to be, and rest content. Self-preservation demands this unconscious routine use of the past, of course. The very perception by each of us that each is a "self" presupposes this continuity of usage and this formation of meanings in perpetuity. Moreover it is certainly true that all practical and many theoretical orders of thinking require this kind of reidentification. But it seems equally clear that unless one breaks this implicit contract with one's own history and with the history of men collectively, there can be nothing new under the sun.

It is a truism that what passes for understanding is often no more than the comfortable recognition of ideas already known, ideas whose power to move us to cognition has long since been neutralized. As I have implied, our technique for defining a thing by referring it to a known may itself be a consequence of the mind's ultimate incapacity to understand in any other way. But it is now a widely held view that it may also be a result of the psychic need to understand "familially." We feel satisfied that all is well if we simply recognize a thing or if we can refer a new thing to the family of things we know and feel at home with. Implicit in the cognition of new things is the disturbance of the psychic order of the perceiver. Presumably one's psyche may be permanently enlarged to include the new thing perceived, or one may still the disturbance by repudiating the newness, referring it reductively to something old, or one may be blind to it in the first place. Given the immense labor and pain of bringing a mind to maturity, particularly an educated maturity, and given the essentially precarious quality of its solutions to the problems represented by profession, family, and whichever of the social and eternal verities it may have considered, would it be any wonder if it were reluctant to admit genuinely new elements into its mechanism? Any wonder if it had a highly developed sub-mechanism for warding them off? And yet there seem to be tranquil moments in every life, during which one sees the world without reference to the secure past—ostensibly immutable deceiver— when one sees with eyes less on the lookout for psychic danger than for whatever will pass through them. Blake calls these the moments "Satan cannot find," and he implies that they alone sponsor new perceptions.

It is obvious that running off unprepared from known to unknown ways is unwise. Almost every one in adolescence has tried at least briefly to find liberty by doing so. And the Fausts of the world have strained to the limits of the experiment. But whether one returns to the high road, as most do, or sticks it out to the edge of things, the result is much the same in that almost none succeed in extracting themselves from their old psychic orientations. In recent years, many young adults have sought to escape from what they took to be the uniform dress and uniform attitudes of their elders. Like the operators on Swift's flayed woman, most of them seem to have changed the surface of things for the worse; but what they meant to overturn—uniformity of perception and behavior resulting from unconscious subscription to group opinion—they have in fact come to celebrate in their own more or less uniform ways. As for Faust, who worked to realize his vision of man uncircumscribed, the failure is equally clear. He coud not conceive a universe without God, when obviously such a universe is a corollary of the principle on which he acts to win his freedom. Or perhaps one had better say Faust ventured beyond the limits of the world for which he had prepared himself psychologically; he wanted absolute liberty, but he could not imagine a universe without moral law, though for a time he seemed to do so. Many have experienced fleeting remission from the control of their established psychic patterns. Relief has not only been short-lived, but from the point of view of functional value, insufficiently or inappropriately remembered.

Unfixing the mind from its fundamental preconceptions in any absolute sense is probably impossible. (I pass over its being thoroughly dangerous.) Each of us depends on these preconceptions for stability, so that they are in one sense "naturally" kept concealed; and the fact of such concealment is of course hidden too, or it is discovered in emotionally neutral conformations and so distanced from our vital centers. The alternative that includes even a partial renovation of the conceptual faculty would require the uncomfortable dismemberment and reconstruction of our "selves," probably for as long as we want to resist intellectual stagnation.

It seems reasonable to suppose that some unconscious sense for the static condition of the self, generally endured without question, has contributed to the expression of several symptoms of perceptual discontent in our time. For the most part this sense appears to have expressed itself non-constructively, if not destructively. The present claim for individualism and the present repudiation of traditional values, for example, seem to me among such non-constructive expressions when the claim for individualism is made by those without individual resources, and when the repudiation is merely iconoclastic. At other times the unconscious sense has found much more immediately useful expression, which has occasionally developed until it includes a consciousness of the very process of which it is a part. Among these I would number educational experiments that grow out of a deep and abiding intellectual curiosity, but not those that merely conform to methods implicit in such experiments. Though having the name without the thing (as Matthew Arnold put it) may do some accidental good, it seems more likely to contribute to the forces of blind uniformity, at the same time that it congratulates itself for pioneering.

If the inter-disciplinary studies of which this volume is a sample indeed developed out of the more or less unself-consciously entertained sense that our fixed psyches and the predictable way of seeing that secures them needed renovation, then they have not succeeded in their basic purpose as I have extrapolated it here. But if they continue the practice of many of the essays that follow by calling for, exemplifying, and discovering the grounds for perspectives alien to their readers, they may quicken a sense for the process of conversion to which I have referred, and they may help to give that process a better understood place in the mind than it presently enjoys. One result may be to improve our partial and intermittent deliverance from habitual ways of seeing. As I have said, most of us have some experience of that deliverance. But none as yet can control the time of its blessing; and the crucial obverse, none can guarantee awareness of its absence.

I wish to thank the colleagues who were kind enough to help with the reading and selection of essays for this volume: Professors George Avery, Hilde Cohn, David Cowden, James Freeman, Timothy Kitao, Paul Korshin, Louis Milic, Henry K. Miller, Jean Perkins, Charles Raff, and David Smith. I owe a special debt to Professor Perkins for seeing the essays of Alice Laborde and Elisabeth Labrousse through the press. Finally, I wish to thank my wife, Judith Egan Pagliaro, for help with proofreading, for a close reading of the preface, and most of all for her support as I did the editor's work during a busy year of leave away from home.

No effort has been made to normalize the form of documentation used in the various essays presented here. There seemed no good reason for requiring a scholar in one field to abandon the form his or her fellow-specialists would expect merely for the sake of levelling to the standard of some other.

Harold E. Pagliaro

Oxford
January 1974

Roy Mckeen Wiles, 1903-1974

Roy Wiles was born on October 15, 1903, in Truro, Nova Scotia; a province noted, like old Scotia, both for its beauty and for the piety and love of learning of its inhabitants. He went to school there, and was an undergraduate at Dalhousie University in Halifax, graduating in 1927. He then spent a year at Harvard, taking an A.M. degree. After a brief period as Instructor at the University of Alberta in Edmonton, where he was also organist and choir-master in the Anglican Church, he returned to Harvard, completing his Ph.D. in 1935, with a thesis on eighteenth-century periodicals—never published, but so authoritative in its fullness and accuracy that it is still consulted and referred to. A short spell back in Nova Scotia, as a church organist, preceded his coming as Assistant Professor of English to McMaster University, in Hamilton, where he remained until his death on 10 March this year: a period of almost forty years.

In 1928 he married Olwen Jones of Springhill, Nova Scotia; they had two sons.

Roy Wiles was one of a generation of teachers dedicated to the establishment of scholarship, research, and speculation throughout Canada. In the early 1930's, only a handful of Canadian universities had large graduate programs; the rest, McMaster among them, were basically undergraduate schools, of slender resources and rather modest aims. Many of the best and liveliest students and faculty tended to drift from the small to the large. Roy Wiles, committed early to the viability of provincial culture, resisted that drift personally, and worked to moderate its effects. He saw that in any university discipline a valid undergraduate program and a functioning, busy graduate school were mutually necessary. It was three decades before his department started extensive graduate work, but from the beginning of his career at McMaster he worked with his colleagues towards an undergraduate English degree that would be a valid training for future specialists and also an ordered, meaningful education for students who did not intend further studies. No one will be surprised that he felt a thorough grounding in eighteenth-century literary studies should be the focal point. Here was a period—largely neglected in the schools—in which a sophisticated and aware society created a literature that was at once lucid and various. It spoke to the young men and women of provincial Canada with the clear voices that Addison and Johnson had used to educate their newly-structured world. It stimulated them with the elaborate modulations of Collins and the manly playfulness of Gay. Certainly, from the eighteenth century much of North American society sprang, and many of the students at McMaster in the '30's and '40's traced their ancestors to eighteenth-century Scotland or Ireland or Wales. The lavish products of Augustan literature, then, were instructive, delightful, and relevant. By 1936 Roy Wiles had created a course, English 2b, described as "A comprehensive study of the main currents of English prose and poetry from the death of Dryden to the publication of the Lyrical Ballads." By 1938 the title had been purified and the boundaries extended—now it was simply English literature "from 1660 to 1800." That year the course enrolled 43 students: a testament to its attraction in a small school. I have a course outline for second-year students, from the old Bredvold, McKillop, and Whitney anthology, which aptly shows the range of his instruction. Much, obviously, from Swift, Dryden, Pope and Johnson, but a large helping of the instructive (various periodical essays and expository poems) and the burlesque joined to provide a delicate lesson in urbanity. Seriousness did not preclude a deft pricking of pomposity, and the sobriety of Ontario life could be graced by the smile of reason.

As an early believer in visual and tactile aids, Roy Wiles always had with him some object to point his classes' imaginations; copies of old books, maps, paintings, coins—splendid shillings to bring John Philips home—and the like. But perhaps the clearest demonstration of the Enlightenment he believed in was his own appearance and style in the lecture room: erect and sprightly, clear voiced and open countenanced, the occasional gesture of a half-raised right hand—in the old days when gowns were worn it seemed that only the wig was missing to make a new, living Kit Kat Club portrait.

During the 1940's and '50's, he and a small group of colleagues at Hamilton developed an English program of enviable quality. But Roy Wiles's energy flowed in many directions. While at Harvard, he had sung with and travelled with the famous Glee Club, under the direction of the great Archibald Davison. From their arrival in Hamilton, he and Olwen Wiles became deeply involved in the musical life of the campus and the city. For twenty years he directed the University choirs, leading them to numerous triumphs, and he played the organ both in the University chapel and local churches. This lifelong commitment he was to see publicly honored in 1971 by his election as a Fellow of the Royal Hamilton College of Music. His service to the church was marked by his fifteen-year tenure of the position of Warden of Lay Readers in the Anglican Diocese of Niagara.

And of course it was during the 1940's and '50's that he undertook the writing of his major work, *Serial Publication in England before 1750.* The preface to this work tells, modestly enough, a familiar story—of research becoming unexpectedly more complex, and of a project's growth from, in this case, an intended brief check-list to a major study and bibliography of a form of publication hitherto ignored by scholars. At the time of publication, it is doubtful whether readers fully realized the implications of his discoveries; that he was presenting evidence of an "information explosion" and how a society coped with and communicated its growing knowledge and awareness to its members. Reviewing the book for *The Library,* Henry Pettit noted a modern way of selling encyclopaedias, and commented shrewdly, "A publishing device which Michael Johnson could offer his frugal customers at the Saturday markets in Ashby de la Zouch in the early eighteenth century and which persists in the American supermarket of today deserves attention." For the serial was a mass medium, and a study of the way it was produced and marketed is of immense sociological significance. Roy Wiles's survey and analysis was timely and well done; naturally pleased by its warm reception, he was, I think, more pleased to see how in the past fifteen years the book has come to have its natural place on the open reference shelves of every library, from the British Museum round the convex world of New Zealand.

Roy Wiles continued to think about the frugal shopper in Ashby—which, far from being at the end of the earth, is indeed at the geographical center of England. As in his personal life in Hamilton he was devoted to a burgeoning world far from Oxford or New Haven, so in his scholarship he became more and more concerned to find and understand the strengths of provincial life in the English past. His painstaking analysis of the provincial newspapers is most fully set forth in his second major work, *Freshest Advices,* handsomely published by the Ohio State University Press in 1965. It is a bumper book, stuck full of jaunty anecdotes and memorable expressions of the country's life and opinions. But beneath the surface constantly is the thesis which he came to hold, and which he expressed in his Rosenbach Lecture, read by James L. Clifford in April of this year; that the newspapers, theatres, concert halls, libraries, and schools of provincial England in the eighteenth century provided the greater part of the nation with its communications, its knowledge, and its enlightenment.

The story of his researches into the provincial newspapers would by itself be well worth telling. Files are widely scattered—in modern newspapers offices, muniment rooms, school, ecclesiastical, and private libraries—usually poorly catalogued and frequently unknown to their present owners. With patience and the instinct of a scholar, Roy Wiles roused dozens of files from obscure, dusty shelves, often leaving behind a surprised and delighted librarian, who had in a few hours become one of his countless colleagues and friends.

With his left hand, as it were, he was also engaged in writing of a more strictly professional nature. It is a happy scholar who produces a best seller —Roy Wiles is probably most widely known for his *vade mecum* of academic mechanics, documentation, and manners, *Scholarly Reporting in the Humanitites,* which first appeared in 1951. Thousands of essays and scores of theses have been better written for the presence of this guide on their writers' desks. Easy to use, clear and good-humored, in its bright yellow cover it is an easily recognized and familiar sight on all Canadian campuses. A similarly useful work is his *The Humanities in Canada, Supplement to 1964,* both a guide to scholarly projects throughout the Dominion and a demonstration of the sophisticated new generation of Canadian scholars. This generation, presumably, is no apter at replying to letters than scholars everywhere, and the immensity and trials of Roy Wiles's task can be well imagined. His vigor and geniality attained the goal. Shortly before his death, he was working with similar vigor on a revised and updated edition.

In 1960, Roy Wiles became Chairman of the English department at McMaster: it was the beginning of an era of expansion through the university world. During his tenure, the size of the department more than tripled, and the undergraduate population similarly increased. Under his direction a graduate program made rapid progress, and the University library holdings in English studies grew in a spectacular way, particularly in eighteenth-century materials. In those fertile days, it might have tempted a chairman to let his department merely flourish like an olive tree, careless of the olive's flimsy roots and fragility. But Roy Wiles foresaw the changing role of humanities studies in the '70's—a student of the eighteenth century will always have a keen nose for revolution—and he took pains to assure the variety and scope of the department, in appointments, programs, and teaching assignments. He was an early booster of student participation, committee decision, and an open administrative structure. As a result he could see, by the early years of this decade, English studies from freshman to the doctoral level undertaken with seriousness and professionalism.

By happy chance, a number of distinguished eighteenth-century specialists in various areas had joined McMaster's faculty in the 1950's and '60's; Roy Wiles was able to become the moving force in the development of a university-wide Association for Eighteenth Century Studies which in the last few years had maintained a regular program, an annual volume, and a reputation for hospitality and vivacity. Since 1969, he had been the Honorary President of this Association.

Roy Wiles had cheerfully filled his administration role in the 1960's, but it was no secret that his preferred positions were before a class and at a library desk. To these he returned in 1967, as a Visiting Professor at Bowling Green State University in 1967-1968 and at the University of Guelph in 1970, and for the rest at McMaster. After his official retirement he remained a cherished colleague, particularly in the graduate program. At his death he had just completed a course, fittingly enough, on Samuel Johnson, whose learning and wit he had emulated for half a century.

Throughout his career, Roy Wiles received a variety of prizes and honors. As a student, he was successively Shattuck, Dexter, and Townsend Scholar at Harvard. In 1952 he was President of the Humanities Association of Canada, and Chairman of the Humanities Research Council in 1960-1962 (he was awarded the Council's Twentieth Anniversary Medal in 1964). In 1962 he was elected to the Royal Society of Canada, and he was President of the Johnson Society of the Great Lakes in 1964-1965 and the Canadian Association of University Teachers of English in 1965-1966. In 1968 he became Honorary Editor of the Royal Society of Canada, and in 1971 he received an Honorary LL.D. of Mount Allison University. When the American Society for Eighteenth-Century Studies met at McMaster in 1973, he was elected President—a position he held at his death. McMaster University had planned the singular honor of awarding him an honorary degree at the Spring Convocation in 1974.

While all these honors pleased him greatly, he was, I think, somewhat surprised by them. He thought of himself as a student of the eighteenth century, rather than the distinguished and creative scholar that he was, and he tended to suppose that it was his subject matter or his University that was being recognized, and not himself and his work. Those who knew him personally knew well how totally he lacked any kind of self-importance. Indeed, one of his most notable characteristics was that he was such a good listener—finding a ready sympathy with varieties of people, and maintaining friendships unimpeded by apparent distances of age-groups, professions, or nations. He was a great traveller: he and Olwen Wiles were familiar and gracious presences at learned gatherings on every continent, turning up—inseparable and tireless—in every corner of the world. His zeal for the journey was a part of his zeal for meeting people of all walks of life and making friends with them. Good travellers abroad, Roy and Olwen Wiles were good neighbors at home, deeply rooted in and involved in many aspects of local affairs. His readers will very properly continue to think of him as a major scholar; those who knew him personally may tend to hold in their memories more the awareness of Roy McKeen Wiles as a Christian and a musician—leading a tuneful life, his undimmed mind and continuing activity through final years of illness until his death founded on spiritual strength and a harmonious decorum.

WRITINGS BY ROY McKEEN WILES

1935

"Prose Fiction in English Periodical Publications before 1750," *Summaries of Theses, Harvard University*, 289-92 .

"Slippers for Cinderella," *McMaster University Quarterly*, 45, 14-22.

1940

"I see by the Papers," *McMaster University Quarterly*, 49, 40-51.

1945

"Enough in Wessex," *McMaster University Muse*, 54, 29-41

1948

"In my Mind's Eye, Horatio," *University of Toronto Quarterly*, 18, 57-67.

1951

Scholarly Reporting in the Humanities, Ottawa, Humanities Research Council of Canada, 50 pp. Second edition, 1958. Third edition, University of Toronto Press, 1963. Revised, 1968.

1955

"Graceful Speech and Golden Apples," *Hamilton Spectator*, 21 May, 9.

1957

Serial Publication in England before 1750, Cambridge, The University Press, xv, 391 pp.

"Eighteenth Century Newspapers: A Neglected Primary Source," *Microcosm*, 3, 1-2.

"Dates in English Imprints, 1700-1752," *The Library*, 5th series, 12, 190-93.

1958

"Freshest Advices, Foreign and Domestick," *Dalhousie Review*, 38, 8-17.

"Sale of a Wife," *Notes and Queries*, 203, 126-27.

"Further Additions and Corrections to G. A. Granfield's *Handlist of English Provincial Newspapers and Periodicals 1700-1760*," *Transactions of the Cambridge Bibliographical Society*, 2, 385-89. Reprinted in *Cambridge Bibliographical Society Monograph* 2, 1961.

Review of P. N. Siegel, *Shakespearean Tragedy and the Elizabethan Compromise*, in *Renaissance News*, 11, 276-77.

1961

Review of L. Dudek, *Literature and the Press: Printed Media and their Relation to Literature*, in *Dalhousie Review*, 41, 85-88.

Review of R. L. Haig, *The Gazetteer 1735-1797: a Study in the Eighteenth Century English Newspaper*, in *Philological Quarterly*, 40, 352-53.

1962

"Perfect Diurnalls," *Dalhousie Review*, 42, 378-84.

1963

"Newspaper Stamps," *Times Literary Supplement*, 19 December, 1054.
Review of M. McLuhan, *The Gutenberg Galaxy: the Making of Typographical Man*, in *Dalhousie Review*, 43, 121-27.

1964

"Measure for Measure, Failure in the Study, Triumph on the Stage," *Transactions of the Royal Society of Canada*, 4th series, 2, ii, 181-93.

1965

Freshest Advices: Early Provincial Newspapers in England, Columbus, Ohio State University Press, xvi, 555 pp.
Reviews of R. R. Rea, *The English Press in Politics 1760-1774* and L. Werkmeister, *The London Daily Press 1772-1792*, in *Modern Philology*, 62, 263-66.

1966

The Humanities in Canada: Supplement to December 31, 1964, Toronto, The University Press, xvii, 211 pp.
"The Earliest Hampshire Newspaper," *Notes and Queries*, new series, 13, 219-22.

1967

"Crowd-Pleasing Spectacles in Eighteenth Century England," *Journal of Popular Culture*, 1, 90-105.
"Felix qui . . . . Standards of Happiness in Eighteenth Century England," *Studies on Voltaire and the Eighteenth Century*, 57, 1857-67.

1968

"The Second International Congress on the Enlightenment," *Studies in Burke and his Time*, 9, 867-72.
"Early Georgian Provincial Magazines," *The Library*, 5th series, 23, 187-95.
"Middle-Class Literacy in Eighteenth Century England: Fresh Evidence," *Studies in the Eighteenth Century*, ed. R. F. Brissenden, 49-65.
"Weekly Entertainments for the Mind," *Journal of Popular Culture*, 2, i, 119-35.
"Manchester's First Newspaper; News from Abroad 1772," *Manchester Review*, 11, 161-66.

"Contemporary Distribution of Johnson's *Rambler*," *Eighteenth-Century Studies*, 2, 155-71.

"Recent Developments in Canadian University Departments of English," *International Association of University Professors of English Bulletin*, 12-14. Continued in 1970, 28-30, and 1971, 3-15.

1971

"Samuel Johnson's Response to Beauty," *Studies in Burke and his Time*, 13, 2067-82.

1972

"The Periodical Esay: Lures to Readership," *English Symposium Papers*, 3-40.

"Provincial Culture in Early Georgian England," *The Triumph of Culture*, ed. P. Fritz and D. Williams, 48-68.

Richard Morton

Studies in Eighteenth-Century Culture

VOLUME 4

The Ivory Tower, New Style

ROY McKEEN WILES

Because most of the sixty or more papers which are being considered during this Annual Meeting of our Society are specialized, I have decided to refrain from making this address one more report on a specific project of research and instead to offer some observations which will, I hope, be of interest to more than one sector of our corporate enterprise. You will be relieved to know that I am avoiding such general topics as unemployment, violence in the streets, pollution, and corruption in government, all of which are very much in the air in our own time and could probably with some interest be investigated as they affected thought and conduct in the eighteenth century. My theme is the Ivory Tower, past, present, and future. Sainte-Beuve's *tour d'ivoire* has for a long time been useful as the scholar's place of contemplation and retreat from unwelcome pressures, but it may have to be remodelled. The reason is that many a scholar who wishes to range freely in the realm of knowledge finds himself hampered in his search for truth if he keeps within the close quarters of the old edifice.

Some months ago, when a group of Canadian scholars undertook to compile an inventory of current projects of research in the humanities, we encountered one scholar who objected to being listed in the section on Classics, though he was member of a Department of Classics and his extensive publications all dealt with a Roman poet. That expert on Catullus protested that his field was not Classics but *Literaturwissenschaft,* and although his protestation

3

was inconvenient for the committee's purposes, we could see that he had a point. Like him, many of us are no longer contented to confine ourselves within a structure that makes it difficult to communicate with others.

Yet I happen to believe that there is still need for *une tour d'ivoire, ein Zufluchtsort*, the Ivory Tower, Old Style. The recognized authority in a particular field must not be distracted from his thorough, intensive study of a person or idea or product of human genius. Research in the humanities and related disciplines will continue to require the independent, sharply focussed inquiry of unprejudiced minds, intent on putting all shreds of evidence on their inferences in order to reach valid conclusions—all of this, naturally, without interruption and with the utmost scholarly integrity.

That word "integrity" reminds me of an entertaining passage in William Congreve's best comedy, *The Way of the World* (1700). If you have recently read or seen that play you will recall that at one point—it is early in the third act—Lady Wishfort hears with some alarm that her maid, Foible, has been seen in close conversation with young Mr. Mirabell, and she fears that Mirabell may have persuaded Foible to betray her. Mrs. Marwood tries to reassure her by telling her that she should not suspect Foible's integrity, but Lady Wishfort cries out, "Ah, dear Marwood, what's integrity to an opportunity? " I shall presently discuss the "opportunity" which I see to be ours; meanwhile a good case can be made for the principle that scholarship of the highest order demands not only integrity in the sense of intellectual probity—which ought to be taken for granted anyway—but integrity in the other sense, which implies undivided attention in order to produce results that will be whole and complete. The scholarly world would suffer immeasureably if the "expert" were to be phased out in this age when so much that seemed permanent is changing. We need, and shall continue to need, the specialist in Diderot, in Lessing, in Vico, in Swift, and in other important personages of the eighteenth century, who must not be left to the dabblers and dilettantes.

But isolation in an Ivory Tower may be dangerous; the "expert" who knows more and more about less and less may be wearing blinkers which cut off areas of research which could reveal important aspects of the whole and complete truth. It may be appropriate for the twentieth-century physicist to block out all but the immediate object of investigation by eliminating distracting elements of the environment; certainly such a procedure is unsuitable for research in the disciplines with which we are concerned. As Francis Bacon, translating Aristotle, said, *"Qui respiciunt ad pauca de facili pronunciant."*[1] That observation, you will remember, came from a man who in a letter to "my Lord Treasurer Burghley," in 1592, wrote, "I have taken all knowledge to be my province"—an ambition which might have seemed reasonable at the end of the sixteenth century but has for a long time been quite unthinkable.

Now what is that "context"? If the student of some particular aspect of the eighteenth-century cultural and intellectual history has to lift his eyes from the page on which he has chosen to concentrate, what must he look for, in what direction should he turn, if he is to correct his otherwise partial view? Samuel Johnson declared in his Life of Cowley that "every piece ought to contain in itself whatever is necessary to make it intelligible."[2] He may have been right; T. S. Eliot said much the same thing in "The Frontiers of Criticism."[3] On the other hand there are those—and I am one of them—who believe that for full comprehension of something written two or three centuries ago one must at least know enough history to perceive the point of a contemporary allusion and must also know precisely what the words meant when they were penned, for it is altogether too easy to read into eighteenth-century records the assumptions and verbal connotations of our own time. One must recognize, moreover, that many of those who left some significant expression of their genius did not themselves live in ivory towers but exhibited a degree of versatility that must be matched by us if we are to meet them on their own terms.

When I speak of the versatility of those who lived in the eighteenth century I mean something less Olympian than the many-sided genius of the intellectual giants of former times. I have in mind the varied interests of a Benjamin Franklin or a Henry Fielding. Neither Franklin nor Fielding engaged in activities quite so diverse as those of Nicolaus Copernicus (1473-1543), who was monk, mathematician, astronomer (sans telescope), physician, advocate of monetary reform, drawer of maps, administrator of episcopal estates. But no one could say of Franklin or of Fielding, any more than of Copernicus, that he was a jack-of-all-trades and master of none. Franklin and Fielding, like scores of their contemporaries in Britain, on the Continent, and in America, achieved eminence in more than one branch of knowledge. If we are to take the full measure of their stature we must come as close as possible to everything they did and wrote.

At last year's Annual Meeting you were told about the various achievements of Samuel Johnson. Let me mention a few other examples of eighteenth-century diversity of interests. Tobias Smollett was not only a novelist but a surgeon's mate in the navy, a physician, an essayist, a poet of sorts, a satirist, a translator, an historian, a dramatist, a traveller, an editor and journalist, and the operator of a profitable "literary factory." Another physician—a less successful one—was also a poet, an essayist, a critic, a reviewer, a dramatist whose best play is being performed again this year at Stratford here in Ontario, the author of a permanently amusing novel, and the compiler of several hack works which brought him many hundreds of pounds. You doubtless recognize Oliver Goldsmith. Most of you can name the man who was a soldier, a dramatist, official Gazetteer, Member of Parliament, knight, moral-

ist, inventor of a method of keeping fish from spoiling while being transported, and the founder of the two most important literary periodicals in the
English language, one of them (the *Tatler*) important because it was the first
of its kind, the other (the *Spectator*) because it was the best. That man was
Richard Steele. And there was another versatile man well known as a prolific
journalist, who was for a time a soldier, a merchant, a manufacturer, a versi-
fier, an essayist, a pseudo-historian, a satirist, an agent of the King, and the
author of several realistic novels. That was Daniel Defoe. All of these lived
and wrote in England. You have already thought of many others in Europe
and America. The versatility which they exhibit stands as a warning that in
order to understand a man one ought to look at all his undertakings.

That is obvious enough. It is likewise obvious that from our point of view in
this Society there would be great folly in neglecting what preceded the year
1701 and what followed the year 1800, since no one can suppose that the
end of one century marked an instant and revolutionary change in taste or
techniques or trends of thought. Time is continuous, and important new ideas
may find their first expression whenever genius produces them, regardless of
the calendar. The past may not be a "burden," to use Professor Bate's term, [4]
but it usually has considerable relevance. How trustworthy would a study of
Jonathan Swift be if the influence of Rabelais and Erasmus had been left
unnoticed? And who could claim our respect as an authority on the significance of Pascal if he neglected the evidence to be found in the following
century?

If I need not labour the argument with respect to the temporal horizons,
the same is true of spatial horizons, for the cross-Channel and transatlantic
and occasionally oriental influences in the eighteenth century must not be
ignored, whether the subject be criticism, music, history, economics, book
publishing, religion, or almost anything else one can think of. The inmate of
an ivory tower will naturally look out of its windows in order to extend his
view in time and space if he is to sustain his scholarly integrity, if his
pronouncements are to be whole and complete.

But looking out of the window may not be enough. And that brings me to
the "opportunity" which I mentioned earlier, though I do not follow Lady
Wishfort in supposing that in seizing an "opportunity" one necessarily abandons "integrity." The opportunity which I have in mind is suggested by
another of Samuel Johnson's observations, this one in the Preface to his
edition of Shakespeare (1765). These are his words: "Every man's performance, to be rightly estimated, must be compared with the state of the age in
which he lived, and with his own particular opportunities." [5] In order to
become adequately acquainted with "the state of the age" we shall from time
to time have to leave our own ivory towers and seek our others. Like the bee
in Swift's *Battle of the Books* (1704) we can profitably range abroad, collecting what will enrich our own productions but doing no injury to the sources

we have drawn upon. And those sources are plentifully diversified, both in the individuals who lived in the eighteenth century and in the period itself. The many-sidedness of the age is reflected in the astonishing array of terms that at one time or another have been used to describe it: the age of prose; the age of satire; the neo-classical age; the age of enlightenment; the age of illusion; the age of reason; the Augustan age; the age of scandal; the great age of forgery; the age of sensibility; the age of improvement—a phrase used in the title of this afternoon's program—; the pre-romantic age; the wickedest age; the age of exuberance; and "that most challenging and puzzling century."[6] The inappropriateness of some of those labels continues to be argued, as well it might. Yet the fact that there are so many "key" words to describe the eighteenth century is not so absurd as it might seem to be; it simply means that the ethos of that century shows itself in many forms; its lineaments are diverse.

In other words one characteristic of the eighteenth century that cannot be disputed in its complexity. That is why a twentieth-century scholar has a distinct advantage if he is at home in more than one discipline. I am not implying that interpreters of the eighteenth century must be masters in each of Lord Snow's "two cultures"—an achievement which George Rousseau has declared to be extremely rare and for most of us impossible.[7] There are some who insist that each of the many divisions of knowledge is in itself a different culture, each with its own vocabulary and investigative procedures.[8] Nevertheless it is gratifying that so many members of our Society—I need not name them—are recognized as trustworthy authorities in related areas of scholarship, such as poetry and music, architecture and history, poetry and horticulture, satire in literature and the pictorial arts.

This combining of solid interests is of course not new. We have always known that it would be foolish to ignore the church in studying eighteenth-century politics, and it is obvious to students of eighteenth-century literature that a knowledge of Greek and especially Latin literature is indispensable for a thorough understanding of what was written by those who had been brought up on the Classics. Some forty years ago Hoxie N. Fairchild published two sizeable volumes in which eighteenth-century poetry and religion were explored together in considerable detail;[9] and about the same time Arthur O. Lovejoy, in the introduction to the first issue of the *Journal of the History of Ideas*, urged that scholars in different disciplines could profitably collaborate.[10] More recently, in the *Times Literary Supplement* toward the end of 1972,[11] John North, Assistant Curator of the Museum of the History of Science at Oxford, deplored the academic barriers which, largely for administrative convenience, still segregate each discipline from all others. He argued, for example, that there are many questions on which historians should seek the assistance of philosophers.

It is the immediate extension of that principle of consultation and collaboration which I recommend strongly. For, as I see it, the opportunity is now upon us in this Society to extend the scope and depth of our individual investigations by consulting scholars in other disciplines than our own. In my opinion more of us ought to be making use of the special knowledge of others who have investigated not only the subject of special interest to us in other countries but also such matters as the size of the population in the eighteenth century, the extent of the reading public, the purchasing power of the franc and the shilling, the political climate, the postal services, and even such things as diet, taxes, weather, the treatment of the poor, sanitation, the workings of the law, book subscription lists, the operation of printing shops—the list is large, too large for any one investigator to deal with adequately. Of course we do take advantage of what the bibliographers and demographers have brought to light (with or without computers), of the careful editing of texts, of the persistent search for biographical details, of what the historians of science, of government, of medicine, of education, of commerce, and of the arts have dug up for us. The process needs to be expanded, and the opportunities are almost limitless. Let me mention one copious source of specific information about "the state of the age" of which little use has thus far been made. That source is the periodical press. I can tell you that a vast quantity of material is waiting to be explored in the newspapers and periodicals, both of which developed enormously in the eighteenth century. And that is only one body of records still demanding examination if we are to continue to demonstrate that many of the facile nineteenth-century generalizations are false.

It is encouraging that the trend toward the interchange of ideas and the intermingling of disciplines has already been firmly set by *Studies on Voltaire and the Eighteenth Century*; by the interdisciplinary bibliography now sponsored by our Society; by the admirable quarterly, *Eighteenth-Century Studies*, now also sponsored by this Society; by other journals, such as the *Scriblerian* and *Studies in Burke and His Times;* by the now firmly established societies—French, British, and Australasian—for eighteenth century studies; by the new Folger Institute of Renaissance and Eighteenth-Century Studies; by the experimental interdisciplinary courses in some British universities and elsewhere; and very particularly by the annual meetings of this Society and its regional branches and affiliates. All of these manifestations of a readiness to enjoy mutual exchanges are exciting both for progress already achieved and for their promise of more to come.

It is that promise of more to come that I urge all members of this Society to recognize; and I am glad to say that I am not the only one to feel confident about the future. In an address at the Istanbul meeting of the International Association of University Professors of English Morton Bloomfield mentioned optimistically "the cross-fertilization of disciplines" and also used the term *symbiosis,* a Greek word used by biologists to mean—as the dictionaries put it—"the consorting together, usually in mutually advantageous partnership, of dissimilar organisms."[12] I am convinced that we can profit greatly from that consorting together; it is in a sense what we try to do in the *plenary* sessions of our annual meetings. While I do not for a moment deplore the arrangement by which we break into sections to hear and discuss communications from members whose interests are the same as our own, what I should like to see is more consultation—perhaps outright collaboration—between individual scholars in *different* disciplines. If each of us tried to master four or five areas of research in addition to our own, there would be danger of superficiality, and the formula which I mentioned earlier of knowing more and more about less and less might be reversed, and the end result would be knowing less and less about more and more. Heaven preserve us from homogenized, two-percent learning! My plea is that individually we establish such cordial relations with specialists in other fields of research that we can on occasion pick their brains and allow them to do the same to us.

Would such practices amount to an invasion of our privacy, an attenuation of our independence, an emaciating of our personal reputations? I see it rather as an opportunity to broaden the basis of our scholarship. We should remain specialists, not with diminished but with increased authority. And who knows but that we might be saved from humiliating mistakes? How many dedicated scholars writing about literature have jumped to untenable conclusions by not knowing that in England there were two considerable changes in the calendar in September 1752? A chat with an historian would have prevented the blunder. As the freshman said at the end of an interview with the President of the University, "It just goes to show that one can pick up an idea from almost anybody." I cannot see that either integrity or independence would be lost or our reputations imperilled by our hobnobbing with exponents of other disciplines.

After all is there any good reason why the "virtuous emulation" that Dryden mentions[13] should not be productive of new insights, exciting discoveries, and fresh interpretations? There are some of you, I am sure, who can testify that such consultations as I am advocating can be not only fruitful but agreeable. Our opposite numbers working in other subjects are not all sour, unapproachable objects of suspicion or envy. You will have heard that when Charles Lamb and a friend with whom he was walking saw another man approaching, Lamb said, "Let us turn down this street. I hate that man! " His companion was surprised and said, "I did not think you knew him." 'I don't,' said Lamb; "I do not hate people I *know*."

And as to the Ivory Tower, what changes are required to improve the opportunities for exchange of facts and ideas? The tower I recommend is not a lofty, isolated column with a narrow, inaccessible lodging at the top, nor is it a squat, windowless, martello tower fortifying the inmate against all comers; it is not a high-rise apartment block filled with would-be but perpetually disappointed troglodytes, nor is it a horizontal condominium complex of separate housing units; it is a single dwelling, with quiet cloisters or pleasant paths leading to the entrances of similar dwellings nearby. It will have a solid oak door which the inmate can "sport" at will to shut out visitors at inopportune times; but it will have a welcome mat at the threshold and a gadget for admitting eager inquirers by opening the door to them when they knock, if their credentials show them to be serious searchers for truth. And if they prove to be "organisms" dissimilar to ourselves, they should be all the more welcome. *Vive la différence!*

The editors of the *Festschrift* which was dedicated to the President of our Society referred to knowledge about the eighteenth century as in a state of "unresolved complexities."[14] In our concerted efforts to understand if not to resolve those complexities some of us will require the Ivory Tower, Old Style, as before; but we should now see the opportunity to make increasing use of the Ivory Tower, New Style, with easier access than ever to other Towers inhabited by scholars willing to exchange ideas. When we seek out, and in turn welcome, that *symbiosis,* that consorting together in mutually advantageous partnership, our scholarship and this Society will flourish as never before.

NOTES

1 *The Proficience and Advancement of Learning Divine and Humane* (1605), in *Francis Bacon: A Selection of His Works,* ed. Sidney Warhaft (Toronto: Macmillan of Canada, [1965]), p. 233.
2 *Lives of the English Poets,* World's Classics (London: Oxford University Press, [1929]), I, 29.
3 *On Poets and Poetry* (London: Faber and Faber, 1957), p. 112.
4 W. Jackson Bate, *The Burden of the Past and the English Poet* (Cambridge: Harvard University Press, 1970).
5 *Johnson on Shakespeare,* ed. Arthur Sherbo, Yale Edition of the Works of Samuel Johnson, VII (New Haven: Yale University Press, 1968), 81.
6 This phrase was used in the announcement that *English Writers of the Eighteenth Century,* edited by John Middendorf (New York: Columbia University Press, 1971), would be available to members of The Readers' Subscription.
7 G. S. Rousseau, "Are There Really Men of Both 'Cultures'? " *Dalhousie Review,* 52 (1972), 351-72 (also published under the title "The Peril of Princes: What Ever Happened to Those Two Cultures? " in the Summer 1972 issue of the *Denver Quarterly*).

8 See for example, F. E. L. Priestley, "Science and the Humanities—are there Two 'Cultures'? " *Humanities Association Bulletin*, 23, No. 4 (Fall 1972), 12-22.
9 *Religious Trends in English Poetry*, Vol. I: 1700-1740 (New York: Columbia University Press, 1939); Vol. II: 1740-1780 (New York: Columbia University Press, 1942).
10 "Reflections on the History of Ideas," *Journal of the History of Ideas*, 1 (1940), 3-23.
11 24 November 1972, pp. 1421-23.
12 The text of Professor Bloomfield's address is printed in the 1973 *Bulletin* of the International Association of University Professors of English.
13 See the discourse of Crites in *An Essay of Dramatic Poesy.*
14 *English Writers of the Eighteenth Century*, ed. John Middendorf (New York: Columbia University Press, 1971), p. viii.

Legends No Histories:
The Case of
Absalom and Achitophel

PHILLIP HARTH

The title of this paper, borrowed from one of Dryden's more irascible contemporaries, Henry Stubbe, is somewhat ambiguous. "Legends No Histories" might easily serve for a Whig interpretation of *Absalom and Achitophel* itself, suggesting that Dryden's account of the Exclusion Crisis in his poem was a pack of lies. My title refers, however, not to legends *in* the poem, but to legends *about* the poem which have passed for history. More particularly, I am going to discuss the most popular and persistent of all legends about that poem, which concerns its occasion and purpose.

Most editions and studies of Dryden's poem today agree that the occasion of *Absalom and Achitophel* was the arrest of the first Earl of Shaftesbury, Dryden's "Achitophel," in July of 1681, just as the occasion of *The Medal* was the same statesman's release from the Tower the following November. They also agree that Dryden's purpose in writing his poem and in publishing it when he did is directly related to the attempt to indict Shaftesbury on charges of high treason four days before he was set free. "It seems clear," writes a recent editor of *Absalom and Achitophel*, "that Dryden's poem was intended and timed to serve as propaganda to prejudice Shaftesbury's case."[1] A random sampling of other modern explanations of Dryden's purpose produces such repetitive phrases as "the design of prejudicing Shaftesbury's

trial," "timed to prejudice the trial," "no doubt timed to influence Shaftesbury's trial," "hoping to influence the outcome of Shaftesbury's trial," and
calculated "for exciting popular feeling against Shaftesbury and thereby
securing his indictment."[2] The nearly identical language in which these syn-
optic accounts are couched suggests the extent to which literary historians
and critics are endlessly repeating a litany each has learned from his immediate predecessor. "Of an opinion which is no longer doubted," Johnson
observed in his *Life of Dryden,* "the evidence ceases to be examined." That
has certainly been true of the case before us, for none of the half-dozen
editors and commentators I have been quoting has seen fit to consider the
reasons behind an opinion regarded as axiomatic. But if we examine the
grounds for this popular belief and retrace the steps by which it acquired the
status of a truism, we shall find ourselves involved in an interesting study of
literary mythogenesis.

Absalom and Achitophel was published on or about November 17, 1681,
the date on Narcissus Luttrell's copy of the poem, a gift from his friend Jacob
Tonson. One week later, on November 24, the case against Shaftesbury was
presented to a grand jury at the Old Bailey. So much is fact; the rest is
speculation: that the close proximity of these two events is not simply a
coincidence, but reflects Dryden's deliberate design. But what was that design?

To the Whigs who dashed off angry rejoinders to *Absalom and Achitophel,*
the fact that the poem was published on the eve of Shaftesbury's inquest was
certain proof that Dryden was trying to inflame public opinion against the
government's intended victim. Less than a month after the poem's appearance,
the Whig author of *Poetical Reflections on a Late Poem Entituled Absalom
and Achitophel,* published on December 14, was indignantly asking: "As to
my Lord *Shaftsbury* (in his collusive *Achitophel*), what does he [Dryden]
other than exceed Malice it self? or that the more prudent deserts of that
Peer were to be so impeach'd before hand by his impious Poem, as that he
might be granted more emphatically condign of the Hangman's Ax; And
which his Muse does in effect take upon her to hasten."[3] But this was not to
say with modern critics that Dryden was "hoping to influence the outcome of
Shaftesbury's trial." Quite the contrary, in fact. According to Dryden's Whig
enemies, the Tory poet must have considered the Whig statesman's approaching indictment so certain that he could slander him without fear of reprisal.
"And if the season be well observ'd, when this Adulterate Poem was spread,"
the Whig author continues, "it will be found purposely divulg'd near the time
when this Lord, with his other Noble Partner [Lord Howard of Escrick,
Dryden's "Nadab"], were to be brought to their Tryals. And I suppose this
Poet thought himself enough assur'd of their condemnation; at least, that his
Genius had not otherwise ventur'd to have trampled on persons of such

eminent Abilities, and Interest in the Nation." Dryden's purpose, then, was to prepare the public for a verdict he regarded as inevitable without his aid.

This was the version of events which suited Whig propaganda in the paper war of 1681 and 1682. Another Whig answer a month later echoed these same charges closely in some execrable verses addressed to Dryden:

> Thou wast Cock-sure he would be damn'd for Ay,
> Without thy presence, thou was then employ'd,
> To Brand him, 'gainst he came to be Destroy'd:
> 'Fore hand preparing him for th' Hangmans Ax,
> Had not the Witnesses been found so Lax.[4]

But in the course of a few years, the charge that Dryden had been engaging in character assassination of a victim already marked for death came to be forgotten along with the memory that the poem had appeared within so short a time of Shaftesbury's inquest, and none of Dryden's eighteenth-century biographers—Thomas Birch, Samuel Derrick, or Johnson—suggested any connection between the two events.

Early in the eighteenth century another piece of information did come to light, however, which was eventually to have important repercussions although its significance was not immediately apparent. In 1716, in a reprint of *The Second Part of Absalom and Achitophel,* Tonson, who had been Dryden's friend, business associate, and publisher, included a note to the reader in which he declared: "In the Year 1680 Mr. *Dryden* undertook the Poem of *Absalom* and *Achitophel*, upon the Desire of King *Charles* the Second."[5] Now even if we accept this testimony, given thirty-five years after the event, as true, it does not, on the face of it, tell us very much.[6] Perhaps the King did ask Dryden to write *Absalom and Achitophel,* but nothing in the account reveals the immediate occasion of the royal request or the purpose the poem was supposed to serve. Although Birch mentioned this information in his life of Dryden in 1736, therefore, he refrained from speculating on its implications.[7]

In 1800, Edmund Malone rediscovered the fact that only a week had separated the publication of Dryden's poem from the proceedings against Shaftesbury. Having been allowed by his friend James Bindley to examine the Luttrell collection with its copy of the poem dated November 17, Malone drew attention to the "critical time" of its appearance "a few days before a bill of indictment was presented against [Shaftesbury]."[8] Malone also repeated Tonson's story that Dryden had written his poem at the King's request, crediting the account to Nahum Tate; but he made no attempt to connect these two facts which now appeared together for the first time. To Malone, indeed, the significant item in Tonson's, or Tate's, information was the year he had mentioned—1680—which suggested to him that the poem was begun no later than February or March of 1681—1680 in the old calendar—long before Shaftesbury's arrest, which in that case could not possibly have been germane to Dryden's purpose. As for the "critical time" of the poem's appearance, its significance to Malone was that popular interest in Shaftesbury just at this moment helped explain why the poem was "read with such avidity."

Seizing on this last suggestion of Malone's, Sir Walter Scott was to show a few years later that Dryden's admirers could draw a more favorable inference from the "critical time" of the poem's appearance than his enemies had done. To Scott the publication of the poem on the eve of Shaftesbury's inquest must have been due to Dryden's deliberate design, but only because as an astute publicist with a keen business sense he had sought a date of publication which would assure maximum interest and publicity for his poem. "The time of its appearance," Scott wrote, "was chosen with as much art, as the poem displays genius," since "the sensation excited by such a poem, at such a time, was intense and universal."[9]

So the matter rested until the middle of the nineteenth century. Then in 1854 there appeared a new life of Dryden by Robert Bell, a journalist and popular historian. James M. Osborn has rightly praised Bell for presenting "some extremely important new evidence about Dryden" but he has also pointed out that he was not "always careful to avoid the quicksands of inference; many times he fell into difficulty where he thought himself on solid ground."[10] So it was in the case we are examining. Fitting together the two discrete facts that the poem was written at the King's request and that it had appeared on the eve of Shaftesbury's inquest, Bell drew a train of inferences which for good or ill was to exert a powerful influence on all subsequent accounts of *Absalom and Achitophel*:

> During the interval that elapsed between [Shaftesbury's] commitment and the presentation of the bill of indictment, the utmost ingenuity was employed to prejudice the public mind against him. It was in this interval, and for this purpose, *Absalom and Achitophel* was written and published. The poem is supposed to have been undertaken at the instance of the king himself; a supposition in some degree sustained . . . by the fact of its having been published a few days before the presentation of the bill of indictment, with the evident design of inflaming the passions of the people.[11]

For the first time, the arrest and commitment of Shaftesbury are assumed to be the occasion of Dryden's poem. Its appearance on the eve of Shaftesbury's inquest appears to Bell, as it had to the early Whig pamphleteers, a sign that Dryden was trying to prejudice the public mind against him, but he goes further, suggesting that this was also the purpose for which Dryden wrote the poem in the first place and for which the King requested it. Unlike the Whig pamphleteers, however, Bell does not assume that Dryden must have considered Shaftesbury's forthcoming indictment a certainty requiring no help from his pen. He thus left the way open for someone else to add the missing ingredient by suggesting that the Tory poet was attempting "to influence the outcome of Shaftesbury's trial."

This man was W. D. Christie, the Whig historian and self-appointed champion for Shaftesbury, who eagerly embraced Bell's story, added the crowning piece, and created the modern legend at a single stroke. In 1870 Christie introduced it for the first time in his life of Dryden prefixed to the influential Globe edition of the poet's works. "The time of publication of this elaborate attack on Shaftesbury," he wrote, "was doubtless chosen for strengthening public feeling against him on the eve of his trial, and increasing the chances of a verdict such as the king wished."[12] The next year Christie returned to the charge again in another life of the poet for another edition of his works, this time declaring that "Dryden's poem was published a very few days before [Shaftesbury's] trial, probably with the deliberate object of inflaming public opinion against him and helping to obtain a condemnation."[13] There can be little doubt that Christie designed his version of events to blacken Dryden's character and win sympathy for Shaftesbury, creating a new Whig legend more effective and more lasting than the one the Whig pamphleteers had hastily pieced together in the heat of the moment. This emerges clearly in Christie's third telling of the story in his life of Shaftesbury: "Just one week before Shaftesbury's happy escape from his persecutors, Dryden had published his 'Absalom and Achitophel', written, it is said, with the benefit of advice from the King, well adapted and probably deliberately designed to injure a formidable adversary who was about to be tried for high treason, and in any case a cowardly attack on a prisoner awaiting trial for life."[14]

Once the tradition was launched, there was no turning back. Subsequent editors and commentators were content to accept Christie's account, divesting it only of the prejudiced colors in which the Whig historian had clothed it. Even George Saintsbury, whose life of Dryden corrects Christie's at many points, accepted the story without question.[15] In this form the legend entered the twentieth century, so firmly entrenched by this time that it had already become a commonplace which the poet's admirers could now turn to his advantage. So Walter Raleigh could praise *Absalom and Achitophel* in 1923 by declaring that Dryden "meant it to do its work, and to procure the conviction of the Whig leader. It is the deadliest document in English literature," he intoned, "splendid in power, unrelenting in purpose."[16]

Legends have a way of accumulating details each time they are retold. In 1946, the British historian Godfrey Davies added some of his own:

Some time in June Charles made up his mind to have Whig leaders prosecuted. His decision did not rest on any popular demand. Addresses and Tory pamphlets had not called for individual victims. Therefore, the King required that his new policy be supported by new propaganda. Having determined to put Shaftesbury on trial for his life, he needed a writer who would make conviction easier by covering the Earl with obloquy .... Therefore, the suggestion is at least plausible that the King turned to Dryden in June or July, perhaps more probably in the latter month .... Thereupon Dryden wrote [and here Davies predictably quotes his own immediate predecessor, Raleigh] "a pamphlet designed to achieve a particular end, pointed to the occasion, topical and allusive in every line."[17]

The King's request has acquired a more definite date, his motives are recounted in some detail, and as the story grows more vivid, it gains in plausibility. We can picture the scene to ourselves, the King turning to Dryden in his difficulty, the poet coming to his aid. It is a memorable account. No wonder that later commentators have accepted it wholesale. Thus a recent critic declares categorically: "This became Dryden's assignment: so to discredit Shaftesbury that it would be easier to convict him of treason."[18]

There is something curiously anticlimactic about the inevitable conclusion to each retelling of the legend about "the deadliest document in English literature." "It failed of its immediate object," according to Bell. Dryden's "calculation was vain," Christie rejoiced. The "pamphlet failed in its immediate purpose," Raleigh explained, for "the Grand Jury threw out the bill." The deadliest document had fizzled out like a squib.

Some measure of the extent to which historians and literary critics alike can be locked in by their own legends is provided by their explanations for Dryden's failure—if it was one. The British historian, Dame Veronica Wedgwood, has suggested, rather surprisingly, that Dryden's artful timing may have been to blame. She has written of the poem: "It came out exactly a week in advance of Shaftesbury's appearance before the Middlesex Grand Jury on a charge of high treason, which seems to allow rather little time for its full impact to be felt, given the small numbers printed and the less advanced organs of salesmanship and publicity known in those days. Whatever the effect of the poem, the Grand Jury refused to find a true bill against Shaftesbury."[19] Within the terms of the legend, this is a perfectly reasonable observation. When we are told again and again that Dryden's poem was calculated "for exciting public feeling against Shaftesbury and thereby securing his indictment," what is meant, presumably, is that Dryden hoped to arouse such intense and universal hostility against the Whig statesman by his incendiary poem that it would be impossible for him to obtain a fair hearing, since any panel of grand jurors would inevitably consist of readers already prejudiced against him. In other words, Dryden envisaged the kind of situation that today would justify the defense in requesting a change in venue. And seven days is indeed a short time in which to hope to accomplish such a design.

It has been more common, however, to suggest that Dryden's carefully-laid plans met an unexpected check in the action of the grand jury. The Whig sheriffs, it is explained, proved so partial to Shaftesbury as to select the grand jury from members of his own party and in these unforeseen circumstances Dryden's eloquent rhetoric fell on deaf ears. The King and his poet laureate had miscalculated.

This notion that the setback to their designs came as a surprise is essential to the legend, since otherwise both king and poet would have been guilty of the greatest folly from the outset. Accordingly, Davies and his successors have insisted that the tide had turned against the Whigs with the dissolution of the Oxford Parliament in March, that a Tory reaction was sweeping the country, that the government was confidently assuming the offensive against a frightened foe, and that Dryden's poem was fashioned as an instrument of the new royal policy. It is time, therefore, to consider just what the King's plans were, the nature of his expectations, and the possibility that Dryden could have contributed to either.

If, in retrospect, the tide had already turned in March, 1681, this was not immediately apparent to the King and his friends, faced with the problem of prosecuting their enemies in the courts by means which were at least ostensibly legal. The responsibility of choosing jury panels for London and Middlesex belonged to the two sheriffs, acting jointly as one officer, who were elected annually by the Corporation of the City of London on Midsummer Day (June 24) and entered office each year on the Vigil of Michaelmas (September 28). In the midsummer election of 1680, the Common Hall of the Corporation, the majority of whose members were Whigs, had chosen as sheriffs Henry Cornish and Slingsby Bethel—Dryden's "Shimei"—both avid Exclusionists. Their responsibility for selecting juries was supposed to be delegated to certain minor officials: in the case of the Middlesex Sessions, held at Hicks Hall and at Westminster Hall, to the undersheriff; in that of the London Sessions, held at the Guildhall and at the Old Bailey, to the secondaries of the two city prisons. But since Bethel and Cornish appointed as undersheriff Richard Goodenough, an eager collaborator, Middlesex juries were regularly assured of a Whig complexion. The two officials charged with the selection of the London juries, Normandsell and Trotman, while politically independent, were nevertheless personally timorous, so that under duress they could be expected to surrender their responsibility to the two sheriffs.[20]

In his portrait of "Shimei" Dryden has immortalized that official's obstructionist tactics whenever the government tried to obtain a conviction:

> If any durst his Factious Friends accuse,
> He pact a Jury of dissenting *Jews*:
> Whose fellow-feeling, in the godly Cause,
> Would free the suffring Saint from Humane Laws.

The situation Dryden describes continued throughout the autumn and winter and into the spring of 1681. Then for a moment light appeared to break. On April 29, Edward Fitzharris, one of Shaftesbury's Irish witnesses to the Popish Plot, was grudgingly indicted under protest by a Middlesex grand jury, and a few weeks later Sir Leoline Jenkins, one of the principal secretaries of state, was able to observe cautiously that although "we are not without our mortifications from the City of London and the Grand Jury of Middlesex . . . that of the City [is] very moderate in comparison of what it was last winter."[21] Soon prospects were to seem even better. On June 9, a Middlesex petit jury convicted Fitzharris, and the time had apparently come for the King to act. Two days later Lord Howard of Escrick was arrested and on June 21 his bill of indictment on charges of high treason was offered to a Middlesex grand jury. But before many hours had passed the government's hopes were dashed. The Attorney General, learning that the jurors were on the point of bringing in a finding of ignoramus, hastily withdrew the bill the next morning and returned Lord Howard to the Tower to await a more favorable opportunity.[22]

The government now turned all its attention to the shrieval elections scheduled for two days later on the 24th. If its plans were to succeed, it was of crucial importance that the new sheriffs, who would assume office the following September, should be favorable to the King's party. In a hotly-fought contest, the government put up its own candidates, Ralph Box and Humphry Nicholson, but to its mortification the Whig candidates, Thomas Pilkington and Samuel Shute, were elected by an overwhelming majority. It was now clear that for the next fifteen months the government's moves must be carried out with circumspection against enormous odds. Their only hope for success lay in a series of cautious maneuvers, probing for weaknesses in their enemy's position, and advancing pawns before they ventured their major piece, the Earl of Shaftesbury. The pawns they chose were two unimportant Whigs, Stephen College, the Protestant Joiner, and John Rouse, servant to Sir Thomas Player, who were arrested on June 29. Three days later, on July 2, Shaftesbury himself was placed under arrest and his home, Thanet House in Aldersgate Street, searched for incriminating papers.

On July 8, the King advanced his first pawn. Stephen College's bill of indictment was offered to the London grand jury meeting at the Old Bailey. Bethel and Cornish, it soon appeared, had chosen its members with their usual care, and a finding of ignoramus was speedily returned. But the government was not easily discouraged. While some of the offenses for which College was charged had occurred in London, others had allegedly taken place in Oxford during the meeting of Parliament there in March. College was now taken to Oxford, where a grand jury proceeded to indict him on July 14. On August 17 he was brought to trial at Oxford and on the following day he was convicted of high treason. His execution took place a fortnight later.

The government's hopes soared. Perhaps Shaftesbury's own activities at the Oxford Parliament in March could yield charges of treason. Rumors that he would be indicted at Oxford began to circulate among the members of the King's party and even to appear in the newspapers.[23] In any event, witnesses were prepared to testify to his treasonable activities in Thanet House in the City of London and it might yet prove possible to reform the sheriffs' jury panels. An attempt of this kind at Hicks Hall on August 26 proved futile in the face of Goodenough's obstinacy, but the new sheriffs, who were to take office in another month, might prove less resolute.

Throughout September and the early part of October, the government's optimism increased while the Whigs experienced growing panic. On October 8, Shaftesbury petitioned the King to allow him to retire into exile on his plantations in Carolina. But the King, sensing Shaftesbury's admission of defeat, replied that the law must be allowed to take its course.[24] He would have done well to have accepted the offer, for the next fortnight was to consist of an unbroken series of disasters for the King and his friends.

Events were about to prove that the new sheriffs were quite as formidable as their predecessors had been. Once installed, they proceeded to appoint as undersheriff Goodenough's brother Francis, who proved in every respect as obdurate as Richard. For nearly two weeks the justices of the Middlesex sessions wrangled with him first at Westminster Hall and then at Hicks Hall over the panel of forty Whigs he had chosen for jury duty and at last, on October 17, they had to admit defeat. No good could be expected of a Middlesex jury this term. The following day, the King advanced his last remaining pawn. John Rouse's bill of indictment was offered to a London jury at the Old Bailey. "It was resolved," the Earl of Longford explained to the Duke of Ormonde, "to taste the temper of this Jury by preferring an indictment against Rouse, in which if there were success, it was believed the bill against my Lord Shaftesbury was to follow."[25] The temper of the grand jury was not long in doubt. It had been packed with obedient Whigs by Pilkington and Shute and quickly returned the bill marked ignoramus.

But worse was to follow. On October 24, the justices at Westminster Hall, worn down by Shaftesbury's repeated appeals for a writ of habeas corpus, at last ruled that he must be indicted before November 28, the last day of Michaelmas term, or be released. The same day the Attorney General gave his opinion that since it had been impossible to discover any treasonable actions committed by Shaftesbury outside London, all hopes of indicting him at Oxford must be abandoned.[26]

Shaftesbury's acquittal was now a foregone conclusion. The government's despair was merely confirmed a few days later when it learned from its informers of the sheriffs' assurance to Shaftesbury's agents that their master had nothing to fear.[27] Halifax gave his opinion that the Whig statesman "had as good be set at liberty upon terms as by a jury, which would be sure to acquitt him."[28] Nevertheless, the government decided, as Longford declared, "to let the world see that the King had reason for his lordship's commitment"; therefore "it is resolved that the evidence against his lordship shall be exposed."[29] But in order at least to minimize a defeat which was now inevitable, the Tory pamphleteers throughout November publicized the certainty of Shaftesbury's approaching release by a grand jury packed with Whigs, lest the government appear to be taken by surprise. A Tory broadside on November 4, for instance, ends with a peroration addressed to his fellow Whigs by the persona of the poem:

> Our Common-Councel lets Summon together,
> To Pannel pack't Jury's, Let's mak't our endeavour,
> For an *Habeus Corpus*, insist on our Power;
> To fetch our Great Patriots out of the *Tower*.
> And then we'le Dispute the Case, for Reformation,
> And make the proud *Torys* Resign us the Nation.[30]

And a few days later, *Heraclitus Ridens,* one of the Tory papers, published another poem, *The Whigs Save-All,* in which another Whig persona declares:

> If we're sworn of a Jury
> To Try a rank Tory,
>   Though no proof, we'l find him ne'r fear it,
> But if by the By
> A Whig we must Try
>   We'l clear him though th' Apostles themselves did swear it.
> If *Tapsky* [Shaftesbury] comes to 't
> I'le warrant ye we'l do 't
>   For the Sheriffs have by their *Mandamus*
> Pick'd up such a Crew
> Of Protestants True
>   That ne'r doubt it the Bill will be found *Ignoramus.*[31]

When the inquest on Shaftesbury met at the Old Bailey on November 24, Pilkington and Shute produced a grand jury for the occasion which offers a model of an ignoramus jury. An analysis of its membership shows why such juries were certain to be proof against adverse influence either within or without the courtroom. All twenty-one grand jurors, needless to say, were Whigs, since the sheriffs had taken over their selection personally from Normandsell.[32] But the core of the jury consisted of a smaller number of prominent Whigs who were figures of importance in the affairs of the City as well as in the fortunes of their party. This phalanx could be depended upon to shelter their fellow jurors from the browbeating expected of Lord Chief Justice Pemberton, who conducted the proceedings, as well as to play the role of party whips in the jury room. The foreman, Sir Samuel Barnardiston, and another juror, Thomas Papillon, had both been leading Whig members of all three of the Exclusion Parliaments. These two men acted as spokesmen for the grand jury throughout the inquest, challenging Pemberton's decisions and cross-examining the witnesses in a manner more appropriate to barristers for the defense. Upon the conclusion of the proceedings, in the words of the court record, "the *Jury* withdrew to consider the Evidence, and return'd the Bill *Ignoramus:* Upon which the People fell a hollowing and shouting."[33]

On the assumption that Dryden was not willfully ignorant of current affairs, we must conclude that he could not conceivably have timed the publication of his poem to influence a grand jury whose commitment to an ignoramus was generally foreseen for at least a month before it met at the Old Bailey. But it is just as implausible that the chances of indicting Shaftesbury could at any time have been enhanced by Dryden's poem or that the King could have suggested, and his poet laureate have undertaken, the writing of *Absalom and Achitophel* for this quixotic purpose. For to assume that Dryden's efforts would ever have been solicited by the King and his friends, even in their most sanguine mood, to aid in the conviction of Shaftesbury is to misunderstand completely the nature of the later Stuart judiciary. The object of the government's unsuccessful maneuvers was not to avoid a packed grand jury but to insure that it would be packed with carefully-selected Tories as immune from persuasion of any kind as were the Whigs actually chosen by the sheriffs. The only hurdle standing in the way of Shaftesbury's certain conviction was in fact the grand jury, since as a nobleman he must, if indicted, be tried by a jury of his peers meeting at Westminster. Unlike the Whigs' victim, Lord Stafford, who had been convicted of high treason the previous year during the sitting of Parliament, Shaftesbury would not have come before the entire House of Lords where he might have been acquitted. Charles's last parliament had been dissolved in March, and in the intervals between parliaments capital cases against peers must be tried in the Lord Steward's Court, consisting of a smaller number of peers chosen by the

Crown. As a government spy discovered, even Shaftesbury, in the Tower, had learned the identity of those whom the King planned to name to that court: the staunchest supporters of the King's party in the upper house, from whom a verdict of guilty was certain.[34]

With only the grand jury standing between Shaftesbury and the block, his opponents considered any means justified which could remove this obstacle so long as it preserved the appearance of legality. We have noticed that the government's efforts during the summer and autumn of 1681 were directed to two possibilities: transferring Shaftesbury's case to another jurisdiction, particularly Oxford, or wresting control of the London and Middlesex panels from the sheriffs. The kind of grand jury they were aiming for in either case can be easily surmised. The King's intentions in the event of an Oxford inquest are starkly revealed by Sir Leoline Jenkins's correspondence on behalf of his royal master during the time that Stephen College's case was proceeding there. In July, a letter of his to Lord Norris, Lord Lieutenant of Oxfordshire and a staunch supporter of the King's party, informed him in no uncertain terms that "His Majesty desires you to have all the care you possibly can" that the grand jury "consist of men rightly principled for the Church and the King."[35] Later, when College had been indicted by a grand jury packed with obedient Tories, Jenkins wrote Norris again to thank him for his "zeal in his Majesty's service" and to declare "Posterity will judge that we owe these subordinate good men to a good lord lieutenant."[36] If the Protestant Joiner was worth such solicitous attention, we can easily guess the kind of care that would have been expended on the selection of a panel for the leader of his party.

Similarly, the goal of the government's efforts to wrest control of the London and Middlesex panels from the Whigs can be judged from the results of a successful renewal of these attempts the following year. In the mid-summer election of 1682, the King's party again put up its own candidates for sheriff against the Whig nominees, Thomas Papillon and John Dubois, both of whom had been members of Shaftesbury's grand jury. This time as the result of a series of extra-legal maneuvers protracted throughout the summer, the Tory candidates, Dudley North and Peter Rich, were declared elected in spite of having secured a minority of votes from the Common Hall. On September 28 the new sheriffs were installed and during the night or early the following day Shaftesbury, his immunity from indictment at an end, went into hiding. As he explained to Lord Howard, who visited him at his hiding place in Wood Street, his life was unsafe "so long as the Administration of Justice was in such Hands as would accommodate all Things to the Humour of the Court."[37] The behavior of the new London and Middlesex juries, now packed with servile Tories, soon proved him right, and a few weeks later Shaftesbury slipped away to Holland, there to die in exile.

In such a situation, with Whigs and Tories locked in a struggle to determine who should have the privilege of presenting a packed grand jury at Shaftesbury's inquest, Dryden's persuasive efforts would have been as needless in the one event as they were useless in the other. The tradition that either Dryden or his patrons ever imagined that a poem could have the slightest influence on such a contest must be dismissed as an improbable fiction.

How are we to account for the persistence of a legend that defies history and even common sense? Legends serve the changing needs not only of those who create them but of those who accept and propagate them. To Dryden's Whig contemporaries, before the modern legend arose, the alleged link between his poem and the proceedings against Shaftesbury had been essential to their picture of the Tory poet as a craven jackal, still smarting from the drubbing he had received in the Rose Alley ambuscade two years earlier for assailing his betters, who only ventured to lampoon the Whig nobleman when he saw him standing at bay, awaiting a fatal onslaught from the King and his courtiers. But to Christie, the father of the modern legend, Dryden's "cowardly attack" would appear more heinous by being portrayed as an advance action against "a prisoner awaiting trial for life" which, as an attempt to prejudice a case while it was still *sub judice*, betrayed a shocking deficiency in that sense of fair play esteemed by his Victorian readers. To understand how later historians, more favorably disposed to Dryden, could have taken over Christie's fiction and turned it to their own account, we might start by remembering that a wish to enhance his subject may entice a historian or biographer into just as much distortion as a desire to denigrate him, and that legends of this kind may serve a larger myth, in this case the myth developed to augment the public poet. This myth, which is a product of our own time, is just as seductive, though not as influential, as that which grew up around the Romantic poet in the nineteenth century, but it is altogether different since the two types of poet are unalike. The Romantic myth that "Poets are the hierophants of an unapprehended inspiration . . . the unacknowledged legislators of the world" depends on the conception of one kind of poet, isolated and apart, the kind celebrated by Shelley when he wrote that "a Poet is a nightingale, who sits in darkness and sings to cheer its own solitude with sweet sounds."[38]

That obviously is not the kind of poet common in the Restoration period and epitomized by Dryden, the public orator who writes occasional poems in which he speaks to his contemporaries on current issues and seeks to influence them. To enhance the importance of this kind of poet, a quite different myth has arisen, that of the counselor to kings and ministers who confide their plans to him, seek his assistance, and depend on him as a necessary instrument of their national policy. If he is Dryden, he responds to crisis by writing "the deadliest document in English literature," a poem designed to effect the downfall of a great public figure and help preserve the state. The public poet as hero and man of action does not simply write about history, he makes it, or just misses doing so because of circumstances beyond his control.

This is not the light in which Dryden's activities were viewed by his earlier admirers. Innocent of any notion that his function was to shape future events, they never exaggerated the role he had assigned to Shaftesbury in his poem. They realized that he had written a poem about Absalom as well as Achitophel, about David and his supporters as well as the King's enemies. For 150 years, they never varied in their view of Dryden's purpose in writing such a poem. For Narcissus Luttrell on the day *Absalom and Achitophel* was published it was "an excellent poem agt ye Duke of Monmouth, Earl of Shaftsbury & that party & in vindication of the King & his friends." [39] For John Mitford, writing in 1832 just on the eve of the legend we have been exploring, *Absalom and Achitophel* was still a poem "the object of which was to gain friends for the King, and discredit the faction of Shaftesbury, Monmouth, and their adherents." [40]

That is a more modest purpose than the other, though not one of which Dryden need have been ashamed. Divested of legend, *Absalom and Achitophel* is not a poem written to influence future action, but party propaganda meant to affect public attitudes toward past events and current policy for which no poet bore any discernible responsibility. This was a goal Dryden shared with other Tory writers in verse and prose who were attempting, in Scott's words, "to place their cause in the most favourable light, and prejudice that of their adversaries." [41] If the King did suggest that Dryden write *Absalom and Achitophel*, it was probably for no more specific purpose than this. Ever since Charles had dissolved his Oxford Parliament in March of 1681 and had issued, early in April, *His Majesties Declaration to All His Loving Subjects*, a white paper defending his action, the government had mounted a massive campaign of propaganda in support of its policy which emphasized that an attempted Whig revolution had been narrowly averted by the King's decisive action. For this purpose it enlisted every Tory writer in its service and it was to be expected that the Poet Laureate and Historiographer Royal should contribute his share to the common effort. If the result of Dryden's labor was incomparably better than that of his fellow workers, this was not because his sources of information were more privileged than theirs or his purpose essentially different, but because he was a greater poet.

The myth of the public poet as man of action can be laid to rest without regret along with the legends that have served it. Their loss cannot affect Dryden's reputation. The measure of his importance, fortunately, is not the extent to which his royal master took him into his counsels and sought his collaboration in accomplishing his plans for the future. Fortunately, for if it were, Dryden would scarcely be remembered today.

NOTES

1 Elias F. Mengel, Jr., ed., *Poems on Affairs of State*, II (New Haven, 1965), 453.

2 James Kinsley, ed., *The Poems of John Dryden* (Oxford, 1958), IV, 1877; Hugh Macdonald, *John Dryden: A Bibliography of Early Editions and of Drydeniana* (Oxford, 1939), p. 20; Ian Jack, *Augustan Satire: Intention and Idiom in English Poetry, 1660-1750* (Oxford, 1952), p. 53; Bernard Schilling, *Dryden and the Conservative Myth: A Reading of "Absalom and Achitophel"* (New Haven, 1961), p. 140; George R. Noyes, ed., *The Poetical Works of John Dryden*, 2nd ed. (Boston, 1950), p. xliii.

3 *Poetical Reflections on a Late Poem Entituled, Absalom and Achitophel* (London, 1681), sig. B1v. The date is that written on Luttrell's copy.

4 *A Key (with the Whip) to Open the Mystery & Iniquity of the Poem Called, Absalom & Achitophel: Shewing Its Scurrilous Reflections upon both King and Kingdom* (London, 1682), p. 24. Luttrell's copy is dated January 13.

5 *The Second Part of Miscellany Poems*, 4th ed. (London, 1716), sig. B2.

6 Tonson's statement receives some collateral support from two other sources. The first is merely hearsay evidence from a priest friend of Pope's reported by Joseph Spence (see *Observations, Anecdotes, and Characters of Books and Men Collected from Conversation*, ed. James M. Osborn [Oxford, 1966], I, 28-29). The other comes from a letter by Richard Mulys dated November 19, 1681, suggesting that the poem was written at the request of Edward Seymour, Dryden's "Amiel," who may have been acting on behalf of the King. See Wallace Maurer, "Who Prompted Dryden to Write *Absalom and Achitophel*?" *PQ*, 40 (1961), 130-38.

7 See *A General Dictionary Historical and Critical*, IV (London, 1736), 680.

8 *The Critical and Miscellaneous Prose Works of John Dryden* (London, 1800), I, i, 141-42.

9 *The Works of John Dryden* (London, 1808), IX, 197.

10 *John Dryden: Some Biographical Facts and Problems*, 2nd ed. (Gainesville, Fla., 1965), pp. 91-93.

11 *Poetical Works of John Dryden* (London, 1854), I, 225.

12 *Poetical Works of John Dryden* (London, 1870), pp. xlviii-xlix.

13 *Select Poems by Dryden* (Oxford, 1871), p. xxxii.

14 *A Life of Anthony Ashley Cooper, First Earl of Shaftesbury* (London, 1871), II, 429.

15 See his *Dryden* (London, 1881), p. 84.

16 *Some Authors* (Oxford, 1923), p. 162.

17 "The Conclusion of Dryden's *Absalom and Achitophel*," *HLQ*, 10 (1946), 71.

18 Schilling, *Dryden and the Conservative Myth*, p. 175.

19 *Poetry and Politics under the Stuarts* (Cambridge, 1960), pp. 162-63.

20 The best contemporary account of these events can be found in the newspapers, particularly the *London Gazette*, Nathaniel Thompson's

Loyal Protestant and True Domestick Intelligence, Richard Janeway's *Impartial Protestant Mercury*, and Langley Curtis's *True Protestant Mercury*. Many, though not all, of these events are also related more briefly by Narcissus Luttrell in his *Brief Historical Relation of State Affairs, 1678-1714* (London, 1857), Vol. I, and in the modern accounts by J. R. Jones, *The First Whigs: The Politics of the Exclusion Crisis* (London, 1961) and K. H. D. Haley, *The First Earl of Shaftesbury* (Oxford, 1968). Valuable information on the legal technicalities involved can be found in Roger North, *Examen* (London, 1740), pp. 89-117 and 582-624.

21 Letter to the Marquess of Worcester, dated May 14, in *Calendar of State Papers, Domestic Series: September 1, 1680 to December 31, 1681, Preserved in the Public Record Office* (London, 1921), p. 277 (hereafter referred to as *CSPD*).

22 See the letter from the Attorney General to Jenkins dated June 22, *ibid.*, p. 325.

23 See the letter of Richard Mulys dated July 11 in Historical Manuscripts Commission, *Calendar of the Manuscripts of the Marquess of Ormonde, K. P., Preserved in Kilkenny Castle*, New Series, VI (London, 1911), 97 (hereafter referred to as *HMC Ormonde*). See also *Impartial Protestant Mercury*, No. 28 (July 26-29, 1681) and *Loyal Protestant and True Domestick Intelligence*, No. 64 (October 15, 1681). The possibility of obtaining an indictment in either Westminster or Southwark was also being considered.

24 See the *Memoirs of Sir John Reresby*, ed. Andrew Browning (Glasgow, 1936), p. 233 (entry for October 13).

25 Letter dated October 18, *HMC Ormonde*, p. 198.

26 See the letter from Longford to Ormonde dated October 25, *ibid.*, p. 208.

27 See the letter of Peter Rich to Jenkins dated October 11, *CSPD*, p. 504, and the information of Laurence Mowbray dated October 28, *ibid.*, p. 538.

28 *Memoirs of Sir John Reresby*, p. 236 (entry for November 6).

29 Letter to Ormonde dated November 15, *HMC Ormonde*, p. 229.

30 *The Whiggs Lamentation for the Death of Their Dear Brother Colledge, the Protestant Joyner* (London, 1681). The date is that written on Luttrell's copy.

31 *Heraclitus Ridens*, No. 42 (November 15, 1681).

32 See the paper by Justice Warcupp, probably dated November 21, *CSPD*, pp. 573-74.

33 *A Complete Collection of State Trials and Proceedings upon High Treason*, 2nd ed. (London, 1730), III, 437.

34 See the letter of Timothy Taylor to Benjamin Herne dated October 20, *CSPD*, p. 524.

35 Letter dated July 11, *ibid.*, p. 353.

36 Letter dated July 26, *ibid.*, pp. 374-75. See also Jenkins's letter of thanks to the Sheriff of Oxfordshire, dated August 22, after College was convicted by the petit jury, *ibid.*, p. 412.

37 See the testimony of Lord Howard at the trial of William, Lord Russell, *State Trials*, III, 639.

38 "A Defence of Poetry," *Complete Works*, ed. Roger Ingpen and Walter E. Peck (New York, 1965), VII, 116 and 140.

39 Written on the title page of the Luttrell copy of the poem, now in the Huntington Library.

40 *The Poetical Works of John Dryden* (1832; rpt. London, 1843), I, lxxxi.

41 *Works of John Dryden*, IX, 197.

A Way of Looking at Some Baroque Poems

OLIVER F. SIGWORTH

I wish to make a few suggestions about ways in which we might read some poetry of the late seventeenth and early eighteenth centuries which today is rather unpopular. I refer to what in England at the time was known as the "great ode." The examples which I hope will occur to you, at least to those readers who are students of literature, are the obvious ones, which I wish to make the center of my discussion for the very reason that they are obvious: Dryden's "To the Pious Memory of the Accomplisht Young Lady, Mrs Anne Killigrew," *Alexander's Feast,* and *Eleonora.* The latter poem, although in form it is not an ode, may be included by Dryden's own testimony, since he remarks that the "whole Poem, though written in that which they call Heroique Verse, is of the Pindarique nature, as well in the Thought as the Expression; and, as such, requires the same grains of allowance for it."[1] Dryden's special mention of the "Pindarique nature" of the poem implies that it is a special kind of poem, and that is indeed the case. I shall briefly discuss below the kind of poem it is, but it is enough to point out here that Dryden himself—and other poets and the audience—saw the genre as distinct, implying that Dryden's original readers came to the poems with certain expectations, a certain set of mind, difficult for us in the post-Romantic world to share. This sort of poem was not, however, purely an English phenomenon; I shall want to mention at least one roughly analogous French example, and I believe examples could be drawn from other literatures.

The problems that most of us have in considering these poems, I think, are in the first place that we generally find it very difficult to shed various preconceptions about poetry, indeed about art, which in the form I intend to discuss them date only from the nineteenth century; and, in the second place, that those of us with literary training, at least literary training in American schools since the early 1940's, generally owe, however faintly, allegiance to a critical method by which it is exceedingly difficult to do the poems justice. I refer in the first instance to the view that art to be good must be "sincere," and in the second instance to the literary-critical method most easily brought to mind by the term "the new criticism," though it is assuredly not new any more. For the benefit of those readers whose chief concern is not with literature, I must mention that some of the chief tenets of the "new critical" approach to a poem are that the poem exists in an autonomous cosmos of metaphor, symbol, and form; that its truth is the truth of coherence rather than of correspondence with something outside itself; and that it can properly be discussed only in the terms which it itself as an art-object generates. These two critical views should be quite incompatible, since the first asks us to consider the author and his emotions, while the second, in its pure form, requires us to imagine the poem as in effect authorless; yet one occasionally finds them side by side in the same mind.

The question of the "sincerity" of these great odes has bothered almost everyone who has commented upon them since the end of the eighteenth century, although we must carefully note that the same question does not seem to have occurred to Dryden's contemporaries. As a matter of fact, it is clear that in modern, romantic terms the poems are *not* sincere; that is, they do not, for instance reflect Dryden's deeply-felt grief at the death of Anne Killigrew or the Countess of Abingdon, and it may be equally true that *Alexander's Feast* does not reflect a genuinely exalted view of the power of music. This "insincerity" bothers even so sensitive a scholar and critic as Earl Miner, for example, who entitles his otherwise enlightening chapter on *Eleonora* "Metaphorical Transport as Surrogate" (surrogate, that is, for genuine, sincere emotion), and begins his discussion by remarking that "we cannot believe that he [Dryden] felt the loss of Eleonora deeply, because he does not make us feel it deeply. Yet," he says, "the poem retains an interest, both for its demonstration by default of the importance of feeling in Dryden's poetry, and for those artistic sides of the poem, other than emotional integrity, which are worthy of admiration."[2] I wonder what lies behind the supposition that we may judge by our reactions to a poem the "sincerity" of an author's emotions upon writing it. The "new critic," indeed, might point out that the ring of sincerity in a poem need have nothing to do with the sincerity of the poet himself, but this view only leads us to another kind of unprofitable subjectivity, and is not in any case the ground upon which Miner and others who fault the poem for insincerity proceed. Miner seems to be leaning in the direction of a "new critical" reading when he speaks of the "emotional integrity" of the poem, but just what "emotional integrity" may be, and in what sense it is an "artistic side" of a poem, we must leave for discussion on some other occasion. Surely, however, it is obvious that Dryden could not have believed *sincerely* that Anne Killigrew's birth inspired joy in heaven because she was "born to the spacious empire of the Nine," or that at the last judgment her artistic merits would entitle her to lead the procession of poets. Anne Killigrew was a very minor poet and artist, and Dryden was too competent not to have known that. In the case of *Eleonora* the lack of sincerity is even more blatant; in fact, Dryden quite freely admits in his dedication that he had never met the lady on whom he was writing a panegyric.

As it happens, both the Anne Killigrew ode and *Eleonora* can be made to respond well to a "new critical" treatment, though such a treatment leaves much unexplored. Each poem does establish an autonomous cosmos for critical investigation, and each has been made to yield significant meanings with reference to itself,[3] although always with the embarrassed reservation that the poems are not "sincere"—a reservation implying that whatever meanings can be extracted are not to be taken quite seriously, and implying a critical inconsistency which I shall pass over as not germane at the moment.

What is germane is that the romantic standards of sincerity simply do not apply to these poems nor to others like them; they do not apply to Milton's "Lycidas," which since the time of Johnson's *Lives* at least has been frequently stigmatized as "insincere" simply because it has been mistakenly considered as an expression of grief for the death of Edward King. Obviously we need another way of approaching these poems. Here the art historians can give us help. It is dangerous to apply to one art the terms of discourse appropriate to another, but I included the term "baroque" in my title advisedly. The question of "sincerity" to those who discuss the visual arts does not seem to be so pressing a matter as it does to students of literature. I do not recall that Wölfflin, or Arnold Hauser, or Robert Rosenblum, to take as examples three art historians from different periods and of different orientations, concern themselves with the artist's sincerity, although they do speak of "expression." Indeed, with what sense could one say of an allegorical representation of Aurora racing across the sky, attended by cupids scattering flowers, leaving her lover Tithonus, and banishing Night (I refer to the Guercino fresco in the Casino Ludovisi in Rome) that it is "sincere" or "insincere"? Does the inclusion of a certain amount of equine anatomy viewed from beneath bespeak the sincere? If so, I suppose we must say that Tiepolo's great ceiling in the Kaisersaal of the Residenz in Würzburg is sincere, since such anatomy is evident in his depiction of Apollo conducting Beatrice of Burgundy to Frederick Barbarossa. There is a good bit of anatomy in this picture in addition to the equine, most of it sitting on, emerging from, or dashing through clouds. Tiepolo may have been quite sincere in his admiration for Frederick, although one hesitates to speculate, given that Frederick died in 1190, and Tiepolo painted the ceiling in the 1750's. Tiepolo no doubt sincerely wanted his commission, and so turned out one of the great, though late, baroque paintings; but to what extent beyond this the question of sincerity arises I do not know.

This is not to say that the paintings are without emotion, however. Michael Kitson of the Courtauld Institute, in writing of the baroque, remarks that while all art appeals in varying proportions "to both the emotions and the mind . . . Baroque makes use of emotional appeal as a means of reaching the mind in a special way. It goes out to meet the spectator's emotional suscepti- bilities; it is 'spectator oriented' to a greater extent than any other style."[4] Among the practices of baroque art, according to Kitson, are an increased emphasis on illusionism, and an interest in the fusion of the arts, particularly the combinations of painting, sculpture, and architecture in tombs, altars, and decorative ensembles. At this point we may turn back to Dryden, and particu- larly to the Anne Killigrew ode.

For the benefit of those readers who are not literary persons, or who may not recall the poem clearly, I shall describe it very briefly. It is written in that irregular, or Pindaric, form which according to Joseph Trapp, writing in 1711, "affects us with its daring colours, its lofty Conceptions, its Choice of Expres- sion, its agreeable Variety of Numbers, and (which is the distinguishing Char- acter of the Lyrics) that Luxuriency of Thought, conducted with the severest Judgement, by which it now and then expatiates into new Matter, connects things it seemed to separate, and falls by Chance, as it were, into its first Subject."[5] The pindaric was supposed to generate a kind of breathless excite- ment; it was expected to sustain the illusion that the poet was so in the grip of his emotions that he was unable fully to sustain the rational connections expected of poetry. And in fact in the Anne Killigrew ode Dryden does exercise the "severest judgment," while constructing an ode, I hypothesize, with much the same set of mind in which a baroque artist constructed a tomb, or a baroque painter painted a ceiling—with the expectation that he would engage the reader's susceptibility to things visible. The poem begins

> Thou Youngest Virgin-Daughter of the Skies,
> Made in the last Promotion of the Blest;
> Whose Palmes, new pluckt from Paradise,
> In spreading Branches more sublimely rise,
> Rich with Immortal Green above the rest:
>
> (ll. 1-5)

With very little effort one may visualize a baroque ceiling, Anne Killigrew ascending with attendant cherubs through the clouds; more difficult to visualize is the discussion of her poetic heritage through metempsychosis which follows in the poem, though the theme is not beyond the efforts of a baroque painter.[6] And also hard to visualize are the joy in heaven at her birth and a digression in which Dryden exclaims: "O Gracious God! How far have we/ Profand'd thy Heav'nly Gift of poesy! " (ll. 56-57) Some lines thereafter Dryden refers to Anne as a painter:

> Born to the Spacious Empire of the Nine,
> One would have thought, she should have been content
> To manage well that Mighty Government:
> But what can young ambitious Souls confine?
> To the next Realm she stretcht her Sway,
> For Painture neer adjoyning lay,
> A plenteous Province, and alluring Prey.
>
> (ll. 88-94)

There follows a description of her paintings, both of landscapes reminiscent of Claude Lorraine and of portraits of the King and Queen. The poem concludes with a picture of her brother at sea, observing "among the *Pleiad's* a New-kindl'd Star"; it is followed shortly by the assurance that on the day of judgment the poets shall lead the way:

> When ratling Bones together fly,
> From the four Corners of the Skie
> When Sinews o're the Skeletons are spread,
> Those cloath'd with Flesh, and Life inspires the Dead;
> The Sacred Poets first shall hear the Sound,
> And formost from the Tomb shall bound:
> For they are cover'd with the lightest Ground . . .
>
> (ll. 184-90)

And of course Anne Killigrew will lead the poets.

Did Dryden *mean* all this? Was he "sincere"? May I say again, the question does not seem to make much sense, particularly when asked with reference to the larger context of baroque art that includes the poem. The quotations from the poem should make it fairly easy to draw a parallel between the poem and a baroque ceiling or a baroque tomb, for the poem can easily be read as if one were "reading" a cartoon for such an exuberant painting as that by Tiepolo, or that by Rubens in the Banqueting Hall at Whitehall—the "Apotheosis of James I," which Dryden may well have seen. I make this last suggestion because it seems likely, as George Watson and others have claimed, that Dryden did not have much opportunity to see painting.[7] He never traveled abroad, and there was not much painting available, available to him at least, in England, although there were a good many engravings of famous paintings circulating. It is not even certain that Dryden's translation of Du Fresnoy's *De Arte Graphica*, to which he prefaced "A parallel of Poetry and Painting" in 1695 (ten years after the Anne Killigrew ode), indicates much more than that Dryden needed the commission, since his "parallels" are neither very interesting nor penetrating. Given his relative ignorance, the parallel between the images employed, and the way they are employed, in the Anne Killigrew ode and in certain kinds of baroque painting and sculpture is the more striking. But in fact Dryden needed only the slightest direct acquaintance with painting or sculpture to work as he did, for a knowledge of baroque style was in the air when he wrote, and that style breathes life into the poems. I may even claim that it was *intended* to be a baroque poem. Certainly Dryden was capable of such intent; in a comment on *Eleonora*, for example, he repudiates the classical for a more nearly baroque designation, just as he might have in a comment on the Anne Killigrew ode, in my opinion: "It was intended . . . not for an elegie; but a Panegyrique; a kind of Apotheosis, indeed; if a Heathen Word may be applyed to a Christian use."[8]

Eleonora itself presents difficulties similar to those presented by the earlier ode, though it hardly seems reasonable that the question of sincerity should come up in discussing a seventeenth-century poem any more than it should in discussing seventeenth-century sculptured tombs in Westminster Abbey. The Earl of Abingdon wanted a panegyrical memorial for his wife, so he commissioned the best poet of the age to write one, just as he might have commissioned the best sculptor of the age to carve her tomb, not expecting that either the poet or the sculptor need have known the subject intimately, or casually, or at all, for that matter. What resulted from the commission is an art object entirely consonant with that ceremonious life of the age which is equally reflected in the galleries and tombs and ceilings, one which is designed to excite admiration by means other than logical. To appreciate the poems, we must suspend our rational skepticism, if not our logical faculties, in much the way we suspend disbelief at a dramatic production. Each of these poems is an artifact creating its own individual cosmos, true, and each can be discussed in its own terms; but each is also an artifact bearing a special relationship to the total artistic life of the age—an artifact of a special kind, perhaps "spectator-oriented" as Kitson has said of works in other arts.

The poems have also a relationship to another, more clearly spectator-oriented (or audience-oriented) art—music. The greatest of Dryden's lyrical compositions, *Alexander's Feast*, was, we know, written to be performed; it was set to music in 1697, by Jeremiah Clarke. I am sure that we all recognize the special sort of music we call baroque. In England Purcell was the greatest exemplar of the style in Dryden's lifetime, and Dryden's respect for Purcell is recorded in a pindaric ode on his death in 1695. As was the custom, that ode was set to music, by Dr. John Blow, shortly after its publication; in the same tradition, Dryden's earlier St. Cecelia ode had been set in 1687, by Giovanni Battista Draghi.[9] The tradition was a vital one, so that more than one composer might provide a setting for the same poem. *Alexander's Feast*, for example, was given its greatest setting by Handel, thirty-five years after Dryden's death. It is a fully elaborated baroque composition, possibly more elaborate than Clarke's original, which has been lost, though there is no particular reason to believe that Dryden's friend Purcell might not have provided just as ornate a setting as Handel's had he had the opportunity, and it was such a setting that Dryden must have had in mind. For my purpose here the most important thing about the coupling of baroque poems to baroque music is the explosive enlargement of the verbal line as it is drawn into the melodic and contrapuntal convolutions of the music. For instance, in Handel's *Alexander's Feast*, which except for repetitions of lines and words adheres in every respect to Dryden's text, the first fifteen lines require seven minutes of performance time, and of these, five are devoted to solo and choral renditions of

> Happy, happy, happy Pair!
> None but the Brave
> None but the Brave
> None but the Brave deserves the Fair.

Obviously there are differences in technique between the poems clearly intended for a musical setting and the Anne Killigrew ode, which was not; yet we must remember that the pindaric was conceived of as a musical form, and it is surely possible that in the back of Dryden's mind as he was writing, he "heard" what a baroque composer would do with his poem—the vast expansion and convolution of the line, the variation and repetition of words, the alternation of recitative, aria, and chorus. Although in the Anne Killigrew ode he does not specify choruses (as he does in *Alexander's Feast*), certainly the concluding lines of most of the ten stanzas could be used as such. Imagine what Handel or Purcell could have done with

> And streight, with in-born Vigour, on the Wind,
> Like mounting Larkes, to the New Morning sing.
> There Thou, Sweet Saint, before the Quire shalt go,
> As Harbinger of Heav'n, the Way to show,
> The Way which thou so well hast learn'd below.
>   (ll. 191-95)

Imagine, for that matter, what a baroque painter might have done with a corner of his ceiling to be filled with that theme! The case in this respect is less clear with *Eleonora,* though here again we must take Dryden's own word that the poem is pindaric as well as panegyric in nature, and we should also recall his saying, ". . . I was transported, by the multitude and variety of my Similitudes; which are generally the product of a luxuriant Fancy; and the wantonness of Wit."[10] Exactly the sort of pindaric suitable for music.

With the music we come to yet another matter. I do not know that on the Continent there was anything like the "pindaric madness" which infected England, but just as the baroque in painting and architecture was an international style,[11] and as baroque music was at home both on the Continent and in England, so there are Continental examples of poetry at least somewhat like that which we have been discussing, though of a slightly later date. In tone and in movement of the verse, *Circé* by Jean-Baptiste Rousseau, for example, approaches the pindaric poems of England, and in Rousseau's case the fact is particularly interesting because his poems in the form were written as *cantate* or *Odes en musique.* We should remember that the poem was indeed set to music by J.-B. Morin as we read a few lines:

> Sur un rocher désert, l'effroi de la nature,
> Dont l'aride sommet semble toucher les cieux,
> Circé, pâle, interdite, et la mort dans les yeux,
>   Pleurait sa funeste aventure.
>   Là, ses yeux errants sur les flots
> D'Ulysse fugitif semblaient suivere la trace.
> Elle croit voir encor son volage héros;
> Et, cette illusion soulageant sa disgrâce,
>   Elle le rappelle en ces mots,
> Qu'interrompent cent fois ses pleurs et ses sanglots:

>   . . .

> Sa voix redoutable
> Trouble les enfers;
> Un bruit formidable
> Gronde dans les airs;
> Un voile effroyable
> Couvre l'universe;
> La terre tremblante
> Frémit de terreur;
> L'onde turbulente
> Mugit de fureur;
> La lune sanglante
> Recule d'horreur.

>   . . .

Ce n'est point par effort qu'on aime,
L'Amour est jaloux de ses droits;
Il ne dépend que de lui-même,
On ne l'obtient que par son choix.
Tout reconnaît sa loi suprême;
Lui seul ne connaît point de lois.

Dans les champs que l'hiver désole
Flore vient rétablir sa cour;
L'alcyon fuit devant Eole,
Eole le fuit à son tour:
Mais sitôt que l'Amour s'envole,
Il ne connaît plus de retour.

It is likely that other examples could be found (I think there are others among the works of those whom Robert Finch calls French individualist poets[12]), and it is also likely (I speculate only as an amateur student of the French literature of the period) that these poems might be seen, as I have tried to see the poems by Dryden, as an integral part of the artistic as well as the intellectual or purely literary life of the age. Certainly in order fully to understand the poems we need to look much farther afield, farther outside the poems, than we have been accustomed and trained to do. The literary theory of the late renaissance, of the seventeenth and early eighteenth centuries, with its emphasis, inherited from antiquity, on the poet as "maker," does ask us to look at the poem as an artifact, as an art object, though not exclusively so. Seeing the poem as one among other art objects of the age, as an expression of the artistic sensibility of an age as well as of a man, seeing it in something like its total artistic, rather than its confined literary or philosophical setting can lead us not only to another sort of evaluation of the poem as an art work, but possibly to a clearer sense of the extraordinarily rich artistic life of the age of baroque.

NOTES

1 *The Works of John Dryden*, vol. III, *Poems 1685-1692,* ed. Earl Miner (Bekerley and Los Angeles, 1969), p. 232. All quotations from Dryden are from this volume. Notice that Dryden writes of the "Pindarique nature" of his poem rather than calling it a Pindaric ode. Dryden seems not to have been aware of the nature of the strict Pindaric ode (see the "Preface to Albion and Albanius [1685], *Of Dramatic Poesy and Other Critical Essays,* ed. George Watson [London and New York, 1962], II, 36), although as early as 1675 Edward Phillips had distinguished the loose Cowleyan "pindaric" from the strict form in *Theatrum Poetarum*, "Preface," sig. **4, and Part II, "The Modern Poets," p. 2.

2 *Dryden's Poetry* (Bloomington and London, 1967), p. 206. A. D. Hope complains of the Anne Killigrew ode, "Anne was undoubtedly a poet, but Dryden has surely overpraised her. If we take the matter of the poem seriously it seems to be little more than a piece of complimentary nonsense" ("Anne Killigrew, or the Art of Modulating," *Dryden's Mind and Art*, ed. Bruce King [Edinburgh, 1969], p. 101). David Vieth gets around the problem by interpreting the poem as ironic, the irony making Anne Killigrew the person more believable amid the conventions ("Irony in Dryden's Ode to the Anne Killigrew," *Studies in Philology*, 62 [1965], 91-100). E. M. W. Tillyard remarks, "Dryden's claims for his heroine are so patently ridiculous that we do not take them seriously, and they are conventionally extravagant rather than thrasonical. They thus turn our minds to those general matters of faith in which Dryden sincerely believed and of whose value no reasonable person can have any doubt: to the faith in the value of good manners and of an ordered way of life" (*Five Poems, 1470-1870* [London, 1948], p. 65).

3 In addition to the works cited in the preceding note, see Alan Roper, *Dryden's Poetic Kingdoms* (London, 1965), pp. 111-12, for a discussion of *Eleonora* in connection with Dryden's use of the story of Eve. Roper does not discuss the Anne Killigrew ode. In *John Dryden's Imagery* (Gainesville, Fla., 1962), pp. 97-128, Arthur W. Hoffman discusses the imagery of the Anne Killigrew ode at length, seldom going outside the poem except to follow in Tillyard's footsteps in relating the poem to Elizabethan and medieval literary and religious traditions. John Heath-Stubbs in "Baroque Ceremony: A Study of Dryden's 'Ode to the Memory of Mistress Anne Killigrew,'" *Cairo Studies in English* (1959), pp. 76-84, at least looks in the direction I am following. Ruth Wallerstein, "On the Death of Mrs. Killingrew: the Perfecting of a Genre," *Studies in Philology*, 44 (1947), 519-28, discusses the poem entirely in context of the literary tradition. Mother Mary Eleanor, S.H.C.J., "Anne Killigrew and McFlecknoe," *Philological Quarterly*, 43 (1964), pp. 47-54, sees the two poems as concerned with the fall and restoration of poetry. Jean Hagstrum discusses the Anne Killigrew ode and *Alexander's Feast* in relation to baroque painting, for the most part easel painting, and elsewhere in his chapter on Dryden makes penetrating observations on Dryden's visual imagination in *The Sister Arts* (Chicago and London, 1958), pp. 173-209, particularly pp. 197-209.

4 *The Age of Baroque* (New York and Toronto, 1966), p. 15.

5 *Lectures on Poetry Read in the School of Natural Philosophy at Oxford. . . . Translated from the Latin . . .* 1742, p. 9. Trapp was the first Professor of Poetry at Oxford, 1708-1718. The *Lectures* were first published in two volumes in 1711-1715.

6 The allegorical portrayal of abstractions was a favorite mode of baroque ceiling painters. See, for example, Pietro da Cortona's *The Triumph of Divine Providence* in the Palazzo Barberini and Giovanni Battista Gaulli's *The Adoration of the Name of Jesus* in the nave of the Gesù, Rome. Both

of these paintings are reproduced (if unsatisfactorily) in Kitson, *op. cit.*, pp. 44 and 45.

7 John Dryden, *Of Dramatic Poesy and Other Critical Essays*, ed. with an introduction by George Watson (London and New York, Everyman's Library, 1962), II, 181.

8 Dryden, *Works, loc. cit.*

9 Ernest Brennecke, "Dryden's Odes and Draghi's Music," *PMLA*, 49 (1934), 1-36, argues convincingly that Dryden profited from his experience with Draghi's setting and put his knowledge to good use in writing *Alexander's Feast*. John Hollander, *The Untuning of the Sky* (Princeton, 1961), pp. 401-22, discusses the two music odes in relationship to their putative settings and as poetry.

10 Dryden, *Works, loc. cit.*

11 See Victor-L. Tapié, *Baroque et Classicisme* (Paris, 1957), *passim.*

12 *French Individualist Poetry* (Toronto, 1971), "Introduction," *passim.*

Swift and the Archetypes of Hate:
A Tale of a Tub

MARTIN KALLICH

I

Like every successful imaginative writer before and after him, Swift uses archetypal symbols to transform the raw and undifferentiated psychic energy that is waiting to be tapped in the collective unconscious for the expression of meaningful emotion and personal value. It is by means of this creative process that he produced his most profound and enduring emotional effects in his satire. It is not only his development of ideas in *Gulliver's Travels* that comes within the scope of this observation—that is, the development within the framework of the allegory of such archetypal fantasies as dwarfs and giants, madmen and beasts, or his allusions in other prose and in verse to classical mythology—but also his frequent use of distorted and grotesque visionary effects that clearly suggest the electrifying presence of the demonic.

For instance, consider this terrifying vision, an emblem of his misanthropic satiric impulse that occurs in a deeply emotional letter to his friend Lord Bolingbroke: "It is time for me to have done with the world, and so I would if I could get into a better before I was called into the best, and not die here in a rage, like a poisoned rat in a hole."[1] The image of the trapped beast is peculiarly appropriate for suggesting the primitive origin of aggressive satire, which in Swift had the tendency to become very destructive. As we visualize the cornered and dying rat, which, of course, is not generally considered an attractive animal inspiring love and admiration, and which is venting its rage futilely at its hopeless predicament, we are made aware of the profound frustration and bitterness, disgust and despair, and resulting anger of Swift, who, snarling, injured, and rendered helpless, was not quite prepared to die as an exile in the odious place of his birth, Ireland. This disturbing animal image effectively conveys a sense of the suppressed but frightful energy inherent in the aggression and hatred which Swift was able to blend into his satire.[2] It is, in short, an evocative archetypal image of hate, and it carries us directly into the presence of a dark and mysterious demonic power.

Even if only ironically, Swift himself, through certain of his speakers, expressed a belief in the significance and potency of archetypal images and figures. It was in the allegorical satire of *A Tale of a Tub* that Swift deliberately laid the foundation of his method of composing what may be called "typical" or "typological satire."[3] In "The Introduction" to the *Tale*, he ridiculed the fantastic typological interpretations of the Bible by the fanatical ministers of the dissenting sects who invoked the inner light for inspiration. Swift here begins his discourse with a witty account of "three wooden Machines" (p. 56), what he calls "Oratorial Machines," Pulpit (or barrel, tub, the Puritan lectern), Stage Itinerant (or raised movable platform for performing mountebanks, like the clever mountebank Peter, type of the Roman Catholic), and Ladder (or a structure that takes criminals up to the gallows and on which they make their last speeches), all devices that elevate writers of various kinds—poets or Grubstreet wits, pedants and dissenting preachers, "our Modern Saints in Great Britain." Swift explicitly admits that he is deliberately expressing himself in suggestive metaphors:

> Now this Physico-logical Scheme of Oratorial Receptacles or Machines, contains a great Mystery, being a Type, a Sign, and Emblem, a Shadow, a Symbol, bearing Analogy to the spacious Commonwealth of Writers, and to those Methods by which they must exalt themselves to a certain Eminency above the inferior World (p. 61).[4]

From their superior eminence, then, preachers and pedantic critics are enabled to discharge their sublime discourse, or wind, which, weighted with words, falls expeditiously into the gaping mouths of their eager auditory below, later in the *Tale* (Sec. 8) identified with the worshipers of wind, the Aeolists.

Moreover, even the title of this work is made to come within the scope of typological description. Thus in "The Preface," Swift semi-humorously offers what he calls a mythological explanation of why he wrote *A Tale of a Tub*, referring as he does so to the method of typological discourse: just as sailors fling a tub into the water in order to divert a whale from attacking their ship, so he wrote his tale to save the ship of state from subversion by "terrible Wits" who use Hobbes' *Leviathan* as their weapon. "The Ship in danger," Swift writes, "is easily understood to be its old Antitype the Commonwealth" (p. 40). That is, the ship is the type or symbol which corresponds with the original, its antitype or the commonwealth.[5] Thus Swift, as he applies it to politics, extends the symbolic meaning of a term originally limited to theology.

To be sure, Swift's ridiculous reference to types, antitypes, symbolic and emblematic description, or what he himself has called "typical Description," has a specific seventeenth-century context. The *Oxford English Dictionary* defines the relevant substantive *type* (deriving from the Latin *typus*, figure, image; and the Greek *typos*, impression, pattern, model) in two ways, as a symbolical prefiguring or as an emblem. Not separated, these two meanings are included together in the first definition as follows:

> that by which something is symbolized or figured; anything having a symbolical signification; a symbol, emblem; *spec.* in *Theol.* a person, object, or event of Old Testament history, prefiguring some person or thing revealed in the new dispensation.

Two examples are cited to illustrate these two closely related senses. One is taken from the commendatory verses to Spenser's *Faerie Queene*, and this suggests the emblematic and allegorical usage: "That faire Ilands right: Which thou dost vaile in Type of Faeryland, Elyzas blessed field, that Albion hight." Another is taken from the work of an early seventeenth-century divine, and this clearly adopts the prophetic usage: "The people of Israel were a tipe of God's people: Canaan a tipe of heauen." The *OED* definitions of the verb *to type* seem to stress the symbolic prefiguring function by placing it first: "To prefigure or foreshadow as a type; to represent in prophetic similitude. To be the type or symbol of; to represent by a type or symbol; to symbolize." But a definition of another related verb, *to typify,* clearly suggests a dual function as emblem *and* prefiguring device: "To represent or express by a type of symbol; to serve as a type, figure or emblem of; to symbolize; to prefigure."[6]

Apparently, the two meanings, *prefigure* and *figure forth*, are not always sharply distinguished, and so in ordinary usage they blend into each other. That is the way Swift must have understood the concept—in two senses very close in meaning, yet not precisely the same, and shading in toward each other. This is made clear in the definition of the word *type* offered in Samuel Johnson's *Dictionary* (1755), which demonstrates conclusively that there were two distinctly separated meanings for the word, however close they must have been, both of which were adopted by Swift. According to Johnson's interpretation of the difference, the first makes emblem or symbol synonymous with type; the second, however, involves prefiguring shadows:

1. Emblem; mark of something.
   Thy emblem, gracious queen, the British rose,
   Type of sweet rule, and gentle majesty. Prior.
2. That by which something future is prefigured.
   Informing them by *types*
   And shadows of that destin'd seed to bruise
   The serpent, by what means he shall atchieve
   Mankind's deliverance.   *Milton.*
   The Apostle shews the Christian religion to be in truth
   and substance what the Jewish was only in *type* and shadow.
                    Tillotson's Sermons.

Johnson also defines *typical* generally as "Emblematical; figurative of something else."[7] Johnson has made clear the two meanings to which Swift refers in his "typical Discourse"—what may be called the general, emphasizing a mystical and symbolic representation; and the specific, emphasizing the mystical correspondence between one event, person, situation in time and a similar event, etc., much later. Both shade into each other through their suggestive connotations, their occult and mystical overtones.[8]

That these definitions of the word *type* and its cognates and approximate synonyms in the seventeenth and eighteenth century anticipate the terminology employed in twentieth-century discussion of the archetypes of the collective unconscious should not seem entirely strange. Nor should their discussion with Jung's views appear anachronistic and far-fetched. Typology was assimilated into the hermetic doctrine of correspondences, an area of seventeenth-century occult learning and alchemical science from which Jung himself drew his ideas. This doctrine assumes that the physical and concrete are allegorical representations of the divine and spiritual, like Swift's three "Oratorial Machines," which are emblematic of a higher reality. Jung was concerned to explain a psychic occurrence similar to that experienced by those who, in Swift's time, were mystically moved by symbolic or supernatural revelation to illuminate the relationship between the Scriptures and their personal lives.[9] Therefore, although the cultural context and times are obviously different, Swift and Jung refer to the same psychic experience, based upon the occult effect of symbols, and draw upon the same mystical tradition for the language that is used to explain it. Moreover, despite the fact that in Swift's opinion Puritan inspiration was both vulgar and false, the result of sheer ignorance and low social status, it is nevertheless true that Swift himself consciously used typological discourse in its general and specific sense and employed several archetypal symbols and images to communicate meaning and emotion in the satire of his *Tale.*

II

Of course, Swift, having adopted the persona of a ridiculous, nameless and faceless, modern author from Grub Street, who, incidentally, is also a type of insane modern hackwriters, is ironic. As he confesses in his own person, some passages in his book "are what they call Parodies, where the Author personates the Style and Manner of other Writers, whom he has a mind to expose" ("Apology," p. 7). Thus he uses silly types, allegories and fables, to illuminate his point, and yet at the same time he has in mind a serious satiric purpose—he wishes to denigrate symbols and images respected in Puritan typological practice and thought, especially Puritan insistence that all wisdom or truth must be sought symbolically below the surface of things.[10] So wisdom, as he says with mock seriousness through his fictional speaker, is sought in such "mystical" but essentially foolish metaphors as a fox, cheese, sack-posset, hen and nut:

> In consequence of these momentous Truths, the Grubaean Sages have always chosen to convey their Precepts and their Arts, shut up within the Vehicles of Types and Fables ("Introduction," p. 66).

Thereupon, after comically reducing to absurdity certain occult tendencies in the writing of his time, he proceeds to jest in earnest with the main narrative line, the allegory of the will and coats. Under the extended metaphor of that allegory is couched "darkly and deeply," he insists (p. 67), the religious satire.

In Swift's mind his satire is integral, and his ironic allusions to types and symbols contributes to its unity. The satire on the abuses in religion is neatly joined with the satire on the abuses in learning and criticism towards the conclusion of "A Digression concerning Criticks," as Swift declares that the symbol of the tailor, representing the tailor-deity of sartorism (a modern system of worship devised by Peter and his brothers to supplant the purity of primitive Christianity and the New Testament), resembles the tailor-critic of modern learning that is in conflict with the excellence of the ancient achievement:

> a True Critick is a sort of Mechanick, set up with Stock and Tools for his Trade, at as little Expense as a Taylor; and . . . there is much Analogy between the Utensils and Abilities of both: That the Taylor's Hell is the Type of a Critick's Commonplace-Book and his Wit and Learning held forth by the Goose (pp. 101-2).[11]

The goose, a common animal symbol, suggests the gabbling silliness of the Grub Street wits. Swift is also punning on the word, which means a tailor's pressing iron, its long handle being curved like the neck of a goose. Thus by means of these ironic references to types and to a kind of typological discourse, Swift provides a degree of unity and integration to the range of the satire embodied in the allegorical narrative about modern religion and in the digressions on modern pedantry and criticism.

Superficially, the persona of the hack writer that Swift adopts when writing the satire seems to make his appeal to reason, and his discourse appears to be logical and aimed at the revelation of truth. But in reality the reverse is true; for he is insane. And one of the rhetorical devices that the hack-persona employs, typological discourse, clearly demonstrates that Swift's real purpose is to have him use it in order to evoke negative feelings, that is, to ridicule what Swift believes to be the madness and depravity of fanatical dissenting preachers and modern authors, to expose them all as authentic quacks. Thus we may say that Swift is not interested in objective truth so much as in emotional persuasion, for the ludicrous types and figures that he deliberately employs are meant to humiliate his targets by triggering feelings of scorn, hostility and disgust towards them. These antagonistic feelings are definitely expressed in an obscene passage, where the persona alludes again to typological discourse, to

> that highly celebrated Talent among the Modern Wits, of deducing Similitudes, Allusions, and Applications, very Surprizing, Agreeable, and Apposite, from the pudenda [genitalia] of either Sex, together with their proper Uses. . . . I have sometimes had a Thought, That the happy Genius of our Age and Country, was prophetically held forth by that antient typical Description of the Indian Pygmies, etc. (p. 147).[13]

That is, Swift means that the potency or achievement of modern critics (alluding ironically to their deformities) is prefigured in the stunted bodies of pygmies with disproportionately large genitalia.

Several archetypes of madness and sexual depravity, which are Swift's two major accusations directed at the psychological vulnerability of his targets, operate in the *Tale* to reinforce thematic meanings and to achieve the desired reductive effect. However, the basic archetype, underlying all the others, not only reflects upon the very meaning of Swift's typological method but also expresses the central theme of the satire—that is, the allusion to the universal experience confirming the opinion that outer or surface images provide a deceitful cloak for the real but hidden essence underneath. That things are not really what they appear to be on the surface is illuminated, for example, in the image of clothes, which in the religious allegory of the three brothers who alter their coats despite their father's will (original Christianity as expounded in the New Testament), is confused with or obscures the genuine person (the true church) underneath (Sec. 2). This typical image reappears frequently and in a variety of contexts, but because it has been discussed so often in essays on the *Tale* it need not be elaborated at this time.[14] Counterpointed with other types and figures, the image of clothes becomes a fundamental symbol conveying rich and complex meanings. It first becomes the object of worship by the disciples of the tailor, those "who madly dote upon matter" in the shape of clothing, which they "devoutly worship" as the unique principle of the universe (pp. 76-78). Then, after the original coats of the three brothers have been completely defaced, the history of the clothes eventually rises to a climax in the ninth section, with the ultimate declaration of despair by the author's speaker, the mad hack, who has come to believe that to achieve happiness reason must be deluded and deceived by the imagination, which is concerned with surface matters. It is here, too, that the memorably vivid types of "a Woman flay'd" and "the stripped Carcass of a Beau" (p. 173) are used for illustrations of his credulity. The net effect of all this typological discourse is emotional persuasion that the reality concerning man cannot be measured only in terms of surface appearance, or clothes alone, without reducing him to self-delusion or insanity, a pitiable target for satire and disgust. Thereupon the *Tale* concludes with the story of Jack, who represents dissent becoming mad—for, failing to restore his coat to its original condition, Jack zealously reduces it to tatters instead, completely debasing what it represents—the Christian religion.

Indeed, one could say that of the two psychological themes in the *Tale*, madness, the result of a delusion that the outside is preferable to what lies beneath, is far more important than the second, sexual depravity, and that therefore it may be considered the central archetypal experience of the satire. It is symbolized and portrayed in such grotesque figures as the maniacal and superstitious fanatics, the dissenter Jack and the Popish Peter, both of whom are also depraved, and the mad hackwriter, Swift's persona, who had only recently been released from Bedlam to become the historian of the *Tale*. Through these types Swift represents a deplorable insanity in religion and learning in his time. For an example of the way in which Swift deliberately uses a typical image for destructive satire, consider the menacing grotesque with which he represents the inspired disciples of Jack, the Aeolists, who affirm "the Gift of Belching, to be the noblest Act of a Rational Creature" (p. 153). By means of an image of a wild-eyed preacher belching wind that is eagerly swallowed by his deluded congregation, Swift is enabled to vent his charge of hate at what he believed was the spiritual madness and hysteria of religious nonconformity.

In accord with his satiric intention, then, Swift first of all reverses the awful archetypal equation of wind with the divine afflatus, genuine religious inspiration, ecstasy, or enthusiasm, reducing it instead simply to a ludicrously vulgar physical disorder, flatulence—intestinal gas and belching: "At certain Seasons of the Year," their ministers may be seen "with their Mouths gaping wide against a Storm. At other times," they perform a disgusting rite, "every Man a Pair of Bellows applied to his Neighbour's Breech, by which they blew up each other to the Shape and Size of a Tun." Thus they "did call their Bodies, their Vessels." Growing "sufficiently replete, they would immediately depart, and disembogue for the Public Good, a plentiful Share of their Acquirements into their Disciples Chaps" (p. 153).[15]

Swift declares of the learning and eloquence of Puritan ministers that their excess of intestinal vapors permitted these enthusiastic preachers to deliver to their pupils

> all their Doctrines and Opinions by Eructation, . . . having first by their Turbulence and Convulsions within, caused an Earthquake in Man's little World; distorted the Mouth, bloated the Cheeks, and gave the Eyes a terrible kind of Relievo (p. 154).

And, in a similar account of the physical effects of ecstasy, Swift describes the face of the "sacred" preacher, when discharging his belches, by comparing it to the sea disturbed by stormy winds, "first blackning, then wrinkling, and at last bursting into a Foam" (p. 156). Their awful facial grotesques, produced by twisted mouths and protruding eyes, is supposed to represent not divine fury, not the violent strain of effecting mystical union or spiritual sublimity through sacred suffering, but disgusting and primitive anality, man as a flatulent and witless hysteric. In short, Swift represents a vision of ugliness and evil in the form of a menacing grotesque, in his opinion emblematic of all that is corrupt and irrational in religion: "All Pretenders to Inspiration whatsoever" (p. 150 n.).

III

Moreover, these are the frenzied and hallucinating followers of Jack, their "Roundhead" leader who not only has the long ears of an ass but who also brays like one. The ass symbolism is especially noteworthy as a device which graphically illustrates and integrates Swift's psychological themes of madness and depravity. At the same time this animal symbol reinforces emotions of horror and disgust at ridiculous corruptions in modern religion and learning. In Swift's allegory, criticism, it will be noticed, is portrayed with asinine attributes.

Far more effective than the pulpit, ladder, and stage platform as emblems of false elevation or inspiration, the immediate cause of madness in both religious and secular oratory, is the false goddess Criticism. She actually appears full blown in *A Battle of the Books*, Swift's other allegory that complements the *Tale*. But because her figure, as well as her spirit, vividly dramatizes the satiric theme of pedantic criticism in the *Tale*, Swift's treatment of the archetypal monster should be discussed at this point. The goddess represents the dread "Prototype" of the true critic, Swift declares with ironic awe (p. 99). Like the disturbing image of the madly belching Aeolists, Criticism also is a menacing grotesque that Swift attempts to recall from the archaic collective unconscious. Electric with emotion, it is a complex mythological monster emblematic of the irrational rhetoric against which Swift was protesting in the *Tale*. But at the same time, because it is so unusually powerful, and charged with so much hate, we could say that it transcends its limited function in these early works by Swift and becomes a symbol of his profound distrust of mankind and the totality of his achievement in satire.

The goddess Criticism, "a malignant Deity," according to Swift, is urged by Momus to inspire the troops of modern writers and critics, her followers, before their battle with the ancients, the occasion of Swift's allegorical narrative in the *Battle of the Books*. Her figure, as Swift describes it, is enriched with a variety of iconic imagery:

> She dwelt on the Top of a snowy Mountain in Nova Zembla; there Momus found her extended in her Den, upon the spoils of numberless Volumes half devoured. At her right Hand sat Ignorance, her Father and Husband, blind with Age; at her left, Pride her Mother, dressing her up in the Scraps of Paper herself had torn (p. 240).

It will be noticed that the minor mythological god Momus plays a significant role as "the Patron of the Moderns" who seek the aid of the archetypal spirit. But in the related section of the *Tale*, "A Digression concerning Criticks," Swift's pedigree of "the True Critick" is slightly different, Momus there playing a more crucial generative role. In the *Tale*, Swift asserts that Momus begat the true critic upon arrogant pride: "Every True Critick is a Hero born, descending in a direct Line from a Celestial Stem, by Momus and Hybris" (p. 94). Momus, the personification of mockery and censure, called by Hesiod the son of Night, the brother of Sleep, of Death, of Dreams, and of Care, could just as well have been used as a symbol of the unimaginative and pedantic fault-finding kind of criticism to which Swift objects. As one eighteenth-century dictionary briefly defines him, Momus is "a Heathen Deity who made it his Business to carp at the other Gods, whence it is used to represent a Fault-finder, or one who snarls at anything."[16] Thus personifying jeering blame, mockery, ridicule, Momus is associated with darkness and shadow, and he recalls the archetype of the true critic, that is, according to Swift's irony, virulent adverse criticism. Clearly, he stands in some relation to nasty and negative satire. Swift, however, as if dissatisfied with the image because it was not adequate to the viciousness of his satiric purpose, felt compelled to create his monstrous version, the goddess, almost the archetype itself.

His imagination drawing upon the emblematic tradition for the details of an elaborate allegory, Swift endows the character with a variety of attributes derived from her father: that is to say, her sister was Opinion, "hoodwinkt and headstrong, yet giddy and perpetually turning," and her children were Noise and Impudence, Dulness and Vanity, Positiveness, Pedantry, and Ill-Manners. As his description continues, Swift allows his imagination to fall deep into the shadow where evil and unpleasant physical and animal details are stressed. As a result, the description becomes grotesque, demonic. The breast image in the following quotation even anticipates that of the ugly Brobdingnagian nurse in *Gulliver's Travels*, II, while the allusion to the ears and voice of the ass recalls Jack and his dissenting disciples:

> The Goddess herself had Claws like a Cat: Her Head, and Ears, and Voice, resembled those of an Ass; Her Teeth fallen out before; Her Eyes turned inward, as if she lookt only upon herself: Her Diet was the overflowing of her own Gall: Her Spleen was so large, as to stand prominent like a Dug of the first Rate, nor wanted Excrescencies in form of Teats, at which a Crew of ugly Monsters were greedily sucking; and, what is wonderful to conceive, the bulk of Spleen encreased faster than the Sucking could diminish it (p. 240).

Surely, all these unpleasant particulars suggest the presence of the menacing grotesque again. But unlike the picture of Jack and the Aeolists, it is so radical as to be incredible. Thus it seems to evoke an ambiguous response— fear mixed with laughter, an ambiguity that often characterizes Swift's satire when it is motivated by an immoderate amount of fury.

Typical of the true daughter of Momus, the angry god of ridicule, the intemperate goddess Criticism "rose in a Rage" when announcing her intention to assist the moderns devoted to her. Approaching one of them, Wotton, in the guise of a book by Bentley, she urges him to the fight; whereupon

> she took the ugliest of her Monsters, full glutted from her Spleen, and flung it invisibly into his Mouth; which flying strait up into his Head, squeez'd out his Eye-balls, gave him a distorted Look, and half overturned his Brain (p. 243).

This last image resembles that of the Aeolist hysterics violently straining for spiritual insight. So similar in some of their ugly details and in their emotional effect, these powerful images or types of modern criticism and modern fanaticism evoke horror and hatred as they reach into the latent depths of the unconscious where their dread archetypes reside. Thus they reinforce with universal significance the manifest themes on the surface of Swift's satire in the allegory on religion and the digressions on learning. But Swift's portrayal of the highly evocative Criticism is unsurpassed in its evil. Buttressed by its association with snarling Momus, the vision of Criticism lies at the emotional center of whatever is memorable in Swift's satiric art, a strangely complex symbol, an archetypal image of primitive rage and its effects into which Swift, apparently without any inhibitions whatsoever, poured his aggression, his hate and hostility. It is in this graphic manner that Swift's satiric imagination operates when it is most effective in his best poetry and prose.

IV

As is well known, Swift's aggressive satiric impulse to destroy his targets is frequently expressed in the form of unpleasant animal images, of which the demonic monster Criticism is one. In the *Tale*, there is a variety of infamous animals used to suggest the malicious archetype of the "True Critick." These, found in "A Digression concerning Criticks," are the serpent whose "Vomit" causes "a certain Rottenness or Corruption" of anything it touches, or terrifying wolves who hunt down large game (great writers), or rats who swarm around "the best Cheese" ("the noblest Writers"), or dogs who "Snarl most when there are the fewest Bones" (the fewest imperfections in a literary work) (pp. 100, 101, 103-4). And, then, too, not to be overlooked is the idol's or tailor's goose (pp. 76, 102, 133), already referred to, and the tame geese that draw the chariot of Criticism (p. 242).

But the most objectionable animal in the opinion of the narrator seems to be the ass.[17] This figure rightly assumes the chief animal role in the satire,[18] because it is the tutelary deity of both the Puritans and the pedantic critics. Therefore if anything figures as the central animal symbol of the *Tale*, it is the ass, whose psychological, sexual, and physical attributes are shared by Swift's satiric targets, the frenzied fanatics and crazy pseudocritics.[19] So, like the monstrous goddess Criticism, Jack the canting Roundhead is portrayed as a braying ass with prominent ears, on which theme the narrator proceeds to elaborate humorous variations, going so far as to transform donkey ears into phallic symbols.[20] This sexual motif, the association of asses with the lust of the "Fanaticks," is pursued further in *A Mechanical Operation of the Spirit*; there, "this distinguish'd Brute" also appears as the means of transporting Mahomet and "a great Number of devout Christians," the "Fanatick Auditory," to heaven. The narrator, it will also be remembered, must have been so obsessed with the subject as to feel compelled to compose a treatise entitled *"A general History of Ears"* (pp. 2, 202).

Previously, however, the narrator had, in tracing the pedigree of the archetypal true critic (a comical parody ridiculing the pedantic method of the scholarly Richard Bentley), cleverly developed the idea of his antiquity through analysis of "Types and Figures" in "Mythology and Hieroglyphick" and arrived at the conclusion that critics in ancient times were so feared that out of caution they had to be portrayed symbolically and figuratively, that is, mystically rather than literally. And so the absurd hieroglyphic of the ass was chosen, thereupon giving Swift the opportunity to speculate learnedly on asses with horns and a redundancy of gall and a remarkable ass whose braying (as recorded by Herodotus) "put to flight in a Panick Terror . . . a vast Army of Scythians"—

> From hence it is conjectured by certain profound Philologers, that the great Awe and Reverence paid to a True Critick, by the Writers of Britain, have been derived to us, from those our Scythian Ancestors (pp. 97-99).

But because of the fear of "too nearly approaching the Prototype," this figure, Swift asserts, was eventually supplanted by others "that were even more cautious and mystical," like a weed with a poisonous scent, and the variety of vicious animals cited before—snakes and wolves, rats and dogs.[21]

As we note the mysterious attraction and psychic energy inherent in types, shadows, figures, and emblems, it is only natural that the ironist who believes that "Rational Creatures, or Men . . . are in Reality the most refined Species of Animals" (p. 78) should use types and signs of ignoble animals to communicate his hostility, particularly a lowly draught animal, the ass. This beast, traditionally notorious for petulance and stupidity, Swift also associates with sexual license because of its long ears, again a traditional notion, and then for good measure adds his personal associations deriving from his culture with its harsh cry, the windy eloquence of raving puritan preachers and the dullness of pedantic critics.

V

Underlying the use of types in religious rhetoric is, of course, the serious assumption that the Scriptures were infallibly inspired by supernatural means to foreshadow the future. In Section 11 of the *Tale* (and elsewhere as noted before), Swift's quarrel is with an arbitrary and fanciful use of types, the result of vulgar ignorance. Thus, for example, in concluding the story of mad Jack, the persona declares that he will literally describe Jack's bizarre behavior, the consequence of Jack's belief that his father's will "was deeper and darker" than it really was; and as he does so, Swift ironically and characteristically has the persona provide an explanation of what he has done. That is, it appears that Swift has playfully used the typological method of ridicule. So the absurd applications of the will (the Bible) by foolish Jack and his Aeolist disciples "in the most necessary, as well as the most paltry Occasions of [contemporary] Life" furnish, he does not deny,

> Plenty of noble Matter for such, whose converting Imaginations dispose them to reduce all Things into *Types*; who can make Shadows, no thanks to the Sun; and then mold them into Substances, no thanks to [Natural] Philosophy; whose peculiar Talent lies in fixing Tropes and Allegories to the *Letter*, and refining what is Literal into Figure and Mystery (pp. 189-90).[22]

But it is clear that Swift does not oppose the use of prefiguring types and shadows or of symbolic types and emblems as such. Swift does not deny in the *Tale* that truth can be expressed more adequately under the forms of imagination, symbol, image, type, and myth, than in propositional and intellectual expression. For obviously he uses these in the rhetoric of his satire. So Swift, impersonating his Grubean sage, argues however paradoxically and humorously, that "where I am not understood, it shall be concluded, that something very useful and profound is coucht underneath" (p. 46).[23] And, again, he has his persona parody humorously and ironically, yet with a good deal of meaning, the character of an occult or "dark," Rosicrucian author who offers "Innuendo's" to help others decipher the mysteries of his work: "For, *Night* being the universal Mother of Things, wise Philosophers hold all Writings to be *fruitful* in the Proportion they are dark" (p. 186). Swift's quarrel, as we have noted, is with fantastic and vulgar typological rhetoric, with the madness that it illustrates.

What Swift clearly scorns is the corruption to base ends of this means of spiritual insight by the "converting Imaginations" of deluded and ignorant fanatics, under the mistaken belief that they were inspired by the divine afflatus. Disgusted by its degeneration into uncontrolled and ridiculous subjectivism, Swift wished by means of his cauterizing satire not only to purify the Puritans but also to bring to their senses whoever among the faithful might have been tempted to defect into dissent.[24]

True, on the manifest level of consciousness, the narrative context, Swift demonstrates the absurdity of the excesses in the typical and emblematic practice attempted by modern critics and sectarian enthusiasts; but at the same time, and far more effectively than he appears to have anticipated, on the latent level of the unconscious, he has endowed his satire with a timeless quality, a universal and continuing potential for emotional appeal, because he had adopted the typical method for reduction.[25] Thus his work has a permanent vitality with all those to whom the symbolic significance of things and words count—and this means all those who are concerned with the ways of the imagination. It is also true, however, that in the *Tale* Swift's compulsion to humiliate the religious mystics and inspired enthusiasts of his time may have carried him further than he intended into the uncomfortable depths of the shadow, thereby converting what could have been a comical satire into something dark, forbidding, and destructive.

What is once written about the contemptible Aeolists can very well be applied to Swift, the genuine author of the *Tale*. The persona notes, for example, that the Aeolists could not sustain their inspired and idealistic vision of God, and so, typically falling to the other extreme, were ridiculously compelled to "provide their Fears with certain ghastly Notions, which instead of better, have served them pretty tolerably for a Devil" (p. 158). Indeed, Swift himself deliberately evokes the devil with menacing visions of grotesque types—of nonconformist preachers, their bodies contorted and their faces grimacing as they frantically strain for mystical transport; of the terror gods, snarling Momus and his monstrous daughter Criticism, who both cast ugly shadows on humane letters; and of the long-eared braying ass, the infernal animal archetype for Puritan lust and degradation and all sorts of foolishness. The savage intensity of Swift's satire suggests that he is projecting his own fears and hatred on to "certain ghastly Notions" representing the numerous offensive and "gross Corruptions in Religion and Learning" that, as he explains in the "Author's Apology" for his satire, he wishes to expose (p. 4). Invariably, therefore, Swift reverses the standard occult procedure of subordinating the letter to the spirit, the literal sense to the allegorical meaning.

Traditionally, madness was both respected and feared because associated with the divine afflatus, the mystical gift of supernatural intelligence that provides prophetic illumination and inspiration. This exalting psychic phenomenon has been described as "enthusiasm" (possession by a god), in allusion to those who, animated in an extraordinary manner with the divine spirit, appear to be enraptured, that is, separated from their bodies and transported from all earthly concerns to engage in a mystic union with the deity.

But in the sceptical world of Swift's *Tale of a Tub* (especially Sections 8, 9, and 11) the possibility of such supernatural vision is denied. On the contrary, the opposite is asserted; and enthusiasm is literally equated with and made to refer either to noxious diabolical possession[26] or to mania or a form of insanity that encourages self-deception. Damned also in the seventeenth and eighteenth centuries by its association with the lower classes and a politically and socially disruptive religious fanaticism, it was thought to be dangerously subversive.[27] Further, those who think they are being ecstatically transported are considered simply deluded fanatics, their souls never really separating from their bodies, but, instead, as in the case of the raving Aeolists, they succumb to the debasing lusts of the flesh and engage in demeaning orgiastic ceremonies. Lastly, because their delusion is so stubbornly persistent, Swift recommends that these mentally disturbed people be thrust away into Bedlam. In this way society can be secured for the sane purveyors of virtue and common sense, that is, all those who support the traditional norm of political, social, and religious stability. In the *Tale*, in short, enthusiasm is reduced to mania and madness, understood literally and medically as mental imbalance, which, because its chief symptom is delusion, results in dangerous fanaticism and a demented pretense at religion. All in all, therefore, it was a type of madness that was disorderly, dark and evil—to be feared, distrusted and despised. [28]

Moreover, air, traditionally thought to be the medium of enthusiasm, inspiration or spiritual rapture, is associated with the creative breath of life, and with smoke, hence with the *anima*, the essence of soul or spirit, the life spirit which animates the universe. So Swift playfully exploits the root meaning of the word "spirit" in his essay on wind and Aeolism (Section 8) and simultaneously with his usual dextrous ambiguity blends a good deal of truth into his satire:

> For whether you please to call the *Forma informans* of Man, by the Name of *Spiritus, Animus, Afflatus,* or *Anima*; What are all these but several Appellations for Wind? Which is the ruling *Element* in every Compound, and into which they all resolve upon their Corruption. Farther, what is Life itself, but as it is commonly call'd, the Breath of our Nostrils? (p. 151).

Thus wind and air also become associated in a dignified and attractive manner with the Original of All Things, the connection between God and Man, eventually sublimating into the archetype of Pure Reason, Pure Spirit, Pure Soul, or God. But again, in the perverse satiric world of the *Tale*, although Swift is certainly aware of the traditional symbolic equation of air with the spirit,[29] air being the medium by means of which man is carried to God, these serious and exalting possibilities are ignored or denied. Instead, Swift literally reduces air to a material substance, vapor or wind, and merely considers it pathologically as it rises from some foulness in the lower faculties of the body to become the cause of flatulence and several species of contemptible insanity, the precise opposite of Pure Reason—and with a suggestion again of darkness and the devil's work.[30]

Thus Swift in the justly celebrated ironic *tour de force*, "A Digression on Madness," declares "a Redundancy of Vapour" (p. 174) causes not only Jack's religious frenzy but also some other varieties, political and intellectual, that are dangerous to the commonwealth; and then, just as we expect him to do, he proceeds to take us into Bedlam, the visible and ultimate result of vapors.[31] And in the preceding essay on Aeolism Swift ludicrously parodies a supposedly scientific treatise as he develops the thesis that wind is air in its most destructive state, therefore properly worshiped by Jack's frenzied followers, "the most Illustrious and Epidemick Sect of Aeolists" (p. 142):

> The learned *Aeolists* maintain the Original Cause of all Things to be *Wind*, from which Principle this whole Universe was first produced, and into which it must at last be resolved; that the same Breath which had kindled and blew *up* the Flame of Nature, should one day blow it *out*.... This is what the Adepti [occultists] understand by their *Anima Mundi*; that is to say, the *Spirit*, or *Breath*, or *Wind* of the World (pp. 150-51).

Swift here is burlesquing Anthroposophia Theomagica (1650), the work of the near contemporary occultist Thomas Vaughan, who described man's soul as "an essence not to be found in the texture of the great world and therefore merely divine and supernatural. Montanus calls it, 'Wind of the Divine Spirit and Breath of Divine Life.' "[32] By explaining Jack's system of belief (the emphasis on preaching and prayer for inspiration), in terms of occult Aeolism which he has rendered comically absurd, Swift hoped to ridicule the fanatics and "All Pretenders to Inspiration whatsoever" (p. 150 n.).

Lastly, the treatment of archetypal images of eyes and light also demonstrates Swift's method of satiric reversal. Light and eyes are standard metaphors for reason and the soul, and reason was often spoken of as the eye of the soul. But these equations are again ironically reversed in the world of the *Tale*. Swift in his devastating attack on predestination has mad Jack declaim against eyes, which he denounces as "blind Guides" and "foolish Lights, which conduct men thro' Dirt and Darkness, til they fall into a deep Pit or a noisom Bog" (pp. 192-94). Being an occultist, Jack criticizes the eyes of the body for their physical limitations on the literal level. Thus he closes his eyes to the light of reason and common sense. Refusing to carry a lantern (another metaphor for reason), he argues that a wise man is his own lantern and must walk in the dark by the illumination of his private inner light. Naturally, of course, because he is deluded, Jack enjoys walking with his eyes closed. With what result? Rendered blind and almost entirely helpless, Jack behaves ludicrously and rationalizes all absurdities.[33]

Thus, upon retrospect, it is felt that the satire in the *Tale* is relentlessly severe, harsh, stinging and scornful, that the religious allegory and the digressions on learning and criticism never present any pleasing images that recall bright archetypes inspiring profound love and veneration. In the religious narrative, Martin, who apparently assumes the relatively attractive middle way of judicious common sense between the inspired idiocy of Peter and Jack, may be intended as the ideal type of patient calm, reasonable moderation and propriety in religion; but in Section 6, where he appears best as the possible satiric norm, he is, in contrast with volatile Jack during the Reformation, "extremely flegmatick and sedate" (p. 139). There is reasonable doubt, it seems, that Martin does represent the archetype of the true Christian Church, for, as Lord Orrery (one of Swift's earliest critics in the eighteenth century) wrote about Swift's probable intention, although "To Martin, he shews all the indulgence that the laws of allegory will permit," Martin simply may stand for "flegmatic stiffness," "the slow and incompleat reformation of the Lutherans."[34] Besides, despite the fact of Swift's insistence that his "Book" "Celebrates the Church of England as the most perfect of all others in Discipline and Doctrine" ("Apology," p. 5), Martin is scarcely maintained with conviction as a noble positive, the necessary vividly imaginative and evocative supporting qualities of an archetypal image being notably lacking.

Likewise, a graphic model of positive secular learning or good criticism never appears definitely, that is, never as a sensuous image or symbol recalling the archetype with all its sublime associations. Whatever model of decent common sense may be found in the *Tale* is so deeply embedded in the extremely baffling irony of Swift's "Digression on Madness" as to be obscured and therefore largely ignored by the commentators.[35] In this digression the model of common sense appears at first non-imaginatively, non-symbolically, as certain abstract norms that have very litle emotional or persuasive impact—what Swift denominates in a neo-Platonic fashion as "common Forms" or "the Pattern of Human Learning." These are archetypes of traditional values, although they are not made sensuous in image or symbol. Thus, Swift can assert with a sneer, being intellectual, these "Forms" are not understood by ignorant and stupid plebeians, the uneducated mechanics, the "British Workmen" (pp. 267, 279) and "The Rabble" (pp. 2, 54) of the lower classes among whom are the asinine and maniacal disciples of Jack and the eccentric private spirit. However, to the approving "Men of Wit and Tast" (*sic*) ("Apology," p. 20) *outside* the *Tale*, as Swift flatters his élitest circle of friendly readers in the Establishment like Lord Somers, who in a bantering dedication by the putative bookseller is fulsomely praised for an almost endless list of virtues, for "Wit and Eloquence, and Learning, and Wisdom, and Justice, and Politeness, and Candor, and Evenness of Temper" (p. 25), these reasonable and decorous norms were supported by authority and upper class tradition and were, no doubt, perspicuously clear and agreeable. But, still, despite this compatibility with patrician taste, as they are presented *in* the

Tale, they lack the usual charge of powerful energy inherent in his sensuous and suggestive images, emblems, and symbols of hate.

> For the Brain, in its natural Position and State of Serenity [unaffected by maddening vapor or wind], disposeth its Owner to pass his life in the common Forms. . . . and the more he shapes his Understanding by the Pattern of Human Learning, the less he is inclined to form Parties after his particular Notion, because that [Pattern] instructs him in his private Infirmities, as well as in the stubborn Ignorance of the People. But when a Man's Fancy gets *astride* on Reason, when Imagination is at Cuffs with the Senses, and common Understanding, as well as common Sense, is Kickt out of Doors, the first Proselyte he makes, is Himself (p. 171).[36]

The image of the rider on a horse at the end of this passage also reappears at the very end of the digression in the figure of reason as "a very light Rider, easily shook off" (p. 180), where it makes Swift's message about man's tendency to madness emphatic. In this image there is an oblique reference to Socrates' fable of the charioteer and the two horses in the *Phaedrus*, which recommends reason as the controlling agent over the furious impulses of desire or the appetitive soul. Perhaps here in the *Tale*, as well as in Plato's dialogue, especially in the account of the unruly passions represented by the wild black steed, Swift found the inspiration in the last voyage of *Gulliver's Travels* for his ironic inversion of the traditional types, man as rational and beast as irrational being, where the Houyhnhnms stand literally for completely fancy-free and passionless creatures—for solid horse sense and reason. That is to say, according to the inversion, the horses become the rational agents and they dominate the totally appetitive man, the antitype of the bestial Yahoos. But in the *Tale* this almost casual image of a horseback rider is the only provision made by Swift for an admirable type corresponding to the reason and common sense which he professes. Indeed, it can only be concluded that in the *Tale*, the allegory and the essays on learning, Swift's normative types and symbols receive little careful or sustained attention, if any at all.

Swift, it is clear, distrusts the evidences of mysticism and sublime emotion in his time and refuses to soar into the airy void. He deliberately rejects all archetypal symbols associated with these experiences, insisting instead upon associating debasing symbols with the objects of his contempt, the assorted "Follies of Fanaticism and Superstition" ("Apology") and pedantry. As a result, anger, disgust, hate are the strong negative emotions that dominate the *Tale*, emotions that are constantly evoked by means of unpleasant and grotesque images, types, and symbols; for Swift seeks to discredit and devalue the thought and behavior of his satiric targets rather than to exalt positive ideals. Expressed with characteristic vigor, Swift's first of many thoughts listed on various subjects provides succinct commentary: "We have just Religion enough to make us *hate*, but not enough to make us *love* one another."[37] In this aphorism probably composed around the time the *Tale* was published, Swift illuminated its satiric spirit with more insight than he was aware.

However, the situation changes in *The Battle of the Books*, in which allegory Swift pursues the secular theme once more. Here he effectively balances the positive and constructive emotions against the negative and destructive aggressive emotions by means of archetypal symbols taken from the insect world, the dark and diabolical spider and the bright and angelic bee, thereby finishing what he had neglected to do in the *Tale of a Tub*.

NOTES

1 21 March 1729/30, *The Correspondence of Jonathan Swift*, ed. H. Williams (Oxford, 1963), III, 383.

2 J. E. Cirlot, *A Dictionary of Symbols* (London, 1962), pp. 259-60: "The rat occurs in association with infirmity and death. It was an evil-doing deity of the plague in Egypt and China. The mouse, in medieval symbolism, is associated with the devil. A phallic implication has been superimposed upon it, but only in so far as it is dangerous or repugnant."

3 The adjective *typical* is the form that Swift and his contemporaries were familiar with. The word *typological*, adopted later to refer to this kind of discourse in Biblical commentary, is in present-day use. See, e.g., the entry "Typology" in the *Hastings Encyclopedia of Religion and Ethics* (New York, 1908-27), XII, 500-501. *A Tale of a Tub, To Which is added The Battle of the Books and The Mechanical Operation of the Spirit, by Jonathan Swift*, ed. A. C. Guthkelch and D. N. Smith (Oxford, 1958), second edition. This edition will be used for all references to the three works which it includes.

4 So Edmund Curll, author of the *Complete Key to the Tale of a Tub* (London, 1710), explains that the elevating oratorial machines (pulpits, ladders, stage itinerants) "emblematicaly [*sic*] represent the various sorts of Authors." See *Tale*, ed. Guthkelch and Smith, p. 299.

5 The word *antitype* is defined in the *Oxford English Dictionary* as "That which is shadowed forth or represented by the type or symbol." One of the examples of usage is precisely this sentence from Swift's *Tale*. In his *Dictionary* (1755), Samuel Johnson defines *antitype* as "That which is resembled or shadowed out by the type; that of which the type is the representation." Apparently, this is the only time in the *Tale* that Swift used this scholastic term derived from theology and occult lore.

6 The OED gives several definitions of *emblem* (sb), the most pertinent being the third, which makes clear its symbolic function: "A picture of an object (or the object itself) serving as a symbolical representation of an abstract quality, or action, state of things, class of persons, etc. b. In wider sense: A symbol, typical representation. Sometimes applied to a person: The 'type' personification (of some virtue or quality)." The verb *to emblematize* is defined as "to express or represent mystically, allusively, or allegorically."

7 In Johnson's definition of *emblem*, the second meaning is relevant: "An occult representation; an allusive picture; a typical designation." Thomas Sheridan, Swift's friend, defines *type* [in his *Complete Dictionary of the English Language* (4th ed., 1797)] in the two usual ways as "Emblem, mark or something; that by which something future is prefigured"; and the verb *to typify* as "To figure, to show in emblem"; and *emblem* as "an occult representation, an allusive picture."

8 Not to belabor the point, it may be said that some early dictionary makers contemporary with Swift can also be cited to prove that the word *type* had a general figurative as well as a specific prefigurative reference, with both of which Swift must have been familiar. For example, Elisha Coles, *An English Dictionary* (1676), defines *type* as "an example, figure or shadow of a thing"; and John Kersey, *Dictionarium Anglo-Britannicum: or, A General English Dictionary* (1708), defines *type* as "the Figure, Shadow, or Representation of a Thing: a Model, or Pattern." Kersey also defines *typical* as "belonging to a Type or Figure." Nathan Bailey's very popular *Universal Etymological Dictionary* defines *type* as "the Figure or mystical Shadow of a Thing; a Model or Pattern"; and *typical* as "emblematical, figurative" (I refer to the twenty-third edition, 1773).

An informative discussion of Swift's adaptation of "typological discourse" for satiric ends is by Paul Korshin, "Swift and Typological Narrative in *A Tale of a Tub*," *Harvard English Studies*, 1 (1970), 67-91. Focusing on Section 7 of the *Tale*, Korshin stresses the more specialized theological use of the word *type* to mean something prefiguring, foreshadowing, or prophetic in time. He is not concerned with its more general symbolic, emblematic, mystical or occult, meaning.

9 In his autobiography, Jung wrote, "The experience of the alchemists, were, in a sense, my experience, and their world was my world. . . . I had stumbled upon the historical counterpart of my psychology of the unconscious. The possibility of a comparison with alchemy, and the uninterrupted intellectual chain back to Gnosticism, gave substance to my psychology." Quoted by Frieda Fordham, *An Introduction to Jung's Psychology* (Penguin, 1966), p. 140. Cf. Jung, *Man and His Symbols* (Garden City, N.Y. 1964), p. 54: "The rediscovery of the principles of alchemy came to be an important part of my work as a pioneer of psychology." For Jung's numerous studies into seventeenty-century occult learning, particularly alchemy, see Mrs. Fordham's book, pp.

80-81, 95, 133, 139-40; cf. also Jung's *Alchemical Studies, Mysterium Coniunctionis*, and *Psychology and Alchemy*. Jolande Jacobi, *The Psychology of C. G. Jung* (New Haven, 1962), also writes about this aspect of Jung's thought.

10 The persona claims to be a modern, having just been made, he admits, "a Member of that Illustrious Fraternity" of Grub Street (p. 63), that is, a hack; and to be "the *Last Writer*" of his time, that is, the most up-to-date, "the freshest Modern" (p. 130). He tries not to "forget [his] character of an Historian" (p. 133), and in Section 9 (p. 176) he cheerfully confesses to madness. Because he takes pride in being "a most devoted Servant of all *Modern* forms" (p. 45), i.e., ideas, he is called by John R. Clark, "The archetype of a broken modernity," in *Form and Frenzy in Swift's Tale of a Tub* (Ithaca, N.Y., 1970), p. 155.

When the speaker calls himself "the *Last Writer*," is he unconsciously parodying Paul, who in Rom. 5:14 describes Adam as the *typos*, "the figure of him that was to come," the antitype Jesus Christ, "the last Adam" (I Cor. 15:45)?

11 This source of unity is briefly mentioned by Miriam Starkman in her study of the *Tale*'s structure: *Swift's Satire on Learning in A Tale of a Tub* (Princeton, 1960), pp. 134-35; but she does not consider the identification of the tailor-deity of sartorism and the tailor-critic of modern learning from the point of view of the scholastic types and emblems.

12 See Sec. 2, p. 76: "This God [a tailor] had a goose for his Ensign; whence it is, that some Learned Men pretend to deduce his Original from *Jupiter Capitolinus.* . . . The *Goose* was also held a subaltern Divinity. . . ." In the *Battle of the Books*, geese also pull the chariot of the goddess Criticism (p. 242). In medieval times, the goose was associated with witches who frequently used these birds for transportation to "the witches' sabbat." Perhaps, then, there is also a similar quality associated with geese. See A. De Gubernatis, *Zoological Mythology* (London, 1872), II, 310: Geese "sometimes do evil, or sometimes are diabolical forms assumed by the witches' deceit."

13 Swift again refers to types in his sexual satire on the dissenters in *The Mechanical Operation of the Spirit*, pp. 284-85.

14 It could be reinterpreted in the light of Jung's concept of the *persona* archetype—the protective coating that makes for easy, natural relations with the outside world. That is, clothes make the man, as the saying goes. Swift satirizes those who identify the self with their office or title or clothes. One recent discussion brilliantly demonstrates that Swift is attacking Hobbes's materialism in the image of clothes: Phillip Harth, *Swift and Anglican Rationalism: The Religious Background of A Tale of a Tub* (Chicago, 1961), pp. 80-85. Another relates it to Hooker's law: Elias J. Chiasson, "Swift's Clothes Philosophy in the *Tale* and Hooker's Concept of Law," *SP*, 59 (1962), 64-82. But basically it appears to me that Swift is merely poking fun at the hermetic doctrine of correspondences between the microcosm and the macrocosm by converting it into

the doctrine of the microcoat and macrocoat. See *Tale*, pp.77-78; and N. J. C. Andreasen, "Swift's Satire on the Occult in *A Tale of a Tub*," *TSLL*, 5 (1963), 410-21, esp. 416.

15 Swift specifically associates enthusiasm with religious fanaticism and air in *Mech. Oper.*, pp. 266 ff. D. J. Dooley, "Image and Point of View in Swift," *PLL*, 6 (1970), 128-30, discusses these grotesque images as evidences of the way in which Swift makes his meaning explicit. D. W. Jefferson, "An Approach to Swift," *From Dryden to Johnson*, ed. Boris Ford (Pelican, 1957), pp. 232-36, likewise considers Swift's use of grotesque images to give force to his arguments, finding in them evidence of metaphysical wit.

16 Bailey's *Universal Etymological English Dictionary*.

17 For a brief discussion of the significance of the ass image, see Ronald Paulson, *Theme and Structure in Swift's Tale of a Tub* (New Haven, 1960), pp. 205-8. But Paulson improperly links it with the dignified horse and rider imagery which conveys an altogether different meaning and emotion. De Gubernatis, *Zoological Mythology*, I, 358-99, devotes one chapter to the myths of the lowly ass, noting the "many blows which . . . it is accustomed to receive, as if to afford a vent for the satirical humour of our race" (p. 360).

18 As it figures in Pope's *Dunciad*. See the title page of the *Variorum Dunciad* (1729).

19 Section 11, pp. 195, 200-202; *Mech. Oper.*, pp. 264-65, 285. Swift also uses the ass figure to satirize the Catholic doctrine of auricular confession. See Sec. 4, p. 108. And in a poem addressed "To Mr. Congreve" (1693), written not too long before the *Tale*, Swift again compares critics to asses, citing their braying and their ears (171-74), and to odious cattle as well (223-26).

20 See the brief note by C. M. Webster, "The Puritans' Ears in *A Tale of a Tub*," *MLN*, 47 (1932), 96-97. Webster simply says that the passage on ears is full of erotic symbolism: "It should be read as Swift's cryptic exposé of the lusts of enthusiasts and especially of the Holy Sisters for the everwilling Puritan preachers." Included in the entry on *ass* in Cirlot's *Dictionary of Symbols* is the idea that "This symbolic animal appears as an attribute of Saturn, in his capacity as the 'second sun.' It is always in heat, and hated by Isis. . . ." Cirlot's source for this idea is Jung's *Symbols of Transformation, Collected Works* (New York, 1956), V, 67. The mythical satyrs had ass's ears; thus the phallic association, as the satyr links the myth of the ass with that of the goat.

21 Bentley, the chief critic mauled in *A Battle of the Books*, is also debased by means of an association with an ass: pp. 254, 257.

22 In his *Key to the Tale*, Edmund Curll declares, "This Passage describes the common Practice of the Fanaticks in Perverting the Scripture." See *Tale*, ed. Guthkelch and Smith, p. 342.

23 Thus Swift also parodies alchemical writings (on p. 114), as Guthkelch and Smith declare (p. 355): "I desire those whom the *Learned* among

Posterity will appoint for Commentators upon this elaborate Treatise, that they will proceed with Great Caution upon certain dark points. . . ." Philip Pinkus, *"A Tale of a Tub* and the Rosy Cross," *JEGP*, 59 (1960), 669-79, discusses the mystical Rosicrucian allusions in the *Tale*. His point is that the allusions to alchemy, mysticism, cabalism, Gnosticism are all considered various aspects of the doctrine of the Rosy Cross and that the *Tale* itself is a Rosicrucian text.

24 This latter alternative is the thesis documented by Harth, *Swift and Anglican Rationalism*, ch. 3, pp. 52-100. But Swift presents both alternatives in his own "Apology," p. 5.

25 This timeless quality is also discussed by Clark, *Form and Frenzy*, pp. 126-33; but it is placed in a different context.

26 See, e.g., *Mech. Oper.*, p. 267,

27 Cf. the entry "Fanatick" in Ephraim Chambers, *Cyclopaedia*, 5th ed. (1741), Vol. I: "a wild, extravagant, visionary, enthusiastical person; who pretends to revelation and inspiration, and believes himself possessed with a divine spirit."

28 Cf. C. M. Webster's articles: "Swift's *Tale of a Tub* compared with Earlier Satires of the Puritans," *PMLA*, 47 (1932), 171-78; "Swift and Some Earlier Satirists of Puritan Enthusiasm," *PMLA*, 48 (1933), 1141-53; "The Satiric Background of the Attack on the Puritans in Swift's *Tale of a Tub*," *PMLA*, 50 (1935), 210-23. See also George Williamson, "The Restoration Revolt Against Enthusiasm," *SP*, 30 (1933), 571-603; Truman Guy Steffan, "The Social Argument Against Enthusiasm," *Studies in English* (Austin, Texas, 1941), pp. 39-63; Harth, *Swift and Anglican Rationalism*, pp. 70-74.

29 Cf. *Tale*, Sec. 9, p. 165: "At last the Vapour or Spirit, which animated the Hero's Brain. . . ." Cirlot, *A Dictionary of Symbols*: "Air is essentially related to three sets of ideas: the creative breath of life, and, hence, speech; the stormy wind, connected in many mythologies with the idea of creation; and, finally, space as a medium for movement and for the emergence of life-processes." The first two are pertinent.

30 The definition of "vapor" in a medical sense was, of course, well known. See, for example, John Kersey, *Dictionarium Anglo-Britannicum, or a General English Dictionary* (London, 1708): "Vapour. . . . In a Medicinal Sense, Vapours is taken for Fits of the Mother, or Melancholy; a Disease." John Harris, *Lexicon Technicum: Or, An Universal English Dictionary of Arts and Sciences* (London, 1725), Vol. I: "Vapours, in a Medical Sense, is now a days [*sic*] used for the Disease called otherwise *Hysterick* or Hypocondraick [*sic*] *Fits* or *Melancholy*. . . ." Robert Burton refers to a type of melancholy (or madness) "that ariseth from the bowles" which he calls "hypochondriacal or windy melancholy" [*The Anatomy of Melancholy*, ed. A. R. Shilleto (London, 1926), I, 3-4]. Chambers, *Cyclopaedia* (1743), Vol. II: "Vapours, in medicine, a disease popularly called *hypo* or the *hypochondriacal* disease; and in men particularly the *spleen*. It is supposed to be owing to a subtile *vapour*, rising from the lower parts of

the abdomen, particularly the hypochondria, to the brain; which it disturbs, and possesses with wild delirious, but generally disagreeable imaginations." See, also, Harth on Swift's possible source for his use of the vapor concept: Ch. 4, pp. 101-17. M. Quinlan has discussed Swift's reduction of inspiration to breathing in "Swift's Use of Literalization as a Rhetorical Device," *PMLA*, 82 (1967), 518b.

31 So in a poem written around this time Swift likewise confesses he himself has been suffering the mad delusion that the Muse was inspiring him to create poetry. In "Lines on Sir William Temple's Last Illness," he describes the Muse in her literal and physical manifestation as "A walking vapor" (102) and renounces her "visionary pow'r; / and since thy essence on my breath depends, / Thus with a puff the whole delusion ends" (152-55).

32 Montanus was an "enthusiastic" ecstatic of the second century, responsible for the Montanist heresy. The passage is quoted by Andreasen (see below) and by Starkman, *Swift's Satire on Learning in A Tale of a Tub*, p. 47. (See Starkman, pp. 24-28 for further discussion of vapors.) Mrs. Starkman emphasizes the contemporary cultural context of Swift's satiric use of the archetypal symbol of air. For more on aeolism and enthusiasm, see Harth, pp. 54-67; Andreasen pp. 410-21, esp. 418; and Swift's reference to Vaughan's mystical work in the *Tale*, p. 127 and note; and the annotation by the editors, pp. 356-58. Pinkus (p. 673) says that the quoted passage from the *Tale* (pp. 150-51) reflects Rosicrucian alchemy, that is, the Rosicrucian search for the first principle, the material basis of alchemy.

33 Cf. Harth, p. 17; Andreasen, p. 418. It should also be mentioned that on the title page Swift offers the strange Gnostic quotation from Irenaeus, an invocation for divine light, which Wotton in his *Observations* (Guthkelch and Smith, p. 323) translated as "I call upon this, which is above all the Power of the Father, which is called Light, and Spirit, and Life, because thou hast reigned in the Body." Thus by quoting this early Church figure who wrote againt the Gnostic heresy, Swift announces in a curiously oblique manner an important occult theme by means of which he hopes to render the Puritans absurd.

34 John, Earl of Orrery, *Remarks on the Life and Writings of Dr. Jonathan Swift*, 3rd ed. (Dublin, 1752), pp. 301, 302. Orrery's association of Martin with the Lutherans and their incomplete reformation of the Catholic Church is quite different from William Wotton's equation of Martin with the Church of England, the one that is usually adopted as Swift's meaning, because Swift used Wotton's interpretation in a note to the text, Sec. 2, p. 73.

As one scholar has pointed out concerning Orrery's opinion, "The effect . . . is to exonerate Swift from any charge of attacking the Anglican faith itself." [Peter Weygant, "Three Kinds of Reply to *A Tale of a Tub*," *The Library Chronicle* (U. of Pa.), 36 (1970), 60.]—Which is precisely what Swift indicated as his intention in the "Apology," p. 5. But the net effect of this interpretation is to deprive the religious allegory of any positives whatsoever!

35 Andreasen, pp. 414-15, 420, remarks on it briefly as Swift's version of the *consensus gentium*, the common notions which all sane men agree upon, Swift deriving his views from Henry More's attacks on the occultist Thomas Vaughan. An excellent discussion of Swift's norms of reason and common sense can be found in Harold D. Kelling's essay, "Reason in Madness" *A Tale of a Tub, PMLA*, 69 (1954), 198-222. Kelling believes that Swift's rhetorical positives tell us what he means by reason and common sense, and the common forms, and these can be found in the contemporary evidence of Anglican pulpit oratory with which Swift must have been familiar. But the fact is that Swift does not provide in the text of the *Tale* a suitable metaphor for these reasonable norms. As a result, they are abstract and, of course, difficult to define precisely.

36 What Swift apparently has in mind in this attack on unconventional thinking may also be seen in his contemporary "Ode to the Honble Sir William Temple" (1692). Referring in this poem to the fruitless search for "the Philosopher's Stone" (15), he shows his contempt for what he calls "The Roguery of alchemy" (25); and, likewise, he attacks "ill-manner'd" pedants who "purchase Knowledge at the expence / Of common Breeding, common Sense, / And at once grow Scholars and Fools" (42-44).

37 "Thoughts on Various Subjects," *Prose Works*, ed. Davis (Oxford: Blackwell, 1957), I, 241.

The Displaced Self in the Novels of Daniel Defoe[*]

HOMER O. BROWN

I Names

> *"A fine Story! says the Governess, "you would see the Child,
> and you would not see the Child: you would be conceal'd and
> discover'd both together."*
>
> *(Moll Flanders)*[1]

Names, false names, absence of names seem to have special importance for Daniel Defoe's novels. None of his fictional narrators, with the exception of Robinson Crusoe,[2] tell their stories under the name he or she was born with. The narrator of *A Journal of the Plague Year* is anonymous, signing his account at the end with the initials "H. F." In the other novels, the narrators receive their names in something like a special christening. Bob Singleton is given his name by one of the series of "mothers" through whose hands he passes after being kidnapped from his true parents. Colonel Jack receives the name "John" from the nurse who is paid to take him by his real parents, who are unmarried "people of quality." Unfortunately, all three of the nurse's "sons," one of them really hers and the other two paid for, are named "John."

Moll Flanders' real name is too "well known in the records, or registers, at

*See the note on p. ix. This essay is reprinted from *ELH*, 38 (1971) by permission of the Johns Hopkins University Press.

Newgate and in the Old Bailey," so she chooses to write under the alias "Moll Flanders" and begs the reader's patience "till I dare own who I have been, as well as who I am." It is by the revelation of this true name (to Moll but not the reader) that Moll recognizes her real mother, who had also adopted an alias, and discovers that she has married her own brother. "Moll Flanders" is the name she takes during her time as a thief in London, when, though already a middle-aged woman, she falls under the tutelage of a woman who refers to her as "child" and whom Moll calls "mother. The title page of *Roxana* is a veritable catalog of her aliases throughout her career. Curiously, the name "Roxana" is the name she bears for the shortest time and one she did not give herself. She received it, in the presence of the king, from the spontaneous cry of a group of men at a masked ball in appreciation of the costume she was wearing. But *Roxana* is a special case, for the reader does learn at least her true Christian name because it is also the name of her daughter, who pursues her through the last part of the book.

At the moment of narration few of Defoe's narrators are living under the name by which they "sign" their stories. Secrecy seems to be an absolute precondition of self-revelation. Or, to put it in a less perversely contradictory way, these narrators seem under a double compulsion to expose and to conceal themselves. Certainly it is a literary convention, a premise of fictional narration, aimed at convincing the reader of their veracity, since Defoe published all these books as the "real" memoirs of their narrators. But it is a curious convention, since it goes beyond a mere premise of narration and becomes an important theme in the narration, an event in the story itself.

Moreover, literary convention cannot explain this practice of concealment in the life of the true author of these fake memoirs, Daniel Defoe, which was not, incidentally, his real name. Before and even after he took up the writing of these books at the age of sixty, Daniel *Foe* served as the agent of various interests, parties, governments, writing and acting under innumerable assumed names and points of view, to the extent that it is difficult to separate fact from fiction in our knowledge of his own life and impossible to go beyond certain limits in ascertaining what he actually wrote.

Robinson Crusoe is a somewhat special instance of Defoe's habit of concealing the true name of his narrators. Robinson has purportedly related the events of his own life under his own name through two volumes—*he* at least has commited no crime and requires no secrecy. In the Preface to the third volume, however, Robinson hints that if the events he has narrated are not strictly true they are allegorically true and that perhaps Robinson Crusoe is not his real name. Many readers have taken this hint to mean that Defoe had written his own spiritual autobiography under the metaphor of the shipwrecked and isolated Crusoe. The question has never been decided. The double project of revelation and concealment of this least sophisticated of novelists was successful. The "real" Daniel Defoe has disappeared into the absence of an irrecoverable time.

We can only probe for the meaning of the double compulsion in the written world of his novel and perhaps ponder the relationship of that compulsion to the project of writing lies that look like truth. Our hopes are limited: if on the one hand we are reduced to a search for the meaning of the name he withheld from us, we know that in the end we will have to content ourselves with no more than the name alone.

What will we find to explain this curious game of names? In a sense it cannot be completely explained or understood because the only real evidence lies in the books themselves and also because, since it is a literary convention, we are touching upon a cultural symptom as well as a personal one and all such symptoms are overdetermined. Two provisional explanations, however, will emerge from an examination of Defoe's fiction. One has to do with a strong fear of the menace of other wills, a pervasive fear in these novels. Another explanation has to do with the way the self becomes somebody else in conversion. In this discussion I will place special weight on *Robinson Crusoe*, for while it provides less mystery about names than the other novels, it offers itself as a kind of myth to explain the fear of exposure, detailing the consequent strategies of the self. In order to discuss this impulse at the source of Defoe's fiction, I will have to defer consideration of the intense fascination with the factual, the most pervasive and already much discussed characteristic of Defoe's writing—defer it, I would hope, only to recover it in a new light.

These provisional explanations might help also to illuminate what is involved in the constitution of imaginary novelistic characters.

II The Myth of Singleness

In my youth, I wandered away, too far from your sustaining hand, and created of myself a barren waste.

(Augustine, *Confessions*)[3]

Defoe's novels are based on a notion of radical egocentricity. Robinson wonders why his isolation on the island was "any grievance or affliction" since "it seems to me that life in general is, or ought to be, but one universal act of solitude":

> The world, I say, is nothing to us as it is more or less to our relish. All reflection is carried home, and our dear self is, in one respect, the end of living. Hence man may be properly said to be alone in the midst of the crowds and hurry of men and business.

> All the reflections which he makes are to himself; all that is pleasant he embraces for himself; all that is irksome and grievous is tasted but by his own palate.
>
> What are the sorrows of other men to us, and what their joy? Something we may be touched indeed with by the power of sympathy, and a secret turn of the affections; but all the solid reflection is directed to ourselves. Our meditations are all solitude in perfection; our passions are all exercised in retirement; we love, we hate, we covet, we enjoy, all in privacy and solitude. All that we communicate of those things to any other is but for their assistance in the pursuit of our desires; the end is at home; the enjoyment, the contemplation, is all solitude and retirement; it is for ourselves we enjoy, and for ourselves we suffer. (*Serious Reflections*, pp. 2-3)

Robinson's thirty years of solitude on a desert island is the metaphor of this selfishness. In fact, his story is based on the etymological metaphor "islanded"–isolated. When Robinson was in Brazil, he "used to say, I lived just like a man cast away upon some desolate island that has nobody there but himself" (VII, 39). The whole book has to do with the progressive materialization of spiritual metaphor for what is implicit in Robinson's condition from the beginning, in the same way that the book itself is a factualization of the metaphors of the whole tradition of spiritual autobiographies.[4]

Selfish, isolated, but is he really alone? Other Defoe narrators are just as solitary in the midst of society. Robinson's island isolation is after all only a metaphor for the solitary selfishness of all men. This seemingly impenetrable selfishness, however, is a Hobbesian "state of nature," transposed into a social world, atomistic, volatile, where the mere existence of another person, for Robinson even the *possibility* of the existence of another person, is a threat to the self. Even Robinson in his wilderness, through all those years of never encountering another human being, is constantly haunted by a sense of menacing otherness. He must always be on guard. He never loses the agonizing sense of being watched. Far from only being a representation of Robinson's egocentric isolation, the book is peopled by *signs* of the constant presence of the other–Robinson's fear, the footprint of a man, the Hand of God, the constant presence of the older Robinson in the double perspective of the narration, the presence of the spectator-reader before whom Robinson rehearses his solitude. In a sense, no Defoe character, not even Robinson, is ever alone.

The need for secrecy at the moment of narration for most of Defoe's "autobiographers" is no mystery. With the exception of Robinson and H. F., they have committed crimes for which they can be called to justice. Near the beginnings of their stories, however, they also are all bereft of family and protection and are thrown into a harsh and dangerous world of deceptive appearances, whose inhabitants are indifferent, conniving, menacing. Some, like Robinson or H. F., orphan themselves seemingly by choice. Others, like Colonel Jack and Bob Singleton, are virtually cut off from their origins, and so, from their true names. Roxana, even as a young girl, long before she is deserted by her husband and left to protect herself and her family, is removed from France and her childhood, bringing with her nothing "but the Language." The separation from any guardian structure is sharp. Their isolation is complete.

No wonder, then, that Defoe has been said to have discounted the importance of personal relationship in his novels.[5] There is no richly complex conflict between wills more or less equal in strength in his fictional world. The Defoe character has to struggle against all the others, against a harsh necessity.[6] There is no sense of an individualized other conciousness confronting the protagonist as there is in Richardson's world or Austen's or George Eliot's. The paradigm is Moll in a crowded London street; her survival depends on her ability to take "the advantages of other people's mistakes" while remaining unseen herself. The value of her story for the reader will be in its warning "to Guard against the like Surprizes, and to have their Eyes about them when they have to do with Strangers of any kind, for 'tis very seldom that some Snare or other is not in their way" (II. 92). Otherness for a Defoe character is generic, anonymous. Individual antagonists like Roxana's landlord, or even her Amy, Moll's various men, Robinson's Moorish captor or Friday can be tricked or subordinated without much apparent difficulty, but a single, anonymous footprint in the sand seizes Crusoe's mind with uncontrollable terror. However easily any Defoe "I" can deal with any individual menace, the unnamed dread remains. Perhaps the most striking example is the London of the plague. The "others" of the *Journal* are anonymous numbers of dead and dying. Any conversation, even the slightest human contact, carries the risk of death.

When Robinson finds himself shipwrecked, almost his first act is to begin to build a wall around himself. He further insulates himself; he creates an island within the island. His action is obsessive. He spends almost three and a half months building the wall—"I thought I should never be perfectly secure 'till this Wall was finish'd" (VII, 87). Although he longs for deliverance from his solitude, he is compelled to hide his presence so "that if any People were to come on Shore there, they would not perceive any Thing like a Habitation" (VII, 87). So, in the midst of a threatening and unknown space, Robinson creates for himself an ordered interior, crowded with things which can be listed and enumerated to his satisfaction. He "furnishes" himself "with many things," as a chapter title phrases it. Like the fallen angels, Robinson sets about to build and secure his own Pandemonium, following the advice of Mammon to "seek / Our own good from ourselves, and from our own / Live

to ourselves, though in this vast recess, / Free, and to none accountable"
(*Paradise Lost* II. 252-55). But, of course, their self-reliance is a sham, their
Pandemonium is a parody of Heaven, founded upon denial of the divine
Other, whose power they can never escape. Like the angels, Robinson's concern with things is a symptom of his fall. Robinson's brave statement "I build
my fortress" echoes ironically Luther's famous hymn based on the Ninety-
first Psalm (cf. *A Journal*, pp. 12-13).

Moll Flanders in disguise in the middle of a crowded London street, H. F. in
his "safe" house surrounded by the plague, Robinson in his fort—the image is
a recurrent one. Earlier in Robinson's account, in Brazil he carves out a
plantation "among Strangers and Savages in a Wilderness, and at such a Distance, as never to hear from any Part of the World that had the least Knowledge of me" (VII, 30). Still earlier, there is Robinson quavering in the hold of
the ship that takes him from home, surrounded by a raging sea.

At the beginning of the book Robinson's father points out to him that his
"was the middle State, or what might be called the upper Station of *Low
Life, . . .* that this was the State of Life which all other People envied" because

> the middle Station had the fewest Disasters, and was not expos'd
> to so many Vicissitudes as the higher or lower Part of Man-
> kind . . . that this Way Men went silently and smoothly thro' the
> World, and comfortably out of it, not embarrass'd with the
> Labours of the Hands or of the Head, not sold to the Life of
> Slavery for daily Bread, or harass't with perplex'd Circumstances,
> which rob the Soul of Peace and the Body of Rest; not enrag'd
> with the Passion of Envy, or secret burning Lust of Ambition for
> great things; but in easy Circumstances sliding gently thro' the
> World, and sensibly tasting the Sweets of living, without the bit-
> ter, feeling that they are happy, and learning by every Day's
> Experience to know it more sensibly. (VII, 2-4)

Then, at the outset, Robinson already possesses the kind of security, freedom from exposure, that most other Defoe narrators and later even Robinson
himself long for. What is given to Robinson is suddenly taken from other
Defoe protagonists by circumstances over which they have no control. Moll
Flanders and even H. F. must expose themselves to danger in order to survive.
Why does Robinson give up so easily what the others have to struggle so hard
to gain? In a sense, this is the same question implicit in the beginning of this
essay: expressing so strong a desire for concealment, why do they offer their
confessions at all? This is as difficult a question as asking why Defoe wrote
novels. The desire for concealment could have been easily satisfied by silence,
by writing or publishing no books at all.[7] The obvious answer to so mani-
festly impossible a question—that Defoe wrote books to make money, that is

to say, like Moll or H. F., to survive—is less satisfactory than it might at first appear. There were other ways to make money, many of which Defoe tried. Much of the other writing Defoe did involved the need for secrecy or masking.

Defoe's narrators seem obsessed with concealing themselves, but the impulse leading them towards exposure appears equally strong. Complete concealment is impossible, perhaps not even desirable. On the one hand there is the insistence on building a faceless shelter around the self, but, on the other, a recurring compulsion to move out into the open. This double compulsion can be expressed as a double fear. When an earthquake makes him fear the security of his cave, Robinson writes that "the fear of being swallow'd up alive, made me that I never slept in quiet, and yet the Apprehensions of lying abroad without any Fence was almost equal to it" (VII, 94). These two fears, however—fear of being swallowed up by the earth, fear of lying in the open— are the same at bottom. Why does Robinson fear sleeping without the protection of a wall? He is afraid of ravenous beasts and cannibals. If one is caught abroad with one's guard down, unconscious (sleeping), one risks loss of self. But the dangers are as great apparently if one never ventures out. Both fears are basically fears of engulfment: one, the fear of being lost in the recesses of one's own nature (the earth), fear of solipsism and anonymity; alternately, fear of being captured, "eaten" by the other. Perhaps behind both, Defoe's fear of imprisonment.[8] Fear of forms, equally strong fears of the formless. The fear of being devoured recurs throughout Robinson's narrative. At the beginning, he is afraid of being swallowed alive by the sea. Near the end, he defends himself against the devouring wolves.[9]

Besides fear or biological need, there are other reasons apparently for venturing abroad. Curiosity forces H. F. constantly to risk infection. Moll learns that the others betray moments of unconsciousness from which she can profit: "a Thief being a Creature that Watches the Advantages of other Peoples mistakes" (II, 92). Why does Robinson surrender his initial security? The reasons are intentionally vague to point to the fact that his motivation is beyond his understanding and ambiguously beyond personal choice, for the reasons are generic and at the same time subject to his accountability. His motivation or lack of justifiable motivation, involving disobedience of the father, is a restlessness of spirit which is simultaneously culpability and its own punishment. He describes the sources of his "meer wandering Inclination" as "something fatal," a "Propension of Nature," symptoms of what he shares with general man, the heritage of the fall. "Design'd" by his father "for the Law," he "would be satisfied with nothing but going to Sea," great symbol of the unformed. The opposition could not be more clear. What is most threatening is also most alluring. Throughout his life, even after his conversion, Robinson will feel the compulsion to leave behind the preformed, the already-given world of law, and face the unknown and undifferentiated, full of menace for the self and simultaneously full of promise. Unable to accept the given definition of himself, the will and legacy of his father, the world of law, Robinson experiences himself as incomplete and searches mistakenly for completion in the world outside. He does not possess himself but is scattered among a world of things. He must externalize himself in the world. He must create a self out of the formless sea of pure possibility, out of the surrounding, anonymous wilderness. The world is for him to make something of—his own.

Here is the source of his egocentricity. His feeling of loneliness in Brazil at being "at such a Distance as never to hear from any Part of the World that had the least Knowledge of me" (VII, 39) suggests that this distance is an alienation from a part of himself held in thrall by the world outside. This alienation and his longing for companionship through his years of isolation on the "Island of Despair" and his fear of the other all testify to his continuing sense of incompleteness but also reveal the lie behind the way he has sought fulfillment.

Fear of the other, determining need for concealment; necessity, allurement of the world offering some form of completion to the self, determining the impulse to risk exposure. This is the explanation of the concealment and exposure or guarded exposure of Defoe's narrators that is revealed by the play of names. Hiding behind the disguise of Robinson and his factual-seeming narrative, Defoe is doing what Robinson does—constructing and hiding inside a "natural" fortification which cannot be perceived as a "habitation" from the outside. In a sense this is as close as we can get to an answer to the problem formulated at the beginning. Pursuit of the mystery might, however, give a fuller sense of the implications of this strategy for the development of the novel.

III   The Necessity of Becoming Other

> I preferred to excuse myself and blame this unknown thing which was in me but was not part of me. The truth, of course, was that it was all my own self, and my own impiety had divided me against myself.
>
> (Augustine, Confessions, p. 103 [Bk. V, Sec. 10])

After fifteen years, after this material and spiritual security has seemed complete, and his only confrontation has been hearing unexpectedly his own name pronounced by his parrot, Robinson experiences the incredible shock of seeing the "naked footprint of a man." The hidden self-other structure of the book is brought into the open. The footprint is the merest sign of the *near* presence of another human being—yet shouting significance for Robinson in the very fact of its inadequacy of signification.

It is the sheerest kind of accident, almost miraculous, as he realized, that he has seen it. Characteristically he sums up the odds: "twas Ten Thousand to one whether I should see it or not, and in the Sand too, which the first Surge of the Sea upon a high Wind would have defac'd entirely" (VII, 179). A footprint in the sand—a partial signature whose power lies in its mystery and ambiguity. A sign of transience—in both the sense that it is the mark of action and also that it is temporary, contingent; it is the static trace of a human movement and a recent movement at that. But rather than being any signal to Crusoe's hopes—of company or of deliverance—in a flash the footprint destroys all his hopes and all his security.

The contradiction between Robinson's desire to externalize himself and his fear of being seen receives sharp definition:

> The first Thing I propos'd to my self, was, to throw down my Enclosures, and turn all my tame Cattle wild into the Woods, that the Enemy might not find them; and then frequent the Island in Prospect of the same, or the like Booty: Then to the simple Thing of Digging up my two Corn Fields, that they might not find such a Grain there, and still be prompted to frequent the Island; then to demolish my Bower, and Tent, that they might not see any Vestige of Habitation, and be prompted to look farther, in order to find out the Persons inhabiting. (VII, 184)

Seized by this terror at the possible presence of another human being, Robinson wants to remove all traces of himself from the island at the cost of destroying all that he has worked for, all that he has created of himself in things. He wants to disappear, to be invisible, to see without being seen. When he recovers his reason, he will try to accomplish this same end by more practical means. He will build a second wall, further enclosing himself; he will go out of it only rarely, when it is necessary, and then only with the greatest caution and circumspection; and he will go to great lengths to provide armed vantage points, hiding places where he can spy on intruders without himself being seen.

Before he conceives of the idea of erasing all trace of himself from the island by destroying his possessions, he imagines more reasonably such destruction by those who left the footprint:

> Then terrible Thoughts rack'd my Imagination about their having found my Boat, and that there were People here; and that if so, I should certainly have them come here again in greater Numbers, and devour me; that if it should happen so that they should not

> find me, yet they would find my Enclosure, destroy all my Corn,
> carry away all my Flock of tame Goats, and I should perish at last
> for meer Want. (VII, 180)

When he considers doing the same thing to himself, it is almost as if he would be acting in place of the others, doing to himself what he most fears at their hands. At this point in his narrative, in a confused way, a dialectic between self and other begins to emerge.

At first Robinson thinks the footprint must have been made by the Devil to frighten him. This idea removes the element of the contingent from the sign, gives it purpose *for* him. Curiously, his idea also mitigates the otherness of the sign. Later, when he is frightened by the dying "he-goat" in the cave, he comments "that he that was afraid to see the Devil, was not fit to live twenty Years in an Island all alone; and that I durst to believe there was nothing in this Cave that was more frightful than myself" (VII, 205). In the *Serious Reflections,* he notes the old proverb "that every solitary person must be an angel or a devil." Here the same association is implicit, for he moves from the idea that it is the Devil's footprint to the persuasion that it is a "meer Chimera of my own; and that this Foot might be the Print of my own Foot" (VII, 182). If this is true, "I might be truly said to start at my own Shadow," but he is unable to convince himself completely of this solution. He records his terrors when he leaves his shelter as if he were seen by someone else: "But to see with what Fear I went forward, how often I look'd behind me, how I was ready every now and then to lay down my Basket, and run for my Life, it would have made any one have thought I was haunted with an evil Conscience" (VII, 183). Roxana also thinks of herself as being haunted by her own evil conscience when the daughter named after her reappears in her life.

All these speculations—the chimera, his own foot, his own shadow, and evil conscience, the curious ability to see himself as another would see him— amount to a confusion between the self and the other. The island, which is an extension of himself, has dark areas Robinson has never explored; he is constantly startled by versions of himself, the voice of the parrot, the dying goat. In the same way the other holds a dimension of himself which Robinson has ignored, a reflection of himself that in his selfishness he has not recognized, and more, the other holds a part of himself in thrall, in an interdependence to which he has been blind. There is also an otherness *in* him. At this point, a brief comparison with an earlier autobiographer might be illuminating. The young Augustine was alienated from himself in his acceptance of the Manichean belief that evil was a foreign substance in the soul: "The truth, of course, was that it was all my own self, and my own impiety had divided me against myself" (*Confessions,* p. 103 [Bk. V, Sec. 10]). As a result of this blindness toward the true location of himself, he had fragmented and scattered himself among the objects of the world.[10] Similarly, Robinson is unable to account for whatever it is in him that constantly leads him to his own misery and destruction, his "foolish inclination of wandering abroad" (VII, 42), which leads to his scattering of self among the objects of his desire and fear.

Recognition of the nature of this otherness and its relation to himself comes gradually as he is exposed to the other in a series of very strange stages over a number of years: first, the footprint, then human bones—"all my Apprehensions were bury'd in the Thoughts of such a Pitch of inhuman, hellish Brutality, and the Horror of the Degeneracy of Humane Nature" (VII, 191)—and then finally the sight of the cannibals themselves from a distance. He is so horrified by them that he thinks of slaughtering them, making himself God's agent of justice, but he realizes both the presumption of this notion and its dangers for himself, so he decides to hold himself hidden and apart from them. To attack the cannibals without direct provocation to himself would not only question the design of God's providence for all creatures but it would also mean that he would be matching their barbarity with his own. Such an action on his part, he realizes, would be like the cruelty shown by the Spaniards in America, "a meer Butchery, a bloody and unatural Piece of Cruelty, unjustifiable either to God or Man; and such, as for which the very Name of *Spaniard* is reckon'd to be frightful and terrible to all People of Humanity, or of Christian Compassion" (VII, 199). The irony of this identification of the enemy as Spaniards and cannibals, both outside the pale of what is human, should be apparent, for Crusoe's first friends on his island, the first human subjects of his "common-wealth," are two cannibals and a Spaniard. He will not only be forced to recognize their humanity, but also will be driven to acknowledge their barbarity in himself or at least in those with whom he identifies.

For the moment, Robinson's two fears of exposure and of being devoured are now focused on this one representative of a cannibalistic nature which is ambiguously human. When another ship wrecks off his island and the entire crew is apparently lost, Robinson is given a strong sense of the possibilities in his own condition. One of his fantasies about the fate of these men is that they might have tried to make the shore in their boat but instead were carried out by the current "into the great Ocean, where there was nothing but Misery and Perishing; and that perhaps they might by this Time think of starving, and of being in a Condition to eat one another" (VII, 216). So, there are circumstances which could turn shipwrecked sailors like Robinson into cannibals. This possibility is reinforced when he and Friday witness the treacherous cruelty of the English mutineers—"O Master! " Friday says, "*You see* English *Mans eat Prisoner as well as* Savage *Mans*" (VII, 42).

On the other hand, it is the humanity of Friday and later of the Spaniard that Crusoe comes to know. The discovery of Friday's loyalty and devotion causes Robinson to reflect that even on savages God had bestowed

The same Powers, the same Reason, the same Affections, the same Sentiments of Kindness and Obligation, the same Passions and Resentments of Wrongs; the same Sense of Gratitude, Sincerity, Fidelity, and all the Capacities of doing Good, and receiving Good, that he has given to us; and that when he pleases to offer to them Occasions of exerting these, they are as ready, nay, more ready to apply them to the right Uses for which they were bestow'd, than we are. (VII, 243)

Robinson must come to see himself in the other and the other in himself. His "social contract," the statement of his subjects' dependence on him, is his covert admission of dependence on them since it is he who insists on it. He also comes to a greater self-knowledge by seeing himself and his works reflected in their eyes. Earlier he had seen himself from the outside as another, totally unsympathetic and possibly hostile, might have seen him. Now he sees himself from the perspective of a friendly providence in the misery of the English seamen who are about to be beached by the mutineers: "This put me in Mind of the first Time I came on Shore, and began to look about me; How I gave my self over for lost; How wildly I look'd round me: What dreadful Apprehensions I had: And how I lodg'd in the Tree all Night for fear of being devour'd by wild Beasts" (VIII, 43). This time he sees his despair in some one else and from the point of view of their and his deliverance. He reflects that just as he did not know that first night that the storm would drive the ship close enough to land for him to receive supply for his needs "so these three poor desolate Men knew nothing how certain of Deliverance and Supply they were, how near it was to them, and how effectually and really they were in a Condition of Safety, at the same Time that they thought themselves lost, and their Case desperate" (VIII, 43). Now, more than twenty-five years after Robinson's shipwreck, he knows that the same thing had been true of him, that he had been "in a Condition of Safety" when he had thought himself lost.

IV The Conversion of Conversion

The good which I now sought was not outside myself. I did not look for it in things which are seen with the eye of the flesh by the light of the sun. For those who try to find joy in things outside themselves easily vanish away into emptiness. . . . But it was in my inmost heart where I had grown angry with myself, where I had been stung with remorse, where I had slain my old self and offered it in sacrifice, where I had first purposed to renew my life

and had placed my hope in you, it was there that you had begun
to make me love you and had made me glad at heart.

(Confessions, p. 188 [Bk. IX, Sec. 4])

Crusoe's ability to stand outside himself is related here to his understanding of the providential meaning of experience. That he is able to see the other Englishmen from the standpoint of a providence of which he is now the agent results from his discovery of the plan of his own life much earlier in the book, when he was still alone on the island. This "objectivity" of the self and the corresponding vision of time's plan, transcending the experience of the isolated self, are the consequences of a conversion which in Defoe never seems a single moment, a sudden and total turning which restructures the self for all time, as it is, for example, in Augustine's *Confessions*. Crusoe does experience something like that moment—there are the misunderstood providential warnings, the despair about his isolation, the new warning in the storm, earthquake, and dream, the sickness that is symbolic of death, the discovery of the biblical message, the prayer and conviction of spiritual deliverance. But in time his certainty is dissipated as if by time itself. And each discovery of a new danger, for example, Crusoe's discovery of the footprint, at least temporarily wrecks all certainty.

Conversion is a recurrent need, a revelation followed each time by another lapse, a forgetting that is like an absence, requiring a new dialectical struggle. Not a completely new conversion, actually—Crusoe must be brought back to the self discovered in the initial conversion and by that movement freed from self-deception, freed in a sense from self. And this must happen again and again. He will suffer the consequences of the original fall, the restlessness, the "foolish inclination to wander abroad," as long as he lives. He must constantly refound himself in Christ and His providence, placing all his reliance on Him.

It is just here that resides buried the curious message of the episode of the corn, curious because it never became completely explicit and because it holds great meaning for Crusoe's egoism. When the corn sprouts first appeared, Robinson thought them miraculous, divine suspension of the laws of nature for his benefit. When he remembered that he had shaken out a bag of chicken feed in the place where the barley and rice were growing, "the Wonder began to cease; and I must confess, my religious Thankfulness on God's Providence began to abate too upon the Discovering that this was nothing but what was common" (VII, 89-90). In the perspective of the narration, Robinson's judgment on the vacillations is that

I ought to have been as thankful for so strange and unforeseen Providence, as if it had been miraculous; for it was really the Work of Providence as to me, that should order or appoint, that

> 10 or 12 Grains of Corn should remain unspoil'd (when the Rats
> had destroy'd all the rest,) as if it had been dropt from Heaven; as
> also, that I should throw it out in that particular Place where it
> being in the Shade of a high Rock, it sprang up immediately;
> whereas, if I had thrown it anywhere else, at that Time, it had
> been burnt up and destroy'd. (VII, 90)

Critics who, like Robinson, attribute spiritual significance to his experience regard the episode as symbolic of the "seeds" of Grace. In this context of Robinson's egoistic blindness against which the episode renders judgment the implications of the passage seem to be more probing. Surely the scriptural reference is to John 12:24-25: "Except a corn of wheat fall into the ground and die, it abideth alone: but if it die, it bringeth forth much fruit. He that loveth his life shall lose it; and he that hateth his life in his world shall keep it unto life eternal." Robinson must die to himself and place all his reliance on God.

Radical individualism in all its isolated inwardness was implicit in Christianity from its beginning; in its emphasis on the brotherhood of all men, the message of Christ explicitly cut across the limits of family, tribe, or nation. One expression of the subjectivist implications of Christianity was in the intense self-exploration of Augustine's *Confessions*, a work which informs Defoe's fictional project.[11] The implications of this individualism were worked out in the Renaissance and in a more radical way in the Reformation, of whose Puritan strain Robinson is a well-known representative. Yet Christianity was also provided with this antidote to the narcissism that threatened it—the notion of the symbolic death of the self. Robinson's resistance to God's call manifested itself in one way in his obsessive fear of the loss or death of self involved in being "swallowed up" or devoured by his beginnings, by the unformed chaos of the sea, by the other. Robinson does undergo a sickness unto death, literally and figuratively, a symbolic death of the self from which he emerges with a truer if temporary understanding of God's plan for him. And as the text from John suggests, and as it was for Augustine, in his sacrifice of self Robinson is given himself for the first time.

The nature of this gift is expressed more explicitly in Moll's conversion in Newgate. Her experience is at first wayward fluctuation between repentance and selfishness. When she discovers that her Lancashire husband is bound to be hanged for a highwayman, she is so overwhelmed by grief for him and by reflections on her own previous life that "in a Word, I was perfectly chang'd, and become another Body" (II, 107). But this transformation is a return to self: "The wretched Boldness of Spirit, which I had acquired, abated, and conscious Guilt began to flow in my Mind: In short, I began to think, and to think indeed is one real Advance from Hell to Heaven; all that harden'd State and Temper of Soul, which I said so much of before, is but a Deprivation of

Thought; he that is restor'd to his Thinking, is restor'd to himself" (II, 107). In as much as she is still concerned about her own fate, she is still selfish and the Moll who narrates doubts the sincerity of her repentance at this point. Finally, when she receives the condemnation of this court it is "a Sentence to me like Death itself" (II, 112) and she feels "real Signs of Repentance" (II, 113). Like Augustine and Robinson, she sees the things of this life in a new way: "I now began to look back upon my past Life with abhorrence, and having a kind of View into the other Side of Time, the Things of Life, as I believe they do with every Body at such a Time, began to look with a different Aspect, and quite another Shape, than they did before" (II, 113).

In his conversion, Augustine is also given a "view into the other side of time." He also is transformed into "another body," which paradoxically is a matter of being "restored to himself."Restored to himself first in this sense, as he says: "O Lord, you were turning me around to look at myself. For I had placed myself behind my own back, refusing to see myself. You were setting me before my own eyes so that I could see how sordid I was, how deformed and squalid, how tainted with ulcers and sores" (169). But he is also restored to himself in a larger sense. Augustine's last doubts before giving himself over to Christ were his doubts concerning his ability to accept continence. For this, he must throw himself on Christ's strength, not try to rely on his own. By being made capable of continence by God, Augustine is given himself, for as he explains: "By continence we are made as one and regain that unity of self which we lost by falling apart in the search for a variety of pleasures" (233).

The similarities between Defoe's fictional memoirs, particularly Robinson's, and their ultimate model, Augustine's *Confessions,* are striking, but their differences are of signal importance. Both Augustine and Robinson have relied upon themselves, upon their own strength and reason, in important, though differing, ways. Each experienced himself initially as incomplete. The early life of each was a wandering, yet for each every erring step was guided by Providence bringing him to the moment of salvation. To each the command of God comes by discovery of a chance word in a Sortes Biblicae. Each is brought by the symbolic death of conversion to an understanding of time and to a self-knowledge, the "proof" of which lies in the act of confession or narration.

For Defoe, however, the gift of self is as "symbolic" as the sacrificial death. Self will continue to reassert itself and be lost consequently in distraction. For it is Defoe's insight that the essential characteristic of a symbolic death is that it is only symbolic and must be repeated *endlessly. All* solutions in this life are symbolic, perhaps "figural" is a better word, and fallen man is never free of the consequences of Adam's sin until he suffers its original punishment, actual death. If he can be "justified" only by God, the promise figured by

Providence can be fulfilled only in Heaven. From this point of view, providence is sight cast forward, into the not yet. Is it too commonplace to say that modern realism is born in the split between the symbolic and the actual, in the despair over the real efficacy of the symbolic?

One consequence is that there is a necessary discrepancy between the allegorical truth and the fact of the story. For example, Tom Jones calls "father" a man named Allworthy, who is squire of Paradise Hall from which he evicts Tom for his wrongdoing. But Allworthy is not omniscient and Tom has not done what he has been accused of. Instead he is a victim of deceit, treachery, and misunderstanding—certainly no orthodox allegory of man's fall. Moreover, in the course of the novel, Tom must acquire wordly wisdom and aspires to Sophia who is not (at least in this novel) wise. Similarly, Richardson's Clarissa disobeys an inexplicable demand of her father and is seduced from her garden by the serpent-like Lovelace. Of course, in this case, the demand of the father is not only inexplicable, it is also patently unjust and Clarissa runs away with Lovelace to escape that injustice. The pattern is there, however, but from this point of view, the realistic story, life in this world, is an incomplete, distorted shadow of its spiritual truth. Hence the traditional dissatisfaction with the "allegory" of *Robinson Crusoe*. The point is not that these writers tried and failed to write novelistic allegories but that life could not be reduced or raised to a spiritual meaning.

The experiences of both Augustine and Robinson find their clear focus against a scriptural and sacred background. For example, the pear tree of Augustine's adolescence, the garden where his struggle with salvation takes place, and the fig tree under which he is saved are types of Adam's tree of forbidden fruit, the garden of Gethsemane, and Christ's "tree" or cross under which man is redeemed. Robinson's story is the story of Jonah and of the Prodigal Son. But it is the "real" Augustine who is offered in the *Confessions* by way of these stories, the real Augustine purged of the accidents of a purely personal life and revealed in the figural patterns of the Scriptures. On the other hand, Robinson is not a real person—the fact of his memoirs is their factitiousness. If, as Robinson insinuates in his *Serious Reflections*, his story is only allegorically true, then it is either true as some have thought of Defoe's own life or the truth of the story is offered as the general truth of everyman's life. If it is Defoe's truth, then the accidents of his own life are given in what is *essentially* true in Robinson's adventures. If it is a general truth, then another reversal has taken place, for this universal essence is offered as the *actuality* of a very eccentric individual life. Symbol and fact are united in Augustine's *Confessions* but forever divided in Robinson's.

This split is demonstrated in a striking way when Robinson appears to the English mutineers "as another Person": "So that as we never suffered them to see me a Governour, so I now appear'd as another Person, and spoke of the

Governour, the Garrison, the Castle, and the like, upon all Occasions" (VIII, 65). Here it is his metaphoric or spiritual condition (as "governor" of the island, "viceroy to the King of all the earth" [*Serious Reflections,* p. 179]), which is held aside, while his disguise, the *other* person he becomes, is his *actuality*, in all the fantastic garb of an eccentricity which has survived almost thirty years of isolation. His disguise is almost like the lies of Odysseus—more plausible than the fantastic adventures he has undergone in the *Odyssey*. I have said that the split is between the symbolic-essential and the accidental-actual, but here the value of these poles has been reversed and the actual has become "other" than the truth. The split in Robinson's being in this passage is also, and not incidentally, the same as the split between the bourgeois *legal person* and the unique individual.

Through his conversion Augustine gains both the true order of life and his true self—one and the same thing in confession, which is the *full* giving of self in speech whose truth is guaranteed by the presence of the Divine omniscient Other. The "real" self of Defoe's various "memoirs," however, is a fictive self. Defoe's confessions are not *his* confessions at all. The pattern of Christian truth has become the design of a lie masked as actuality, the plot of a novel. The symbolic death of the Christian pattern has become truly symbolic on another level, in as much as even actual death in fiction is still a symbolic death. And the symbolic deaths of Robinson's or Moll's conversions are the doubly symbolic deaths of surrogate selves.

The full implications of this death by proxy are revealed in the story of Roxana, where the death is carried a step more distant and conversion is either impossible or no longer necessary. Roxana makes her escape into the curious oblivion of the end of that book disguised by the clothes and sanctimonious speech of a Quaker, symbols of a conversion she cannot attain. The split in Roxana, indicated by disguise, is more complicated than Robinson's self-division. She appears as the self she would like to be (her "spiritual truth") at the same time she is confronted by her past self projected onto the form of her daughter who bears Roxana's true name, whom she deserted as a child, and who later appeared again as her servant at the moment she became the notorious Roxana. Now, it is this poor scapegoat of a daughter, the alter ego of a fictional character, yet the only truly individualized "other" of any of Defoe's fictions, who is made to suffer a sacrificial death for which Roxana will never be forgiven.

The death is brought about in a curious way—curious, in the light of the dialectic between self and other in Defoe's novels. The witness to Roxana's first crime against morality was her servant Amy. Roxana felt compelled to force Amy to sleep with her seducer: "As I thought myself a Whore, I cannot say but that it was something design'd in my Thoughts, that my Maid should be a Whore too, and should not reproach me with it" (47). As witness to her crime, Amy would become the dangerous other—seducers or seducees never seem to have enough self-consciousness to appear as threats to the self in Defoe. The witness is the dangerous other. Roxana, by watching Amy's seduction by the same man who has ruined her, has rendered Amy "safe." She has made her an accomplice, an adjunct to her own will. When, at the end of the book, Amy does away with the daughter by some means that Roxana can't bear to think about, Amy has become like an element of Roxana's personality capable of acting autonomously (somewhat like the daughter herself). That Amy is enacting Roxana's secret will is proved by Roxana's overwhelming sense of guilt. The book ends in the uncertainty of the unspeakable. It is either the most resolved of all the dialectical struggles between self and other in Defoe's fiction or the most unresolvable.

What is certain is that the symbolic death has been moved a step farther away from the "I" who narrated all of Defoe's books. The conversion has disappeared completely, although Roxana, beyond her Quaker costume, does become another person. Near the beginning of her account of her life, but speaking from the obscurity into which she disappears at the end, Roxana says: "Being to give my own Character, I must be excus'd to give it as impartially as possible, and as if I was speaking of another body" (6). What has replaced the conversion is the act of narration itself.

And what can be said of Defoe? In the Preface to *Roxana*, he describes himself as the "Relator" who will "speak" the words of the Beautiful Lady. Unable to give a true account of the self, he is doomed to speak the words of "another-body" as if they were his own, putting on the disguise of one fictive self after another.

V Providence and Writing: A Natural Habitation

> *Roxana's maxim, "That Secrets should never be open'd, with-out evident Utility." Robinson's maxim, "The prudent man for-seeth the evil and hideth himself."*
> *Speech was given to man to disguise his thoughts.*
>
> (Tallyrand)

When Robinson began to ponder the mystery of the footprint found on the beach, he discovered that he could not be certain that he had not left the print himself. Like the mystery of causality itself, the footprint is a trace of an intentional act seen from the outside: "Again, I consider'd also that I could by no Means tell for certain where I had trod, and where I had not; and that if at last this was only the Print of my own Foot, I had play'd the Part of those Fools, who strive to make stories of Spectres, and Apparitions; and then are frighted at them more than any body" (VII, 182). The enigmatic footprint is like a ghost story, a genre most interesting to Defoe, whose power is great enough to deceive even its own teller. The footprint then is similar to a myth, told by an individual who yet cannot claim authorship, like the dream from its source by disavowal. In short, the footprint is a figure for the book of Robinson's adventures. Did Robinson leave the footprint or was it left by the threatening other? Are the adventures authored by Defoe, who disavowed them, by the Robinson who signed them, or by the other in whose constant presence they are structured and who is their destination?

Perhaps there is already on Defoe's part a glimmmer of that suspicion of the concept of the unified and identifiable "subject" with which it has been seen by later thinkers, particularly by Nietzsche and Freud and more recently by Derrida. For Defoe's project seems to have involved the creation of more or less autonomous voices, themselves without a center, that is to say, irredeemably eccentric voices. Or, rather, voices whose center is a felt lack of center, the absence of which could be explained by the *insertion* of the myth of fallen man, yet voices created without the distance or structure of a consistent irony, a fact which has troubled the criticism of Defoe's books. Voices calculating a world of facts but who are themselves fictions after all. Books whose ambiguity is deep, thorough, and finally unresolvable.

The problem of Defoe criticism is well stated by the title of an early twentieth-study, William Trent's *Daniel Defoe: How to Know Him.* My strategy has been to chip away at the hard flint of that ultimately unanswerable question in the hope that the sparks would illuminate, if only slightly, the surrounding terrain.

How can Robinson tell for certain where "I had trod and where I had not"? Time, the shifting sand on the beach, how indeed can they afford a true history or a stable identity to a mind isolated in a subjectivity, the subject is so elusive? An heir of Adam, Robinson has lost the opportunity of "sensibly tasting the sweet of living, without the bitter" offered by his father at the beginning of the book. He can only come to knowledge dialectically, by contraries. He can only know good, his good, by experience of evil. Robinson's obsession with reason as *ratio*, measurement, his sometimes comical "accounting" point not only to his empiricism but also to the curse of fallen man. All evaluations of his condition are relative. When he considers himself ruined, he must acknowledge that there are others who are worse, just as in the beginning when his father tried to convince him he was set for life, he thought he could become better. In order to account for his condition after the shipwreck, he *has* to draw up the famous profit and loss sheet, the spiritual bookkeeping for which he (and Defoe with him) has been so often derided. The curiosity of this debit-credit sheet lies in its slipperiness. One *fact* is not registered against another. The facts are the same on both sides of the sheet; each side merely interprets the fact in a different way. There are no true alternatives present. Instead of representing Robinson's ingenuous calcu-lation, the sheet does give a true account of the flux of moods, moods considered as facts, the dizzying back and forth of a subjectivity deprived of an external gauge of truth.

Robinson's journal itself is another form of this spiritual bookkeeping. If one cannot gauge the meaning or portent of each moment, perhaps the pat-tern formed over longer periods of time would reveal the truth. Such an accounting might provide a true profit and loss tally of the spirit. Crusoe's journal not only documents his recall of day by day events as he recounts them more than thirty years later, it also represents an attempt to give the shifting moments of a subjective time something like a spatial ordering in the same way that he carves notches into a post to mark each day he is on the island. The journal is an attempt to define a situation by ordering the present as it becomes the past. Writing also means to Robinson a deliverance from the agonizing and vconfusing impact from momentary impressions about his con-dition: "I now began to consider seriously my Condition, and the Circum-stance I was reduc'd to, and I drew up the State of my Affairs in Writing, not so much to leave them to any that were to come after me, for I was like to have but few Heirs, as to deliver my Thoughts from daily poring upon them, and afflicting my Mind" (VII, 74).

Robinson wants what Sartre's Roquentin, one of his heirs, desires: "I wanted the moments of my life to follow and order themselves like those of a life remembered. You might as well try and catch time by the tail."[1 2] Cru-soe's journal, like the greater account of which it is a part, is an attempt to do precisely that—catch time by the tail. The events of each day are recorded into the journal, already culled and selected, already abolished by the past tense of language and presented to us, a legacy to heirs that the Crusoe *living* each moment could not expect. We can never, however, get close to the lived moment and neither can Robinson capture it. Even the journal shows signs of a later editing, at the time of the principal narration, from the perspective of a story already closed. Moreover, such a perspective inheres in the narrative past tense. As Roquentin observes, "You have started at the end . . . and the story goes on in the reverse: instants have stopped piling themselves in a lighthearted way one on top of the other, they are snapped up by the end of the story which draws them and each one of them in turn, draws out the preceding instant" (57-58). The whole book is caught up on a past tense suggesting an end which renders significant each sentence.

Crusoe's story, however, goes backwards in more obvious senses than that meant by Roquentin and Sartre. We are given no fewer than four accounts of Robinson's first day on the island, each differing in some small detail: the main account in Robinson's narrative, *two* journal accounts, and finally when Robinson relives his plight as he watches the English mutineers and their victims. First, we have the account in the chronological course of Crusoe's narrative, written years later, long after even his return from the island to civilization.

The second version is composed at the same time. This is the journal that might have been, if he had started it when he first landed on the island and it curiously is the one most different although it is ostensibly contemporaneous with the narration of the book. The reason that he did not begin the journal the first days was that he was too busy then making himself secure but also that he was "in too much discomposure of mind, and my journal would have been full of many dull things." The writing of the journal then is the result of the *composition* of his mind and although it has precedence in time over the other two versions, it is still separated from the event by an extensive period of time, for Robinson doesn't begin it until he is more or less settled on the island—perhaps six weeks after the shipwreck, after he finished the table and chair, probably November 12 according to the journal itself.

The differences between these accounts of his first days, mainly concerning whether he wept with joy or with terror, despair or thanksgiving, whether he slept on the ground or in a tree, are less significant than the fact that there *are* differences. What are we to make of this confusion, other than to see it as an emphasis on the elusiveness of even the facts of this narrative and an admission of an irreparable tear between the written account and the naked, lived moment? The journal—trace of the event—is vacant like the footprint. In fact, it is marked by a double absence. The writing of the account releases Robinson from the pain and confusion of experiencing—"to deliver my thoughts from daily poring upon them, and afflicting my mind." The journal serves the same purpose. And it is also removed from the event. It objectifies and orders both Robinson's thoughts and his daily experiences.

The gap cannot be closed. Narrative language removes the contingency and absurd inconsequence of the lived moment by abstracting that moment from the field of open possibility and directing it toward a certain outcome which will define it and give it significance. As Roquentin comments, " 'It was night, the street was deserted.' The phrase is cast out negligently, it seems superfluous; but we do not let ourselves be caught and we put it aside: this is a piece of information whose value we shall subsequently appreciate. And we feel that the hero has lived all the details of this night like annunciations, promises, or even that he lived only those that were promises, blind and deaf to all that did not herald adventure" (58).

Annunciations, promises, and one might add, portents and warnings—for that is precisely the way Crusoe lives, or rather relives in his narrative, each event of his experience. What in the already realized end guarantees the significance of each event is identical with the ordering of written narrative and the opposite of the subjective flux of the lived moment—the discovery of

God's plot, His Providence. The point of view of narrative is precisely a providence. In God's plan, Robinson's end *is* in his beginning—each step along the way is either a promise or a warning, but always an annunciation of a divine structure which exists outside of time, but which operates in and through time. Sartre's argument with narrative is that the foundation of the passing moment in narrative language bestows on it a privilege, robes it with a destiny, that is altogether false to experience, but Robinson's discovery of a special providence saves the moment, placing on each moment a heavy burden of significance.

Providence not only underwrites Robinson's narrative, it is also discovered by means of the writing of the journal. The subject caught in the flow of time is blind to the providential meaning of his experience. Crusoe suffers the flickering onrush of momentary sensations and is driven by selfish appetites and fears which change as rapidly as circumstances change: "Everything revolves in our minds by innumerable circular motions, all centering in ourselves" (*Serious Reflections,* p. 2): "And by what secret differing Springs are the Affections hurry'd about as differing Circumstances present! To Day we love what to Morrow we hate; to Day we seek what to Morrow we shun; to Day we desire what to Morrow we fear; nay even tremble at the Apprehensions of" (*Robinson Crusoe*, VII, 180).

Though Crusoe is given many warnings, many chances for repentance, as soon as the warning danger has passed, so dissolve Robinson's resolutions and promises. The Defoe self in isolation is the self of Hobbesian sensationalism. The order revealed one moment is obliterated by the new sensations crowding in the next. It is the function of narrative, with its double perspective, to remember.

By means of his journal, Robinson discovers the startling concurrence of his "fortunate and fatal days":

> As long as it [the ink] lasted, I made use of it to minute down the Days of the Month on which any remarkable Thing happened to me, and first by casting up Times past: I remember that there was a strange Concurrence of Days, in the various Providences which befel me; and which, if I had been superstitiously inclin'd to observe Days as Fatal or Fortunate, I might have had Reason to have look'd upon with a great deal of Curiosity.
>
> First, I had observed, that the same Day that I broke away from my Father and my Friends, and ran away to *Hull*, in order to go to Sea; the same Day afterwards I was taken by the *Sallee* Man of War, and made a Slave.
>
> The same Day of the Year that I escaped out of the Wreck of that Ship in *Yarmouth* Roads, that same Day—Years afterwards I made my escape from *Sallee* in the boat.

The same Day of the Year I was born on (*viz.*) the 30th of *September,* that same Day, I had my Life so saved 26 Years after, when I was cast on Shore in this Island, so that my wicked Life, and my solitary Life begun both on a Day. (VII, 153-54)

Later, when Robinson leaves the Island of Despair, he is "deliver'd from this second Captivity, the same Day of the Month, that I first made my Escape in the *Barco-Longo*, from among the *Moors of Sallee*" (VIII, 74). Robinson will justify our belief in such amazing coincidences by detailing examples in his essay on Providence from the long tradition of such concurrences, beginning with the Scriptures and continuing into modern political history. The scriptural example alone marks the meaning of this pattern in Robinson's life. It is in Exodus 12: 41-42 and has to do with the children of Israel leaving their exile and imprisonment in Egypt the same day of the year, 430 years after they entered into it. Robinson's isolation has also been an exile and imprisonment, but the justification has a larger meaning as do all the scriptural parallels. Robinson's exile from himself and from the truth has been a type of the exile of the chosen people and of everyman, but as the real history of a man, as it is presented, it represents a figural truth. In the Preface to his *Serious Reflections* when he admits the story is allegorical, Robinson does not give up the claim to its authenticity. He simply claims to have "displaced" its literal truth:

> All these reflections are just history of a state of forced confinement, which in my real history is represented by a confined retreat in an island; and it is as reasonable to represent one kind of imprisonment by another, as it is to represent anything that really exists by that which exists not. The story of my fright with something on my bed was word for word a history of what happened, and indeed all those things received very little alteration, except what necessarily attends removing the scene from one place to another. (xii)

One is reminded that among the earliest meanings of *figura* was its usage in rhetoric to conceal the truth (in a figure of speech).[18] It usually had to do with suggesting without actually expressing a truth which for political or tactical reasons or simply for effect could not be expressed openly. This was precisely Defoe's purpose.

Any discussion of the question necessarily collapses into the ambiguity Defoe left surrounding it.[14] No sooner are we satisfied with his admission of allegorical truth in the Preface to Robinson's *Serious Reflections* than we discover that among the reflections it prefaces is "An Essay upon Honesty" and another on "the Immorality of Conversation," which contains a section about "Talking Falsely." No oversight on Defoe's part. In case we miss the point, he at first distinguished from the lying tales he is attacking such "historical parables" as those in the Holy Scripture, *Pilgrim's Progress*, or, "in a word, the adventures of your fugitive friend, 'Robinson Crusoe' " (101). But then he makes the standard Puritan attack on realistic fiction: any fiction that offers itself as historical truth is a dangerous and damning lie. Lest we dismiss the discrepancy as mere ingenuousness on the part of Defoe, he adds the following disclaimer: "If any man object here that the preceding volumes of this work seem to be hereby condemned, and the history which I have therein published of myself censured, I demand in justice such objector stay his censure till he sees the end of the scene, when all that mystery shall discover itself, and I doubt not but the work shall abundantly justify the design, and the design abundantly justify the work" (103). Does that settle the issue?

Ambiguity aside, it is possible to say that while Defoe is impersonating Robinson Crusoe, he is also impersonating on another level Providence itself. Just as the double vision made possible by the Christian conversion is replaced by the double vision of narration, the structure of narration has stood in place of providence.

It is no accident and may in fact be "the end of the scene" Robinson alluded to earlier that the last story he tells in his *Serious Reflections* concerns a young man who speaks to an atheist in the voice of a mutual friend and is taken instead for the voice of a spirit, messenger of God and medium of His Providence, by the disbeliever who is thereby saved.

Defoe's fortress is complete, constructed according to the laws of nature and concealing the plot of Providence. It is a natural habitation, in which like Robinson, Defoe can live in the open but unseen and unmolested by devouring eyes. In this essay on "Solitude" Robinson countered the voluntary withdrawal into the desert wilderness of the religious hermit by the voluntary exile in the midst of society by means of something like disguise. Peaceful solitude "would every way as well be supplied by removing from a place where a man is known to a place where he is not known, and there accustom himself to a retired life, making no new acquaintances, and only making the use of mankind which I have already spoken of, namely, for convenience and supply of necessary food; and I think of the two that such a man, or a man so retired, may have more opportunity to be an entire recluse, and may enjoy more real solitude than a man in a desert" (13-14). Defoe's fiction has provided him with such a hermitage.

Many novelists who followed Defoe were strangers in a strange land and found means of both concealing and exposing themselves in their novels. Pseudonymity and anonymity haunt the novel throughout the eighteenth and nineteenth centuries. Perhaps these novelists too confronted the necessity of becoming other persons in their narrators. There was Richardson's "editorship," for example, and while Jane Austen's and George Eliot's concealment of their names was perhaps only conventional for lady writers, Stendhal's need for pseudonyms was obsessional. Scott, already a famous author, concealed himself behind the tag of "the author of Waverley" and became the most visible "great unknown" of his day. Defoe's discoveries about the nature of narrative and its plots made the novel an apt genre for a society of isolated and mutually suspicious individuals. Perhaps all novelists begin in anonymity and construct for themselves the personality of their works.

NOTES

1 Shakespeare Head edition (Oxford and New York, 1928), I, 188. All citations of *Moll Flanders* and *Robinson Crusoe* refer to this edition and are identified by volume and page number in my text. Quotation of the third volume of *Robinson Crusoe, Serious Reflections*, are taken from the George A. Aitken edition (London 1895) and are identified by title and page number. Quotations from *Roxana* and from *A Journal of the Plague Year* are taken from the Oxford English Novels series: *Roxana*, ed. Jane Jack (London, 1964), and *A Journal*, ed. Louis Landa (London, 1969), and are identified in my text by page number. The writing of this paper was made possible by a grant from the Center for Advanced Study, University of Illinois.

2 Actually, Robinson was born under the name *Kreutznaer*, "but by the usual Corruption of Words in *England*, we are now called, nay we call our selves, and write our Name *Crusoe*."

3 Trans. R. S. Pine-Coffin (Baltimore, 1961), p. 53 (Bk. II, Sec. 10). All further quotations of the *Confessions* are taken from this edition.

4 See G. A. Starr's *Defoe and Spiritual Autobiography* (Princeton, 1955) and J. Paul Hunter's *The Reluctant Pilgrim* (Baltimore, 1966).

5 Ian Watt, *The Rise of the Novel* (Berkeley, 1959), p. 133.

6 At least part of the impulse behind Defoe's fiction is the desire to explore human possibilities in the face of a necessity so harsh as to suspend normal laws. The whole question of natural right has been examined in Maximillian E. Novak's *Defoe and the Nature of Man* (Oxford, 1963).

7 The pressures against Defoe's writing these novels seem multiplied when one remembers that Defoe was violating the Puritan ban against realistic fictions. For a discussion of this problem, see Hunter, *The Reluctant Pilgrim*, pp. 114-24. For other accounts of Defoe's ambivalence about "feign'd Histories," see Maximillian Novak's "Defoe's Theory of Fiction," *SP*, 61 (1964), 650-68, and the chapter on Defoe in Alan McKillop's *The Early Masters of English Fiction* (Lawrence, 1956). For a discussion of the background of this problem, see William Nelson's "The Boundaries of Fiction in the Renaissance: A Treaty Between Truth and Falsehood," *ELH*, 36 (1969), 30-58.

8 See James Sutherland, *Defoe* (London, 1950), p. 91.

9 Frank H. Ellis has revealed in the Introduction to his *Twentieth-Century Interpretations of Robinson Crusoe* (Englewood Cliffs, 1969), pp. 12 ff., the extent to which Defoe organized this book on the basis of images of devouring.

10 I make a more extensive comparison with Augustine's *Confessions* later on. Augustine's influence on the Puritans is well known. In addition, however, there are structural similarities between Augustine's *Confessions* and Defoe's "autobiographies." This influence was conveyed, if not directly, by way of the confessions and spiritual autobiographies of the seventeenth century, as Starr and Hunter have shown. On this point, see also Paul Delaney's *Briitish Autobiography in the Seventeenth Century* (London and New York, 1969).

11 See note 10.

12 Jean-Paul Sartre, *Nausea*, trans. Lloyd Alexander (New York, n.d.), p. 58. Further quotations refer to this edition and are identified by page number in my text.

13 See Erich Auerbach's essay on "Figura" in his *Scenes From the Dream of European Literature* (New York, 1959), p. 45.

14 See note 7.

The Problem of the Environment in Les Rêveries du promeneur solitaire

EVE KATZ

Jean-Jacques Rousseau's life was one long conflict between his sense of self and the external circumstances of his existence. It was this tension—which he recognized as common to all men, in varying degrees—that Rousseau had hoped to explore and resolve in a book he projected when he was about forty-four years old, and which was to be called *la morale sensitive* or *le matérialisme du sage*. He had planned to use the instability he had observed in himself as a point of departure. If he could define what it was that caused a man's nature to change on different occasions, Rousseau reasoned, then he could help men learn how to prevent unworthy desires from developing. Familiar with the sensationalism of Locke and Condillac, Rousseau explained man's nature as being—to a large extent—(and it is Rousseau who adds this qualification), the effect of impressions made by the environment, "des objets extérieurs," as he puts it.* These impressions may be subsequently modified. With the use of observed data, Rousseau hoped to determine the *general* external conditions ("régime extérieur") which could then be varied according to *specific* circumstances and would be able to put or keep a man's

*Jean-Jacques Rousseau, *Oeuvres complètes*, Pléiade, I, *Confessions*, 409. All subsequent quotations from Rousseau will be from this edition unless otherwise indicated. The volume, title of the work, and page number will be given in parentheses immediately following the quotation.

character in a state likely to advance virtue. His dream, then, was to find a way of modifying all those physical impressions which, in his words, effect our body and hence our soul:

> Que d'écarts on sauveroit à la raison, que de vices on empêcheroit de naitre si l'on savoit forcer l'économie animale à favoriser l'ordre moral qu'elle trouble si souvent! Les climats, les saisons, les sons, les couleurs, l'obscurité, la lumiére, les élemens, les alimens, le bruit, le silence, le mouvement, le repos, tout agit sur notre machine et sur notre ame par consequent; tout nous offre mille prises presque assurées pour gouverner dans leur origine les sentimens dont nous nous laissons dominer. (I, *Confessions*, 409)

Some years earlier Rousseau had written a short piece on the influence of climate on civilization, in which he affirmed the total dependence of man on his environment—although he did remark that this is perhaps less true of individuals than of peoples: ". . . l'homme tient à tout ce qui l'environne. Il dépend de tout, et il devient ce que tout ce dont il dépend le force d'être" (III, *Fragment politiques,* 530). Later, he often refuted the idea of man's total passivity to outside impressions, distinguishing sensation, what he calls a "sensibilité physique et organique," which is purely passive, from sentiment, a "sensibilité active et morale" (I, 2e *Dial.,* 805). In the *Profession de foi* the vicar distinguishes ideas, which come from the outside, and are acquired, from feelings, which come from within, and are natural. It is these innate moral feelings which actively direct man to the good once it is brought to his rational attention and which Rousseau calls "conscience" (IV, *Emile,* 598-600).

Rousseau never wrote the *morale sensitive*, but he did explore the awesome possibility of establishing a system of correspondences between the physical and psychological world in three other books on which he worked simultaneously and which were published within a year of one another in 1761-1762: *La Nouvelle Héloise, Emile, Le Contrat social.* Wolmar deliberately places St. Preux in a carefully planned situation in order to cure him of his love for Julie. He closely supervises, together with his wife, all aspects of the communal life of Clarens: all its members are obliged to conform to a clearly formulated design for a society in which the practice of virtue ensures a constant example for all to emulate. In *Emile*, it is the tutor who so arranges things that his pupil will react as he should. In the *Contrat social,* consonant with the project of *la morale sensitive,* Rousseau proposes a *general* political scheme which could be adapted to *specific* circumstances, one in which, with the legislator's superior vision, citizens are helped to overcome the selfishness of ordinary civil society and are guided back to the practice of natural virtue.

As early as 1754, in what has been called his pre-constructive period, Rousseau ascribed to environmental, and specifically physical, environmental conditions some of the responsibility for the development of human society. In his *Discours sur l'inégalité,* it is fortuitous changes in the external environment which set off the inherent "perfectibility" of man and which start him on that calamitous road toward civilization. Rousseau speaks of topographical differences and climatic transformations which force changes in primitive man's habits. A chance thunderbolt or volcanic eruption, he conjectures, may have shown man fire. Thus, Rousseau suggests, the delicate balance by which the moral and intellectual dimensions of man were kept from developing was upset by external physical forces. The development of society is explained not by man's nature alone, but by the interaction between his primitive instincts and his physical milieu.

The period which Rousseau describes as the happiest for man was one in which, curiously, time seemed to come to a temporary halt, and in which a precarious balance was maintained between man's natural and social qualities (III, *Discours sur l'inégalité,* 171). It is this lost equilibrium which the *morale sensitive* was to help man recapture. When Rousseau describes unhappiness in *Emile,* he speaks of an improper relationship between man's actual powers and his psychological desires:

> c'est [. . .] dans la disproportion de nos desirs et de nos facultés que consiste nôtre misére. Un être sensible dont les facultés égaleroient les desirs seroit un être absolument heureux. (IV, 303-4)

Happiness, then, is harmony between man's physical and psychological situation, between his objective and subjective state. In so far as this tensionless ideal of equilibrium is associated, in Rousseau's mind, with an earlier condition of mankind, one can relate it to Freud's notion of the death instinct, defined as a regressive tendency toward the reinstatement of an earlier condition which man had to abandon under the influence of external disturbing forces.

The last of the twenty-seven playing cards on which Rousseau jotted down some thoughts for his *Rêveries* has five notations which suggest a thematic scheme for the promenades. The second and fifth notation are the same words: "morale sensitive." Thus, twenty years after conceiving the project, Rousseau was still trying to solve the problem of the individual's adjustment to his environment. No longer young in 1776, feeling himself near the end of his life, Rousseau increasingly assimilated the ideal of mankind's lost childhood with the salvation of a state free from the conditions of mortal existence. Furthermore, the problem of adjustment which is, in this last work, an intensely personal one, was so aggravated by Rousseau's feeling of persecution that it had to be reformulated.

Just as the equality which reigns at the wine-gathering festivities in Clarens is a *consolation* for those who in fact must obey the rules conceived by others (II, *La Nouvelle Héloïse,* 608), so the various moments of happiness evoked in *Les Rêveries*—the gratification of self-knowledge, the comfort of joyful memories, the delight of encounters with children, the contentment while botanizing, the ecstasy of the reveries themselves—all are conceived as means of soothing the pain of alienation from other men. "Il y a compensation à tout," says Rousseau in the 9th promenade (I, *Rêveries,* ix, 1090).

In each of his main public writings, Rousseau examined the breach that had developed between man as he was originally and man as he had become. The problem of the reintegration of the urban European with his environment and his own history would be overcome by first recovering a sense of self, and this could best be done by a cultivation of sensual experience in nature. In the winter of 1756-57, Rousseau advises madame d'Houdetot to take periodic retreats in the country, to commune with herself: "commençons en un mot par nous rassembler où nous sommes, afin qu'en cherchant à nous connaître, tout ce qui nous compose vienne à la fois se présenter à nous" (*Corr. générale,* éd. Dufour, Lettre morale VI, 369). This is what Emile must do before he can join society. Yet Rousseau fails to concretize the second step in positive experience. Emile's existence in society, for example, is an unhappy one, and in the generalized conceptions of the *Contrat social,* the life of the citizen is never described.

Ideally, solitude and community are always complementary in Rousseau. "Recueillez-vous," he continues telling Sophie d'Houdetot, "cherchez la solitude: voilà d'abord tout le secret, et par celui-là seul on découvre bientôt les autres" (Lettre VI, 370). Only through "recueillement" can one learn the "sentimens expansifs" which truly join us to other men. By the time Rousseau undertakes his *Rêveries,* however, this second step has become impossible. Society has refused to recognize the real Jean-Jacques, in whose place it has substituted a fictional monster; mankind has systematically undermined every attempt at reconciliation. In the process of writing the *Rêveries,* Rousseau formulates a suspicion he had long resisted, namely, that he is unfit for civil society as it exists. He is consequently obliged to resolve his relationship to his environment in an un-social way. I should like to outline some of his solutions as proposed in the *Rêveries du promeneur solitaire,* keeping in mind the *morale sensitive* so much in his thoughts as he was writing these last pages.

The environment in which Rousseau now dwells has cosmic dimensions. Pain comes from other men; relief can come only from avoiding them. The extreme wickedness of mankind renders licit, even dictates, Jean-Jacques' flight into the comfort of a union with the Eternal Being, of identification with a universal order. Feeling himself near the end of his life, Rousseau is approaching communion with the one being who knows him as he knows himself, whose judgment can be no more severe than his own– God. Like Julie, Rousseau will be able to eradicate the tensions of mortal existence only by a direct contemplation of the Eternal Being. In expectation of this sublime encounter, Rousseau seeks the ecstasy of union with "la nature entière" (viii, 1066). Because the orderly world of the stars is far away and difficult to study, Rousseau explains in the 7th promenade, he concentrates on the world of plants. It reflects a consoling universal order to one constantly threatened by the nightmare of chaos (vii, 1069). Jean-Jacques can actually *feel* the cover of anonymity, realize the fantasy of invisibility, as the shadows and branches enclose his body (vii, 1070). The "vieux enfant" of the second dialogue (I, 800) is at war with all his brothers. More than ever he needs to *feel* the comfort of mother nature: "me réfugiant chez la mère commune j'ai cherché dans ses bras à me soustraire aux atteintes de ses enfants . . ." (vii, 1066). The sight, even the memory, of her other children threatens to come between this child and his consolation (viii, 1082-83).

The experience of reverie in the promenade is well known. Exploiting his physical nature, his dependence on physical stimuli, Rousseau reaches a state of timeless consciousness, a feeling of harmony between subjectivity and objectivity, activity and passivity, in which all distressing distinction between the self and the universe is overcome. In the 5th promenade, Rousseau takes pleasure for a moment in thinking he could realize such ecstasy in the Bastille or a dungeon, far from outside stimuli, but then recognizes how difficult it would be to achieve this fulfillment in barren isolation (v, 1048). In any case, now that old age has weakened Rousseau's imagination, reverie has become harder and harder to experience. But what is of particular interest to us is the fact that Rousseau conceives of his alienation and the solution to it in cosmic terms. His environment is one in which other men have become "nuls" to him (i, 995) and in which he has become "nul" to them (i, 1000). He must establish a relationship with a universe empty of men. This he can do through concrete physical experience. It is by returning to the world of sensation of early natural man that Rousseau's isolation from mankind can be made tolerable. It is sensual contact which keeps his isolation from being unbearable. For without it, far from fusing with the cosmos, he is lost in it: "Je suis sur la terre comme dans une planète étrangère où je serais tombé de celle que j'habitais" (i, 999). Rousseau frequently evokes this feeling of having fallen, of having lost solid contact. But, as he explains in the 6th promenade, the links which occasionally have joined him to others (in a relationship born of a kind act, for example) soon become chains, "la chaine des devoirs," "des chaines d'engagemens" (vi, 1051). He reaches the implicit conclusion that the gap between himself and others is not only to be explained by the plot against him. His nature was not made for social life; or rather, it is society, he concludes again, that corrupts nature: "C'est alors que j'eus lieu de connoitre que tous les penchans de la nature sans excepter la bienfaisance ellemême portés ou suivis dans la societé sans prudence et sans choix changent de nature et deviennent souvent aussi nuisibles qu'ils étoient utiles dans leur premiére direction" (vi, 1052).

In his *Discours sur l'origine de l'inégalité parmi les hommes*, Rousseau describes the first men as pre-moral beings, limited to a sensual existence. Similarly, as he demonstrates in *Emile*, every individual begins life on a purely physical basis. In the *Rêveries*, written in his mid-sixties, Rousseau attempts to recover a state in some ways close to infancy. He tries to divest his environment of its moral dimensions and to establish a relationship to it on a physical basis alone. This may be irresponsible, he recognizes, but it is excusable, he explains in the 5th promenade, because others have cut him off from society. Clearly, the mechanical occupations, so like childrens' games, of copying music and botanizing (which has all the advantages of taking place in nature) are potentially less threatening than writing, which stimulates the memory and can summon up painful as well as pleasant experiences. One might say, in the most general terms, that Rousseau's objective becomes to dehumanize his existence. Wolmar, the legislator, and Emile's tutor had earlier understood that de-personalized authority is the most successfully imposed. Man does and should accept only "la nécessité des choses." In the *Rêveries*, Rousseau attempts to create such an illusion for himself, to practice on himself the "duplicity" critics have accused him of condoning in his public writings.

Consistent with the *morale sensitive*, in *La Nouvelle Héloise*, *Le Contrat social*, and *Emile*, virtue is encouraged, even created by manipulation of an environment; and the environment is made to appear an objective necessity. In *Les Rêveries*, Rousseau uses a similar tactic in coming to terms with his painful situation. The stratagem can be used as effectively to endure pain as to promote goodness. Since *ignoring* the world of men through reverie or distracting activities is only partly successful, Rousseau also attempts to *redefine* it by ridding it of all moral intention.

It is in the 8th promenade that Rousseau takes up several of the themes of the first two and reformulates them in mechanical terms. From the start of the work he had de-personalized the enemy: "la race humaine," "la canaille," "une génération entière," become "les corps qui m'ont pris en aversion" (i, 998). In this late promenade, Rousseau explicitly rids his enemies of all moral intention. "Pressé de tous côtés," he sees them as a purely mechanical force: ". . . je compris que mes contemporains n'étoient par rapport à moi que des êtres méchaniques qui n'agissoient que par impulsion et dont je ne pouvois calculer l'action que par les loix du mouvement" (viii, 1078). There is of course great comfort in this reduction of hostility to physical, non-moral activity:

...je devois regarder tous les détails de ma destinée comme autant d'actes d'une pure fatalité où je ne devois supposer ni direction, ni intention, ni cause morale, [...] il falloit m'y soumettre sans raisonner et sans regimber parce que cela seroit inutile, [...] tout ce que j'avois à faire encore sur la terre étant de m'y regarder comme un être purement passif je ne devois point user à résister inutilement à ma destinée la force qui me restoit pour la supporter. (viii, 1079)

The passivity which Rousseau saw as a weapon against his enemy at the beginning of the *Rêveries* is expressed again here, but in mechanical terms:

Je cède à toutes les impulsions présentes, tout choc me donne un mouvement vif et court, sitot qu'il n'y a plus de choc le mouvement cesse, rien de communiqué ne peut se prolonger en moi. Tous les evenemens de la fortune, toutes les machines des hommes ont peu de prise sur un homme ainsi constitué. Pour m'affecter de peines durables il faudroit que l'impression se renouvellat à chaque instant. (viii, 1084)

Rousseau will not meet force with counter-force; relief will come as *stasis*.

There is however an inconsistency in this tactic of reducing the relationship between self and other to a purely physical one. The ultimate aim of *la morale sensitive* was to promote virtue. In *Les Rêveries*, Rousseau is true to this aim in his attempt to use the examination of his relationship to his environment for self-improvement: "Heureux si par mes progrès sur moi-même, j'apprends à sortir de la vie, non meilleur, car cela n'est pas possible, mais plus vertueux que je n'y suis entré" (iii, 1023). But this moral objective cannot be reconciled with the de-moralization of the environment. Virtue cannot come from a purely physical relationship. What is more, since as long as he writes Rousseau cannot pretend to have eliminated his own moral dimension, there can be no true harmony between him and the artificially de-moralized milieu he posits. The reflexivity signified by each written word belies the purely physical relationship affirmed.

Rousseau *does* evoke his destiny or the will of God to explain his suffering: "Dieu est juste; il veut que je souffre; et il sait que je suis innocent. Voila le motif de ma confiance, mon coeur et ma raison me crient qu'elle ne me trompera pas. Laissons donc faire les hommes et la destinée ..." (ii, 1010). But, just as often, he chooses a different vocabulary, that of the physical sciences and sensationalist psychology, in order to express the notion of fate and to explain and come to terms with his painful predicament.

In the *Rêveries*, as in his other writings, Rousseau constantly affirms his responsiveness to sense impressions. This may of course bring relief. In the days when he had a more active imagination, Rousseau used to be able to use physical reality to flee reality. Rousseau used the "objets environments" as a way of fixing his attention and reaching a kind of hypnotic state in which these same external stimuli were forgotten. Thus, in the 5th promenade, he says of the reverie: "Il y faut des dispositions de la part de celui qui les éprouve, il en faut dans le concours des *objets environnans*" (my italics; v, 1047). And two lines further on: "Si le mouvement est inégal ou trop fort il réveille; en nous rappelant aux *objets environnans*, il détruit le charme de la rêverie . . ." (my italics; v 1047). Now that his imagination is weaker, botanizing allows Rousseau to substitute pleasant sensations for painful ones. As he puts it in the 7th promenade, "Mon imagination qui se refuse aux *objets de peine* laissoit mes sens se livrer aux impressions légéres mais douces des *objets environnans*" (my italics; vii, 1063).

His great sensitivity to physical impressions is, however, also vulnerability: "Cette action de mes sens sur mon coeur fait le seul tourment de ma vie" (viii, 1082). For Rousseau experiences the conflict I have already characterized. As he seeks to reduce his reaction to the law of inertia, he wants to limit his impressions to sensual ones. But he discovers that he is unable to separate his "sensibilité physique" from his "sensibilité morale." The only solution is to get out of his enemies' range, as he explains in the 6th promenade: "Leur aspect frape mes sens et par eux mon coeur d'impressions que mille regards cruels me rendent pénibles; mais le malaise cesse aussi tot que l'objet qui le cause a disparu. Je m'occupe d'eux et bien malgré moi par leur présence, mais jamais par leur souvenir. Quand je ne les vois plus, ils sont pour moi comme s'ils n'existoient point" (vi, 1056-57). Now that the gift for reverie and imaginative creation is gone, Rousseau depends more than ever upon his sensations: "Mon ame morte à tous les grands mouvemens ne peut plus s'affecter que par des objets sensibles; je n'ai plus que des sensations, et ce n'est plus que par elles que la peine ou le plaisir peuvent m'atteindre ici bas" (vii, 1068). But since Rousseau cannot control the sense impressions which come his way, he is at their mercy. Chance and the deliberate manipulation of his enemies are working against him: ". . . j'échape rarement à quelque atteinte sensible, et lorsque j'y pense le moins un regard sinistre que j'apperçois, un mot envenimé que j'entends, un malveillant que je recontre, suffit pour me bouleverser" (viii, 1082). What is more, he can no longer even trust the evidence of his senses, for the stimuli are being controlled by hostile forces: ". . . certain qu'on ne me laisse pas voir les choses comme elles sont, je m'absteins de juger sur les apparences qu'on leur donne . . ." (vi, 1056). With his contemporaries, Rousseau had often noted man's dependence upon his senses, limited in number and subjected to external contingencies. His description of a hysterical seizure at the end of the 8th promenade makes clear how literally he was at the mercy of the physical manifestations of his mental state. In a less acute

way, too, Rousseau experiences his anguish as physical constriction and op-
pression: "Mon âme offusquée, obstruée par mes organes s'affaisse de jour en
jour et sous le poids de ces lourdes masses n'a plus assez de vigueur pour
s'élancer comme autrefois hors de sa vieille envelope" (viii, 1075).

In the first promenade, Rousseau discusses his purpose in undertaking the
Rêveries. He will apply a barometer to his soul in order to understand its
"modifications" and "leurs successions" (i, 1000-1001). The *morale sensitive*,
it will be remembered, was to be a study of the causes of the "variations" in
men and an attempt to determine those which could be controlled. While
rejecting *bodily* action at the beginning of the *Rêveries*, Rousseau still takes
pride and comfort in his active *soul*: "... elle produit encor des sentimens,
des pensées, et sa vie interne et morale semble encor s'être accrue par la mort
de tout interest terrestre et temporel" (i, 1000). But self-examination can be
painful, as the 4th and 6th promenades reveal, and as we have seen, the later
promenades propose to eliminate this distressing moral activity. The solution
proposed in the 8th promenade is that of *stasis*, a mechanical notion which
expresses spatially an ideal similar to the temporal notion of *permanence:* the
absence of change marks both. The reverie is the privileged experience which
most approaches this state of timelessness. All feeling of succession—the very
thing the written *rêveries* were intended to study—is abolished. This state
comes very close to being an extinction even of vital physical sensitivity. All
that remains is a consciousness of existence which one prepares oneself to
experience by brushing aside "toutes les impressions sensuelles et terrestres
qui viennent sans cesse nous en distraire et en troubler ici bas la douceur" (v,
1047). The harmony of the individual and his environment which *la morale
sensitive* was intended to realize is achieved in these rare moments: "Il y faut
des dispositions de la part de celui qui les éprouve, il en faut dans le concours
des objets environnans" (v, 1047). Although the feeling of permanence
brought about by the reverie is temporary, Rousseau can call it happiness
because it makes him want to say "*Je voudrois que cet instant durât toujours*" (v, 1046). This wish to suspend time is analogous to the desire to
eliminate movement by avoiding the impact of outside forces.

The theme of time is of course present in every one of Rousseau's writings,
and it is intimately connected with his views on politics and psychology.
What should be noted here is that in the *Rêveries*, as elsewhere, Rousseau
clings to the idea of the permanence of his own being despite all the vicis-
situdes of existence. Thus, time does not change Jean-Jacques: "De quelque
façon que les hommes veuillent me voir ils ne sauroient changer mon être, et
malgré leur puissance et malgré toutes leurs sourdes intrigues, je continuerai
quoi qu'ils fassent d'être en depit d'eux ce que je suis" (viii, 1080). The
radical disharmony between him and his milieu comes from a change in the
environment; it is the others whom time has altered. Of his former friends

Rousseau says: "De vrais et francs qu'ils étoient d'abord, devenus ce qu'ils sont, ils ont fait comme tous les autres et par cela seul que les tems sont changés, les hommes ont changé comme eux" (vi, 1055). If Jean-Jacques has changed at all, and he hesitatingly admits the possibility, it is because he has reacted to a change outside of him (vi, 1054). It was impossible for him not to react to treachery.

Rousseau devotes his 3rd promenade to a discussion of his famous "reform"—his decision to quit the world and its false values, his search for new principles according to which to live his life. The religious principles he develops are able to bring the physical world, mortal and immortal existence, into a harmonious relationship: "Non, de vaines argumentations ne détruiront jamais la convenance que j'apperçois entre ma nature immortelle et la constitution de ce monde et l'ordre physique que j'y vois régner" (iii, 1018-19). Rousseau sees his reform as a rule of conduct to be valid once and for all: "j'entrepris de soumettre mon intérieur à un examen sévère qui le réglat pour le reste de ma vie tel que je voulois le trouver à ma mort" (iii, 1015). He speaks of "une régle fixe de conduite pour le reste de mes jours" (iii, 1016), of "la régle immuable de ma conduite et de ma foi" (iii, 1018), and it is the permanent validity of his principles which he calls upon for assurance in the distress of his last years.

By evoking his timeless principles, Rousseau is doing on a moral level what he did on a quasi-mystical level in the moments of reverie. He is perpetuating a moment. It is precisely this which Emile wished to effect when he made a kind of pact with his tutor: "Je veux obéir à vos loix," he said, "je le veux toujours, c'est ma volonté constante" (IV, 651-52). Rousseau explains how he conceived of his reform: "Fixons une bonne fois mes opinions, mes principes, et soyons pour le reste de ma vie ce que j'aurai trouvé devoir être après y avoir bien pensé" (iii, 1016). But one cannot fix the will; man cannot deny time or refuse change. Rousseau demonstrates this himself in the 6th promenade, when he discusses how his instinct of generosity is modified by the feeling of obligation. He explicitly speaks of "une espéce de contrat . . . entre le bienfaiteur et l'obligé" (vi, 1053). But it is a contract he cannot honor, for he cannot tolerate the constraint of precedent and suffers from the expectation of others that he will act tomorrow as he has acted today. This promenade reveals how vain, in reality, is the dream of eternalizing the will of the moment. It is as vain as seeking the security of permanence in a mechanical ideal of stasis, for as Rousseau himself discovers, a physical body can never eliminate all outside impulses and a reflective human being cannot suspend all moral reaction.

In the process of writing his *Rêveries*, Rousseau keeps coming to the same, for him disquieting, realization that where there's life, there's hope. For life is change. And when change appears as a threat, one can speak, as he does, of "l'inquiétude de l'espérance" (i, 997). Tranquillity can come only from the elimination of moral intention, the cessation of physical sensation, and a deliverance from the fragmentation of time in a union of the ego and the cosmos which transcends all tensions of mortal existence. Ultimately, it can come only from death.

It is not by chance that the last two promenades deal almost entirely with memories of human encounters or that the last one was left unfinished. The various attempts Rousseau had made to modify, so to speak, his present environment had failed. Writing himself into a vicious circle, he kept returning to the very need for personal relationships which were bringing such unhappiness.

In the 7th promenade, he describes his ambivalent reaction upon discovering a stocking mill (the presence of man) in a setting where he thought himself the only mortal. There is an interesting passage in the 8th promenade, which seems to echo the famous description of the reverie on the lac de Bienne:

> Quand tout étoit dans l'ordre autour de moi, quand j'étois content de tout ce qui m'entouroit et de la sphére dans laquelle j'avois à vivre je la remplissois de mes affections. Mon ame expansive s'étendoit sur d'autres objets, et sans cesse attiré hors de moi par des gouts de mille espéces, par des attachemens aimables qui sans cesse occupoient mon coeur je m'oubliois en quelque façon moi-même, j'étois tout entier à ce qui m'étoit étranger et j'éprouvai dans la continuelle agitation de mon coeur toute la vicissitude des choses humaines. (viii, 1074-75)

As in the reverie, Rousseau experiences a kind of self-forgetting ("je m'oubliois en quelque façon moi-même"). As in the reverie, he seems to incorporate the movement outside him. But in the reverie the outside movement is rhythmic and peaceful, and it chases inner turmoil. Here it is otherwise: "j'éprouvai dans la continuelle agitation de mon coeur toute la vicissitude des choses humaines." The relation is the same, but the result is not. "Cette vie orageuse ne me laissoit ni paix au dedans ni repos au dehors. Heureux en apparence je n'avois pas un sentiment qui put soutenir l'épreuve de la reflexion et dans lequel je pusse vraiment me complaire," explains Rousseau (viii, 1075). The mortal world which penetrates Rousseau's soul in society is "la vicissitude des choses humaines," it is mutability and not continuity. In a social environment, receptivity invites invasion, expansiveness means self-dissipation.

The last written memory with which Rousseau consoles himself in the 10th promenade is that of the time spent with madame de Warens. Here, in recollected experience, Rousseau sees himself as happy, briefly, in a human context:

> Le gout de la solitude et de la contemplation naquit dans mon coeur avec les sentimens expansifs et tendres faits pour être son aliment. Le tumulte et le bruit les resserrent et les etouffent, le calme et la paix les raniment et les exaltent. J'ai besoin de me recueillir pour aimer. (x, 1099)

The *resserrement* that in a corrupt social environment becomes selfish *amour-propre* is here the justified solitude of *amour de soi*, the self-cultivation which he had counseled Sophie d'Houdetot to strive for and which is compatible with, indeed necessary to, true community. The *expansion* which in a corrupt social environment becomes dissipation is here the generosity which resembles the instinctive "pity" of natural man and which, again, is compatible with, indeed necessary to, true community. But this experience with madame de Warens, too, succumbs to the destruction of time: "Ah! si j'avois suffi à son coeur comme elle suffisoit au mien! " (x, 1098).

Although Rousseau lived for more than two months after he wrote that line, he never finished the *Rêveries*. He put down his pen and gave himself to the more repetitive, less reflective, activity of botanizing in Ermenonville. The project of the *morale sensitive* had been on his mind until the end of his life. It had been explored in various ways in his novel, in his books on education and political theory. In each case the environment was one in which the individual was intended to dominate his weaknesses, to transcend his "moi personnel" and become part of the "moi commun." But in each case the system posited the existence of an individual who was outside the pattern of corrupted mankind and who was able to identify the point at which the individual and his milieu were in optimal relationship one with the other. One might, of course, study the role of Rousseau as outsider even in the *Rêveries*. Nevertheless, the problem of the relationship between the individual and his environment is now posed in personal terms, and Rousseau is, here, inside the system. The manipulation of external conditions cannot be done successfully by the one who will be subject to those conditions, for he is, to put it most simply, conscious of the very stratagem which he is intended to experience.

Rousseau conceived of the harmony between the individual and the collectivity or between man and his environment in static terms. Yet this ideal was to be realized in a world of flux. If the democracy of the *Contrat social* seems a curious one, it is because it rejects debate as a means of inquiry; it makes no provision for a search for changing solutions to changing problems. There is a famous passage in *La Nouvelle Héloïse* in which St. Preux laments the fate of a sensitive soul in this mortal world. He describes himself as victim first of his physical environment, next of false social values and corrupted humanity, but finally, and unavoidably, as victim of his humanity:

> O Julie, que c'est un fatal présent du ciel qu'une ame sensible! Celui qui l'a reçu doit s'attendre à n'avoir que peine et douleur sur la terre. Vil jouet de l'air et des saisons, le soleil ou les brouillards, l'air couvert ou serein regleront sa destinée, et il sera content ou triste au gré des vents. Victime des préjugés, il trouvera dans d'absurdes maximes un obstacle invincible aux justes voeux de son coeur. Les hommes le puniront d'avoir des sentimens droits de chaque chose, et d'en juger par ce qui est véritable plutôt que par ce qui est de convention. Seul il suffiroit pour faire sa propre misere, en se livrant indiscretement aux attraits divins de l'honnête et du beau, tandis que les pesantes chaines de la nécessité l'attachent à l'ignominie. Il cherchera la félicité suprême sans se souvenir qu'il est homme: son coeur et sa raison seront incessamment en guerre, et des desirs sans bornes lui prépareront d'éternelles privations. (II, 89)

St. Preux's words describe Rousseau, whose final struggle with his own situation was in large part, as we have seen in *Les Rêveries,* a struggle against his humanity.

Etude du rituel sadique dans ses rapports avec les rituels des sociétés primitives*

A. M. LABORDE

L'étude comparative que je présente ici est légitime dans la mesure où nous savons, et de source sûre, que Sade lisait avec avidité les récits de voyage des explorateurs et missionnaires de son temps et s'en inspirait largement pour composer ses romans, qu'il écrit très vite mais révise et augmente constamment. Le détail des listes de livres dont il pouvait disposer soit en prison soit au château de la Coste nous est connu. Il prend soin, d'autre part, surtout dans *l'Historie de Juliette,* de citer ses sources. [1]

Voulant, à l'encontre de Rousseau, prouver la méchanceté naturelle de l'homme, il emprunte une multitude d'exemples de cruauté humaine à ses lectures. La fameuse diatribe du Pape à Juliette, dans *l'Histoire de Juliette,* est un modèle du genre.[2] Mais le romancier ne se borne pas à cette forme d'emprunts pratiquée d'ailleurs par nombre de philosophes avant lui (voir Bayle, Voltaire, Diderot, etc...). Il reprend au monde archaïque des attitudes types, des symboles, des images, des structures mentales qui suggèrent au lecteur une analogie subtile entre le monde sadique et le monde archaïque. C'est le détail de cette analogie que je voudrais mettre en évidence ici. Elle me paraît essentielle à qui veut saisir l'originalité foncière d'un roman tel *la Nouvelle*

*This essay is part of a chapter entitled "Le Rituel Sadique" from a book entitled *Sade Romancier* published in Fall 1974 by Les Editions de la Baconnière (Neuchâtel-Suisse) in the Collection Languages.

Justine ou *l'Histoire de Juliette.* En m'appuyant sur les travaux de Mircéa Eliade, éthnologue spécialiste des religions primitives, j'examinerai tout d'abord ce que représente le rituel pour le primitif. Cette réflexion d'Eliade nous l'indique:

> Pour toute l'humanité primitive, c'est l'expérience religieuse qui fonde le monde: c'est l'orientation rituelle, avec les structures de l'espace sacré qu'elle révèle, qui transforme le "Chaos" en "Cosmos" et, partant, rend possible une existence humaine (c'est-à-dire l'empêche de régresser au niveau de l'existence zoologique).[3]

Cette attitude, qui cherche à mettre de l'ordre dans le désordre, qui cherche à donner un sens à ce qui semble dénué de sens, me paraît très proche de la démarche sadienne.

Il semble, en effet, que l'effort de l'auteur soit comme une réaction instinctive au chaos de sa vie comme à celui que la révolution de 1789 entraînera pour les Français et surtout pour la noblesse française dont il porte si nettement les stigmates. Sa conscience aiguë de ces bouleversements, qui mettent en question sa propre sécurité aussi bien que les structures politiques et sociales du pays, me paraît avoir offert le terrain propice à cette reconversion systématique entreprise par la magie de l'écriture; ceci donnerait à l'oeuvre sadienne la portée d'une ontologie révélant "ce qui est réellement" et cherchant à fonder "un monde qui n'est plus évanescent et incompréhensible" mais à imposer, au contraire, une structure nouvelle susceptible d'apporter l'ordre, l'apaisement. L'intention, dans les romans sadiens et particulièrement les plus sadiques est bien de dévoiler les mystères de l'homme, je préférerais dire les signes de l'homme, à savoir sa cruauté, sa volonté de puissance, son érotisme, son imagination créatrice. L'auteur revendique avec entêtement cette prérogative. Il revendique aussi le droit d'offrir ces signes selon des modes susceptibles d'engendrer, chez le lecteur, une émotion choc nécessaire à l'appréhension de *l'authentique.* Nous dirions à l'appréhension de l'en-soi des manières et des modes de l'humain.

Nous comprenons mieux, dans ce contexte, les raisons de l'injection à doses massives des formes les plus variées d'expressions érotiques-cruelles en tant que moyens d'expression de l'être et moyens de structuration d'un nouvel équilibre de l'être. C'est que l'activité érotico-cruelle qui forme l'un des ingrédients essentiels du rituel sadique présente dans les sociétés primitives un caractère qui n'est pas étranger à l'utilisation qu'en fait Sade. Compte tenu des proportions surhumaines que lui donne, à dessein, le romancier qui veut créer un monde allégorique, "un sortilège," et non pas une fiction vraisemblable, je crois que l'écrivain a respecté nombre des aspects les plus caractéristiques des emplois de l'érotisme et de la cruauté tels qu'ils sont réalisés par les primitifs dans leurs rituels.

Sade observe et respecte, en effet, la loi première de toute pensée mythique selon laquelle:

> Rien ne peut se créer que par immolation, par sacrifice... L'idée fondamentale est que la vie ne peut naître que d'une autre vie qu'on sacrifie... En d'autres termes, on retrouve ici le schéma cosmogonique bien connu de la "totalité" primordiale brisée et fragmentée par l'acte de création.
>
> (Eliade, *Mythes, Rêves et Mystères*, pp. 245-46)

Cette conception de l'homme archaïque rappelle l'essentiel du poème *la Vérité* (1787) dans lequel Sade rejette le concept de mort tel que nous l'entendons au nom d'une reconversion perpétuelle. Nous retrouvons, au sein de la société primitive, cette même idée de régénération constante que Sade appelle phénomène de *Transmutation*. Dans ce contexte, déclare Eliade:

> La mort arrive à être considérée comme la suprême initiation, c'est-à-dire comme le commencement d'une nouvelle existence spirituelle. Plus encore: génération, mort et régénération ont été comprises comme les trois moments d'un même mystère, et tout l'effort spirituel de l'homme archaïque s'est employé à montrer qu'entre ces moments il ne doit pas exister de coupures.
>
> (Eliade, *Mythes, Rêves et Mystères* p. 303)

Cette façon de concevoir le phénomène de mort permet une réappréciation de la signification des sacrifices humains. Elle retire à cet acte sa valeur de transgression que notre société lui donne pour en faire "un geste de nature" aux implications essentiellement métaphysiques. Le libertin sadique emprunte au monde archaïque cette interprétation de ce que nous considérons nous-mêmes comme un crime. Mais en appartenant, d'autre part, à un groupe social qui rejette cette vision, n'oublions pas que le libertin est aussi un homme de son siècle, il jouera sur ces deux interprétations afin de mettre en évidence la complexité du problème total et de permettre en fin de compte au lecteur une réappréciation de cette complexité.

Il est un autre phénomène particulièrement choquant pour nos mentalités d'hommes "dits civilisés" que le libertin sadique partage avec le primitif. Il s'agit de l'intervention des sens en tant qu'aspect essentiel du rituel. Celui que nous appelons un sorcier (terme péjoratif, remarquons-le) s'adonne à des gestes, à des cris, à des mimiques qui nous paraissent grotesques, contre nature. En fait, comme le remarque Eliade, il faudrait considérer ces "manifestations" dans le contexte des intentions du sorcier lui-même, qui est de retrouver par le truchement de ces cris d'animaux et autres activités à première vue aberrantes le moyen d'établir une correspondance intime entre l'être historique qu'il est devenu et le cosmos. N'est-ce pas là l'intention essentielle du Marquis de Sade? Les débordements érotiques et cruels, auxquels s'adonne le libertin ne sont alors que la manifestation extérieure de ce besoin de l'être de dépasser sa forme historique, en transgressant tout ce qui s'attache à cette forme historique. L'ivresse *sadique* devient alors la manifestation consciente d'une réalité métaphysique. Grâce au processus du rituel le libertin comme le primitif se voit entraîné à la redécouverte de ses forces originelles, de celles dont il pouvait jouir dans un état antérieur, au moment de la création. Le rituel sadique comme le rituel archaïque devient alors une technique susceptible de faire découvrir à l'homme des vérités connues mais oubliées dans la nuit des temps, c'est-à-dire de susciter chez lui un état propice à l'expérience ontologique.

A cette analogie qui lie l'esprit dans lequel s'accomplissent le rituel archaïque et le rituel sadique fait pendant une analogie de structure.

Dans les sociétés archaïques, les cérémonies d'initiation comportent toujours un certain nombre de séquences typiques, comme le "dépècement du corps du néophyte et renouvellement de ses organes; mort rituelle suivie de résurrection et plénitude."[4]

Nous retrouvons ces étapes dans le rite sadique. Elles correspondent à la destruction systématique des concepts moraux jusque là respectés et acceptés par la victime, et à la perpétration du viol de l'intimité sexuelle de la victime. Il y a attentat "aux organes" foulés, et régénérescence de ces mêmes organes par l'expérience sadique qui leur est imposée. Nous avons affaire à deux formes simultanées de "dépècement" du néophyte, celui de sa pureté morale, celui de sa pureté physique, en vue d'initier une mentalité neuve chez l'individu soumis au rituel. L'idéal, en effet, pour le libertin sadique est de profiter des victimes mais aussi et surtout d'en faire des initiés, et seuls ceux qui montrent des dispositions pour ce rôle seront conservés. Le sadique réclame souvent aussi la faveur de se faire victime de ses victimes. Les sévices qu'il leur inflige, il aime à se les voir infliger. L'expérience sadique n'est pas complète sans cet échange de rôles, sans cette réciprocité. Il faut fermer la boucle, il faut clore le cercle de l'expérience. Le but ultime de cette initiation de la victime du sadique n'est pas autre chose que la réalisation chez l'initié de l'état *d'Apathie*. L'Apathie n'est pas seulement l'endurance à la douleur des autres mais aussi à sa propre souffrance:

> Qui sait s'endurcir aux maux d'autrui devient bientôt impassible aux siens propres, et il est bien plus nécessaire de savoir souffrir soi-même avec courage, que de s'accoutumer à pleurer sur les autres.
>
> (*Juliette,* Vol. VII-VIII, p. 104)

Un long apprentissage, une étude attentive des marques extérieures de l'impassibilité et de ses progrès sont essentielles. Ce flegme parfait, ce détachement est à rapprocher de celui présenté par le futur chaman face à la douleur physique au moment des rituels initiatiques. Dans l'un et l'autre cas il s'agit d'atteindre à un stade de sensibilité nouveau, phase marquante des progrès de l'initié.

Dans l'expérience sadique comme dans celle du primitif les rapports entre individus sont strictement codifiés. Le libertin Saint—Fond énonce ici les modalités de ces rapports:

> [...] je vous préviens qu'il ne faut jamais vous écarter du profond respect que j'exige et qui m'est dû à bien plus d'un titre; je porte sur cela l'orgueil au dernier point. Vous ne m'entendrez jamais vous tutoyer; imitez-moi, ne m'appelez, surtout, jamais autrement que monseigneur; parlez à la troisième personne tant que vous pourrez, et soyez toujours devant moi dans l'attitude du respect.
>
> (*Juliette, op. cit.*, p. 209)

Pourtant quelques pages plus loin, content de la fête qu'elle vient de donner, Saint-Fond se met à tutoyer Juliette et lui permet d'en faire autant. Le tutoiement devient alors la marque des progrès de Juliette en tant qu'initiée.

On ne saurait nier l'importance du respect des différentes étapes du rituel dans la mentalité sadique. Il s'agit tout d'abord de faire acte d'obéissance, une sorte de serment d'allégeance est prononcé par Juliette devant la Delbéne:

> "Je fais serment entre tes mains de ne m'effrayer de quoique ce puisse être."

Remarquons que ce serment implique nettement l'Apathie. Le néophyte se voit alors soumis à une première cérémonie celle de la *réception:*

> "Laisse-la donc, dit Volmar [...] laisse-la donc; il faut qu'elle soit reçue avant que nous nous en servions."
>
> (*Juliette, op. cit.*, p. 33)

L'ordonnance des différents moments de la réception et le respect de cette ordonnance sont essentiels:

> "Un moment, dit la supérieure; ceci est une cérémonie de récep- tion. J'admets Juliette dans notre société: il faut qu'elle remplisse les formalités d'usage."
>
> (*Juliette, op. cit.*, p. 33)

Juliette passera d'autre part un *mois d'épreuve* [sic]. Cette période rappelle le temps de préparation nécessaire au néophyte des tribus primitives qui quitte son village et sera soumis pendant un temps bien déterminé à certaines épreuves qui préludent à son initiation.

Le secret de ces activités est la condition sine qua non de l'initiation:

> tu choisiras dans le couvent celle dont tu voudras cueillir les
> prémices, et ce sera moi qui flétrirai les tiens... les déchirements...
> les blessures... tranquillise-toi, j'arrangerai tout. Mais *ceci* [sic]
> *sont de grands mystères*; pour y être initiée, il faut ta *parole*
> *sacrée* que, dès ce moment-ci, tu ne parleras plus à Sainte-Elme:
> autrement, je ne mets point de bornes à ma vengeance.
>
> (*Juliette, op. cit.*, p. 37)

L'activité sadique est donc considérée comme sacrée par les protagonistes:
(Je m'excuse d'employer ce terme qui paraîtra à certains offensant. Il faut se
rappeler pourtant que si Dieu n'existe pas dans le contexte sadique la notion
d'être souverain en parlant de l'homme nous amène à une similitude de
démarche et d'intention qui nous rapprochent beaucoup de la mentalité
religieuse.) C'est qu'il s'agit bel et bien d'une initiation à un mystère. Ce
terme est particulièrement significatif ici. La mort suivra la violation du secret
que le néophyte détient. Cette attitude se retrouve exactement vis-à-vis du
néophyte des rituels archaïques.

L'organisation des réjouissances se fait sur les ordres d'une ou d'un meneur
de jeu comme dans les cérémonies initiatiques des primitifs où le chaman
préside aux différentes étapes du rituel, tout en veillant à l'ordonnance
rigoureuse des choses.

> "L'extrême vénération que l'on avait pour les ordres de la supé-
> rieure fit mettre à leur exécution la *ponctualité* la plus entière."
>
> (*Juliette, op. cit.*, p. 34)

La position des corps formant souvent une sorte de chaîne fermée sur
elle-même peut-être interprétée comme une nécessité physique mais à laquelle
les protagonistes donnent une valeur symbolique. Cette chaîne d'êtres, fermée
sur elle-même, sans commencement ni fin, est la figure parfaite de ces activités qui ont pour but de narguer la mort en donnant à l'être qui s'y soumet le
sentiment d'un infini de puissance et de jouissance, susceptible d'éliminer
toute appréhension de la mort, partant toute notion de mort au profit de la
notion de Transmutation. Elle symbolise aussi la domination par les êtres qui
s'y soumettent de la notion de temps historique. Elle devient enfin la manifestation fondamentale de l'idée de souveraineté de l'homme, l'un des messages essentiels de la dialectique sadienne.

Le goût pour l'ordre et l'organisation en séquences bien réglées est très
évident dans ces deux extraits choisis dans *Juliette*:

> N'importe, suivons *nos opérations*; que chacune de vous mainte-
> mant se place sur le lit; Juliette exigera d'elle tour à tour ce qui
> lui conviendra, vous serez contraintes à vous y prêter; mais

comme elle est encore bien neuve, je la conseillerai; *le groupe* se formera sur elle ensuite, comme il vient de se former sur moi.

(Juliette, op. cit., p. 35)

Un peu d'ordre à tout ceci, dit Noirceuil, [. . .] *Il fait mettre un tapis, au milieu de la chambre, et nous formons un cercle autour d'elle.*

(Juliette, op. cit., p. 218)

Nous retrouvons chez le primitif cette fidélité à la place assignée à chacun et le règlement systématique des activités selon certaines figures géométriques dont celle du cercle.

On donne, d'autre part, dans les mentalités sadiques et primitives une importance énorme à la topographie des lieux où se déroule l'initiation, puis le rituel lui-même, c'est que la sécurité qu'accorde l'isolement et le secret n'est pas seule en jeu. La topographie choisie prend une valeur symbolique. A sa manière, le rituel sadique réitère le rituel de la descente aux enfers:

Si nous nous engloutissons au fond de la région des morts [déclare Delbène], c'est pour être le plus loin possible des vivants.

(Juliette, op. cit., pp. 63-64)

La clôture des lieux est encore renforcée par leur circularité qui se reflète d'ailleurs à l'infini, grâce à des systèmes de miroirs bien conçus:

"Le cabinet où le duc nous reçut était rond, absolument environné de glaces."

(Juliette, op. cit., p. 190)

On ne saurait confondre pourtant la valeur provocatrice de l'image du crime reflétée, à l'infini, grâce au jeu des miroirs, avec le désir de s'exposer en pleine lumière. Le sadique évite le soleil, le lumière éclatante, et préfère la demi-obscurité des retraites bien closes, la pénombre des bosquets, les ombres de la nuit pour se livrer à l'activité sadique:

[. . .] l'obscurité convient au crime et vous en jouirez dans touté son horreur; allons, prince, égarons-nous dans ces labyrinthes, et que là rien n'arrête l'impétuosité de nos emportements.

(Juliette, op. cit., p. 234)

Nous trouvons dans cette citation non seulement l'idée de la nécessité d'une retraite obscure mais aussi une référence explicite au labyrinthe qui symbolise dans le contexte des sociétés archaïques le retour à la terre-mère:

Pénétrer dans un labyrinthe ou dans une caverne équivalait à un retour mystique à la mère—but que poursuivaient aussi bien les rites d'initiation que les rites funéraires.

(Eliade, *Le Chamanisme,* p. 228)

Si cette interprétation d'Eliade est exacte il me semble que les gestes sadiques sont bel et bien les manifestations physiques d'une conscience mythique qui se reconnaît et s'expose comme telle en choisissant d'opérer selon un cérémonial et dans des conditions topographiques typiques.

J'ai distingué jusqu'ici dans l'initiation du primitif comme dans celle du libertin sadique la nécessité d'un isolement physique: le néophyte est retiré à sa famille; le libertin sadique est sûr que ses victimes n'ont plus de liens avec la société. Dans ce désir d'abolir ce qui lie au passé, comme au monde de l'homme historique on change volontiers de nom, on se limite au prénom. On va plus loin. On apprend une langue nouvelle. La langue ordurière et toutes les infractions à la rhétorique de l'homme historique forment dans l'oeuvre de Sade la base d'une langue originale homologue de celle que le chaman enseigne au néophyte. Imitée des cris d'animaux, la langue du chaman représente un effort particulier en vue de retourner aux origines et de communier avec les forces originelles. En employant les termes les plus primitifs (empruntés souvent à la langue du Moyen-Age) Sade refait, à sa manière, la même démarche que le chaman apprenant à ses disciples les subtilités du langage des initiations. L'intention dans les deux cas me semble similaire:

> détruire les cadres "profanes" de la sensibilité; [. . . afin de] créer un milieu sensoriel ouvert au surnaturel.
>
> (Eliade, *Le Chamanisme*, p. 116)

Le rôle joué par la parole dans ce contexte est particulièrement intéressant. La parole rend ivre, on s'enivre en parlant, c'est là un stade essentiel dans la préparation au rituel. L'audition des blasphèmes et des élucubrations sadiques est la première phase indispensable à la préparation du néophyte. Tous les moyens verbaux sont bons en vue d'induire un état de demi-conscience chez l'initié. L'ambivalence des termes est l'un des processus les plus communs. C'est qu'il s'agit d'obtenir du néophyte des capacités sensibles bien au-dessus de la normale. Les sens sont explicitement conçus comme des outils susceptibles d'inaugurer des métaphores du cosmos qui seront transmises par le signe linguistique, d'où cette exubérance volubile des uns et des autres.

Les chiffres, enfin, dans le rituel sadique forment une sorte de cadre théorique qui renforce de son aspect scientifique une expérience qui ne serait autrement que vulgaire. Ils donnent une auréole à l'acte, lui confèrent le mystère et, en même temps, renforcent sa puissance suggestive, lui impriment une sorte de validité en l'inscrivant dans un cadre de références familières. La valeur symbolique de la répétition systématique des gestes selon un nombre établi est une caractéristique évidente des rituels primitifs où la portée magique des chiffres vient renforcer de son mystère la "sacralité" du geste.

Chez Sade ce ne sont pas seulement les situations, les positions qui sont multipliées d'une manière mathématique, sans aucun respect d'ailleurs pour la vraisemblance mais les mots eux aussi se voient juxtaposés dans un ordre exponentiel qui défie le réel.

Les personnages sadiens sont des champions, de véritables athlétes du discours; et ce sont leurs performances qui, tout en réflétant l'une des caractéristiques de l'être énergique tel que le conçoit Sade, offrent un intérêt, tout particulier, pour le critique littéraire. Le romancier invite le lecteur à faire une sorte d'exploration des possibles jusqu'à la limite non plus seulement de son imagination mais de l'infini mathématique. Il le force à une redécouverte de l'authenticité des choses par l'usage d'un système de combinaisons imité des lois mathématiques.

Nous ne trouvons pas cette forme combinatoire dans la mentalité primitive mais seulement le respect de la mesure exacte en vue de réitérer précisément les différents moments du rituel. Cette différence est fondamentale. Pour le primitif le rituel se doit de rester statique en tant que moyen de restructuration périodique du réel. Le rituel sadique n'est pas rivé à cette rigidité. Chacune des expériences vécues par Juliette, chacune des parties du roman de sa vie est imitée de la structure des rituels primitifs mais à partir de cette structure s'élabore une oeuvre qui s'impose par son autonomie, sa spécificité et l'intention affichée de l'écrivain de se commettre à un renouvellement, à des variations, à des modifications profondes, à des "transmutations" à partir d'une mentalité, d'une structure mentale, philosophique et littéraire fermement établie.

L'artiste Sade emprunte donc à l'ethnologie, aux mathématiques, le cadre, l'essence même de leurs modes mais sén libère tout à la fois par le soin qu'il met à renouveler, dans le détail, les données rigides, que lui imposait la structure du rituel archaïque. C'est que l'artiste Sade entend exercer, en toute liberté, ses prérogatives d'artiste créateur en ne mettant aucun frein à son imagination (voyez ce qu'il dit, à ce sujet, dans *l'Idée sur les romans*). Enfin, n'oublions pas que *la Nouvelle Justine* ou *l'Histoire de Juliette* sont, avant tout, des tentatives de démystification au même titre que *l'Histoire des oracles* ou *Candide*. Voilà une différence fondamentale et essentielle qui marque, à sa manière, les limites de l'analogie que je viens de tracer.

NOTES

1 Voir, par exemple, Sade, *Oeuvres complètes* (Cercle du livre précieux, Paris, 1966), VII-VIII, 78; note, p. 178; p. 572.
2 Sade, *Oeuvres complètes* (Cercle du livre précieux, Paris, 1967), IX-X, 187 et suivantes.
3 Eliade, *Mythes, Rêves et Mystères* (Gallimard, Paris, 1957), p. 13.
4 Eliade, *Le Chamanisme* (Payot, Paris, 1951), p. 49.

The Forgotten Genre:
The Poetic Epistle in
Eighteenth-Century German Literature

MARKUS F. MOTSCH

Among Goethe's contributions to the first two volumes of the *Horen*, the literary periodical edited by Schiller, were two poetic epistles. Making use of a humorous and slightly ironic style, these two pieces consider the influence that literature, particularly the novel, exerts on the reader. Appended to the second epistle is the remark "Die Fortsetzung folgt" (to be continued), a promise that was not kept; in the 1815 edition of his poems, Goethe introduces the two epistles with the lines: "Gerne hätt' ich fortgeschrieben, / Aber es ist liegen blieben" (gladly would I have continued, but never got around to). Presumably it was pure coincidence that Goethe, preoccupied with other tasks, did not continue his epistles. On the other hand, his omission may have been symptomatic of the declining interest in this genre, for although a number of verse epistles were written by nineteenth-century authors (and even by twentieth-century authors such as Bert Brecht and Erich Kästner), German literary scholarship has not much concerned itself with the genre since the middle of the nineteenth century. Only recently, one German scholar introduced an article on the epistle by stating that to judge from modern reference works standard in the field, he was about to discuss a subject that did not even exist.[1] Despite his interest in the subject, apparently even he was unaware of the tremendous popularity the poetic epistle has enjoyed during the entire eighteenth and much of the seventeenth century, for he treats the time span between Horace and the nineteenth-century poet Eduard Mörike with silence.

To Horace, of course, together with Ovid, belongs the credit for having made the poetic epistle a popular genre of literature. The tradition of the subject matter, tone, and form chosen by the two Roman poets for their epistles can be traced in epistolary poetry throughout the ages, as is evidenced, for instance, by a letter of November 10, 1714, to *The Spectator,* offering "some remarks upon the epistolatory way of writing in verse." The anonymous author differentiates between two types of epistles, the one comprising "love-letters, letters of friendship, and letters upon mournful occasions," for which Ovid is cited as the best example; the other, for which Horace serves as model, includes "epistles in verse, as may properly be called familiar, critical, and moral; to which may be added letters of mirth and humour. . . . He that is ambitious of succeeding in the Ovidian way," the author continues, "should first examine his heart well, and feel whether his passions (especially those of the gentler kind) play easy; since it is not his wit, but the delicacy and tenderness of his sentiments, that will affect his readers. . . . The qualifications requisite for writing epistles, after the model given us by Horace, are of a quite different nature. He that would excel in this kind must have a good fund of strong masculine sense: to this there must be joined a thorough knowledge of mankind, together with an insight into the business, and the prevailing humours of the age."[2] Among the host of other qualifications stipulated by the author of the letter are "the finest precepts of morality," "a lively turn of wit," and to "appear a man of the world throughout." Later in the century, in 1770, Christoph Martin Wieland summarized all this by saying that one has to be a Horace in order to write poetic epistles like Horace.[3]

Given that both Horace and Ovid were, next to Virgil, the most widely read poets of Antiquity throughout the Middle Ages, it is not surprising that the poetic epistle survived well as a genre in medieval Latin literature. Hexameter epistles were written by the members of Charlemagne's Court Academy, and they were part of the correspondence between learned monks, clerics, noble ladies, and nuns. Frequently, these epistles contain exchanges of scholarly thoughts and philosophical ideas, sometimes they offer witty remarks and friendly advice, and occasionally they are simply letters of friendship and love. The influence of both Horace and Ovid is evident in most. The art of writing poetry was part of the training of the educated person of the Middle Ages. It was taught in school; indeed it was a prerequisite to one's being accorded the status of *clericus* and *literatus* and to one's corresponding with one's colleagues and peers. The poetic epistle served all these needs. Of the few known verse letters in medieval German—some are love letters, some are didactic—none seem to root in the classical tradition of Horace and Ovid. But in the sixteenth century, the poetic epistle, with the ode, elegy, eclogue, and epigram, became one of the preferred forms in the neo-Latin poetry of the German humanists. In contrast to many of the earlier, medieval Latin verse letters, the epistle at this time was quite often consciously conceived as a poetical work, intended not only for the addressee—who at times was fictional—but for a wide literary audience and for posterity. And depending on the subject matter, tone, and form, either Horace or Ovid might serve as model. But at present there is no evidence that sixteenth-century attempts to render classical poetic forms in German verse looked to the epistle for their model; the known examples of such attempts are rare, in any case.

The earliest epistles in New High German date from the seventeenth century, and Gottsched is probably correct when he says of Martin Opitz (1597-1639): "Unter unseren Landesleuten hat Opitz uns den Weg in poetischen Briefen gebahnet" (among our countrymen, it was Opitz who cleared the way for the poetic epistle).[4] In fact the genre became so popular that it would take less time to enumerate those poets of the seventeenth century who did not write epistles, than those who did. Much of this profusion of epistolary poetry must be classified, however, as occasional poetry in the strictest sense of the term—and accordingly much of it is bad. Panegyrics, petitions and dedications, congratulations on weddings, birthdays and promotions, and messages of sympathy were composed in the form of verse letters, quite often ghost-written on order for the signature of the third party. The poetic quality of most of these leaves much to be desired. But many uncommissioned epistles, written by competent poets who sought primarily to express certain of their own thoughts and feelings, are quite good. Often these poems refute the cliché that Baroque rhetorical formality makes it inevitable that "the poet's personality remained separate from his work," that "he did not in any way give expression to his inner self."[5] The generalization simply does not hold true for the majority of epistles written by such men as Opitz, Fleming, Gryphius, Mühlpfort, and others. Many of these poets looked to the neo-Latin *poetae* of the preceding century, rather than to Horace, for their models. It seems worth observing here that Ovid, by contrast, was much admired by another group of seventeenth- and early eighteenth-century poets, the writers of gallant and love poetry. Among them are Hofmannswaldau (who indeed was given the epithet of "German Ovidius" by his contemporaries), Gottlieb Siegmund Corvinus, better known under the pseudonym "Amaranthes," and Gottlieb Stolle, who signed himself "Leander." But there were exceptions to the general ignoring of Horace. For example, Horatian subject matter and tone permeate the epistles of Friedrich Rudolf Ludwig von Canitz, who also translated one of Horace's epistles. Probably no other poet of the time made as much use of the genre of the poetic epistle as Johann Christian Günther, who though he began as an admirer of Lohenstein and his contemporaries, soon turned to the classics, particularly to Horace and to Ovid, for his models. "Saepe mihi Nasonis erant fata omnia votum, / Si mihi tam felix flere Thalia foret" (often I wish all the fates of Ovid upon me, if only Thalia grant me to sing as mournfully), he wrote as a student.[6] His unfortunate life provided him with more than enough occasion to mourn the fate that befell him, so that the elegiac tone in many of his epistles echoes Ovid's *Tristia* and *Epistulae ex Ponto.* It was from Horace, however, that Günther borrowed his more mature stoic-epicurean philosophy of life, so evident in his epistles. More than anyone else, Günther, whose dates (1695-1723) place him on the line dividing the Baroque from the Classical period, combined the influences of Ovid and of Horace, both in his epistles and in his poetry generally. And later, writers of epistles looked almost exclusively to Horace as their master.

Because of the increasing popularity the poetic epistle enjoyed among the poets, the genre was also given attention in the handbooks of rhetoric, in treatments of the art of poetry, and in other theoretical works, which the age produced in vast numbers. At first, during the earlier half of the century, the epistle usually appeared under the general subject heading of "letters," where it was described as a poetically elevated form of epistolography. Thus, Gottsched, in his *Versuch einer Critischen Dichtkunst,* finds that "So gut andre Leute in ungebundner Rede an einander schreiben können, so leicht kan ein Poet solches in gebundner Schreibart thun" (a poet can correspond in poetry just as easily as others can in prose).[7] Gottsched does insist, though, that the epistle should not convey a merely private message, but that it concern itself with such matters as are useful and agreeable to many readers. This Horatian formula of *prodesse et delectare* was, of course, applied in one way or another to practically all the literature of the time, but for the epistle in the Horatian tradition it constituted the essence. Gottsched, like the author of the letter to *The Spectator,* considers Ovid to be the master of elegiac epistles of tender and mournful character, Horace to be the model for serious, moral, and satirical epistles. Of the German poets of epistles, Gottsched selects Canitz, Neukirch, and Günther as not only equal to the best of the Roman and French poets, but as surpassing them on occasion. The eighteenth-century treatises and remarks on the writing of poetic epistles are too numerous to mention here. Nevertheless, at the end of the century, the learned Professor Manso, if one may judge from the title he gave his fifty-five page essay on the subject, offered the world all that had been said and all that could be said about the topic.[8]

By that time, the epistle had long since freed itself from its lowly association with occasional poetry and had achieved the status of a respected genre in German literature. More than a thousand epistles are known to have come from the pens of over a hundred poets of the eighteenth century, from

Gottsched's and Gellert's letters in alexandrine verse to Stolberg's blank verse and Goethe's hexameters. Most popular by far were rimed iambic meters of various lengths, meters which lent themselves to the conversational tone and natural style, the *genus medium,* generally recommended for the epistle. The difficulty in the art of writing poetic epistles was considered to lie primarily in fulfilling all the rhetorical, stylistic, metrical, and other requirements of poetic composition, and at the same time maintaining an air of casualness, effortlessness, and naturalness. In essence, there was to be an harmonious balance of art and nature. In addition, the epistle, while addressing or pretending to address a particular recipient, had to appeal to a general audience.

There was practically no limitation on the subject matter other than its having "to teach and to delight." The poets and writers had assumed the noble task of enlightening their fellow men in the quest for the perfection of mankind. All agreed with Pope that "The proper study of Mankind is Man." This settled, the eighteenth-century German writers of verse epistle indulged their obsession for "Truth" as it affected men. "True happiness," "true virtue," "true liberty," "true wisdom," "true love," "true friendship," and the "true destiny" of man occupied their attention. They argued the advantages of country life versus city life, censured the court and the aristocracy, flayed folly and vice, discussed marriage and the status of women, and debated political issues. They approached the inexhaustible topics of philosophy and religion in every conceivable manner, and, being men of letters themselves, they devoted much attention to the world of literature and literary criticism. Sometimes, the moral and didactic intent prevails to such a degree as to overshadow the personal character and tone of the epistle. Such is the case, for instance, in Wieland's *Moralische Briefe.* But the opposite is true of many of the epistles exchanged among the poets of the *Halberstädter Kreis,* especially of those by Johann Ludwig Gleim, Johann Georg Jacobi, and Leopold Friedrich von Goekingk; and the opposite is also true of the eighty-some epistles of the farmer-poet Isaak Maus. Here it is the personality of the writer and his relationship to the recipient that controls the tone of the epistle.

Of particular interest to the literary scholar are the epistles dealing with the literary life of the period, because they not only further illuminate factors already known, but quite often reveal new information. It would be difficult to think of a literary topic they do not touch upon. They include references to the poet, his qualifications, his tasks, and his station in life; discussions regarding the theory of literature, its essence, its function, and its influence; and finally the controversies and the feuds. As one might expect, these controversies range widely. They cover *la querelle des anciens et des modernes,* the question to rime or not to rime, the polemics of Gottsched and the Swiss, the quarrel between the moralists and the Anacreontics, especially between the young Wieland and Johann Peter Uz, the conflict of the generation gap between the older classicists and the angry young men of the seventies and eighties, and, of course, the perennial feud between the poets and the critics. All this and much more is reflected in poetic epistles, which provide an intimate picture of the diversity of German intellectual life in the eighteenth century—a picture which frequently does not correspond with present day concepts of that era. No age can be appraised by its masterworks alone. Recognizing this fact, literary scholarship in recent years has redirected its attention to poets and works that for too long have been ignored. They had not been ignored by the great poets who lived when these lesser works were written, and consequently they were more influential than has been allowed until a few years ago. To be sure, the rediscovery of the poetic epistle as a minor genre at one time exceedingly popular in German literature is not an event to shake modern scholarship. Still, providing as it often does unexpected insights into the cultural and literary life of past centuries, frequently revealing personal attitudes and perspectives hitherto overlooked, the entertaining and instructive poetic epistle deserves a better fate than it has heretofore endured as a forgotten genre.

NOTES

1 Gerhard Rückert, "Die Epistel als literarische Gattung Horaz-Mörike-Brecht," *Wirkendes Wort* (1972), 1. Heft, p. 58.

2 "[Letter] No. 618. Wednesday, November 10 [1714]," *The Spectator* (London, 1771), VIII, 216.

3 "Vorbericht zur dritten Ausgabe" [1770], *Sämtliche Werke* (Leipzig, 1855-58), XXV, 141.

4 *Versuch einer Critischen Dichtkunst vor die Deutschen* (Leipzig, 1730), p. 435.

5 Curt von Faber du Faur, *German Baroque Literature* (New Haven, 1958), p. xxii.

6 "Vitae Curriculum Guntheri P.L. Caes. a se ipse scriptum. A. 1716." *Sämtliche Werke*, ed. Wilhelm Krämer (Leipzig, 1930-37), IV, 62.

7 *Dichtkunst*, p. 434.

8 Johann Kaspar Friedrich Manso, "Ueber das Wesen der Horazischen Epistel," *Nachträge zu Sulzers allgemeiner Theorie der schönen Künste* (Leipzig, 1802), VI, pt. ii, 395-450. Many of the theoretical treatises here alluded to are discussed in my forthcoming book, *Die poetische Epistel Ein Beitrag zur Geschichte der deutschen Literatur und Literaturkritik des achtzehnten Jahrhunderts* (Bern: Herbert Lang, 1974); the book also provides numerous examples and quotes in attempting to illustrate the reasons for the attractiveness of the genre.

Hamann's Views on Human Reason

S. SUE NEBEL

Johann Georg Hamann (1730-1788), the intellectual, philosopher, and theologian from Königsberg often known as "der Magus im Norden," is traditionally linked with the *Sturm und Drang* and with Romanticism in Germany. Certainly there is some justification for such interpretations, for Hamann shared with the writers of the *Sturm und Drang* strong objections to the doctrines of Rationalism and a firm belief in the value of spontaneity and direct experience. His arguments were an inspiration and a stimulus to Herder and others in the latter half of the eighteenth century. An unfortunate result of identification with a specific group or with the appearance of new ideas is that we begin to think of a man like Hamann principally, or perhaps even exclusively, in terms of his significance for these developments and thus neglect to study him in his own right. Specifically, such an approach to Hamann's works has led to a narrow, restricted consideration of his views on human reason. Attention has been focused mainly on his anti-Rationalist position and those highly critical, negative statements on reason which support it. But to understand and appreciate Hamann, one must go beyond such statements and attempt to find the basis of his reaction to Rationalism and his own conception of the proper place and function of human reason as well.

Hamann's is one of the strongest among the critical voices protesting the ideas of the Enlightenment. He finds it impossible to accept the premises that reason is the superior faculty and that it serves as the basis of all knowledge. These concepts and all that follows from them are not the only object of his attacks; he goes further and criticizes Rationalist thinkers for the methods by which they reach such conclusions about the human mind. By employing analytical methods, these philosophers have succeeded in isolating reason from all other human powers and from the world and the tradition of which the human being is part. Hamann considers this a damaging process. He takes Rationalist thinkers, especially the faculty psychologists, to task for pursuing an analysis of man's inner make-up to the point that they lose sight of the essential unity of the various mental powers. They become enthusiastic about their discoveries and theories and neglect the integration of *all* human faculties, which Hamann himself puts before all other considerations. This notion of the "undivided soul" is a fundamental principle, on which much of Hamann's own thought rests. No less an admirer than Goethe observes:

> Das Prinzip, auf welches die sämtlichen Äusserungen Hamanns sich zurückführen lassen, ist dieses: "Alles, was der Mensch zu leisten unternimmt, es werde nun durch Tat oder Wort oder Sonst hervorgebracht, muss aus sämtlichen vereinigten Kräften entspringen; alles Vereinzelte ist verwerflich."[1]

In his attempt to reestablish this idea, Hamann goes beyond the level of mental powers, claiming the essential unity extends to include man's physical nature as well. Moreover, he understands this harmony of all human faculties—mental and physical—to represent an ideal towards which one should strive. He says of this integration and of its place in his scheme of values,

> Unsere Gesundheit ist ein Gut, das in einer Harmonie des körperlichen Baues und der Vereinigung mit der Seele besteht. Alles dasjenige, was selbige zu zerstören und zu ändern fähig ist, heisst daher ein Uebel; und im Gegenteil ist dasjenige ein Gut, was selbige erhält oder wiederherstellen kann.[2]

Reason cannot be considered apart from man's entire mental and physical make-up; that would be to regard it as operating in a vacuum. Obviously man employs the powers of mind and body in a variety of activities during his lifetime. According to Hamann, man first encounters the world through the senses and then formulates thoughts and ideas about his sense experiences; these formulations he in turn expresses in language. Throughout this process, man strives to understand himself in relation to others, to the world, and finally to God. It is important to stress that the firm belief in God is a constant theme in Hamann's works, and it can be traced to a specific source: an intense religious experience in 1758, the turning-point in his life. At the time of his conversion Hamann recorded many of his thoughts in a series of essays which make up the *Tagebuch eines Christen*. In these writings he expresses basic concepts, to which he continually returns; among them are the assertions that man is a creature of God, his powers of thought and speech a divine gift, and that the world of nature is a visible expression of the Creator.

For Hamann, God and His creation of the world stand at the beginning of all things. The world of nature is an outward, visible expression of God, which Hamann terms "divine language." Hamann speaks variously of language, expression, communication, and revelation, but all of them, it becomes clear, are terms for the fundamental process of outward expression of an inner, subjective nature. Divine language is God's revelation in concrete objects, or as Hamann prefers to describe it, in concrete images. Man, created by God, comes into the world uniquely organized for the task of acquiring knowledge of that world. The beginning of human life is experience, which initially at least is man's encounter with nature; as a result, he gains impressions of the external world through the sense organs. Thereafter he must create order out of this welter of sense-data, by formulating concepts about that which he has perceived. At this point, the mind begins to develop a complex activity involving many different, yet closely related processes: reflection, judgment, testing, comparison, and conclusion. For Hamann this is a harmonious—an integrated—activity; that is, though he makes distinctions between the functions of the senses and those of reason, between perceptive and reflective activity, he insists on their essential inseparability. In one sense, then, he not only redefines the relationship of reason to other faculties, he also enlarges the faculty of reason itself, in that he conceives of it as including many orders of operation.

But as one becomes intrigued with the complexity of human mental functioning and attempts to describe it, one must not forget the external world which serves both as the stimulus and the subject-matter (*Stoff*) for it. This, Hamann feels, is the mistake of the Rationalists. As I have said, Hamann understands that world to be the expression, the language of God. This revelation of God is revelation *to* and *for* man. ("Gott hat sich *Menschen* offenbaren wollen."[3] God created man so that he could know and enjoy creation, and God expressed Himself in terms that are comprehensible to man. The external world is divine, created by God; but it is also human in that these visible "images" are specifically suited to man's perceptive ability. Once again we see Hamann's emphasis on an essential harmony, that between the divine and the human:

Alles Göttliche ist aber auch menschlich; weil der Mensch weder wirken noch leiden kann, als nach der Analogie seiner Natur, sie sei eine so einfache oder zusammengesetzte Maschiene, als sie will. Diese communication göttlicher und menschlicher idiomatum ist ein Grundgesetz und Hauptschlüssel aller unsrer Erkenntnis und der ganzen sichtbaren Haushaltung.[4]

Through the use of his own faculties man achieves a certain level of knowledge, but Hamann maintains that there is another level beyond this. Human reason working with the senses provides the individual with knowledge of the physical world and of himself, but it does not give him insights into the essential nature of the world and of man. Man cannot and does not know by means of these processes alone that nature and human life come from and are ultimately dependent upon God. In order to gain this wisdom, man must make the transition to the state of faith. The first step in this process is the recognition of the limitations of human knowledge. Comments on the inadequacy of human reason can be found in many of Hamann's works, but the clearest statements on the subject occur in the essay *Sokratische Denkwürdigkeiten.* Hamann felt a certain kinship with the Greek philosopher because of the similarity of their experiences. Socrates, living according to the ancient maxim "Know thyself," was great in Hamann's eyes because he had attained a degree of self-knowledge probably unsurpassed. Socrates recognized and acknowledged that he knew nothing. He realized, as Hamann relates it, that human knowledge actually amounts to very little, for man, through reason, only knows and understands the world in a limited way. This admission, the Socratic *Nichtwissen,* is, on the one hand, negative; man admits the inadequacy of his knowledge. On the other hand, it is essentially a positive experience because it marks the beginning of new, higher knowledge.

This realization of the inadequacy of reason is not a simple conclusion of the human mind. It is a feeling (*Empfindung*); it must be experienced. This was the experience of the young Hamann in his own religious conversion. In the writings of that period, he emphasizes the negative aspect—the inadequacy of human reason—and often claims that the conclusions of human reason must conflict with the convictions of faith. Comparing man with God, Hamann finds the powers of man amounting to very little. Man is nothing without God: "Alles ist Weisheit in deiner [Gottes] Ordnung der Natur, wenn der Geist deines Worts unsern aufschliesst. Alles ist Labyrinth, alles Unordnung, wenn wir selbst sehen wollen."[5] Taken without the further explanations in later works, assertions such as this support the generalization that Hamann's view of human reason is completely negative, that man, when faced with the conflict between reason and faith, must choose faith as the source of true knowledge. And this implies that reason as a means of acquiring knowledge is entirely rejected. But Hamann does not deny reason, As his ideas develop, he comes to understand that the very ways in which the human mind conceives ideas are the basis for faith.

Hamann describes how an individual reaches the state of faith in terms of his own personal religious experience; on the other hand, he also confesses that, in the final analysis, one cannot explain the process completely. The experience of faith is one of knowing God directly, feeling that one belongs to the divine, and admitting that God is at the center of all things. Nature is one revelation of God to man; another is God's word in the Bible, and this, Hamann proclaims (without explaining very much about the basis of his view) is the key which opens the door to real understanding. In the teachings of the Bible the individual human being finds the meaning of Creation; it is God's direct expression to man. He also finds accounts of God speaking to him through the words of other men (e.g., Moses) and of man's dependence on God (Job). In the New Testament he learns of God's final revelation in the person of Christ. Belief in Christ is the basis of wisdom and true knowledge; it is also the means of understanding what man is and what place he occupies in the scheme of things.

Inherent in this act of faith as man accepts his dependence on God is the recognition of his insignificance in comparison to the divine. We have already seen that Hamann considers it essential for man to acknowledge the limitations of human reason. To take this step is not to repudiate knowledge which has already been acquired, but rather to place it in proper perspective. Once an individual accepts this view of God and the world, his sense organs and his mind do not cease functioning. He continues to acquire knowledge of the universe around him, but in such a state, he considers it evidence for his belief in God.

Attainment of the state of faith is for Hamann the real aim of human life, and the highest achievement possible. It is the most difficult task, but the most fulfilling as well:

> Wenn der Geist Gottes in unsern Seelen wohnt, so genüssen selbst die äussersten Grenzen unsers Gebieths den geistlichen, göttlichen und übernatürlichen Frieden, der höher, denn alle Vernunft und bewahrt unsere Herzen und Sinnen, unsere Affecten Gedanken, sensa mentis et animi.[6]

The person who reaches this goal possesses that quality which Hamann calls *gesunde Vernunft*. The individual with "healthy reason" understands the place of the human mind in the process of acquiring knowledge and the relationship of that knowledge to God. Hamann compares this condition to that early state of man as depicted in the Biblical figures of Adam and Eve, when man still lived in harmony with God. The quality of *gesunde Vernunft* is not the early, innocent state of man, but a state reached only after the long struggle in which the individual develops his mind, acquires knowledge and accepts the limitations of his reason. The individual who achieves this condition, who becomes aware of the inner unity of his powers and their harmonious relationship to the world, realizes Hamann's ideal and his hope for the future. Hamann pronounces this judgment on his own time and the future: "Das verflossene Jahrhundert war das Reich des Genies; das nächste wird vielleicht unter dem Scepter der gesunden Vernunft blühen."[7]

NOTES

1 J. W. von Goethe, "Dichtung und Wahrheit," *Goethes Sämtliche Werke,* ed. Eduard von der Hellen (Stuttgart and Berlin, 1902-7), XXIV, 8.
2 Johann Georg Hamann, *Sämtliche Werke,* ed. Josef Nadler (Vienna, 1949-57), I, 305.
3 *Ibid.,* I, 9.
4 *Ibid.,* III, 27.
5 *Ibid.,* I, 70.
6 *Ibid.,* p. 234.
7 *Ibid.,* II, 153.

Feijoo, Voltaire, and
the Mathematics of Procreation

A. OWEN ALDRIDGE

Modern scholarship has relegated the Spanish phase of the famous quarrel of the ancients and moderns to the period prior to the eighteenth century. Yet Benito Jerónimo Feijoo, sometimes known as "the Spanish Voltaire," took a vigorous interest in the controversy and kept it alive in Spanish letters throughout the eighteenth century. Opinions are divided as to whether the comparing of Voltaire to this talented Benedictine monk is apt or incongruous.[2] The chief resemblance between the two men is their ability to portray in readable prose the most interesting philosophical notions of the time, that is, concrete topics as distinguished from systems. Voltaire's championing of the moderns in the debate concerning the old and the new is well known. Feijoo refrained from adopting an unequivocal defense of either side in the controversy, and therefore his extensive writings on the subject have not lent themselves as readily to scholarly attention. He nevertheless devoted four of his major essays to the dispute: "Degeneration of the World," "Moral Degeneration of the Human Race," "Against the Modern Philosophers," and "Resurrection of the Arts and Defense of the Ancients." In addition, he treated the linguistic aspects of the controversy in "Parallel of the Castillian and French Languages" and "Dissuasion of One of His Friends from the Study of Greek and Persuasion of the Study of French."

My interest in the present essay will focus itself on only one narrow aspect

131

of Feijoo's preoccupation with the theme of human development from the remote past to the historical present of the eighteenth century—the topic of human reproduction, or, to be even more specific, the rate at which human reproduction has occurred and the manner in which the process takes place. Feijoo discusses the first of these notions in his essay on "Degeneration of the World," the second, in "Against the Modern Philosophers."

The seventeenth century in both England and France had revived from earlier times a theory that the world was wearing down physically and morally and would eventually decay into nothingness. As one English pessimist expressed it, "the world is decrepit, and, out of its age & doating estate, subject to all the imperfections that are inseparable from that wracke and maime of Nature."[3] In France, the theory was related to the question of the preeminence of ancients and moderns, and the answer was presumed to lie in discovering "whether the trees which formerly existed in our countryside were larger than those of today."[4]

Among the arguments used to prove the degeneration of the world was that of shrinking population. Those who believed in degeneration maintained that the ancient nations were densely peopled, in contrast to countries in their own times, in which every generation was thought to reveal a lessening productive capacity. Since no national population statistics existed for either ancient or modern times, Feijoo, in attacking the hypothesis of the decaying world, was forced as usual to depend on the meagre evidence of printed sources and on his own deductive reasoning. In regard to population, his method was disastrous.

The most prodigious propagation to occur in ancient history, he reported, was that during the three centuries after the Flood. When Noah died 350 years after this universal deluge, according to Philo's *Biblical Antiquities*, the progeny of one of his sons, Ham, amounted to 240,900, an enormous figure, which Feijoo indicated had been rejected as an exaggeration by the scholars of his time. Feijoo's second example was that of Ninus, king of the Assyrians, who came to the throne 249 years after the Flood. According to Diodorus Siculus, when Ninus gave battle to the king of the Bactrios, the king had 400,000 troops under arms, and Ninus, one million seven hundred thousand, divided between infantry and cavalry. Although Feijoo considered these numbers prodigious, considering that the multiplication of population had taken place in less than three hundred years and that other people were on earth besides these battalions, he, nevertheless, would not reject as fabulous or inaccurate the computation of his ancient authorities. Instead he tried to prove that the modern world could equal or exceed this enormous rate of propagation. He offered as evidence two examples. First of these was a tombstone in Paris marking the grave of a woman who had died at the age of 88, leaving behind 288 descendants. The second was the story of a shipwrecked mariner, taken from *Le Grand Dictionnaire historique* of Louis Moreri. According to the article cited by Feijoo, a fleet of four English vessels was shipwrecked off the coast of an island near Madagascar, which is now called Pines. Only one sailor and four women survived, including two maids, a black slave, and the captain's daughter. They were nourished on this otherwise uninhabited island chiefly by fruits and eggs, "and appetite, together with freedom, conferred upon this lone male marital rights over four women." Seventy-seven years after this shipwreck, another vessel touched at the island and discovered a population of eleven thousand inhabitants, all descendants of the English captain, whose name was Pines.

Feijoo carried the numerical progress further than his source and calculated that after another period of seventy-seven years, that is, after 154 years, the population of the island would amount to more than a thousand million, and after two hundred and thirty years, it would be three times greater than the total number of troops engaged in Assyria three centuries after the flood.[5]

As we have said, Feijoo freely admitted the unreliable character of his ancient historical and Biblical authorities. What he failed to realize is that his modern story of the prolific island has even less foundation in real life. He had been taken in by a gigantic hoax! The ultimate source of Feijoo's story of the shipwrecked mariner is a pornographic novel by Henry Neville, entitled *The Isle of Pines*, which had appeared in England in 1668. The name of the mariner-husband is also Pines, an obvious anagram of the male organ of reproduction. Everything recounted by Feijoo concerning the fertile island has its origins in Neville's equally fertile imagination and nowhere else.[6] Neville's novel enjoyed instantaneous success, both in England and on the continent, and it served as the basis for an episode in Grimmelshausen's seventeenth-century picaresque novel, *Simplicius Simplicissimus.*[7] To be sure, Moreri, in his *Dictionnaire*, was equally a victim of Neville's hoax, and as late as July, 1758, an adulterated version of the exploits of Pines was reproduced in the *Grand Magazine* as a travel article. Feijoo, however, prided himself both on his sophistication and on his mission to expose vulgar errors.[8] He devoted an entire essay, for example, to exposing the gullibility of various authors for accepting traditions concerning imaginary lands and cities. In this essay, entitled "Fables of the Batuecas and Imaginary Countries," he particularly criticizes the absurdity of another article in Moreri on a mythical fertile valley in Spain known as the Batuecas, a kind of Spanish Lubberland.[9] Accordingly, Feijoo should hardly be exempted from criticism for his observations on the isle of Pines. He was naive in accepting the story, and his statistics on population growth as a result are dead wrong.

One very appropriate comment on Feijoo's mathematics is a remark which Voltaire made in a completely different context: "Children are not made by a stroke of the pen."[10] Voltaire is famous for the social skepticism of his satirical works and the caution of his scientific investigations. As a result of these traits, he challenged accounts of extraordinary population growth in both the ancient and the modern worlds. Montesquieu had argued that population had reached its peak during the period of Julius Caesar and that Roman marriage laws brought on a decline. But even during the times of Charlemagne, Montesquieu argued, Europe had more inhabitants then during the seventeenth century.[11] A French theologian Denis le Peteau (1583-1652), had calculated that the population of the world 290 years after the Flood had been about seven hundred billion. Voltaire ironically assured his readers that it was not as a continuation of the *Arabian Nights* that Peteau had printed this handsome enumeration. The good Jesuit, Voltaire remarked, knew nothing about either making children or rearing them.[12] The brunt of Voltaire's attack was delivered against neither Montesquieu nor Peteau, however, but against a Scottish demographer, Robert Wallace (1697-1771), who had argued that population had already begun to diminish in Roman times. Voltaire pointed out the great fallacy of population estimators in assuming that propagation takes place in geometric progression. It never does, Voltaire affirmed, and all calculations based on this assumption are chimerical absurdities. "If a family of men or of apes multiplied in this fashion, the earth at the end of two hundred years would not have resources to nourish them."[13] Voltaire believed that the numbers of men, like those of apes or caterpillars, went up or down according to the ecological conditions in which the species live—a consideration which virtually none of the statistical reasoners had taken into account. Voltaire believed that the population of Germany, France, and England in the eighteenth century exceeded that in Roman times because of important social changes: "the prodigious extirpation of forests, the number of large cities built or enlarged during eight hundred years, and the number of arts augmented in proportion."[14] This was Voltaire's "precise reply to all the vague declamations which are repeated daily in books in which the authors neglect truth in favor of showing off their wit." Even though Voltaire devoted a considerable amount of attention in several of his works to problems of demography, he did not think it important to decide whether at any given time there was a large or a small number of men on the earth: "the essential is that this poor species live in the least misery."[15]

Feijoo in the essay following his discourse disproving the decay of the world, wrote against what he considered to be modern philosophy, particularly the system of René Descartes. In the early eighteenth century the Cartesian philosophy was considered radical in Spain, and to a certain extent in France, even though it had already been outmoded in England by Newtonianism. Voltaire attacked Cartesianism because he considered it to be discredited and supplanted by Newton's system. Feijoo, to the contrary attacked Cartesianism for its inherent weaknesses, chiefly in that it implies the gradual destruction of the world, but he did not propose that Newton's hypotheses were more acceptable. One of the notions of Descartes disputed by Feijoo was that concerning the method of procreation, a corollary of the corpuscular system. According to the notion Feijoo rejected, the seeds of every living thing existed as embryos in the seed of the first parent. This Chinese box theory was ordinarily known in the eighteenth century as "emboîtement des germes." Here, in Feijoo's words, is the theory he opposed: "God created in the beginning of the world, enclosed one in the other, the seeds of all the living forms that were to have existence in all the duration of the centuries, in such a way that the seeds of all plants of the same species that were and would be until the end of the world existed not only virtually but formally in the first plant of each species. And what is more in each of these innumerable seeds was perfectly formed the plant with its stem, roots, leaves, flowers and fruits." Feijoo did not know who was the first author of this opinion, but he had encountered it in Jacob Rohault and in Malebranche and assumed that it was accepted by most Cartesians. Actually the theory of preformism goes back to Hippocrates and that of preexistence was first developed by Malebranche. Preformism assumes that the parent himself fashions the embryo within the seminal fluid; whereas preexistence assumes that the embryo was created by God at the beginning of the world.[17] Feijoo makes no distinction between ovistic and animalcule preexistence, but the distinction is a vital one: the former assumes that transmission is carried on by the female ovum, and the latter, by the male sperm. Both theories were being advocated at the time Feijoo wrote his essay, even though Aristotle, and in modern times Harvey as far back as 1651, had supported epigenesis or gradual development of the embryo, with both male and female contributing to the process.

Feijoo's major objection to the theory of *emboîtement* is, as far as I know, an original one. Relying on mathematics, it is at least superficially comparable to his treatment of the Isle of Pines—although he uses his calculations in one instance without much commonsense reference to the real world, whereas in the other he is nothing if not practical. He argues that unless one accepts the concept of the infinite divisibility of material, it is impossible to conceive of millions and millions of plants preformed in the first seed of each species. The example he offers to prove his point is that of an average oak, which produces acorns for a period of 100 years, approximately ten thousand a year or a million in its lifetime. The first acorn which existed in the world would then require one million embryo acorns for the first production. Inside of each of these would be another million for the second generation; and each of these in turn would contain another million for the third generation. An acorn becomes a producing tree only after ten years. Therefore, every ten years after the first one hundred and ten, the previous number of acorns must be multiplied by one million. In order to produce the first series of generations the number of acorns required would extend to nineteen figures. Every two years the preceding number must be multiplied by a million. To illustrate the staggering immensity of these figures, Feijoo observed that if God created a firmament that was a thousand billion times greater than the present sky, and if He filled this cavity with grains of sand so small that a thousand together would not weigh as much as a grain of mustard, the space could not accommodate even one-tenth of the grains of sand represented by his colossal number. Without assuming the infinite divisibility of matter, Feijoo asked rhetorically, would it be possible for the first acorn to contain as many embryo acorns as represented by a number comprising three thousand figures.

Feijoo appended three other objections to his refutation of the preformationist theory, but considered them less significant than his mathematical demonstration: the theory cannot account for the production of monsters; it cannot explain hybrids or animals of mixed species; and it cannot account for the likenesses of progeny to both parents.

The notion of preformation was not as closely linked to Cartesianism as Feijoo suggested, for it was accepted by many scientists and writers who were not Cartesians at all. One of these was the Swiss naturalist Charles Bonnet (1720-1793), who utilized preformationism as the basis of his *Considérations sur les corps organisés,* 1762. Bonnet was the disciple of another Swiss naturalist, Albrecht Haller (1708-1777), but was less dogmatic. He admitted that his work could be accepted as nothing more substantial than a novel, but modestly asked whether any other hypotheses could serve any better.[18] Voltaire was not on good terms with either Haller or Bonnet. After reading Haller's reflections, Voltaire affirmed that "men still do not know how they make either babies or ideas."[19] In a printed review of Bonnet's *Considérations.* Voltaire attacked the preformationist theory with arguments resembling Feijoo's but he did so in an ironical fashion. The reader who approaches his remarks without due caution is in danger of assuming that Voltaire is accepting rather than ridiculing the emboîtement theory.

According to Voltaire's ironical review,

> the extreme and inconceivable smallness of the last seeds contained in the one which serves as father need not at all startle one's reason. The infinite divisibility of matter is not a truth of physics; it is only a metaphysical subtlety entertained in geometry. But it is true that an entire world may be contained in a grain of sand in the same proportion as the universe which we see exists. It will probably require centuries to exhaust the seeds contained one within the other, and it is perhaps then that, nature having arrived at its last period, the world of which we are a part will have its end as it has had a beginning.
> ... Perhaps this ingenious and profound author does not pro-

vide in this system convincing enough reasons to explain the formation of monsters, or the resemblance of children sometimes to the father and sometimes to the mother. But what system has ever properly explained these secrets of nature? [20]

Voltaire attacked preformationism more directly in two of his satirical works, *L'Homme aux quarante écus*, 1768, and *Dialogues et entretiens philosophiques (Dialogues d'Ephémère)*, 1777, but concerned himself with a more sophisticated version, that of animalculism, based on the pioneer microscopic experiments of Leeuwenhoek and Hartsoeker. In the former work, he expressed doubts that the active little men presumably contained in the seminal fluid would submit to remaining inactive for nine months after entering the egg, and suggested that there is something repulsive about reducing man in his earliest stages to a caterpillar.[21] In reference to *L'Homme aux quarante écus*, Voltaire remarked to one of his friends, "All the systems on the manner in which we come into the world have been destroyed by each other: it is only the way in which one makes love that has never changed."[22] In his dialogue on generation, Voltaire repeated most of his objections to the major systems and concluded, "we must decide to remain in ignorance of our origins; we are like the Egyptians who derive so much benefit from the Nile, but are still not acquainted with its source; perhaps they will discover it some day."

Obviously the mysteries of generation have been to a considerable extent clarified in our time, so that the remarks of Feijoo and Voltaire on the theory of preformationism have value only as literary history, and perhaps as a small part of the history of science. Yet the basic question which led to Feijoo's reflections on human production—whether the ancient world is preferable to the modern or vice versa—still has considerable appeal for many people. The question cannot be answered as Feijoo tried to answer it—by mathematical reasoning; but one may say in his defense that empirical evidence has so far been proved no more conclusive.

NOTES

1 J. A. Maravall, *Antiguos y Modernos. La idea del progreso en el desarrollo inicial de una sociedad* (Madrid, 1966), pp. 16, 99; Otis H. Greene, *Spain and the Western Tradition* (Madison, Wis., 1965), III, 278-79.

2 Américo Castro, *Lengua, enseñanza y literatura* (Madrid, 1924), p. 31, "habría merecido el nombre de Voltaire español." G. Marañón, *Las ideas biológicas del Padre Feijóo* (Madrid, 1934), p. xx.

3 Henry Reynolds, *Mythomystes*, cited in Gordon L. Davies, "The Concept of Denudation in Seventeenth-Century England," *JHI*, 27 (1966), 279.

4 A. Lombard, *La Querelle des Anciens et des Modernes: L'Abbé du Bos* (Neuchatel, 1908), p. 15, attributes the remark to Fontenelle, who was probably one of Feijoo's main sources.

5 The translator of a French edition of Feijoo's *Teatro critico* in 1742 disagreed with his multiplication; according to the translator's application of the rule of proportion, after the first 154 years, there would be only 48,400,000 individuals, and after 231 years, only 72,600,000. See *Théâtre Critique* (Paris, 1742), pp. 29-30.

6 A. O. Aldridge, "Polygamy in Early Fiction: Henry Neville and Denis Veiras," *PMLA*, 65 (1950), 464-72.

7 Bk. VI, Chaps. 19-22.

8 *Para desengaño de errores communes.*

9 Sec. IV.

10 Theodore Besterman, ed., *Voltaire: Correspondance* (Paris, 1963), letter 6723.

11 *L'Esprit des Lois*, Bk. 23, Chaps. 17-26.

12 M. Beuchot, ed., *Oeuvres de Voltaire* (Paris, 1829-40), V, 65a.

13 *Ibid.*, VIII, 148a.

14 *Ibid.*, VIII, 146a.

15 *Ibid.*, V, 63.

16 F. J. Cole, *Early Theories of Sexual Generation* (Oxford, 1930), p. 50.

17 Jacques Roger, *Les Sciences de la vie dans la pensée française du XVIIIe siècle* (Poitiers, 1963), pp. 325-36.

18 *Oeuvres* (Neuchatel, 1779), V, 114.

19 Besterman, ed., *Correspondance*, letter 4324; the title of Haller's piece is "Reflexions sur la système de la génération de M. Buffon."

20 *Aux Auteurs de la Gazette littéraire*, 4 April 1764.

21 *Romans et Contes* (Pléiade ed.), pp. 333-34. In the next year, 1769, Diderot in *Le Reve de d'Alembert* rejects as completely false the opinion that each foetus is a completely formed tiny creature originally tucked away in a remote ancestor, and he substitutes epigenesis as the true explanation of generation.

22 To Thierot, 15 September 1768.

Quantities of Qualities:
Nominal Style and the Novel

CAREY McINTOSH

One of the most important of general indexes of style is the degree to which the language of a given passage entrusts meaning to nouns or verbs. In a nominal prose style, nouns and noun phrases predominate; what counts is not action, which is so far as possible diluted or hidden or masked, but *relationships* between things or qualities. Nominal sentences rely on being verbs and stative verbs; they express meaning in terms of static conditions variously arranged and distributed. An energetic "verbal" style is, for the literary critic, easier to talk about and appreciate, in part because its energy is likely to break through the literal sense into metaphor, as in the second clause of this sentence. The best writing handbooks of our time attack nominal constructions. Many of the "Bad Sentences" that Sheridan Baker corrects in the fifth chapter of *The Practical Stylist* use a nominal syntax, and George Orwell's translation of a verse from Ecclesiastes into "Gobbledygook" makes painfully obvious the miserable weakness of some pseudo-scientific modern nominal styles.[1]

Nothing in the nature of things decrees, however, that nominal styles must always be flabby, vague, and colorless. They are a large family of styles, characterized by many degrees and kinds of nominalness; in skillful hands they may perform necessary functions and achieve effects—some of them quite beautiful—that would be destroyed by the use of strong, active verbs. I shall confine myself in this essay to a few variants of nominal prose that play a role in a few novels, beginning with *Clarissa.* The first variant may be defined in lexical as well as grammatical terms because it leans heavily on a small number of abstractions derived from the social environment of the court, "honor," "favor," "service," "interest"; I shall call this kind of nominal style "courtly-genteel." In the early volumes of *Clarissa,* courtly-genteel prose adds a certain presumptive dignity to venal middle-class maneuverings within the Harlowe family. In later volumes of the same novel, Clarissa uses a more complicated nominal style to express more complicated feelings and states of mind. Henry Fielding puts courtly-genteel phrases in the mouths of his wicked aristocrats, but in a different context some of the same constructions embody true politeness, and signal a new stage of maturity in Tom Jones. Later novelists turn nominal prose to their own purposes, all of which have something to do with politeness, pedantry, or self-consciousness.

One of the aims of nominal prose in the eighteenth century was to rise above the coarseness and vulgarity of market-place lanaguage, as if on the premise that abstractness and passivity contribute to true refinement of style. I think it could be shown that eighteenth-century prose in general is more nominal than Elizabethan prose. Clarissa's letters, however, aspire to something higher than the norm of clarity and correctness established by (for example) Joseph Addison, whose celebrated "middle style" is not designed for ceremony but for "ease." Clarissa, by contrast, is set up—rather painfully at times—as "an Exemplar to her Sex," as a model of true elegance; her language transcends simple correctness; it is a medium for the extraordinary "Delicacy of Sentiments" by which she excels her peers.[2] And yet it never rises to the loftiest heights of the "high style"; by design as well as by incapacity, it falls short of the authentic splendors that we expect in the language of heroism or prophecy.

Clarissa is recounting the history of her family's quarrel with the rake Lovelace. James and Arabella Harlowe have insulted Lovelace, who makes sure that Clarissa knows he has swallowed the affront for her sake. "I was sorry for the merit this gave him in his own opinion with me," writes Clarissa (I, 23). She could have said, "I regretted that he believed . . ." "I was sorry" is more nominal than "I regretted," simply because it uses the verb 'to be' not a "real" verb, and therefore describes, at least on the surface, a stage of being, not a form of behavior. The "merit" that Lovelace thinks he has acquired "with" Clarissa is clearly a commodity that *can* be acquired or lost; the presence or absence of so many units of merit is a nominal substitute for active—and therefore 'verb-ish'—admiration or disapproval. Some pages further on, James Harlowe "bid me deserve his love, and I should be sure to have it" (I, 46): this is not at all the same as saying, 'behave yourself, Clarissa, and I shall love you,' because it is phrased in terms of static conditions, not actions; it says in effect that if Clarissa attains the condition of 'deservingness,' a certain commodity, her brother's "love," will come into her possession.[3]

A number of commonplace locutions in Clarissa's prose use the verb 'to have' plus an abstract quality in place of an active verb: "I had interest enough to disengage myself from . . ." (I, 27); "He has not the sense to say any-thing to the purpose" (I, 49); "he had a command of his passions which few . . . would be able to show" (I, 23); "I am sorry to have occasion to say it" (I, 34); "the man they had all so much reason to hate" (I, 42). By focusing on what a person 'has,' such expressions direct our attention to status, not process.[4]

If the 'possession' of an abstract quality is crucial, then it matters intensely how much of a given abstraction one has or does not have; some of the most characteristic idioms of Clarissa's prose measure out quantities of qualities. There may be an excess (Lovelace "was supposed to have given *too much* cause for their ill opinion" (I, 22); Solmes's family "stands in *too much* need of his favour" (I, 87)), or a deficiency ("they have begun so cruelly with me, that I have *not* spirit *enough* to assert my own Negative" (I, 48). In particularly delicate cases, the writer does not presume to say how much of an abstraction is present except in terms of its *results*: under great pressure from her father Clarissa cannot "even . . . make *such* an expression of my duty to him *as* my heart overflowed with" (I, 52). A few pages further on, she muffles an uncomfortable sum of pounds, shillings, and pence in the same periphrasis: "And surely I will not stand against *such* an accession to the family *as* may happen from marrying Mr. Solmes" (I, 87).

Two other means of diluting action are favored by this courtly-genteel style. The human agent can be replaced by a personified quality: it is not James Harlowe himself who refuses to wait for Lovelace to tire of his suit; rather, "my Brother's *antipathy* would not permit him to wait for such an event" (I, 26). Whether Clarissa herself may be trusted or not, we are not told; rather her Aunt Hervey affirms that "my Cousin Clary's *prudence* may be confided in" (I, 39). The personified quality does the work here, just as an eighteenth-century gentleman employed "his" servant to perform certain menial actions that he considered below his dignity; and the higher the rank, the fewer everyday actions he could permit himself. An action may also be placed at one remove from its agent by inserting a motive or emotion between them: "my Father *was pleased* to hint . . ."; "he *thought fit* . . . to make . . . enquiries"; "he *is willing* to hope you to be all obedience" (I, 26, 27, 50).

We are now in a better position to see affinities between Clarissa's prose style and the language of the court. These last two mannerisms seem to be borrowed directly from the courtier, who speaks of 'his Majesty' rather than

bluntly referring to the king, 'his Reverence,' not the bishop. Pronouncements from the throne are habitually phrased to give at least syntactic promi-
nence to royal emotions or motives, the will or pleasure of the monarch: his
royal Highness is pleased to signify . . . ; his Grace is willing to grant. Moreover relationships within the Harlowe family are defined in courtly terms, in
terms of service, honor, desert, obligation, favor, indulgence, duty, and interest. Clarissa remarks ruefully to Anna Howe early in the first volume of the
novel that "if we have the power to *oblige* those we have to do with," "we
may make the world allow for and respect us as we please" (I, 33). She
justifies herself in courtly terms: "I hoped I should always have a just sense of
every one's *favour* to me, superadded to the *duty* I *owed* as a Daughter and a
Niece" (I, 45). Before Lovelace appears on the scene, she "had *interest*
enough to disengage herself from the addresses" of unwanted suitors (I, 27).
"How difficult is it," she exclaims as the thumbscrews are being tightened,
"to give a negative where both *duty* and inclination join to make one wish to
oblige" (I, 47). Her mother distresses her by "expatiating upon the com-
plaisance I *owe* her for her *indulgence*" (I, 63). The very delicacy that distinguishes her from other women sharpens her predicament: "My *duty* will not
permit me *so far* to suppose my Father arbitrary, *as* to make a plea of that
arbitrariness to you" (I, 116).

The courtier displays his craft of courtesy most conspicuously in ceremonies, not in common conversation; and so some of the most elaborately
elegant passages in Clarissa's letters occur when she bows herself off stage;
notice how many of the idioms and mannerisms we have been describing are
combined in the following: "I am sure of your kind construction," she writes
to Anna Howe,

> and I confide in your discretion, that you will avoid reading to or
> transcribing for others, such passages as may have the appearance
> of treating too freely the Parental, or even the Fraternal charac-
> ter, or induce others to censure for a supposed failure in duty to
> the one, or decency to the other,
>
> Your truly affectionate,
Cl. Harlowe.
>
> (I, 91)

Often the closing words of eighteenth-century letters, by convention, make
fragmentary allusions to what were originally courtly ties—'and remain, my
dear Sir, / *Your* most *obliged* and humble *Servant*.' Many twentieth-century
letters close with a petrified remnant of the same formula: '*Yours* truly' and
'Sincerely *yours*' preserve the grammatical signs of a relation between a noble
lord and "his" bound servant that is legally speaking five or six hundred years
out of date.

We have talked about courtly-genteel prose as a language of mutual obligations, a special kind of nominal prose, in which people "give," "have," and
"owe" various quantities of duty, service, interest, honor, and favor. The
history of this style is complicated. Nothing that I have been able to find out
weakens a working hypothesis to the effect that courtly-genteel language is
almost as old as courts; that, in other words, when the 'favor' of a noble lord
and his ability to confer 'obligations' and 'honor' and to advance a lesser
man's 'interests' in return for 'service' and 'duty'—as these social and political
relationships came into existence, so did a set of conventional phrases and
periphrases that corresponded to these daily realities of court life. Analogies
may be drawn between the courtly ideal and the religious conception of man
as a 'servant' of God.[5]

The oldest examples of courtly-genteel prose in modern English that I know
of occur in letters written under the early Tudors, including one from Henry
VII and one to Henry VIII; in 1517 Thomas More applies the language of
courtly patronage to friendship:

> That in your letter you thank me so carefully for my services on
> behalf of your friends is a mark of your great courtesy. What I
> did was quite trifling: it is only your goodness that exaggerates it.
> But you scarcely do justice to our friendship, for you seem to
> think that what I may do puts you under an obligation, whereas
> you should rather claim as your own and service due you.

Here are most of the important traits of Clarissa's courtly-genteel prose
style, a heightened consciousness of quantities of service and obligation
rendered and due, nominal phraseology, actions attributed to personified
qualities. On the other hand, More's language is loosely connected; it is un-
likely that Richardson would start a sentence with 'But' and splice on successive 'for' and 'whereas' clauses; but the courtly formulas in More and Richardson are very similar. "Formula" is perhaps the wrong word for More's and
Richardson's use of such expressions, since they stand for strongly-felt relationships. Nevertheless, by 1640 such expressions had been codified in phrase
books and courtesy manuals, and thereby widely disseminated to all who
wished to learn such an "Elegant and Compendious way of writing."[6]

We can distinguish four areas of experience outside the court itself where
these formulas come frequently into play: ceremonial friendships, dedications
and patronage, diplomacy, and courtship. In each case the writer sets himself
up to pay his obeisances to the addressee; and form—establishing a climate of
honorable respect and reciprocal politeness—is at least as important as content. In each case the relationship between writer and addressee may be
traced back to the court, historically, or by functional derivation, or by

simple imitation. And in each of these transactions one party offers itself up to the other with a sweeping bow of elegant humility; courtly-genteel style reflects (as content) abject dependence—which is as often a matter of politeness as of actual inferiority.

Since in the early eighteenth century almost every one literate was trying to be or seem polite, Richardson, whose ear for nuances of language was exceptionally keen, could have picked up such elements of courtly-genteel style as he needed for *Clarissa* from any one or more of a dozen sources. It is not hard to collect examples of courtly-genteel prose from eighteenth-century drama, periodical essays, dedications, and letters. One of the oddities of Pope's 1717 Preface is his attempt to speak both as patron and as poet: "I wish we *had* the humanity to reflect that even the worst authors might, in their endeavour to *please* us, *deserve* something at our hands." Cruel critics, he remarks, discourage beginning authors, "till *such* talents *as* they have are *so* far discredited *as* to be of small *service* to them." Courtly-genteel mannerisms play no small part in Pope's efforts to sweep all disagreeables under the rug. A letter from Lady Hertford to Elizabeth Carter (dated 1739) shows how elaborate such mannerisms could be, even in private correspondence:

> I have received so much pleasure from the few Poems I have seen of yours, that if I were not afraid of asking too great a favour, I would tell you that I should (when you have a leisure hour) take it for a great obligation if you would communicate a copy to me sometimes; and let me have the satisfaction of knowing that you are so just as to believe me denying myself the honour you offer me, does not proceed from a want of a real regard to your merit, which will always make me, with the utmost sincerity,
>
> Madam,
> Your most obliged humble Servant.

Courtesy here translates into an epistolary curtsey so excruciatingly polite that I am not sure whether it really comes off or not. The phrases quoted from Pope serve a purpose; they muffle stridencies and provide a sort of padding for the sharp edges of their author's anxiety, like the velvet lining of a case of knives. Lady Hertford's letter illustrates the same verbal gestures in unskilled hands, almost pure form, almost no content at all.[7]

So far, I have emphasized the social context of nominal prose; let's turn now to aesthetics, to ways in which a nominal style improves *Clarissa* as a work of art. The conclusion to Clarissa's letter quoted above—where she trusts that Anna's discretion will prevent her from transcribing such passages as may have the appearance of treating too freely the paternal character—is authentically graceful in its branching symmetry, in the measured agility with which it weaves among measured quantities of freedom, duty, and decency. The difference between a nominal sentence and its verbish equivalent may count as heavily in setting tone or expressing point of view or defining character as any number of violent actions or transcendent metaphors. The courtly-genteel style of Clarissa's letters contributes to plot also, taking 'plot' in an Aristotelian sense as the central complication of the action; Clarissa's predicament is that she must reward the 'service' Lovelace has done her by enabling her to circumvent her brother's 'interest' without compromising her own 'honor' or failing in her 'duty' or destroying her chances of regaining her parents' 'favor.'

Nominal prose is among the most effective instruments by which the characters of *Clarissa* express complicated feelings and judgments. The only action any one in *Clarissa* performs before our very eyes is the act of writing letters; epistolary style is therefore a dramatic element in the novel, and it is through virtuoso convolutions of nominal style that we gain access to many of the most intense and private moments of the psychological and moral drama of the novel. I shall give two examples of Richardson's higher virtuosity as an artist in nominal prose, drawn from later volumes of the novel, where the abstractions being balanced and arranged are not courtly but psychological and moral. Since by this time Clarissa has left far behind the struggle to adjust her social 'obligations' and settle what she 'deserves' from her family, courtly-genteel formulae are much less in evidence than they were in the first volume.

Seven weeks before Clarissa's death, Anna Howe takes it upon herself to inform Arabella Harlowe that her unhappy friend is "dangerously ill." The first paragraph of Arabella's reply is curt, blunt, brutal ("We are told he [Lovelace] has remorse, and would marry her. We don't believe it, indeed. She may be very ill"); for the second she pulls herself together to express stinging disdain, in nominal prose: "I cannot say, Miss, that the notification from you is the more welcome for the liberties you have been pleased to take with our whole family, for resenting a conduct, that it is a shame any young Lady should justify." The insolence of this letter is more than Anna can bear, but she does not "rave" (as Lovelace does, under provocation, later on); rather, she replies in kind, in nominal prose; but her anger pulls the sentence out of shape, and overflows into parentheses:[8]

> If you had half as much sense as you have ill-nature, you would (notwithstanding the exuberance of the latter) have been able to distinguish between a kind intention to you all (that you might have the less to reproach yourself with, if a deplorable case should happen) and an officiousness I owed you not, by reason of freedoms at least reciprocal.

The sentence has an almost convulsive imbalance. Clause number one is the nominal translation of a cry of rage, 'you stupid bitch,' or words to that effect; what follows tries to modulate from hot outrage to freezing contempt: it begins to lecture and then chokes itself off in "freedoms at least reciprocal," a tight-lipped acknowledgment of complicity, as Anna becomes aware that her correspondent really is below contempt, and feels humiliated, and stifles the feeling.

That is a brief explication of what this nominal sentence expresses in human, dramatic terms. To appreciate its linguistic artistry, try to paraphrase it in less nominal language. 'You are so stupid and malicious that you couldn't understand my good intentions (I hoped to lighten your future burden of self-reproach, if Clarissa should die) or my helpfulness, which you did not deserve since you and I have been insulting each other right along.' Richardson's sentence is subtler and carries more meaning than my paraphrase: I have had to leave out a good many of Anna's ideas in order to make sense (e.g., the "exuberance" of Arabella's ill-nature); I have blunted the edge of Anna's irony by choosing, among twenty meanings implied by a given understatement or periphrasis, one or two for translation into explicit, verb-ish language: "freedoms at least reciprocal" scores points not only by its conciseness but also by its ambiguity.

One of the special strengths of nominal prose is its capacity to make fine moral and psychological discriminations. Clarissa's talents as a moralist emerge as she is forced to pick her way among temptations that are likely to turn her own virtues against her or against her family; and some of her nicest judgments could hardly be expressed except in nominal prose. For example: having escaped from the brothel, Clarissa, in hiding, is checking up on Lovelace, and has written to the real Lady Betty about her supposed visit to London twelve days earlier. The letter consists of a formal self-introduction, three questions of fact, and then a paragraph justifying the inquiry, of which this is a part:

> I think I owe it to my former hopes (however deceived in them) and even to Charity, that a person [Lovelace] of whom I was once willing to think better, should not prove so egregiously abandoned, as to be wanting, in *every* instance, to that veracity which is an indispensable in the character of a gentleman.

Again, a less nominal paraphrase necessarily simplifies, because there is no way to express with active verbs some of the things this sentence means to say. 'At one time I hoped that Lovelace, whom I wanted to admire, would in *some* instance tell the truth like a gentleman.' Richardson's sentence is more intricate and poignant: if her "hopes" that Lovelace may not prove "in *every* instance" deficient in a virtue that no gentleman should lack in *any* instance, if these hopes are "former," i.e., defunct, why should she trouble herself? Conscious perhaps that her letter makes her liable to cross-examination on this and other more painful subjects, she adds another motive, capital-C "Charity." In what way is this sincere? I do not doubt it is, at bottom, but she can hardly expect Lovelace to be exonerated; that is, since she must know with part of her mind that her inquiry will almost certainly expose Lovelace as a liar, it is disingenuous of her to claim "Charity" as a motive for writing. A more obvious motive for her letter, a sense of injured merit, is introduced not as a motive at all but as a part of the network of substantives and modifiers that explain what her "former hopes" were: that he not *be so* "egregiously abandoned" *as* to *be* totally deficient in that "veracity" which *is* "an indispensable" in a gentleman. The feelings are so intense here, and so strenuously knotted up in *politesses*, that whatever irony may have inhered in these hyperbolical "hopes" vanishes completely.

Brief discussion of five later novels will show that nominal style continued to be a resource for the writer who values indirection. We might expect that comic novels have recourse to nominal style less frequently than do novels of sensibility. But this is not true, for several reasons. Nominal prose styles as a general phenomenon deal with abstractions of many kinds, only a few of which originate in the court, and some of which fall pat to the purposes of comedy. Very rarely, moreover, do comic novelists limit themselves to an exclusive diet of 'low' characters and actions; they pay their respects to middle-class values, and dabble in romance.

Roderick Random thrives on low company and rough-neck adventures, but preens himself on "advantages of birth and education," and in his first undisguised words with the insipid Narcissa is careful to identify himself as "an unfortunate *gentleman*."[9] Since the novel consists of Random's own history narrated in his own words, the defensive-aggressive pride he takes in his gentility can scarcely fail to color the language of the novel as a whole. Perhaps it is responsible for the ungainly, low-bourgeois, shabby-genteel nominal idioms that may be found on almost every page of the novel, idioms that fail both to achieve elegance and to say plainly what they mean: "My mistress *took occasion*, from this detection, to rail . . ." (p. 144); "which, however, we *find means* to clear . . ." (pp. 231, 260); "*with* a *resolution* of *taking* the first *opportunity* to . . ." (p. 263); "would have *done my business*" (p. 266); "*to* their great *satisfaction*" (pp. 212, 232, 244, and *passim*). Only the very lowest of rascals is allowed to talk plainly in *Roderick Random:* " 'I only want to taste the purser's rum; that's all, master,' " says the carpenter's mate as he chops his way into a storeroom with a hatchet (p. 262). On the next page our hero draws a pistol and leaps into a crowded lifeboat 'swearing' that he "would shoot any man who should *presume* to *obstruct* my *entrance.*" Nominal constructions in *Roderick Random* support Random's pretensions to gentility, and when he cultivates a patron (Book II, Chapter 15) and hunts for a wife (Book II, Chapters 20, 31, 32), courtly-genteel language plays the role we might expect, though it seems more stilted in Random than in Clarissa.

In *Tom Jones* a number of different nominal styles are ingeniously subordinated to a variety of artistic purposes. The courtly jargon of Lord Fellamar is as empty of meaning as his pursuit of Sophia is devoid of true affection—"do not accuse me of *taking* an ungenerous *advantage* while I *have* no *thoughts* but what are directed to your *honour* and *interest.*"[10] Sentiments like these the narrator does "not perfectly understand"; perhaps, he insinuates, they "could not all be strictly reconciled either to sense or grammar" (Book XVII, Chapter 8; p. 780). Nightingale exposes Lady Ballaston to Tom in a delicious parody of the same jargon: "You are not the first upon whom she hath conferred *obligations* of this kind . . . . Her *favours* are . . . prudently bestowed"; and Tom is so disgusted by these discoveries that he turns himself "out of her *service*" (Fielding's italics) (XV, 9; p. 701).

This is not to say that courtly language and nominal style in Fielding are always signs of decadence or foppery. Some obligations, in *Tom Jones,* are honorable; both Mrs. Miller and young Nightingale express their gratitude for Allworthy's generosity in variations on the courtly-genteel style. Allworthy himself favors a nominal style; it suits his dignity (" 'I am afraid, Miss Western, my family hath been the occasion of giving you some uneasiness, to which, I fear, I have innocently become more instrumental then I intended' " XVIII, 9; p. 823). In the crisis of Tom's and Sophia's betrothal the words that burst from him are more courtly than usual; "I hope, madam, my nephew will merit so much goodness, and will be always as sensible as myself of the honour you have done my family.' " Nobly spoken—but not, in Fielding's comic world, the last word on the subject. " 'Yes,' cries Western, 'but if I had suffered her to stand shill I shall I, dilly-dally, you might not have had that *honour* yet awhile.' " Worthy as Allworthy is, he lacks the indisputably vulgar energy, linguistic as well as sexual, that brings the lovers together despite modesty, despite justice, despite principle: Tom Jones himself is by now so thoroughly converted to prudence, honor, and a nominal way of expressing himself that for a very brief moment he hinders his own happiness: " 'Let me beseech you, sir,' says Jones, 'don't let me be the occasion—' 'Beseech mine a—,' cries Western, 'I thought thou had'st been a lad of higher mettle than to give way to a parcel of maidenish tricks. I tell thee 'tis all flim-flam. Zoodikers! ' " (XVIII, 12; pp. 844-45). Thus the passive, genteel rewards in store for Tom—honor and favor in abundance, "mutual esteem," discretion, prudence, a lifetime of static conditions and honorable abstractions—depend on the *active* interference of a comic country squire whose language is as earthy as the Somerset loam.

Polite and ironic passages in Jane Austen make an impression as much by what they leave out or paint over as by what they say directly. In Darcy's second, his successful, proposal to Elizabeth, the abstractions that the two lovers maneuver into position and assign to proper places as part of their new intimacy are motives and emotions and moral virtues: "Let me thank you," says Elizabeth, "for that generous *compassion* which *induced* you to take so much *trouble*..."; and Darcy does not attempt to deny "that the *wish* of giving *happiness* to you, might add force to the other *inducements* which led me on." Dummy verbs again: trouble is *taken*; happiness and uneasiness are *given*; sentiments are *given to be understood.* Darcy is sorry that Mrs. Gardiner told Elizabeth about his part in patching up a marriage between Lydia and Wickham, but in the words he uses to Elizabeth he omits Mrs. Gardiner altogether, by means of passive voice, and converts a scandal into the sources of a lady's discomfort, by noun-clause periphrasis: "I am sorry that you have been informed of what may have given you uneasiness." Here is how Elizabeth and Darcy say 'I love you':

> Elizabeth feeling all the more than common awkwardness and anxiety of his situation, now forced herself to speak; and immediately, though not very fluently, gave him to understand, that her sentiments had undergone so material a change, since the period to which he alluded, as to make her receive with gratitude and pleasure, his present assurance. The happiness which this reply produced, was such as he had probably never felt before; and he expressed himself on the occasion as sensibly and as warmly as a man violently in love can be supposed to do.

Taken out of context, the passage has its quaintnesses; in context it is very moving, because its use of nominal prose first draws attention, by oblique allusion, to the hard human facts that have humbled Darcy's pride (and muted Elizabeth's gaiety); and then, by demonstrating to the civilized-ness that controls those hard facts and strong emotions, softens them. In Jane Austen's world, self-control and the capacity to harness socio-psycho-moral abstractions (including 'desires') within a nominal syntax are by no means incompatible with passion; we feel that Elizabeth's love is far deeper and richer than the love that Lydia so unrestrainedly, so artlessly announces for Wickham ("I am going to Gretna Green, and if you cannot guess with who, I shall think you a simpleton, for there is but one man in the world I love, and he is an angel").[11]

In Dickens, the polite indirections of nominal prose become circumlocutions on the part of characters who wish to say something impressive and dignified, but don't know what that something is. There is no equivalent to the Harlowe family in Dickens, no three generations of haughty bourgeois inter-impaled on each other's patronage and service, interest and favor. Personal antipathies, private affections have replaced the quasi-political relationships within Clarissa's family, leaving no other function for courtly-genteel formulas than the simple heraldic ones they perform nowadays on engraved invitations—except as the stuffing in stuffed shirts like Mr. Veneering of *Our Mutual Friend*, who appoints Twemlow to give away Sophronia in the following passage:

> But . . . there is a tried friend of our family who . . . is the friend on whom this agreeable duty almost naturally devolves. That friend is now among us. That friend is Twemlow. . . . And I cannot sufficiently express to you, my dear Podsnap, the pleasure I feel in having this opinion of mine and Anastasia's so readily confirmed by you, that other equally familiar and tried friend who stands in the proud position—or I ought rather to say, who places Anastasia and myself in the proud position of himself standing in the simple position—of baby's godfather.[12]

This sounds like perfect nonsense, but isn't. Veneering's problem is that of the politician who wants to oblige one of the people in his service, without diminishing the favor that a rival feels himself to enjoy; he must juggle with the status of each to make both feel they have gained something. His speech confers a favor on Twemlow, and turns somersaults to appear to confer an equivalent favor on Podsnap: a noteworthy piece of social gerrymandering, achieved by adding sections and coupling on segments of nominal syntax until the sentence buckles of its own weight.

Norman Mailer is not so pompous as Mr. Veneering, but much more self-conscious. Nominal syntax in *The Armies of the Night* enables him to play with categories of identity, arrange them in patterns, decorate them, and then move on, without necessarily affecting the main plot of the novel, except—and it is an exception almost important enough to destroy the rule—that what Mailer calls the "cathedral" of his own "personality" is thereby endowed with one more in a long series of colorful grotesques. In the following passage Mailer uses the word 'image' to mean the picture of oneself that projects to one's own consciousness and to other people; this central abstraction is almost inert. But Mailer invents metaphors for it, and then stages a set of tiny 'happenings' around the metaphors; these 'happenings' are not static but feverishly active:

> As a corollary of his detestation of the telephone was his necessity to pick it up once in a while. Mailer had the most developed

sense of imagery; if not, he would have been a figure of deficiency, for people had been regarding him by his public image
since he was twenty-five years old. He had in fact learned to live
in the sarcophagus of his image—at night, in his sleep, he might
dart out and paint improvements on the sarcophagus. During the
day, while he was helpless, newspapermen and other assorted
bravos of the media and the literary world would carve ugly
pictures on the living tomb of his legend. Of necessity, part of
Mailer's remaining funds of sensitivity went right into the war of
supporting his image and working for it. Sometimes he thought
his relation to this image was not unlike some poor fellow who
strains his very testicles to bring in emoluments for his wife yet is
never favored with carnal knowledge of her. In any event, Mailer
worked for the image, and therefore he detested the portrait of
himself which would be promulgated if no one could ever reach
him. So, on impulse, thereby sharpening his instinct as a gambler,
he took spot plunges: once in a while he would pick up his own
phone.[13]

The paragraph as a whole includes flashes of intense activity, darting, painting, carving, straining. Mailer's 'image' changes somewhat bewilderingly from
a sarcophagus into an abstract cause, then into a woman who in a deliberately
stilted or old-fashioned euphemism, denies the writer her 'favors.' The
'image' itself does not act, however, but is acted upon; its function is to be
cast into adventurous relationships with 'people,' newspapermen, and the
narrator, as a part of a very extensive and complex exposition of the mind
and art of Norman Mailer himself.

It is fair to propose that nominal style contributes significantly to the power
and beauty of Richardson's best novel. If Clarissa's tragedy takes place in a
hot-house atmosphere, it is a hot-house ornately decorated, almost weed-less
and bug-less—thanks in part to Richardson's aptitude for genteel but meaningful periphrasis. Sometimes the gentility of nominal prose *is* its meaning; elegance and delicacy justify themselves in Richardson's ideal of true nobility of
soul. Elsewhere the complicated ordeals of Anna and Clarissa are reflected in
contortions of syntax only possible in nominal prose; the language of Clarissa's "tragic quest for identity . . . , the tragedy of personality,"[14] is sensitive
to minute details in the interior drama it mirrors. Nominal prose helps Jane
Austen to embody high decorum and austere moral values in human beings
who suffer and love as intensely as any one could ask them to, but express
their feelings elliptically; the reader is frequently required to infer the true
depth of their emotions, and to catch oblique allusions to what actually
happened. In eighteenth-century comic novelists, courtly-genteel phrases are
still reliable signs of social class; in Dickens they indicate empty pretensions

to an almost meaningless rank in society. During the nineteenth century, courtly-genteel terminology may have lost the place it once occupied in civilized discourse, but other abstractions multiplied, and continue to multiply, and since nominal syntax provides a framework for "dealing" with abstractions, it may be very useful to a writer who is trying to sort out states of consciousness.

NOTES

1 See Rulon Wells, "Nominal and Verbal Style," *Style in Language*, ed. Thomas A. Sebeok (New York, 1960), pp. 213-20; for stative verbs see Martin Joos, *The English Verb: Form and Meanings* (Madison and Milwaukee, 1964), pp. 102-15; Roderick A. Jacobs and Peter S. Rosenbaum, *English Transformational Grammar* (Waltham, London, Toronto, 1968), pp. 63-65. For a statistical approach to nominal and verbal styles, see Louis T. Milic, *A Quantitative Approach to the Style of Jonathan Swift* (The Hague, 1967), pp. 195-98 and p. 164, Table 6.8.

2 Preface to *Clarissa; or, The History of a Young Lady*, 3rd ed. (1751, rpt. Oxford, 1930), I, xiii. All subsequent references to *Clarissa* will be provided in parentheses, citing volume and page of this edition. In two or three cases I have reduced Richardson's italics to roman type, so that I am responsible for typographical emphasis throughout this essay, except as specifically noted. For some interesting changes in English after 1640, see G. L. Dillon, "The Seventeenth-Century Shift in the Theory and Language of Passion," *Language & Style*, 4 (1971), 131-43. Recent publications that deal with contrasting styles in Richardson: W. J. Farrell, "The Style and the Action in *Clarissa*," *SEL*, 3 (1963), 365-75, and Irwing Gopnik, *The Theory of Style and Richardson's Clarissa* (The Hague, 1970), esp. p. 76 f.

3 To many linguists, sentences like 'John considers Mary's feelings' "are understood in the same way" as sentences like 'John is considerate of Mary's feelings': see George Lakoff, *Irregularity in Syntax* (New York, 1970), p. 115 f. For some of the peculiarities of the verb 'to be,' see Emmon Bach, "*Have* and *be* in English Syntax," *Language*, 43 (1967), 462-85; F. R. Palmer, *A Linguistic Study of the English Verb* (Coral Gables, Fla., 1968), pp. 142-47. See also Otto Jespersen, *A Modern English Grammar on Historical Principles*, Part III: Syntax, vol. II (Heidelberg, 1927), pp. 319-404.

4 For some of the peculiarities of the verb 'to have,' see Bach and Palmer as cited in note 3; Charles Fillmore, "The Case for Case," *Universals in Linguistic Theory*. ed. Emmon Bach and Robert T. Harms (New York, 1968), pp. 22-23 (possessor-as-subject sentences: 'The beauty of her eyes dazzled us') and 74-80 ("sentences which assign attributes to obligatorily possessed elements": 'she has beautiful eyes').

5 See Marc Bloch, *Feudal Society*, trans. L. A. Manyon (Chicago, 1961), I, 145-47; David Lyle Jeffrey, "The Friar's Rent," *JEGP*, 70 (1971), 600-606.

6 For example, [Jean Puget] de la Serre, *The Secretary in Fashion* [trans. John Massinger] (1640; rev. London, 1654). Among his "Answers to the Letters of Complement [*sic*]": "SIR, / Though I give you very humble thanks for the Honour of your Remembrance, yet I shall always remain indebted to you, as making more account of the least of your favours, then all the respects I am able to render you. Continue onely in obliging me of that fashion (though I be intirely yours already) and believe (if you please) that I shall never be capable of other resentment, then which shall witnesse the quality that I bear / SIR / of / your most humble servant" (p. 7). For texts cited in the preceding paragraphs, see *Original Letters, Illustrative of English History*, ed. Henry Ellis (1st series, London, 1825), I, 21, 93, and *St. Thomas More: Selected Letters*, ed. Elizabeth Francis Rogers (New Haven, 1961), p. 91.

7 See Alexander Pope, *Pastoral Poetry and An Assay on Criticism*, ed. E. Audra and Audrey Williams (New Haven, 1961), pp. 4-5; *Memoirs of the Life of Mrs. Elizabeth Carter*, ed. M. Pennington (London, 1807), p. 35. For courtly-genteel style in the drama, see Colley Cibber, *The Careless Husband*, ed. W. W. Appleton (London, 1966), pp. 88-89; and in the periodical essay, Richard Steele, *Guardian* 47.

8 Compare "self-embedding" in Henry James for a quite different effect: see Richard Ohmann, "Generative Grammars and the Concept of Literary Style," *Word*, 20 (1964), 436-37.

9 Tobias Smollett, *The Adventures of Roderick Random* (1748; Oxford World Classics, 1959), pp. 3, 288. Subsequent references to *Roderick Random* will be to this edition

10 *The History of Tom Jones*, ed. Frank Kermode (New York, 1963), Bk. XVII, Ch. 8 (p. 779). For a careful account of Fielding's ideas on good-breeding and gentility, see C. J. Rawson, "Gentlemen and Dancing-Masters: Thoughts on Fielding, Chesterfield, and the Genteel," *ECS*, 1 (1967), 127-58.

11 *Pride and Prejudice*, ed. R. W. Chapman (3rd ed., 1932; rpt. Oxford, 1959), pp. 365-66, 291. See also Philip Waldron, "Style in 'Emma',", in *Approaches to the Novel*, ed. John Colmer (Edinburgh, 1967), pp. 60-62.

12 *Our Mutual Friend*, ed. Stephen Gill (Penguin English Library, 1971), p. 162 (Bk. I, Ch. 10).

13 *The Armies of the Night* (New York, 1968), pp. 15-16 (Part I, Ch. 2).

14 A. D. McKillop, *The Early Masters of English Fiction* (Lawrence, Kansas, 1956; rpt. 1962), p. 74.

Courtly-Genteel or Moral-Didactic?
—A Response to Carey McIntosh

ELIZABETH MacANDREW

It is a pleasure to see the nominal style with all its subtleties defended and the advocates of the verbal style and "Anglo-Saxon vigor" answered with cogency. I agree with Mr. McIntosh that the nominal style has great versatility and is actually essential to some types of expression, in particular the presentation of abstractions. We are faced then, as he says, with a need to distinguish between nominal styles. An immediate difficulty arises, however. In attempting to come by a "discrimination of nominalities" we are plunged into the central problem of stylistic analysis—its tendency to circularity.

For example, Mr. McIntosh's description of the style of *Clarissa* as "courtly-genteel" is, I think, dependent as much upon an understanding of Richardson's novel as it is upon analysis of its style. That is, we can only say that it is a "courtly-genteel" style because we know the importance of gentility at least to the Harlowes, and probably to Richardson himself as well. Analysis of the style enables us to explain the feeling we have that Richardson has succeeded in his purpose. The "static style" Mr. McIntosh describes fits well with the characterization of Clarissa, and this is a strong mark of Richardson's achievement. But we cannot say that the style creates its effect without having first felt or experienced the effect by understanding the novel's themes.

Once we recognize this circularity as inevitable, we can perhaps make a parallel analysis of style and of theme such that each supports the other. Looking at it this way, I would still agree that the highly static style maintains our sense of Clarissa's gentility. However, I see a quite different designation for the style when it is considered in relation to the theme.

Mr. McIntosh gives us some excellent examples (pp. 141-44) of the courtly-genteel style. A look, however, at that most prevalent of eighteenth-century devices, personification, as used by Richardson, will show, I think, that he uses it, as Johnson and others so often do, because, ultimately, he wishes to discuss abstract qualities and not people. Mr. McIntosh quotes the sentence, "My Cousin Clary's *prudence* may be confided in," as an example of courtly-genteel personification, used to "dilute action." Now, Richardson could have written: "We may confide in my Cousin Clary's *prudence*," a sentence which is only less nominal than the former to the extent that the active voice is associated with the verbal and the passive with the nominal style. If, on the other hand, Richardson had written, "Our confidence in my Cousin Clary's *prudence* is not misplaced," the sentence would be decidedly more nominal. But it would not have served Richardson's purpose. By opening his sentence with "My Cousin Clary's *prudence*" he has given maximum emphasis to the abstract quality of prudence, rather than to the human beings involved.

A similar process is at work in "my Father *was pleased* to hint . . ."; "he *thought fit* . . . to make . . . enquiries"; etc., which Mr. McIntosh quotes as typifying the Harlowes' use of forms which express the relationship of a courtier to his monarch. We should note first that the action is "placed at one remove from its agent" by the addition of adjectives, not nouns (here, "pleased" and "fit"). While, again, adjectives *are* associated with the nominal style, these are participial adjectives in the first place, and, besides, adjectives cannot be taken, apart from a nominal context, as indicating nominality in themselves.

But more important, while these locutions *may* be equated with royal authority, and the use of verbs like "oblige" with the humility of the courtier, to do so is surely rather distracting here. Richardson has as the central problem of his novel a different authoritative relationship, which is just as real: Clarissa's filial obedience, and her, his, and our recognition of her father's authority. Without this, the novel's theme is destroyed. Richardson wishes us to criticize the *abuse* of authority, but not the authority itself. This is central to the novel and explicit in it as a theme, and if it is linked by analogy to a higher authority, it is not the relation of a courtier to his king, but that of a humble Christian to his God. Hence, Clarissa's pun about returning to her "Father's house," which she does not consider an unconscionable deception of Lovelace. Mr. McIntosh himself notes an analogy between the courtly-genteel in general and "the religious conception of man as a 'servant' of God" (p. 143). He appears to consider this analogy peripheral to *Clarissa*, however, whereas I think it is central. To me, it binds together the social and religious themes of the novel.

Mr. McIntosh quotes another example of courtly-genteel style in Clarissa's letter asking Anna not to pass on to others Clarissa's disrespectful remarks about her brother and father. This passage is truly nominal in style, but is it courtly? I think it is directly expressive of Richardson's central point and again works to make abstractions central instead of people. It is not of her father or her brother that Clarissa is afraid to be disrespectful, but of "the Parental, or even the Fraternal character." In this there is certainly a parallel with notions like "allegiance to the crown," a metonymy that makes clear that the relationship is to the monarchy, not to the man who is king. But we do not need this analogy. In Richardson's view, it is a social and moral fact that Clarissa must show respect for James Harlowe, senior and junior, in their respective capacities as her father and her brother. Their human qualities as individuals, loving or hating, are beside the point. Clarissa's entire dilemma rests on the conflict between the duty she owes them, which is absolute and outside the personal relationship, and their abuse of their authority which forces her to defend her integrity as an individual and so depart from the duty as an absolute. This, not the family relationships of the Harlowes as such, is Richardson's point, which he presents in abstract personifications so that the moral lesson of the novel may be seen to be applicable to all parents and children. There is, too, incidentally, that covert sarcasm here which this paragon could not possibly allow herself if she expressed it directly, but which she frequently indulges under the cloak of this diffuse form.

We are thus faced with a double question. How nominal is the nominal style of *Clarissa*? And what is its effect? Just how far can one go in attributing "nominality" to the use of parts of speech which are not nouns? For instance, about "I was sorry for the merit this gave him," Mr. McIntosh says (p. 140) that " 'I was sorry' is more nominal than 'I regretted,' simply because it uses the verb 'to be' not a 'real' verb, and therefore describes . . . a state of being, not a form of behavior." But if we look at the state of being and the form of behavior, we see that each can be followed by the same two noun phrases:

(1) I regretted that this gave him merit
(2) I regretted the merit this gave him

(3) I was sorry that this gave him merit
(4) I was sorry for the merit this gave him.

The addition of "for" in the last sentence only demonstrates the versatility of the English system of prepositions and is irrelevant here. When we compare the sentences we can see that (3) and (4), starting "I was sorry," describe a state rather than an action not because they are more nominal than the others but because they are more adjectival—a conclusion which is not really surprising.

Similarly, expressions are made nominal by the use of an active verb followed by an infinitive. The examples Mr. McIntosh gives are: "[He] bid me deserve his love, and I should be sure to have it"; "He has not the sense to say anything to the purpose"; "He had a command of his passions which few . . . would be able to show"; and "The man they had all so much reason to hate." These forms do, indeed, make the style more static. But while verbs like "bid" and "have" do demand a noun followed by an infinitive verb-form, a still greater degree of nominalization can be achieved by using the verb "to be." Thus, the first of these sentences could become: "Possession of his love should be the consequence of desert." "He has not the sense" could be "His sense is not sufficient," "He had command of his passions" equals "His command of his passions . . . ," and "The man they had all so much reason to hate," could be "The man who was the object of their hatred for so many reasons." Can we really argue, as Mr. McIntosh does, that Richardson is trying to hit a sort of middle nominal style here, which avoids the high, heroic style of full-scale nominalization? I am not even sure that the notion of degrees of nominalization will hold. But even if it will and this *is* "middle nominal," how do we determine the purpose and the effect of it?

I submit that we do so, inevitably, through meaning. It is certainly more important to have seen the static quality of this prose, than to have measured its nominality. But, as I have said, I think it is made static to serve the novel's didactic function, which demands a higher degree of abstraction and impersonality than appears in later, less didactic novels. Certainly, later novels make use of nominal styles but, as Mr. McIntosh shows, they do so for a variety of purposes and effects. I see this style, in Richardson, as directly related to the abstract moral theme of this one novel. Consequently, I do not feel that a type of style, such as courtly-genteel, can be drawn from the analysis.

Perhaps such words as "favour," "oblige," "owe," "bid," "deserve," and "have," do, as Mr. McIntosh says, make of qualities commodities "that can be acquired or lost," perhaps "some of the most characteristic idioms of Clarissa's prose measure out quantities of qualities." But how do we know that they thereby indicate the courtly-genteel? Perhaps they portray the merchant origins of the Harlowes. Certainly, the cost-accounting verbal habits of Defoe's characters have often enough been said to reflect their creator's mercantile spirit. But we do not find this said of Richardson because we do not expect it from him. And, in fact, we are right not to. If these words in *Clarissa* were intended to reflect the language of Exchange, then they would constitute an ironic satire of the Harlowes as social-climbing merchants. This would undercut that central moral theme about the abuse of parental authority in matters of marriage. The Harlowes may *be* social-climbing merchants, but if Richardson satirized them as such he would be criticizing the class-structure itself. And if the class-structure is wrong, then abuse of it is not an important moral issue.

Thus, to decide what the nominal style is doing, we have had to turn to the novel itself. We may say, as Mr. McIntosh does so well, that the nominal style can convey gentility. We can extend the notion, as he does, and find it used in other novels for a variety of purposes. He mentions high moral values, abstract thoughts, and states of consciousness. I hope he would agree that it is one of the eighteenth century's prime means of pursuing its moral-didactic purpose in literature. We could continue to multiply examples. Among moderns, John Updike, for instance, has some nominal passages which are as striking in their effect as they are different from the Mailer passage which Mr. McIntosh quotes. Indeed, the instrument of measurement is too imprecise. The use of nominal structures is so extensive because they can do so many things—almost anything except create a crisp sense of intense activity, for which the use of active verbs is essential.

The usefulness of the nominal in our scientific world, which tries to construct systems, and therefore abstractions, out of every aspect of life, has led to widespread abuses. These, in turn, have evoked a hundred glib articles with titles like "How to Write Like a Social Scientist," which attack the style instead of the misuse of it. Across the country composition teachers have been insisting for generations that students write short sentences with active verbs—as if vigor were the only attribute to look for in a piece of writing. It is consequently refreshing to see the usefulness of this flexible style reaffirmed.

Nevertheless, the very versatility of nominal style forbids us to make out of our observations of it a set of categories. The idea that there are degrees of nominality is questionable in itself, but more important, we cannot tell from the style alone what purpose the author has in using it. Only through meaning can we determine the effect of a particular arrangement of particular parts of speech. Instead of discriminating among nominalities and creating categories and subdivisions of the nominal style, we must, willy nilly, start our analysis anew with each new work.

The Gateway to Innocence:
Ossian and the Nordic Bard
as Myth

JOHN L. GREENWAY

Few now tremble at the dauntless heroism of Fingal, and none of us, I fear, are tempted to don Werther's yellow vest and share the misty signs of Temora. Indeed, the noble passions of this Last of the Bards have been treated with a neglect less than benign. Though we no longer read Ossian, we do read writers who, convinced of his authenticity, attempt to recapture what they imagine to be that synthesis of vigor and sentiment possessed by their Northern ancestors. As I have already implied, I propose to take Ossian seriously, and to suggest that he functioned as a mythic narrative for a modern era—"mythic" not in the Enlightenment sense of "falsehood," but in the more recent sense of "symbolic apprehension of reality." But what can Ossian have to do with reality?

Let us consider for a moment the nature and function of mythic narrative. The myths of a culture provide an orientation for man's moral experience in that they bestow an objective status upon values of the present, preserving them from relativism.[1] Myths of gods and heroes show that the paradigms for human action not only exist outside man, but can be a part of genesis itself; that is, present values are legitimized, transferred from the profane world to

161

the sacred by projecting them *in illo tempore* (to use Mircea Eliade's term): a static time of creation when a culture's truths were established. I see Ossian and his imitators as doing essentially the same thing, and on a pre-rational level of cultural consciousness—legitimizing the values of sentimental primitivism through a mythic narrative (the Ossianic poems) which showed that sentimental views of human nature, virtue, and vice were really present at the dawn of Northern, *non*-classical civilization.

This brings us to a second point about myth, one which in a sense distinguishes modern myths such as Ossian from pre-scientific myths. The anthropologist Malinowski has noted that while we see myth, rite, and ritual as symbolic, the believer does not: to him, the constructs of myth are empirically real.[2] Modern man, however, defines truth in terms of rational thought, and either tends to see myth as falsehood, or as symbolizing an empirical or conceptual content. But, as Cassirer and others have shown, the impulse to myth-making is not negated by reason, for modern myths must maintain their objectivity in *two* realms: first, as narratives expressing spontaneously the world of feeling, and second, as historical, empirical fact. As an illustration of this, the assumed literary merit of Ossian was predicated upon his historicity; indeed, this was the most important single fact about the forgeries, in that Ossian's status as historical document objectified values, much as ritual validates rites by presenting them to a receptive audience as reenactments of sacred paradigms of the *illud tempus*. As a means of organizing values, myth is neither true nor false—it is expressive or inexpressive.

Ossian validated and gave factual status to several primitivist fantasies of the Nordic past. Basically, the Ossianic poems fused in one symbolic universe what had been a paradox since the first humanist attempts to build a national past upon Tacitus' *Germania*, first edited in the fifteenth century. This paradox, simply stated, was that enthusiasts for Germanic valor such as Conrad Celtis could admire our heroic ancestors for their martial vigor and, at the same time, following Tacitus, point to tribes of chaste, democratic, freedom-loving (Humanist) Teutons.[3] Obviously, one part of this mythic construct ran counter to another, older view, which helps to give substance to the paradox; that is, this very martial vigor destroyed classical culture, and brought on what Renaissance scholars called those dark "Ages in the Middle." In the eighteenth century, Shaftesbury was not alone in identifying "Gothic" with "barbaric,"[4] and the dual nature of the myth continued even into the next century.

Before Ossian, the "nobler qualities of the mind" necessary to complement the fascinating barbarity of the North in a primitivist myth had to be supplied by conjecture. In 1763, the year of *Temora's* appearance, Bishop Percy complained that "many pieces on the gentler subjects" must exist, but that they simply have not been edited.[5] With the appearance of the Ossianic poems, however, there was no longer need for apologies or conjectures such as the German Humanists of the sixteenth and Swedish historians of the seventeenth-century Great Power Era had had to make,[6] for the mythic imagination had received its document.

As myth, Ossian was more expressive than Homer, his southern counterpart, in that his poems expressed no moral ambivalence. The Humanists had seen history in terms of a struggle between virtue and vice (witness the popularity of Virgil), but this makes a balanced conflict difficult to portray in a moral narrative. In *Temora*, Macpherson is ingenious; in the first book he kills off the villain, whose noble brother Cathmor is obliged by honor to oppose the mighty Fingal. Macpherson was then able to sustain his narrative by more than token opposition to Fingal's moral (hence, martial) invincibility.

Fingal fights only defensive wars (*Fingal*), or he fights the *bellum justum* to further social justice (*Temora*). "My arm was the support of the injured," he says, "but the weak rested behind the lightning of my steel."[7] Fingal thus functioned paradigmatically, in fulfillment of one of the great Enlightenment axioms that emancipated valor must triumph over tyranny and idolatry. This Fingal does, always.

The legacy of barbarism, which was an integral part of the myth of the Nordic past, is also present in the Ossianic poems. Macpherson assigns this role to the Scandinavians; and Starno, in the poem "Cath-Loda," is a repository for all the pejorative connotations of "Gothic." But even though we find that his Scandinavians are barbaric, tyrannous idolaters, Macpherson's "Caledonians" are not, as his notes make clear. And though Ossian believes in spirits, Fingal's defeat of the Scandinavian chimera "Cruth-Loda" indicates that neither Fingal nor Ossian was an idolater nor obnoxiously superstitious.

Within this large universe legitimizing truths that the Enlightenment held to be "self-evident," Ossian also validated several other literary myths, among them that of the spontaneous perception of nature by the primitive poet.[8] W. K. Wimsatt has pointed out that in eighteenth-century literature it was not easy to express a sense of animate or "souled" nature, for the conscious use of mythology was generally restricted to decorative, intellectual allegory.[9] When the setting of the poem was temporalized, however, and the narration placed in the *illud tempus* of the Nordic past, it was possible to create the illusion of the naive experience of Northern nature for the modern reader, by giving him the impression that the poem is being narrated by a naive *Volksdichter* as the reader reads it. Northrop Frye calls this technique that of "poem-as-process," saying that "Where there is a sense of literature as process, pity and fear become states of mind without objects, moods which are common to the work of art and the reader, and which bind them together psychologically instead of separating them aesthetically."[10] Herder used this technique in his *Abhandlung über den Ursprung der Sprache* to recreate for the reader the illusion of the creative process of the primitive mind:

> Since all of nature sounds, nothing is more natural to a sensuous human being than to think that it lives, that it speaks, that it acts. That savage saw the tall tree with its mighty crown and sensed the wonder of it; the crown rustled! There the godhead moves and stirs! The savage falls down in adoration! Behold, that is the story of sensuous man, the dark link by which nouns are fashioned from verbs.[11]

Herder was not the only critic attempting to convey the illusion of process in essays describing the creative process of the primitive, though what others did was sometimes derivative; for example, certain data concerning the "wild" Nordic nature appear to have been taken from *The Castle of Otranto*. But Macpherson employed the illusion in what became mythic narratives. The belief in Ossian's authenticity implied that "poem-as-process" had been an actual technique of the primitive Northern poet.

Macpherson's creation of the illusion of process and his validation of the technique are actually rather sophisticated—sophisticated in that the reader is taken through time by several devices. The first element is his use of the mythic figure of the naïve *Volksdichter*, the Bard. Bishop Percy and Thomas Gray had been central in establishing this persona in the 1760's.[12] Here I will mention only briefly Thomas Gray's ode "The Bard" (1757), which was central to the establishing of the *Volksdichter* as a narrative persona in the 1760's. Gray employs the knavish Edward I and the naïve national Bard of the Golden Age, and as the last of the bards "plunged to endless night," the Golden Age ended and the modern, fallen world began.

Ossian as Bard was a principal part of Macpherson's mythmaking, establishing a psychological tie from the historical present to the mythic past, and part of the success of the "ancient epics" was owing to Macpherson's structuring of these poems. By means of a fairly complex point of view, he managed to create the illusion that the reader was experiencing directly the "raw nature and noble passion" of his ancestors. Ossian, near death, a death that will mark the end of the Golden Age (it always does, in these cases), is singing to Malvina, the fiancée of his dead son Oscar, "a song of the days of old," in which Fingal, Ossian's father, is the principal character. In all this, the illusion of the spontaneous process is maintained by several devices: Ossian can make himself a character in his own poem and by doing so remind one that there is a narrator ("I walked over the heath"); or he can remind one of the narrator by breaking his own narration ("Malvina! Why that tear? Oscar is not dead yet"). We participate in the Golden Age through the naïve songs of the Bard, yet we are constantly made aware that it is coming to an end, and our own unheroic time is beginning.

Ossian as myth legitimized as being "Nordic" not only the naive Bard and the illusion of process, but a particular kind of imagery used to express this spontaneous relationship to nature. Indeed, one of the merits of Ossian, and and one of the inadequacies of his imitators, was just this use of sympathetic imagery (where nature is an extension of character or mood) to integrate landscape into the action. For instance, when things are going badly for the noble Cuchullin, Macpherson's use of sympathetic imagery both amplifies the impending disaster and isolates the warrior by focusing down upon him: "The winds came down on the woods. The torrents rushed from the rocks. Rain gathered round the heads of Cromla. And the red stars trembled between the flying clouds. Sad by the side of a stream whose sound was ecchoed by a tree, sad by the side of a stream the chief of Erin sat." (One of the facts that had filtered out of Antiquarian editing was that Northern poetry was alliterative.)

Macpherson's notes are an integral part of Ossian-as-myth, for they provide a constant empirical commentary, emphasising the historicity and verisimilitude of the poems. They also make of Ossian an epic counterpart to Homer, Virgil, and Milton, showing that though Ossian expressed a superior Northern morality, he obeyed the "general rules" of the epic. A growing accretion of appended commentary elaborated upon this, beginning with Hugh Blair's essay. In Germany, Denis translated the poems into hexameters, adding his own notes and those of Cesarotti to the poems and to Blair's essay as well.

Initially, then, Ossian served to provide an epic Northern counterpart to Homer, unifying the genesis of the primitive Nordic genius in the minds of the primitivists, as Madame de Staël illustrates in *De la littérature.*[13] Secondly, and more importantly, Ossian's mythic function as the objectification of the Northern muse helped break down the stigma of Northern barbarity, in that he either modified the view of the Nordic past or shaped reactions to it. Ossian could animate the nostalgia of Denis for the lost Lieder of Charlemagne, while in Denmark, Blicher saw the same virtues celebrated in Ossian and in the Icelandic sagas. Ossian's main function, however, was as a mythic paradigm, a touchstone for contemporary poets. If we look at the Ossianic poems and those they inspired, we see that Macpherson enjoyed a relationship to the Golden Age unavailable to other moderns. He was actually a kind of modern folk poet, transmitting primal truth in a quasi-oracular form, not creating on his own. In the Swedish poet Thomas Thorild we can see this difference between Macpherson and his imitators. Though Thorild felt himself to be part of Ossian's Golden Age ("You should have seen me . . . when I first saw the sun set in Glysisvall, when with Ossian I can feel [*sic*] the shades of heroes about me"), his creativity was limited to incantation, not recreation of the naive experience:

Stream exultation! To You, ah, You immortal, gentle, All-eleva-

ting; you Nature, my trembling harp is tuned. Silently weave
about me, spirit of Ossian![14]

The Ossianic muse came to dubious fruition in Germany with the "Bardic
Movement," sustained by a group of mediocre poets who were primed by a
bowdlerized version of Herder's concept of *Volkspoesie,* but who were not
galvanized into imitation until they encountered the paradigms of Ossian, the
Bard, and Germania. Most of these poets exist today only in literary histories
and dissertations, for their poetry functioned as myth for only a few years in
the 1760's—during the first Ossianic craze—and was particularly vulnerable to
the dialectic process that ultimately overtook Ossian himself.

The mythic aspect of the Bardic lyrics was almost immediately inadequate;
as it not only objectified contemporary literary values (Ossian being the
paradigm), but also depended upon an assumption of historical objectivity,
the Bards' myth was fatally vulnerable in two areas. First, it succumbed to
the revolutionary effects of Herder's conjectures concerning the literary
imagination; second, to philology.

The idol of the Germanic Bards was Klopstock, who read Ossian before
reading about Norse mythology: Klopstock's "Nordic" poems and dramas are
predicated upon the superiority of an Ossian-constituted Teutonic muse to
that of the artificial South. In "Der Hügel und der Hain" (1767), the Southern poet is defeated in the battle for a modern poet's soul by a Bard who
sings of "souled nature," and whose Telyn (a musical instrument) sounds
"Fatherland."

Though Klopstock is widely cited as inaugurating a new sensibility of nature into German poetry, it is clear that his poetic convention could not
assimilate a subject-matter intrinsically "Teutonic," not even such a Teutonic
subject mater as the Golden Age of Ossian's invention. In 1767, for instance,
Klopstock "Nordicized" his ode "An des Dichters Freunde" (1747), merely
by removing Apollo and plugging in Braga: "Would you be verses, O song?
Or, / Unsubmissive, like Pindar's songs, / Like Zeus' noble, intoxicated son, /
Whirl free from the creating soul? " became "Would you be verses, O heroic
song? / Would you soar lawless, like Ossian's flight, / Like Uller's dance upon
sea-crystal, / Free from the poet's soul? "

But such was the momentary power of this myth to constitute reality that
Lessing could praise lines like the following from Klopstock's drama *Her-
manns Schlacht* (1769) as being "completely in the ancient German manner"
(Hermann speaks): "Noble lady of my youth! Yes, I live, my Thusnelda!
Arise, you free princess of Germany! I have not loved you before, as today!
Has my Thusnelda brought me flowers?" Klopstock, too, was convinced
that this was pretty accurate dialogue, and footnotes the morality of his
Teutons.[15] The central role of Ossian in this drama is obvious, except that

Klopstock has choruses of Bards chanting "Höret Thaten der vorigen Zeit! " whereas Macpherson had been content with Ossian's beginning "A song of the days of old! "

The most common effect of the Ossianized Nordic muse was what Northrop Frye calls "psychological self-identification." As an example we may consider the otherwise forgettable masterpiece of K. F. Kretschmann, *Gesang Ringulph des Bardens, als Varus geschlagen var* (1768).[16] Again, the mythic world here derives much of its texture from the defeat of Southern tyranny by Northern freedom, thanks both to the hero Hermann and to the Ossianic Bard, Ringulph, who implements the transition to the sacred *illud tempus*. "Ha! " Ringulph begins, giving the sense of process by recalling the scene in present tense, "There they lie, yes! / The legions lie slain! " "Ha's" and "Ach's" dot the narrative to support the illusion of spontaneity. But the fundamental contradiction in the Bardic myth is obvious; that is, despite the ostensible epic purpose of the poem—"Allvater" tells Ringulph to quit singing about his beloved Irmgard and sing about Hermann—only a small part of the fourth *Gesang* (out of five) concerns the battle. The rest is mostly about Ringulph himself.

Central to the "poetics" of the Bards was that their function as poets and their literary products were reincarnations of an actual Teutonic genius, Ossian, of course, being the paradigm. Denis emphasizes in his well-informed essay "Vorbericht von der altern vaterlaendischen Dichtkunst" that the modern Bard must not betray his muse through anachronisms. But it is a singular commentary on the power of this myth to regulate rational inquiry that Denis, the most philologically oriented of any of the Bards, cites the poems of Klopstock and Kretschmann as exemplary for those who wish a "complete transition of oneself into other times."[17] Denis was correct in a sense he did not intend, for the mythic world given symbolic form by Ossian, Klopstock, and Kretschmann was for a time *more real* to the general perception of the age than historical fact.

Even though myth's truths are not primarily validated by reason, a modern myth must maintain a factual superstructure to complement that part of it which operates extra-rationally. This requirement implies a separation of Faith and Reason, which in fact worked to render the Bardic myth inexpressive. And the separation was ultimately to undermine Ossian himself. Concerning Denis, Gleim wrote to Jacobi in 1768, "my Herder, who has long sighed deeply for such a Bard, will rejoice."[18] But Herder, though unaware of Ossian's role as myth, sensed the great discrepancy between the lyrics of the Bards and those of his idol: they are not *Volkspoesie*, but *about Volkspoesie*, he maintained. His response to lines such as these by Kretschmann is also telling:

> I crept in the forest
>
> . . . . .
>
> In the high peaks roared
> The spirits of airy night;
> Then a chill broke out on my brow,
> And strongly beat my heart.
> And look! It seemed to me
> As though there stood a man . . . Are you a man? An elf
> Of midnight? [19]

Herder sensed the great flaw in Kretschmann's myth: "Where Ringulph, the Bard, sings well, he sings modern."[20]

If one thinks of them in the context of eighteenth-century primitivism, *Fingal* and *Temora* were indeed folk-epics, but because of their pretense to historicity, both Ossian and the Bardic Movement were vulnerable to the latent sundering of the temporary accommodation between myth and reason. In 1800, Kretschmann in effect defended the myth in an article asking "Did the Germanic Peoples have Bards and Druids or Not?"[21] He supported his affirmative argument with sources dating from the days of the Humanists. The next month, H. Anton argued persuasively that "The Germanic Peoples had no Bards and no Druids," attacking not only Kretschmann's methodology (argument by analogy), but the veracity of his sources—his "factual" base: "I assumed," Anton says, "That we in our criticism at the end of the century must be more advanced than we were at the beginning."[22] His view heralds the Twilight of the Bards.

Herder and others were able to dispatch the Bardic lyrics by the sheer force of individual critical acuity. More theoretical criticism of the Bards was taken up by philologists, who tested the paradigm of the myth with an informed methodology. That basis was Ossian himself. Earlier assaults on Ossian, Hume's, for example, had been based upon aesthetic distaste. But these empiricist attacks were philological. In the 1780's, John Pinkerton concentrates what he terms the "fierce light of Science" upon the vision of the Nordic past and finds error wherever he looks. Conversant with the recent Scandinavian scholarship of Suhm, Schøning, and others, Pinkerton demolishes the Ossianic universe by showing the Norse myths to be "merely" myths, and not real at all. He then attacks Ossian's "costume." Since historicity was an integral part of Ossian's mythic significance, the exposure of anachronism was mortal: "Eternal ladies in mail, where no mail was known," writes Pinkerton, "sicken one at every turn."[23]

In 1817, the Swedish poet and critic Erik Gustaf Geijer could look back upon this period as closed, and describe it as an unsuccessful attempt to "return to ourselves."[24] His comments upon the ineffectiveness of the Klopstock method of studding manuscripts with "By Thor! " are an index to the increased sophistication with which a new generation viewed the Nordic past. Though the figure of the Bard, perched at the end of the sacred Golden Age and at the beginning of profane, historical time, continued (Hugo, Scott, and Geijer himself, among others, used the persona), the assault on Ossian was symptomatic of a larger process, the calling into question of the whole moral universe of sentimental primitivism. Geijer and others saw that the simple structure of good *vs.* evil, virtue *vs.* vice was inadequate to explain the colliding contraries of moral experience. For a later generation Ossian was, in important ways, dead. Yet, in the myth of Ossian's synthetic spontaneity we can see a lasting legacy—the genesis of the contemporary attempt to merchandise both electronic Bards and the sentimental naive.

NOTES

1 See the discussion of "symbolic universes" in Peter L. Berger and Thomas Luckmann, *The Social Construction of Reality* (Garden City, N.Y., 1967), pp. 88-104, and Mircea Eliade, *Cosmos and History*, tr. Willard R. Trask (New York, 1963), Ch. IV: "The Terror of History," pp. 141-62.

2 Bronislaw Malinowski, *Magic, Science and Religion* (New York, 1954), p. 100.

3 See Frank L. Borchardt, *German Antiquity and Renaissance Myth* (Baltimore, 1971), and Paul Joachimsen, "Tacitus im deutschen Humanismus," *Neue Jahrbücher für das klassische Altertum*, 14 (1911), 695-717.

4 Josef Haslag, *"Gothic" im siebzehnten und achzehnten Jahrhundert* (Cologne, 1963).

5 *Five Pieces of Runic Poetry* (London, 1763), pp. x-xi.

6 The Swedish historian Johannes Magnus, in his *Historia de omnibus Gothorum Sveonumque regibus* (Rome, 1554), began a century and a half of pseudo-scholarship designed to eradicate the stigma of Gothic barbarity, an effort culminating in Olof Rudbeck's mammoth *Atlantican* (Uppsala, 1679-1702), which poved that all classical culture was of Swedish origin. See Johan Nordström, "Gotisk Historieromantik och Stormaktstidens Anda," in *De Yverbornes Ö* (Stockholm, 1934).

7 Citations from the Ossianic poems will be from the editions of *Fingal* (London, 1762), and *Temora* (London, 1763).

8 See Lois Whitney, "English Primitivistic Theories of Epic Origins," *Modern Philology*, 21 (1924), 337-78, and Lars Gustafsson, "Schillers bestämning av det naive i Ueber naive und sentimentalische Dichtung," *Samlaren*, 82 (1961), 101-32.

9 "The Structure of Romantic Nature Imagery," in *Romanticism and Consciousness*, ed. H. Bloom (New York, 1970), p. 79.

10 "Towards Defining an Age of Sensibility," in *Fables of Identity* (New York, 1963), p. 135.

11 *On the Origin of Language*, tr. Alexander Gode (New York, 1966), p. 133.

12 Demonstrated in detail by Anton Blanck, *Den nordiska Renässansen* (Stockholm, 1911), pp. 72 and 368.

13 See Chapter XI, "Literature of the North," for instance.

14 "The Passions," 1st song. See Theodor Hasselqvist, *"Ossian" i den svenska dikten och litteraturen* (Malmö, 1895), pp. 79-80.

15 Lessing's comment is in a letter to Nicolai, 4 August 1767; the text of *Hermanns Schlacht* is in *Deutsche National-Litteratur*, ed. Kürschner (Berlin and Stuttgart [no date]), XLVIII, 53-146. This speech is from scene xi.

16 Text in *DNL*, XLVIII, 325-69.

17 *Ossian und Sineds Lieder* (Vienna, 1784), IV, xci.

18 Cited in *DNL*, XLVIII, xvi.

19 "Ringulph's Lament," in *DNL*, XLVIII, 77.

20 *Allgemeine deutsche Bibliothek*, 17, (1779), 451.

21 *Der neue teutsche Merkur* (November, 1800), 168-92.

22 *Der neue teutsche Merkur* (December, 1800), 292-93.

23 *Inquiry into the History of Scotland* (London, 1789), II, 85.

24 "Betraktelser i afseende på de nordiska Myternas Användande i skön Konst," *Samlade Skrifter* (Stockholm, 1875), I, 176.

The Legal Status of the English Woman in Early Eighteenth-Century Common Law and Equity

JANELLE GREENBERG

While law may be defined in several ways, it is reasonable to view it both as reflecting and reinforcing the norms of society. It is for this reason that a study of the legal status of women can prove fruitful: the treatment which the law accords women reflects society's perception of women and of what if means to be a woman. This paper will describe the legal status of English women in the first half of the eighteenth century, with a view to ascertaining the ideology reflected in this status. In order to do this it is necessary to deal with two interrelated bodies of law: 1) the common law, administered primarily in the courts of King's Bench and Common Pleas, and 2) equity, administered by the Lord Chancellor in the Court of Chancery. It is the thesis of the paper that all too often the study of women's rights has produced an inaccurate picture of their legal status. There appear to be two reasons for this distortion. First, the common law and its treatment of women are often misunderstood or misinterpreted. Second, and perhaps more important, the common law is usually emphasized to the exclusion of equity. These tendencies have resulted in a general misunderstanding which is manifested in current descriptions of women as chattels and legal nonentities. It will be argued here that although the prevailing ideology mirrored in English law was indeed paternalistic, women were accorded more legal rights than is generally acknowledged.

The Legal Status of Women in Common Law

It is frequently said of women in the eighteenth century and earlier that they were chattels, mere property, devoid of a legal existence. For example, a lawyer specializing in women's rights recently stated in her testimony before a United States Senate Sub-committee that "under the old English common law, women were not regarded as persons under the law; women were regarded as chattels, as property."[1] Similar statements abound.[2] Such descriptions are, however, inaccurate. In no period of English history, at least not since the Norman Conquest, have women been given the legal status of chattels. To be sure, they have not been treated as the legal equals of men. But neither have they been regarded as mere things, either in common law or in equity.

For a description of the common law status of the early eighteenth-century woman, one can do no better than to rely on Sir William Blackstone's monumental *Commentaries on the Laws of English*, published between 1765 and 1769.[3] This treatise, which greatly influenced American as well as English lawyers, contains some of the most frequently cited passages on the legal status of women. Before turning to these passages, it is necessary to make two distinctions: the first is between the single and married woman, the *feme sole* and *feme covert*; and the second is between public and private law. The public law position of all women, *sole* and *covert*, may be easily described: in public law there was no place for them, except on the throne. They sat neither in the Council nor in the House of Commons or the House of Lords (though if they were peeresses and they married commoners, their husbands might sit in the Lords by courtesy). Neither did they serve on juries or vote.

In private law the status of women varied according to whether they were married or single, *covert* or *sole*. The *feme sole* enjoyed, for the most part, the same rights and responsibilities as did men. She owned property and chattels, which she could bequeath by will. She made contracts; she sued and was sued.

The situation changed dramatically when a woman married. At that time and by that action she surrendered those rights and fell prey to a whole series of disabilities which placed her in the same legal category as wards, lunatics, idiots, and outlaws. This radical alteration in her status is usually explained by reference to the doctrine of a unity of person. In the words of Blackstone, who gave the doctrine its most famous enunciation,

By marriage, the husband and wife are one person in law: that is, the very being or legal existence of the woman is suspended during the marriage, or at least incorporated and consolidated into that of the husband: under whose wing, protection, and *cover* she performs everything; and is therefore called in our law French a *feme covert* . . . ; [she] is said to be covert-baron, or under the protection and influence of her husband.[4]

An anonymous author of a seventeenth-century tract on women's legal rights expressed the same idea in a rather different way:

When a small brook or little river incorporateth with Rhodanus, Humber, or the Thames, the poor rivlet looseth her name, it is carried and recarried with the new associate, it beareth no sway, it passeth nothing during coverture. A woman as soon as she is married is called *covert* . . . that is, bailed, as it were, clouded and over-shadowed, etc. She hath lost her stream, she is continually *sub potestate* . . . .[5]

The doctrine of a unity of person, or coverture, is sometimes pointed to as reflective of the woman's common law status as chattel. The validity of this view can be ascertained by examining the precise legal effects of the doctrine. What, exactly, did Blackstone mean when he stated that "the very being or legal existence of the woman is suspended during the marriage, or at least incorporated and consolidated into that of the husband"? What were the specific legal consequences of the doctrine?

First, it had certain implications for the relationship between husband and wife. If husband and wife were one at law, it followed that neither could grant anything to the other. Nor could they contract with one another. On the other hand, a wife could serve as her husband's attorney because such an action implied a representation, not a separation. Moreover, a husband could bequeath personal and real property to his wife, since the will was not executed until after his death, when the woman resumed the status of *feme sole*. Further, because of the unity of husband and wife, each was generally prohibited from testifying in court against the other.[6] Yet where the husband committed an offense against the person of his wife, the rule was disregarded and the wife permitted to testify against her husband, and *vice versa*. Further, if a wife feared that her husband might do her bodily harm, she could have security of the peace against him, as he might against her.[7]

There were still other consequences of the doctrine of a unity of person. A *feme covert* could not, generally speaking, make a contract, except for such necessaries as food and clothing. For such expenses her husband was obliged to pay. There seemed to be two reasons for this rule. First, because the law assumed that the woman was under the power of her husband, it was therefore unreasonable for her to be bound by any contract, since it might have been the result of coercion. Moreover, if the wife could contract, she would be liable to arrest, which would subject her husband to the loss of her services. This rationale also explains another rule of common law. If a person harmed a *feme covert*, her husband was likewise injured, and any action against the offending party had to be brought in the names of the husband and wife jointly. But if the injury or maltreatment of the wife was so severe that the husband was deprived of her company and assistance, the law gave him a separate remedy by an action of trespass.[8] The law's presumption of a husband's power over his wife mattered in another way. Sue her and you sued her husband, for her behavior was, to a large extent, his responsibility. Similarly, if she committed a misdemeanor or even a capital offense in his presence, she was presumed to be acting under his coercion and was, therefore, not liable. Exceptions were treason, the keeping of a brothel, and offenses which were *mala in se*, for example, murder. In these instances the wife was liable as well as the husband, the reason being that such actions were viewed as so reprehensible that she had to assume sole responsibility for her behavior, even though it took place within his presence. If she committed an offense when she was not in his company, she alone was liable, unless it could be proved that she was acting under his orders.[9]

The effects of the doctrine of a unity of person were also evident where property rights were concerned. To a large extent the *feme covert's* interest in property, personal and real, passed under her husband's control. That personal property which a wife brought to her marriage became her husband's absolutely, just as if he had purchased it himself. His title further extended to personal property given to his wife after marriage, unless the gift was to her separate use.[10] In real property of which she had a fee simple, a fee tail, or a life estate, he gained only a title to rents and profits. If, however, a child was born of the union, who would inherit the wife's estate, the husband became tenant for life by curtesy.[11] The wife, on the other hand, gained certain rights to her husband's property upon marriage. While she had nothing during his life, she was entitled to one-third of his personal property if he died intestate and with issue. If he died without issue, she received one-half of his personal property. Moreover, upon her husband's death, she became entitled to her dower, which consisted of one-third of the real property which he held in fee simple or fee tail during his life. Her right to dower was absolute in that her husband could not lawfully deprive her of it by will or by any conveyance, except one to which she consented.

There were several ways in which her dower might be barred. If her husband committed treason, she lost the dower, she being presumed to be privy to the plotting.[12] Or, if she eloped with another man, she also forfeited her dower.[13]

The law provided a mechanism by which the wife, in conjunction with her husband, might convey her dower, or other property which she held, to a third party. This was the fine, or final concord, an instrument of conveyance which was in the form of a covenant. A fine decided title to land once and for all. It served a peculiar purpose where the *feme covert* was concerned: it was the only method by which she could convey estates in which she had a right. The uniqueness of the fine was that it required that the judges examine the wife separately from her husband in order to ascertain whether her consent to convey had been obtained under duress. That is, the law, upon consideration of the fact that the wife was under her husband's control and authority, took special pains to protect her interest by trying to ensure that her consent to convey was voluntary.[14]

In sum, the doctrine of a unity of person visited upon the *feme covert* a number of disabilities. She was in no way the legal equivalent of her husband. Her rights to her personal and real property were conditional and qualified. In her relationships with other people she was sometimes severely restricted. If husband and wife were indeed one, that one was, as Justice Hugo Black once remarked, the husband. Yet the *feme covert* was not a mere chattel, a thing. Her husband could not do with her or her property whatever he would. While he might attempt to influence and control her behavior in a number of ways, he might not do her violence. Moreover, where her own estate was concerned, the common law gave her special consideration in the form of the fine.

Because lawyers and judges seldom remark on the assumptions which underly their pronouncements on the law, it is impossible to determine with certainty the ideology and set of values which the legal status of women mirrors. It does seem safe to suggest, however, that the ideology reflected in the doctrine of a unity of persons was one of paternalism. The *feme covert* related to her husband as a child to her parents, an apprentice to her master, a ward to her guardian. When a woman married, she entered into a relationship with a person who was assumed to be more intellectually and physically capable than she of exercising the rights and responsibilities which accompanied a full legal existence. Consequently, she was assumed to be weaker than her husband in the sense that she acted under his coercion.

Yet if a woman remained a *feme sole*, she escaped the disabilities of private law. To be sure, she was excluded from public life. She retained, however, as complete control over her goods and land as did a man. Neither were her relationships with others any more restricted than his. It would seem, then, that it was not women *per se* who were subject to disabilities at common law but rather married women, *feme coverts,* who were disabled because of their association with people presumed to be more capable than they, namely, their husbands. It was for this reason, it seems, that the doctrine of a unity of person relegated the *feme covert* to second class citizenship.

The Status of Women in Equity

The common law was not the only law which England knew. The law administered in the Court of Chancery—equity—constituted a vital part of English justice. Very briefly, equity was that body of rules which supplemented, or as Maitland said, fulfilled the common law. In order to draw an accurate picture of the legal status of the eighteenth-century woman, it is essential, as Mary Beard observed, to turn to equity.[15] For it is equity which afforded the *feme covert* her most effective legal protection. Indeed, a survey of Chancery cases in the first half of the eighteenth century indicated that where private law was concerned a woman occupied a legal status not unlike that of a man.

That equity mitigated the common law disabilities to which a *feme covert* was subject is apparent in cases concerning the husband's common law right to dispose of his wife's personal and real property. There were certain methods by which a woman might retain control of her estate. One of the most popular vehicles was the marriage settlement, in which the future wife and husband agreed that she should keep certain goods or lands "to her own separate use and enjoyment." Or, the woman might, before marriage and with her husband's knowledge, convey lands to trustees in trust, to pay the rents and profits to her sole and separate use. If the husband at some later date attempted to circumvent or defeat the marriage settlement, the wife could petition the Lord Chancellor to do justice. In such cases the court would likely enforce the articles of agreement.[16] Similarly, Chancery would enforce those marriage settlements which gave a wife a separate cash allowance, or the proceeds from such enterprises as the selling of eggs.[17]

The *feme covert's* control over her own estate could be achieved in another way. Occasionally a relative would bequeath a personal estate to a woman, stipulating in the will that the heir was to hold the estate to her particular and separate use. Chancery would likely enforce the conditions of the will by prohibiting the husband from interfering with his wife's legacy, even to the extent of barring his curtesy.[18] A representative case is that of *Sheppard vs. Gibbons, et al.,* heard in 1742. It concerned one John Bromwick, who made a will in which he decreed that two trustees, their heirs and assigns, should permit his three sisters "to hold and enjoy the said premises, and to receive the rents thereof to their sole and separate use . . . notwithstanding their coverture, to the intent that the said three husbands might have nothing to do with the said premises or the rents thereof." The Court of Chancery adjudged both the will and the trust good in equity.[19]

Another mechanism by which a *feme covert* could circumvent the common law rights of her husband was a marriage settlement in which the husband agreed that he would take only a certain portion of his wife's estate, with the remaining portion to be disposed of by her last will and testament. Here, again, the *feme covert* could rely on the support of the Lord Chancellor should her husband attempt to defeat the terms of the agreement. If, however, the husband's agreement to the making of the will followed marriage, it seemed that he was bound to honor his promise only in conscience, not in law. Moreover, such a marriage agreement applied only to that estate which the wife possessed at the time of her marriage, not to any properties to which she became entitled during the coverture.[20]

Equity mitigated the harshness of the common law's treatment of women in still another way. While at common law a wife could not sue her husband, there was a mechanism by which she could proceed against him in Chancery, namely through the use of a *prochein amy,* or next friend, who would bring suit on her behalf.[21] As the Lord Chancellor stated in a case heard in 1742, while neither husband or wife could sue one another at common law. "in equity the constant experience is that the husband may sue the wife, and the wife the husband."[22] Further, Chancery was careful to ensure that the *prochein amy* was indeed acting on behalf of the *feme covert,* who was permitted to dismiss her *prochein amy* if she feared that she or he was acting in collusion with her husband. This she might do even if the case had proceeded considerably past the initial phase.[23]

Finally, the Court of Chancery balanced the common law treatment of women by insisting that when husband and wife conveyed property in which she had an inheritance, the mode of conveyance be properly attended to—by fines which she levied of her own will and volition. A representative case is that of *Penne and Peacock,* heard in 1734. Here the Court of Chancery agreed that a fine levied by husband and wife of land which she held to her own separate use was void if she, when questioned apart from her husband, claimed that she was forced by duress to join in the fine.[24]

When equity is taken into account, the legal status of the English woman appears less distressing than it does when one assumes she had to rely only on common law protections. When she took sufficient precautions in the form of marriage settlements, and when those who bequeathed estates to her took similar care, a wife could retain some degree of control over her interests. Moreover, through the use of a *prochein amy*, she might protect her rights by bringing suit against her husband.

The summary nature of case reports makes it difficult to ascertain the ideology which Chancery judgments reflect. While that court was clearly tender of the rights of married women, it is doubtful that the judicial officers ruled as they did because they believed women to be the legal equals of men. This was not a century for views of that sort. A more cogent explanation for the treatment of women in equity lies in the distinction between the *feme sole* and the *feme covert.* It would seem that Chancery treated the *feme covert* differently from the common law courts because of the special arrangements often made on her behalf. That is, in many instances the *feme covert* had entered into a marriage settlement which guaranteed her right to control her property, either by herself, through trustees, or by will. This being the case, Chancery would consider her not as a *feme covert* but rather as a *feme sole*. Such property she held as a *feme sole* because of special marriage arrangements made in her favor. Consider a statement made in *Ross vs. Ewer,* heard in 1744: "Where there is a trust for the wife's separate use, this court looks upon her as a *feme sole."* Tapping Reeve, a nineteenth-century American commentator on the law of husband and wife, echoed that sentiment in stating that "a wife, as to her separate property, is a *feme sole;* and must be so considered, in all her actions respecting it, to act freely and without coercion."[26] It seems likely, then, that Chancery's treatment of the *feme covert* was a result of the fact that, for certain purposes, she was regarded as a *feme sole*.

This interpretation is given added weight when one considers the function of equity and its relationship to common law. As mentioned earlier, equity was seen as a body of rules which complemented and supplemented the common law, not as a competing system of justice. For this reason it is untenable to argue that Chancery administered a law which contradicted common law principles, that is, that equity would contravene the common law rules concerning the *feme covert*. The most probable explanation is that under certain circumstances and for particular purposes, Chancery regarded the *feme covert* as a *feme sole*.

This paper has been concerned with legal reality, with the way in which eighteenth-century law and lawyers regarded women. There is, of course, another reality. For a woman to have been accorded legal protection, for her to have the benefits of common law or equity, she must ultimately have been willing and able to bring suit. And then, as now, law was an expensive business. A mitigating factor was that she could sue in Chancery in the form of a pauper. But something more was likely to be required. Very often, the person from whom she sought protection, the perpetrator of the wrong for which she sought redress, was her husband. In such circumstances she would need not only a certain amount of strength to initiate and carry through proceedings but also a degree of awareness that a wrong had been done her. Given the prevailing view of a wife's proper relationship with her husband, given the likely tendency for her to view herself as "Other," that is, as a mere reflection of her husband, it is doubtful that many women would prove equal to the task. To be sure, there exists a multitude of Chancery cases involving women who sought to protect their own interests, and in such cases these women could count on the support of the Lord Chancellor. But this legal reality must not be allowed to obscure the fact that most of life's activity takes place outside the court, unregulated by the rules of equity.

In sum, then, the ideology reflected in early eighteenth-century legal and judicial pronouncements created certain social and psychological realities. The general acceptance of the assumptions of paternalism meant for the English woman relegation to a status decidedly inferior to that of a man. In addition to a total exclusion from public life, she was subjected upon marriage to the disabilities implicit in the doctrine of a unity of person. Her presumed inferiority and incompetence *vis à vis* her husband spelled a life of second-class citizenship. But more than this. Her own likely internalization. of the prevailing ideology meant that she herself probably failed to perceive the nature and extent of her disabilities.

NOTES

1 Jean Whitten's testimony in *The Equal Rights Amendment: Hearings Before the Subcommittee on Constitutional Amendments of the Committee on the Judiciary, United States Senate, Ninety-First Congress, Second Session on S. J. Res. 61 To Amend the Constitution So as to Provide Equal Rights for Men and Women* (Washington, 1972-73).

2 See, for example, Barbara Kirk Cavanagh, " 'A Little Dearer Than His Horse': Legal Stereotypes and the Feminine Personality," *Harvard Civil Liberties Law Review*, 6 (1971), 261; and Jean Murphy and Susan Deller Ross, "Liberating Women—Legally Speaking," in Bruce Wasserstein and Mark J. Green, ed., *With Justice for Some: An Indictment of the Law by Young Advocates* (Boston, 1970), p. 106.

3 For assessments of Blackstone's work see Sir William Holdsworth, "Some Aspects of Blackstone and His Commentaries," *Cambridge Law Journal*, 4 (1932), 261-85; and A. V. Dicey, "Blackstone's Commentaries," *ibid.*, 286-307. A much less sophisticated assessment can be found in Mary Beard, *Women as Force in History* (New York, 1946), Chapters 6 and 8.

4 Sir William Blackstone, *Commentaries on the Laws of England* (Philadelphia, 1879), I, 442. This notion of coverture was common in the seventeenth century as well, as were most of the common law rules regarding women's rights. See, for example, Sir Edward Coke, *Institutes on the Laws of England* (Philadelphia, 1836), I, 12 (this tract is commonly known as *Coke on Littleton*).

5 *The Lawes Resolutions of Womens Rights: Or, The Lawes Provision for Women* (London, 1632), pp. 124-25. This tract has been attributed to Sir John Doderidge, who served as solicitor-general and justice of King's Bench in the reign of James I.

6 Blackstone, *Commentaries on the Laws of England*, I, 442-43. The statute

of 16 and 17 Victoria, cap. 83, altered this rule by enacting that husbands and wives could give evidence on behalf of and against one another in civil proceedings. They could not, however, be compelled to disclose any communication during marriage, nor could they testify against one another in proceedings concerning adultery.

7 Blackstone, *Commentaries on the Laws of England*, I, 442-45. Before the reign of Charles II a husband could give his wife "moderate correction," just as he might his apprentices and children. But this power had to be confined within "reasonable bounds," and the husband must not use violence against his wife.

8 *Ibid.*, III, 140. For seventeenth-century statements of the rule see Coke, *Institutes on the Laws of England*, I, 133.

9 Blackstone, *Commentaries on the Laws of England*, I, 443, 444.

10 *Ibid.*, II, 433-34. See also Coke, *Institutes on the Laws of England*, I, 351b. Gifts to a woman's separate use are discussed below, 176.

11 Blackstone, *Commentaries on the Laws of England*, II, 126-27. Curtesy referred to the common law estate to which a man was entitled in his wife's lands and tenements of which she was seised in possession in fee simple or fee tail, providing they had lawful issue born alive which was capable of inheriting the estate. An exception occurred if the wife held her land by gavelkind tenure, in which case the husband gained title by curtesy before the birth of a child.

12 It was also suggested that this rule resulted from an attempt to dissuade men from plotting treason.

13 Blackstone, *Commentaries on the Laws of England*, II, 129-37.

14 *Ibid.*, 348-57, especially 355. Jointure was another method of barring dower. It consisted of a marriage settlement made upon the wife, accompanied by the stipulation that she would not take her dower. Blackstone, *Commentaries on the Laws of England*, II, 137-39.

15 Beard, *Women as Force in History*, pp. 209-13.

16 See, for example, *Penne and Peacock*, Mich., 1734, *A General Abridgment of Cases in Equity* (London, 1902, English Report Series), II, 116; an unnamed case in *ibid.*, 128; *Powell and Hankey and Cox*, Mich., 1722, *ibid.*, 129; *Christmas and Christmas*, Trin., 1725, *ibid.*, 130; *Susanna Elizabeth Vanhessen, Wife of Casimer Abraham, Count of Shippenbeck, and the South Sea Company vs. Count of Shippenbeck and the South Sea Company*, Dec., 1725, John Dickens, *Report of Cases and Determined in the High Court of Chancery* (London, 1794, English Report Series), 222; *Combe vs. Combe*, June, 1741, *ibid.*, 516-18; *Tyrell vs. Hope*, May 1743, *ibid.*, 735-37; *Wrottesley*, June, 1743, *ibid.*, 749-51; *Guidot vs. Guidot*, Trin., 1745, *ibid.*, 948-50; *Aston vs. Aston*, Hil., 1745, *ibid.*, 976. An exception occurred if the wife eloped, in which case the Court of Chancery would not assist her in recovering property settled to her own separate use. *Lee vs. Lee*, Dec., 1758, *ibid.*, 292.

17 *Wilson and Pack*, Trin., 1710, *A General Abridgment of Cases in Equity*, 133.

18 *Harvey and Harvey*, Trin., 1710, *ibid.*, 127; *Relf and Budden*, Hil., 1725, *ibid.*, 131; *Bennet and Davis*, Mich., 1725, *ibid.*, 131-32; *Ross vs. Ever*, July, 1744, John Atkins, *Reports of Cases Argued and Determined in the High Court of Chancery* (London, 1794), I, 892-97.

19 *Sheppard vs. Gibbons et al.*, Nov., 1742, *ibid.*, 666-67.

20 *Petts* (alias Potts) *and Lee*, Hil., 1725, *A General Abridgment of Cases in Equity*, 128. See also an unnamed case in *ibid.*; *Balch and Wilson*, Mich., 1697, *ibid.*, 134; an unnamed case, Trin., 1723, *ibid.*, Related issues were adjudicated in *Rich and Beaumond*, Feb., 1727, *ibid.*, 134; and *Cotton and Layer*, Trin., 1731, *ibid.*; *Pilkington and Cuthbertson*, Mar., 1711, *ibid.*, 163.

21 *Kirk and Clark*, Hil., 1708, *ibid.*, 124; *Cannel and Buckler*, Mich., 1724, *ibid.*, 117; *Angier and Angier*. Trin., 1718, *ibid.*, 129; *Watkyns by her next friend, vs. Ferdinando*, Dec., 1740, Atkins, *Report of Cases Argued and Determined in the High Court of Chancery*, I, 460-61.

22 *Cannel and Buckler*, Mich., 1724, *A General Abridgment of Cases in Equity*, 117.

23 An unnamed case, Mich., 1731, *ibid.*, 124.

24 *Penne and Peacock*, Mich., 1734, *ibid.*, 116. The judges were not agreed, however, on whether the wife or the trustees had an interest which could be conveyed. See also *Ortread and Round*, Mich., 1717, *ibid.*, 124; *Drybutter and Bartholemew*, Easter, 1723, *ibid.*, 113.

Lessing's Conception of Revelation as Education

HENRY E. ALLISON

I

The Education of the Human Race is generally regarded as the final and most authoritative expression of Lessing's religious-philosophical position. Its central theme is the analogy between revelation and education. This analogy is used as a vehicle for presenting a progressive or developmental conception of religious truth and thereby for ostensibly answering the objections which were raised against the notion of revelation in general, and the Jewish and Christian revelations in particular, by Hermann Samuel Reimarus.[1]

Neither the analogy itself, nor the purpose for which it is apparently used, were original with Lessing. Probably the first thinker to make use of it was Clement of Alexandria, in his response to Gnostic criticisms of the Old Testament. The Gnostics, in striking anticipation of deists such as Reimarus, challenged the revealed character of the Old Testament on the grounds that it presented an overly anthropomorphic conception of God and failed to include a doctrine of immortality. Clement responded to this criticism by presenting the Old Testament as a preparatory revelation, accomodated to the primitive level of development of the Hebrew people.[2] A similar conception, together with a doctrine of stages of revelation, was developed by Origen, and is also to be found in Tertullian and Irenaeus.[3] In more recent times, we find Locke using a similar analogy in order to counter the deistic objection that a God who makes salvation dependent upon the acceptance of an historical

183

revelation, which must of necessity remain either inaccessible or implausible to the vast majority of mankind, is an arbitrary and immoral tyrant. Locke responds to this by admitting that, since the truths which it contains are all accessible to reason, divine revelation is not absolutely necessary to salvation. He also claims, however, that revelation has an important pedagogical function, as without its assistance most men would never be able clearly to apprehend these truths.[4]

These thinkers all seem to have taken the analogy between revelation and education with full seriousness, viewing revelation in theistic fashion as the communication from God to man of a body of propositions and moral principles. This naturally gives rise to the question whether Lessing likewise construed the analogy in this sense, that is to say, whether he really accepted a theistic conception of revelation. The vast bulk of the Lessing literature of the present century has, of course, answered this question in the negative. Since the work of Frederick Loofs,[5] the prevailing opinion has been that Lessing's conception of revelation is merely an exoteric cloak for a theory of human development. This prevailing interpretation has, however, been acutely challenged by Helmut Thielicke.[6] The latter views Lessing's approach to the concept of revelation in light of the contemporary debate over the demythologization, and attributes to Lessing a view of revelation which is in many ways similar to Bultmann's.[7] Moreover, in reviewing the secondary literature, Thielicke makes the telling point that merely characterizing Lessing's use of "revelation" as an exoteric expression for a conception of human development hardly resolves the problem. For even if this is accepted, the question still remains whether this process of ethical and religious development, which for Lessing constitutes the education of the human race, requires an appeal to the idea that a transcendent deity entered into history.[8] Thielicke believes that it does, and he endeavors to justify this by an analysis of *The Education of the Human Race*, together with some of Lessing's other writings.

Now, as I have argued elsewhere, a consideration of Lessing's overall position and strategy in the theological controversies stemming from the publication of the fragments from Reimarus cannot bear out any such interpretation.[9] His whole approach to the question of religious truth is grounded in his adaptation of the Leibnizian perspectivalism, which he held together with a basically Spinozistic conception of God. Accordingly, there is no place in his scheme for the traditional conception of revelation. The present study, however, shall deal solely with *The Education of the Human Race*. Its goal is to show that Lessing provides us with several clues which point to the fact that the analogy between revelation and education is to be construed in such a way as to indicate Lessing's rejection of the traditional conception of revelation. More specifically. I shall try to show that the belief in revelation as a pedagogical act on the part of a transcendent deity, like the belief in any particular historical revelation, is to be understood as a stage which must itself be overcome or abandoned with the further development of the religious consciousness.

II

Let us begin with a brief review of the structure of the work. The actual essay consists of one hundred numbered paragraphs. These were published anonymously, although somewhat in the fashion of his later admirer, Kierkegaard, Lessing affixed his own name as editor. He also includes an editorial preface, in which he speaks in his own name, and the entire text is preceded by a quotation from St. Augustine. In his preface, Lessing reflects that the anonymous author stands on a height from which he can see further than his contemporaries, but that his vision is still not absolutely clear. The latter point is expressed poetically by the suggestion that he sees "from the immeasurable distance which a soft evening glow neither entirely conceals nor wholly reveals to his gaze."[10] What he sees in the "immeasurable distance" is apparently religious truth, and the "soft evening glow" would seem to be the contemporary religious perspective which is still essentially Christian. In short, Lessing (the editor) characterizes the author of the work as one who is viewing the problem of religious truth and development from a determinate standpoint within religious history, rather than from any absolutely privileged transcendent position. Moreover, in so locating the author, Lessing is, implicitly at least, placing himself at a somewhat higher, if not totally transcendent, standpoint. This is reflected in his significant query:

> Why are we not more willing to see in all positive religions simply the process by which alone human understanding in every place can develop and must still further develop, instead of either ridiculing or becoming angry with them? In the best world there is nothing that deserves this scorn, this indignation we show. Are the religions alone to deserve it? Is God to have a part in everything except our mistakes.[11]

The main text presents and develops the analogy between revelation and education as a device for interpreting the history of religion. "Education," it is claimed (§2), "is revelation coming to the individual man, and revelation is education which has come, and is still coming to the human race." In light of this analogy, the Jewish and Christian revelations are treated as successive stages in the moral and religious education of humanity. Each is seen to contain a partial truth, adequate for mankind at a particular level of develop-ment. Finally, although a warning is addressed to those who are overly eager to abandon the Christian perspective, the work closes with the affirmation of the eventual advent of a post-Christian stage of religious development. This is characterized as the era of the "Eternal Gospel," a glimmer of which was already caught by "some enthusiasts of the thirteenth and fourteenth cen-turies," who "only erred in that they predicted its arrival, as so near to their own time" (§87).

This analogy between revelation and education is justified in terms of its "advantages" for theology (§3), and these turn out to be precisely the con-siderations which led the previously mentioned thinkers to this conception, viz., the defense of the revealed character of the Old Testament, and the determination of a function for revelation which does not yield any truths that are not, in principle at least, accessible to human reason. This latter task is resolved by comparing revelation with an essentially Platonic conception of education:

> Education gives man nothing which he could not also get from within himself; it gives him that which he could get from within himself, only quicker and more easily. In the same way too, revelation gives nothing to the human race which human reason could not arrive at on its own, only it has given and still gives to it, the most important of these things sooner. (§4)

It has often been claimed that this conception is contradicted by the later suggestion (§77) that despite the dubious nature of its historical claims, the Christian revelation may have led to the discovery of truths "which human reason would never have reached on its own."[12] Nevertheless, even if we discount the extremely tentative manner in which the author makes this suggestion, there is no real contradiction. Both passages can be readily under-stood in light of the Platonic-rationalistic conception of an "occasion." Qua rational, these "revealed" truths are not derived from without, and in this sense education (revelation) does not provide man with anything that he cannot acquire for himself. However, since education (revelation) does pro-vide the occasion which first enables man to recognize these truths, it is perfectly consistent to argue that without this occasion human reason might never, in fact, have come to recognize them. The situation is precisely the same as in the famous slave boy episode in Plato's *Meno*. Although the point of the story is that the slave boy "recollected" the geometrical truths rather than acquired them from Socrates (the occasion), it is equally clear that without the prodding of Socrates, or someone like him, he would never have been able to do so.[13]

But, if this be the case, then it would appear that *The Education of the*

Human Race does contain a basically theistic conception of revelation after all. For to give to revelation the function of an occasion, in the above sense, strongly suggests that it is to be conceived as the act of a transcendent deity, through which the human race is led to the apprehension of rational truths which are appropriate to its particular level of development. This brief survey of the "argument" of the work therefore hardly confirms the original contention that it contains a radical critique of the traditional conception of revelation.

III

The first, and perhaps most basic clue that this "argument" is not to be taken at face value is provided by the quotation from St. Augustine: "All these things are in some respects true precisely because they are in other respects false."[14] This is taken from a portion of the *Soliloquies* wherein St. Augustine is discussing, among other things, the sense in which the notions of truth and falsity are applicable to works of art. The cited passage constitutes the essence of "Reason's" (St. Augustine's partner) answer to this question. Reason provides several examples from the arts, which are designed to illustrate this principle. Typical of these, and of the whole line of argument, is the example of the painting of a horse. Here the point is simply that in order for such a painting to count as a "true picture," or a genuine work of art, it must not contain a real horse. As a work of art, its truth depends upon its success in creating an illusion, and in this sense upon its being false. But this applies to all works of art, as well as to things such as jokes and mirror images. In regard to this whole class of things it can be said: "To establish their truth, the only thing in their favor is that they are false in some other regard. Hence, they never succeed in being what they want or ought to be, as long as they refuse to be false."[15]

This principle is obviously applicable to the Jewish and Christian revelations as presented in *The Education of the Human Race*. Their "truth" is therein seen to reside in their suitability for molding the moral and religious consciousness of their recipients. They do this by initially presenting themselves as the absolute, revealed word of God. The whole analysis, however, assumes that they can only fulfill their pedagogic function if they are not in fact what they present themselves as being, i.e., not the absolute word of God, but merely historically conditioned expressions thereof. These revelations then can be said to be in some respects true precisely because they are in other respects false. The key question, however, is whether the same thing can be said about the very conception of revelation as education, which is the central theme of the essay. Must we not likewise say of *this* conception that it is in some respects true precisely because it is in other respects false? Otherwise expressed, the question is whether the conception of revelation as an historically conditioned means for the moral and religious education of the race can itself be maintained, without this conception turning out to be something quite different from what it is initially presented as being.

The answer to this question can be derived by an analysis to the specific pedagogical function which is attributed to revelation. This function is to lead the recipient to the eventual recognition of a rational content implicit in the revealed teaching. "When they were revealed," the author notes (§75), "they were certainly not truths of reason, but they were revealed in order to become such." This theme is supported by an appeal to the analogy with the "facit" or sum which the mathematics teacher uses to initiate his pupils into the subject. The point here is simply that the function of a revelation, like that of a facit, is to make itself dispensable; to bring the pupil to the point where he can grasp the truth for himself.

There are, however, two obvious differences between the two cases, which are glossed over in the text. First of all, in order for the facit to help the pupil eventually attain some knowledge of mathematics, it must express the correct sum. With regard to revelation, however, it is only important that it be *believed* to be true. Unless the believer takes the revelation for the absolute word of God, that is, accepts it as a revelation, it can never serve as the occasion for the development of his own moral and religious consciousness. But it can fulfill this function simply by being believed to be true, without having actually to be true. Secondly, as Kierkegaard so astutely pointed out, in the case of revelation, one cannot neatly separate the teaching from the teacher.[16] When God is in fact regarded as the teacher, the claim that this is the case must be itself an essential part of the teaching or revelation. It must therefore also be an integral part of the *content* of one's belief, and not merely an extrinsic reason for holding that belief.

The latter point, which is not explicitly developed in the essay, but which was certainly recognized by Lessing,[17] has some interesting implications for the program of religious education outlined in the essay. For with the development of truths of revelation to truths of reason we do not have one and the same content apprehended in two manners, i.e., at one time on the basis of authority and at another time through reason. Rather, we have two distinct contents, the second of which explicitly excludes an essential ingredient of the first, namely, the claim that it is revealed by God. We are thus brought to see that, while the belief in the revealed character of a religious truth is necessary if the human mind is ever to be drawn to that truth, once this truth is understood and seen to be rationally grounded, the belief in its revealed character, just like the trust of a student in the authority of his teacher, must be discarded. The author himself does not, of course, explicitly assert this as a general principle, but he certainly implies as much when he asks whether we may not find in the New Testament, as we have already found in the Old, truths "which we are to gaze at in awe as revelations, just until reason learns to deduce them from its other demonstrated truths, and to connect them with them?" (§ 72) To express the general point in a Hegelian manner, which here seems quite appropriate, the concept of revelation is shown to undergo a dialectical development wherein it eventually overcomes itself. Like the work of art in St. Augustine, revelation achieves its truth, or what it "ought to be", only in so far as it does not "refuse to be false." Thus, the defense of revelation offered in *The Education of the Human Race* does, indeed, issue in the complete rejection of the traditional conception.[18]

IV

For some one of Lessing's Spinozistic persuasions, the basic difficulty with the notion of revelation is the concept of God which it entails. We would therefore expect to find some hints in this direction in *The Education of the Human Race.* Such an expectaion is not disappointed, although, in typical fashion, Lessing manages to convey his message to the discerning reader through the very structure of the work, and ironically, through what is omitted more than through what is said.

The work as a whole traces the religious development of the race in terms of three concepts: God, morality, and immortality. According to the basic schema, each of these concepts ought to be grasped in an increasingly adequate manner at the successive stages of development. Thus, the ancient Hebrews initially had a very crude conception of God. He was known merely as Jehovah, the private tribal deity of the Hebrew, and was worshipped more for his power than for his wisdom. It was only under the Persian influence, the author suggests, that the Hebrews were led to a genuinely monotheistic position. Once this position was attained, however, the Hebrews were able to realize that this conception was implicit in their scripture all along. With regard to morality and immortality the situation was somewhat different. Here the author asserts that the Old Testament really lacks a doctrine of immortality, and that its moral teachings do not rise above the level of a doctrine of temporal rewards and punishments, for the obedience, or lack of it, to the divine commandments.

The New Testament, according to the author, reflects a higher level of the religious consciousness. He places special emphasis on the doctrine of the immortality of the soul, of which "Christ was the first *reliable, practical* teacher" (§58). This goes together with a spiritualization of the principle of morality, i.e., the emphasis on inward purity of heart rather than merely outward conformity. There is also, however, a development of the concept of God. In a manner reminiscent of Lessing's early fragment, the *Christianity of Reason*, the author suggests that "God cannot possibly be One in the sense in which finite things are one, that even his unity must be a transcendental unity which does not exclude a sort of plurality" (§73). This plurality, we are told, is grounded in the divine self-consciousness. As an infinite being, God must have a perfect conception of himself, but as perfect, it must contain all of his attributes, including necessary existence. God's concept of himself thus turns out to be "a true double" rather than merely an empty representation. There is therefore a real plurality within the divine unity, and this, it is suggested, is the rational content of the Christian doctrine of the Trinity.

It seems worth pointing out that Jacobi referred to precisely this passage as evidence for Lessing's Spinozism, suggesting that it implies a denial of the distinction between God and the world.[19] As Thielicke has shown, however, this is simply not the case. What emerges from God's conception of himself is not the world, as a pantheistic position would presumably require, but merely the Logos.[20] Nevertheless, the point to keep in mind is considering this extremely obscure but suggestive passage is that it is presented as a reflection of the *Christian* stage of religious development, and therefore from a point of view which is itself destined to be overcome.

According to the ground plan of the essay, this overcoming should take place during the third period of religious development, the time of the "Eternal Gospel." This occurs explicitly with regard to the conceptions of morality and immortality. Thus, we are told that at this time men will love virtue for its own sake, "will do right because it *is* right, not because arbitrary rewards are set upon it" (§85). Moreover, the belief in an after life, wherein the individual is rewarded or punished in accordance with his deeds on earth, is to be supplanted by a doctrine of metempsychosis, wherein the same individual is held to appear many times on earth, and is thus able to progress through the whole course of education.[21] There is, however, no mention of the conception of God which is appropriate to this level of development. Nevertheless, the reader is able to supply this conception for himself simply by applying the formula which is at work. The Christian conception of God, it will be recalled, was held to be superior to the Hebrew conception because it contained a more adequate view of the divine unity, and it was more adequate because it included plurality within it. Now, by a process of extrapolation, one may conclude that a still more adequate conception of God would be one which included an even greater plurality within it. But then the most adequate conception of all would be the one which reconciled the divine unity with the greatest possible plurality, and this is precisely the Spinozistic conception wherein "all things are in God." It is therefore the

God of Spinoza which is to be found in the "Eternal Gospel," and with such a God there is no place for the traditional conception of revelation.

V

In view of these considerations, we can conclude with some degree of confidence that Lessing's strategy in *The Education of the Human Race* is to lead the discerning reader to the point where he can reach certain conclusions for himself, which go considerably beyond the explicit teaching of the text. His goal is thus to educate the reader in the most profound sense of the term. Like many of Lessing's works, *The Education of the Human Race* is therefore at once a philosophical treatise and a work of art.

Furthermore, it is only by considering this aspect of the work that we can come to understand why Lessing published it anonymously. Since he presented himself as editor, and changing the stance he had adopted as commentator on the fragments from Reimarus, expressed general agreement with its contents, this anonymity cannot simply be seen as a device for avoiding further conflict with the orthodox clergy and the authorities. Rather, we must view this anonymity as an integral part of the meaning of the work. This becomes possible when we recall that in his preface, Lessing explicitly locates the author within the Christian perspective. It is from this perspective that the author endeavors to defend the concept of revelation against the Reimarus type of objections. It is therefore no wonder that he (the author) takes the concept of revelation seriously and fails to note the Spinozistic conception of God which is implicit in the Eternal Gospel.

But the position of Lessing (the editor) and, one hopes, that of the discerning reader, is not completely identical with that of the author. This is the crucial point that is generally overlooked in interpreting *The Education of the Human Race.*[22] From the more exalted perspective which Lessing adopts, and to which he endeavors to lead his readers, one can see clearly what the author of the work fails to grasp fully, viz., the untenability of the traditional conception of revelation, even when viewed as a pedagogic device. Moreover, by presenting this thesis in such an oblique fashion, Lessing is able to suggest a major point which raises his analysis far above the level of the *Aufklärung.* This point is that, although erroneous, the belief in a divine revelation ought not to be simply repudiated in the literal-minded manner of the deists, as though it were a mere aberration. Rather, as he suggests in a manner which anticipates a central feature of the Hegelian dialectic, the concept of revelation can, and must, be shown to contain within itself the seeds of its own destruction. Its inevitable destiny, its historic function, and therefore its "truth," is to overcome itself. This is the "esoteric" message of *The Education of the Human Race.*

NOTES

1 In his capacity as ducal librarian of Wolfenbuttel, Lessing published anonymously between 1774 and 1778 a number of fragments from Reimarus' *Schutzschrift für die vernunftigen Vereher Gottes.* It was this fact together with the comments which he annexed to the fragments that set off the controversy in which Lessing was embroiled during the last years of his life. The first part of *The Education of the Human Race* was initially published (1777) in response to one of these fragments. For an analysis of the content of the fragments, Lessing's criticisms of them, and the ensuing polemic with the orthodox theologians, see my *Lessing and the Enlightenment* (Ann Arbor: Univ. of Michigan Press, 1966).

2 Cf. Charles Bigg, *The Christian Platonists of Alexandria* (Oxford, 1886), pp. 55-56.

3 For a discussion of this conception in Origen see Bigg, *op. cit.,* p. 223; for Tertullian and Iranaeus see Adolph Harnack, *History of Dogma,* Eng. trans. by Neil Buchanan, Dover edition (New York, 1961), II, 103 and 305-7.

4 John Locke, *Reasonableness of Christianity as Delivered in the Scriptures, Works,* 9th ed. (London, 1794), VI, 144 ff.

5 Frederick Loofs, *Lessings Stellung zum Christentum,* Theol, Studien und Kritiken Jahrg., 1913, 1. Heft (Gotha, 1912).

6 Helmut Thielicke, *Offenbarung Vernunft und Existenz,* Studien zur Religionsphilosophie Lessings, 4th ed. (Gütersloh, 1957). Thielicke also provides (pp. 16-28) an excellent review of the whole literature.

7 *Ibid.,* p. 150 ff.

8 *Ibid.,* p. 22 ff.

9 Allison, *Lessing and the Enlightenment,* esp. Chapters 3 and 4, pp. 80-166.

10 Henry Chadwick, *Lessing's Theological Writings* (Stanford: Stanford Univ. Press, 1957), p. 10. This and other references to *The Education of the Human Race* are taken from Chadwick's revision of F. W. Robertson's 1858 translation of the essay.

11 *Ibid.*

12 Cf. Thielicke, *op. cit.,* p. 33; Chadwick, *op. cit.,* p. 39.

13 For a fuller discussion of this point see *Lessing and the Enlightenment,* p. 58 ff.

14 St. Augustine, *Soliloquies*, Bk. II, Chap. ¹⁰, Eng. trans. by T. F. Gilligan, *The Writings of St. Augustine*, Vol. I, *The Fathers of the Church* (New York, 1948), p. 401.

15 *Ibid.*

16 S. Kierkegaard, *Philosophical Fragments*, Eng. trans. by David F. Swenson, 2nd ed., rev. Howard Hong (Princeton: Princeton Univ. Press, 1962), p. 17 ff.

17 In fact, it underlies his whole critique of neology, and is clearly developed in his counter-assertion to the first fragment of Reimarus, *Von Verschreiung der Vernunft auf den Kanzeln*, Rilla, VII, 816-20. For a discussion of this text see *Lessing and the Enlightenment*, pp. 93-95.

18 This strategy of presenting a defense which is actually a disguised attack is typical of Lessing. We find it in especially clear form in his youthful *Rettung des Hieronymous Cardanus*, 1754, Rilla, VII, 201-28, and *Leibniz von den ewigen Strafen*, 1773, Rilla, VII 454-88, where he "defends" Leibniz's doctrine of eternal punishments against Eberhard's rationalistic attacks. For a discussion of these texts see *Lessing and the Enlightenment*. pp. 54-58, and 83-91.

19 Cf. Thielicke, *op. cit.*, p. 94.

20 *Ibid.*, p. 94 ff.

21 Lessing apparently seriously entertained the doctrine of metempsychosis at that time. In a remark added to *Dass mehr als fünf Sinne für den Menschen sein konnen*, a fragment which is dated around 1776, Lessing remarks: "Thus my system is certainly the oldest of all philosophical systems. For it is actually nothing but the system of the pre-existence of souls and metempsychosis, which was not only taught by Plato and Pythagoras, but even before them by the Egyptians and Chaldeans and Persians, in short by all the wise men of the Orient." For a full discussion of this issue see Heinrich Kofink, *Lessings Anschaungen über die Unsterblichkeit und Seelenwanderung* (Strassburg, 1912), and *Lessing and the Enlightenment*, pp. 131-33.

22 Thielicke comes close to this, pointing out (p. 44) that the author of *The Education of the Human Race* is writing from a definite historical perpective, but he fails to take the further step, to question whether the position assigned to the author is that of Lessing himself.

Edelmann and the Silent Reimarus

WALTER GROSSMANN

Edelmann is not a forgotten figure in German intellectual life of the eighteenth century. Of his *Moses mit aufgedeckten Angesichte*, published in 1740, Emanuel Hirsch observes, "Never before had a book been published in the German language that, like the *Moses*, entirely denied biblical faith and Christian dogma."[1] The literary historian Hermann Hettner sees in him a "courageous thinker . . . far too far ahead of his time"[2] to be understood and appreciated; and Paul Hazard sketches his life as that of a theologian who, departing from Lutheran orthodoxy, reached the heights of enlightened and independent religious thinking.[3] Ernst Barnikol has demonstrated Edelmann's influence on the left—on the Hegelian Bruno Bauer;[4] and Ernst Benz has linked Friedrich Nietzsche's ideas of Christianity and Christ to those of Bauer and Edelmann.[5]

It has been especially encouraging recently, for one who is spending some time on this much abused and still little read maverick, to find Hans Kohn, in "The Multidimensional Enlightenment," calling attention to Edelmann;[6] and it is encouraging as well to find Franco Venturi in the newly published *Europe des Lumières* admonishing his readers "Il faudrait réétudier Edelmann."[7]

The question I want to raise in this paper is, why was Edelmann not fully acknowledged by the leaders of German enlightenment as their courageous precursor? Or to put it differently, why did Lessing, who was familiar with Edelmann's works, publish fragments from Reimarus' *Apologie oder Schutzschrift für die vernünftigen Verehrer Gottes*[8] but not call attention to Edelmann, who at least thirty years earlier had taken a similar position on the Bible, the apostles, the divinity of Jesus, and the economy of salvation? An attempt to answer this question will bring out differences as well as similarities between these two almost precise contemporaries—Edelmann (1698-1767) and Reimarus (1694-1768). I hope such an attempt will also contribute to the characterization of the intellectual and political scene of Germany in the four decades after 1740, a period whose first year saw the publication of Edelmann's *Moses,* and which includes the beginning of the reign of Frederick II.

Paul Tillich, in *A History of Christian Thought* says, "The great movement of historical Bible criticism began around 1750. Lessing, who was the greatest personality of the German Enlightenment, was the leader against a stupid orthodoxy which stuck to traditional terms."[9] In linking Lessing's contribution specifically to historical Bible criticism. Tillich refers to Lessing's having published, between 1774 and 1778, fragments from a manuscript of Hermann Samuel Reimarus entrusted to him by the Hamburg scholar's children. Lessing concealed the authorship of the fragments by claiming that they were found in the Wolfenbüttel library and that the writer was unknown, thus keeping his promise to Reimarus' children, who feared for the reputation of their father. David Friedrich Strauss (1808-1874), a great admirer of Reimarus, wrote that he "was not frank with his contemporaries; he preferred to transmit his thoughts to posterity only through unpublished manuscripts."[10] In his brilliant sketch of earlier research, with which he introduces his own *Das Leben Jesu* (1835), Strauss gives Reimarus the credit for introducing to a German audience the "Deistic attacks on the Bible and on its divine authority."[11] Strauss learned of Edelmann's writings only later, as he makes clear in his *Die Christliche Glaubenslehre,* (1840-41), which includes the following footnote: "The writings of this frail and restless personality from the midst of the last century have been called to my attention by the pamphlet of W. Elster, dean of the gymnasium at Clausthal: *Erinnerung an Johann Christian Edelmann.* Its purpose is to discredit me as the Edelmann redivivus. I am indebted to that publication for an interesting acquaintance—not perhaps with the dean, but with this alleged precursor, who has been abused much more than he has been studied."[12]

In 1906 Albert Schweitzer, following the Strauss of *Das Leben Jesu,* programmatically called his history of research of the life of Jesus *Von Reimarus bis Wrede, Eine Geschichte der Leben Jesu Forschung.* This book, which was to become the classic in its field, thus firmly established Reimarus' reputation as the first who applied historical methods to the study of the Bible tradition.

A comparison between the writings of Edelmann and the *Apologie* of Reimarus discloses some striking similarities. For Edelmann as well as for Reimarus one of the strongest arguments against Orthodox teachings that regard the Bible as inspirational are passages that run counter to the ideal of a loving God and the unchangeable laws of nature. Both Edelmann and Reimarus addressed their arguments in particular to the image of Moses as it emerges from the Old Testament. Edelmann points to passages that show Moses demanding "inhuman legislation devoid of all natural charity."[13] Among the passages to which Edelmann referred are the ones in which Moses reprehended the military after their victory over the Midianites for sparing the lives of women and children (Numbers 31: 17) and the call for utter destruction of seven nations (Deuteronomy 7: 2). Having quoted these and other passages, Edelmann concludes with the question, "Can you imagine that these barbaric laws were dictated by a God of whom Scriptures says that He is anxious to help all men . . . by the same God who through Christ has demanded that we bless our enemies? "[14] In a similar vein, Reimarus observes, "It is not divine to ask that the Israelites should beg the Egyptians to let them borrow silver and gold vessels without intending to return them. It is unjust and cruel that they should plot to take away land by force from people who have done them no harm, but the contrary, whose ancestors have shown kindness and hospitality towards them, yet that they should go even further and wish to strangle their wives and children." Reimarus continues, " . . . when the words are added, 'God has appeared to me, God has said or ordained,' does that turn lies into truth, and make of the worst ungodly actions deeds pleasing to God? Thus it is not difficult to make out of phantasy a revelation, of deceit virtue . . . and as a consequence all real distinctions between godly and ungodly are eliminated. How can we be asked to take Moses: miracles and divine mission for truth? "[15]

In the *Glaubens-Bekentniss* Edelmann set out to demolish the entire accepted order of salvation—the belief in the Bible's account of paradise, the fall, damnation, and salvation. In his opinion the church's teachings of a wrathful God whom humans can insult are contradicted by all that natural reason tells us about the Creator and his creation. This contention of Edelmann "that God was never separated from his creatures"[16] negates the orthodox economy of salvation and leads to the re-evaluation of Jesus' role in the history of mankind. Edelmann's attacks are directed against the doctrine of the devil, the fall, and Jesus' death as instrument of redemption. "If one proclaims that Jesus has promised to men the forgiveness and the taking away of their sins, because he himself suffered the sacrifice of redemption for them, then one makes of Jesus a liar. It is evident before the eyes of the world that he neither has freed man from sin nor has united him with God. On the contrary we have never before had more poor sinners and a more angry God (according to the clergy) than since the Gospel was proclaimed and the so-called sacrifice of redemption was preached."[17]

Reimarus, in his rejection of the Christian economy of salvation, started out as Edelmann did, declaring the doctrine of the estrangement of man from God, as accounted for in the story of the fall, a fabrication unworthy of the benign Creator. He rejects the accusation "that the miserable fall has made us blind in matters religious and that this is why the order of salvation appears to us unreasonable and even foolish. Yes, it is indeed correct that we have to become first blind and convinced that we possess no healthy reason before we can be made to accept such contradictory teachings."[18]

Reimarus, like Edelmann, argued vigorously for the autonomy of reason over blind faith and against the Orthodox demand for acceptance, because "obedience to faith makes a captive of reason."[19] He condemns intolerance and the persecution of those who express different views on matters of religion and faith, and he paints a picture of the Orthodox clergy's tactics in grim terms: "Thus they rally to the suppression of reasonable religion a whole army of themselves, and the civil authorities as the defenders of faith are asked to interdict the circulation of writings by freethinking authors, the bookstores are threatened with severe punishment in case of transgression, and the books are burned by the executioner; worse fate may be in store for the authors, who will be chased from their office, put into jail, and left to their misery."[20] Actually this is an accurate description of how Edelmann was persecuted by the Orthodox clergy and how those who printed and distributed his book were taken to task and punished.

Edelmann, pointing to the contradiction between claim and reality in the Christian concept of the messianic role of Jesus, writes, "What reasonable explanation have the Christians to offer, why Jesus, having conquered sin, death, devil and hell, has not kept his word . . . ? Why does the devil, whom he allegedly overcame 1700 years ago, still rule the entire world?"[21] Concerning Christianity's power to improve man's moral behavior, Reimarus arrives at the same conclusion Edelmann did, and the words he finds recall those just quoted from the *Glaubens-Bekentniss*. Reimarus expressed the dilemma thus: "If we look today upon the influence and the moral benefits the Christian religion has exercised to improve the human heart, then we must acknowledge that from the history of these 1700 years and from today's experience nothing indicates that Christianity has increased man's reverence for God, morality, virtue and conduct, or has made man more devout, just, loving, and more moderate."[22]

Edelmann and Reimarus both subscribed basically to Spinoza's concept of Jesus. Edelmann emphasized in Jesus' message the transvaluation of values, its radical aspects. Reimarus, though much more cautious in his evaluation of Jesus, also proclaims, "See what pure and sublime holy morality Jesus is preaching. He seeks to close the source of evil, the sordid desires of the heart, and instead imbue it with self and neighborly love."[23]

The similarities in Edelmann's and Reimarus' position are not confined to major points; throughout their Bible criticism they are also alike in their use of examples and arguments. Even a cursory inspection of the sources demonstrates their knowledge and use of the same works. It seems proper to add here that Edelmann's scholarship was considerable, though he was not as erudite as Reimarus, professor of Hebrew and oriental languages, and lecturer in philosophy, mathematics, and natural sciences at the Akademische Gymnasium at Hamburg. On the other hand, Reimarus showed little interest in documentation.

If it is true that in 1740 Edelmann published ideas that anticipated those of Reimarus, whose *Apologies* did not appear until about 1774, only after Lessing discovered the manuscript hidden away in a desk by the author, one may raise the question why it is Reimarus and not Edelmann who is credited with introducing radical Bible criticism in Germany. As has been suggested, the answer is linked to the historical situation of the period. Above all it must be sought in the differences between Edelmann's and Reimarus' work. Albert Schweitzer, praising those parts of Reimarus that Lessing had made known, wrote: "Of the grandeur of the work enough cannot be said. This work is not only one of the great events in the history of criticism, it is also a masterpiece of world literature."[24] Indeed Reimarus' almost serene tone, on occasion lightened by wit and irony, must have appealed to Lessing tremendously. When he read this systematic investigation of the New and Old Testament, written from the vantage point of the Enlightenment in a splendid German style, he must have felt compelled to share what he had found with his contemporaries. None of Edelmann's major work could lay claim to such distinction as one readily concedes to Reimarus' *Apologie*. Edelmann never intended to offer his readers a systematic and thorough critique of all the books of the Bible. Even his style had evolved only slowly, moving from baroque opulence to more sober, rational diction. On the other hand, he did have virtues as an author. Edelmann often coined a fortunate phrase, gave forceful expression to what he wanted to convey, and linked his arguments together skillfully; in short, he was a fine philosophical writer. His style suited its purpose—to instruct his readers by convincing them of what he thought to be true. In addition, he wanted to combat their prejudices and open their minds to receive a message of reason and freedom. If one is surprised that a certain enthusiasm every so often shows itself in Edelmann's writing, it may be well to remember that even Lessing could be carried away when envisioning the advent of a truly enlightened mankind. Edelmann addressed himself to a lower class audience, and though his ambition to reach people did not restrict his interest to any particular group, he wanted to be sure of being understood by those who lacked education though not the willingness to listen and learn.

When Reimarus wrote his *Apologie*, he definitely did not want it to be published then, and did not anticipate its publication in the near future. He did not mean to become, like seventeenth-century English radicals, a "publisher of truth." "The manuscript," he wrote, "may remain in secrecy available to a few understanding friends. It will not be made public in print with my consent, before times become more enlightened."[25]

"Dippel and Edelmann," Strauss remarked, "were free thinkers and enthusiasts and therefore they found it easier to put up with the insecure existence that their frankness demanded as its price."[26] That is too cavalierly said. Dippel suffered from imprisonment, and Edelmann certainly would have preferred a place where he could live and work peacefully to the almost constant moving about he endured.

Yet Strauss had put his finger on the neuralgic spot. Edelmann, right at the beginning of the *Glaubens-Bekentniss,* draws a portrait of the ideal teacher the pleasures and inconveniences of whose life he was probably willing to accept: "His estate is a free one and consists more in doing than mere talk, he loves truth in everyone, bears the errors of others with patience, although he exposes them with candor and without hesitation . . . , hates all violence and persecution and proves by deeds and not pompous oratory that he is a true lover of the impartial and frank Jesus."[27] By contrast, Reimarus' estate was not free, he was attached to a highly reputable gymnasium, and his values were deeply embedded in the commercial bourgeois society. These values are given high visibility in many passages of the *Apologie*. One example will suffice: "Never has he [Jesus] made it a general rule for all Christians to give away all their goods. Such generosity dries quickly at the source. Who gives out of what he can spare has a long time to give. He who just disburses his goods and makes himself a beggar is callous towards wife and children and becomes a burden to human society. I want to go a step further: community of goods, a 'Saviour's' cash box in private hands, deprives the state of taxes from well-to-do citizens, makes for a state within a state, and is a dangerous thing, not to be tolerated anywhere."[28]

Reimarus paid for his silence. In a moving sentence in the *Apologie* he gave this feeling expression, a luxury he otherwise did not permit himself: "The Herrn preachers should well know that it is not small suffering that an honest man has to inflict on his soul if he has through all his life to feign and pretend." Reimarus projects the consequence if the honest citizen would reveal his true thoughts: "Friendship, kindness, confidence, sociability, his very economic existence would be denied to him, he would be avoided as a wicked and despicable malefactor."[29] Such ostracism the beloved family head and honored Hamburg citizen could not visualize as his lot. The real motive for his writings, which were buried in his desk, was, he confessed, his "own peace of mind."[30] He had to unburden himself of what he found true, in this manner; otherwise the frustrations of the great scholar and writer would have become unbearable.

Lessing did not publish the *Fragments* without encountering opposition from the clergy. As a consequence he became embroiled in a controversy with the Hamburg Pastor Goetze that brought him into conflict with the Braunschweig authorities. Under the threat of losing the privilege of publishing his own journal, *Für Geschichte und Literatur,* free of censorship, Lessing was forced to deliver the Reimarus manuscript to the authorities.[31]

Let us return to the question asked at the beginning: Why did Lessing, who was familiar with Edelmann's work, not give him the credit that was due to him as a radical critic of Orthodoxism and champion of reason? The answer is partly implied in the qualitative differences between the works of Edelmann and Reimarus. The political hazards in German states and towns, including the Prussia of Frederick II, that a German champion of natural religion had to face were not greatly reduced between the 1740's and the 1770's. The story of Lessing's publication of the *Fragments* is the best example in point.

Edelman's case is further complicated: First by his frank acknowledgement of Spinoza's contribution to Bible criticism. Secondly, by his attempt to redefine Spinoza's interpretation of the relation of God to his Creation. The stigma of materialism rightly or wrongly was pinned on Edelmann. To be a Spinozist or materialist was still the worst allegation that could be made against an intellectual.

In 1785, Friedrich Heinrich Jacobi reported a conversation with his friend Lessing, dating back to July 1780, the year before Lessing died. Jacobi reported Lessing's comment, prompted by Goethe's poem *Prometheus:* "The view from which the poem arose, is my own . . . . The orthodox views of divinity are not for me, I can not bear them anymore: Hen Kai Pan [one and all] I do not know anything else . . . ." Having heard this unexpected remark, Jacobi probed further: "Then you are in accord with Spinoza? " To this Lessing replied, "if I shoud identify myself with anybody, I would not know anyone else."[32] The next morning, when Lessing visited Jacobi, he reaffirmed his declaration for Spinoza: "There is no other philosophy than Spinoza's."[33] Jacobi's report was immediately challenged by another of Lessing's friends, Moses Mendelssohn, who felt that these apocryphal sayings would endanger Lessing's reputation. He exclaimed in indignation, "the editor of the *Fragments,* the author of *Nathan,* the great admirable defender of theism and the religion of reason, a Spinozist, atheist and blasphemer! "[34] A few years after 1787, Immanuel Kant, in the preface to the second edition of the *Critique of Pure Reason,* expressed the view that speculative reason would find a better reception when recommended as a tool in combating the potential dangers "of materialism, fatalism, atheism, libertine disbelief, enthusiasm, and superstition."[35] Although radical Bible criticism and natural religion became acceptable within the decade following the appearance of Kant's preface, Spinozism did not. It was associated with atheism and materialism even in the minds of intellectuals like Mendelssohn. Herder's and Goethe's admiration for Spinoza's work were the exceptions. The "public" silence"—*öffentliches Schweigen*—of Lessing on his Spinozism, to use Lukacs' expression,[36] is indeed the forced silence of a man who certainly cannot be accused of cowardice and hypocrisy. Rather than reflecting on the character of Reimarus and Lessing, their public silence says a good deal about the society they lived in.

Edelmann, we assert, was the precursor of Reimarus and Lessing. The fact that it was still too dangerous in 1780 to write and say what Edelmann had dared to say in 1740 indicates that despite the growing Enlightenment, toleration had not increased. "Germany," as Heine wrote in 1832, "had for a long time displayed an aversion to materialism and therefore for the last 150 years had become the true playground of idealism."[37] One consequence of this tendency was that it wandered farther and farther away from the radical thought of Spinoza and Edelmann.

NOTES

1 E. Hirsch, *Geschichte der neueren evangelischen Theologie* (Gütersloh, 1951), II, 413.
2 H. Hettner, *Geschichte der deutschen Literatur im achtzehnten Jahrhundert* (Braunschweig, 1872), part III, book I, 272.
3 P. Hazard, *European Thought in the Eighteenth Century* (New Haven, 1954), 56-58.
4 E. Barnikol, *Das entdeckte Christentum im Vormärz* (Jena, 1927), 57-62.
5 E. Benz, *Nietzsches Ideen zur Geschichte des Christentums und der Kirche* (Leiden, 1956), 125-33.
6 H. Kohn, "The Multidimensional Enlightenment," *JHI*, 31 (1970), 473.
7 F. Venturi, *Europe des Lumières* (Paris, 1971), 15.
8 H. S. Reimarus, *Apologie oder Schutzschrift für die vernünftigen Verehrer Gottes*, herausgegeben von Gerhard Alexander, 2 vols. (Frankfurt am Main, 1972; quoted as hereafter Reimarus, *Apologie*). The full text of Reimarus' manuscript has now been published for the first time, two hundred years after Lessing made parts of it known. Substantial parts (Vorbericht, I, II, III Buch Kapitel 1-4) were published by Carl Rudolph Wilhelm Klose in *Zeitschrift für die historische Theologie 1850-1852*, vols. 20 (pp. 519-637), 21 (513-578), and 22 (380-494). It was also

Klose's merit to publish the manuscript of Edelmann's *Selbstbiographie*, Berlin 1849.

9 P. Tillich, *A History of Christian Thought* (London, 1968), 292.

10 D. F. Strauss, *Gesammelte Schriften* (Bonn, 1877), V, 233.

11 D. F. Strauss, *Das Leben Jesu* (Tübingen, 1837), I, 15.

12 D. F. Strauss, *Die Christliche Glaubenslehre* (Tübingen, 1840), I, 99.

13 J. C. Edelmann, *Sämtliche Schriften*, hrsg. v. W. Grossmann (Stuttgart-Bad Cannstatt, 1972), VII, I, 109.

14 *Ibid.*

15 Reimarus, *Apologie*, I, 285-86.

16 J. C. Edelmann, *Sämtliche Schriften*, hrsg. v. W. Grossmann (Stuttgart-Bad Cannstatt, 1969), IX, 313.

17 *Ibid.*, 250. The evident indebtedness of Edelmann and Reimarus to Johann Conrad Dippel deserves attention. Such study is helped by Karl-Ludwig Voss *Christianus Democritus, Das Menschenbild bei Dippel* (Leiden, 1970).

18 Reimarus, *Apologie*, II, 468. On Reimarus cf. also the introduction by G. W. Buchanan to H. S. Reimarus, *The Goal of Jesus and His Disciples*, introduction and translation by G. W. Buchanan (Leiden, 1970)

19 *Ibid.*, I, 104.

20 *Ibid.*, 129.

21 J. C. Edelmann, *Sämtliche Schriften*, IX, 206.

22 Reimarus, *Apologie*, II, 482.

23 *Ibid.*, I, 35.

24 A. Schweitzer, *The Quest of the Historical Jesus* (London, 1954), 15.

25 Reimarus, *Apologie*, I, 41.

26 D. F. Strauss, *Gesammelte Schriften*, V, 249.

27 J. C. Edelmann, *Sämtliche Schriften* IX, 12.

28 Reimarus, *Apologie*, II, 365.

29 *Ibid.*, I, 29.

30 *Ibid.*, 41.

31 *Ibid.*, 15.

32 F. Jacobi, *Spinoza-Büchlein*, hrsg. v. F. Mauthner (München, 1921), 65-66.

33 *Ibid.*, 67.

34 *Ibid.*, 201. For a full discussion cf. Alexander Altmann, "Lessing und Jacobi: Das Gespräch über den Spinozismus," *Lessing Yearbook*, 3 (1971).

35 I. Kant, *Kritik der reinen Vernunft*, hrsg. v. Th. Valentiner (Leipzig, 1913), 39.

36 G. Lukacs, *Die Zerstörung der Vernunft* (Neuwied, 1962), IX, 89.

37 H. Heine, *Werke und Briefe* (Berlin, 1961), V, 221.

Note sur la théorie de la tolérance chez Pierre Bayle

ELISABETH LABROUSSE

Comme on le sait, le plaidoyer des Lumières en faveur de la tolérance religieuse n'a guère fait que diffuser, monnayer, vulgariser des conceptions exposées dès la fin du XVIIe siècle (en 1686 et 1689, respectivement) par Bayle et par Locke, le premier sous un pseudonyme, le second sous le voile de l'anonymat. Bayle a décrit la cruauté des persécutions, tout en soulignant leur inutilité, si l'on avait vraiment cherché à persuader leurs victimes; il a aussi frappé ses lecteurs par les analyses où il montrait que les efforts immenses déployés pour asseoir le monopole d'une religion d'Etat sont complètement superflus, pareil monopole n'entraînant aucun avantage réel pour celui-ci, à qui, en revanche, le pluralisme religieux est profitable. Le programme utilitariste et pragmatiste des hommes du XVIIIe siècle accorde une importance majeure à de tels arguments, qui cependant ne sont pas les plus décisifs pour Bayle. On ne retrouve au XVIIIe siècle ni la logique rigoureuse de ses considérations spéculatives, ni la hardiesse de ses conclusions: ainsi la plupart des ténors des Lumières renoncent à réclamer la tolérance pour les athées que la problématique de Bayle exigeait.

La pensée de Locke est directement tributaire des théories développées en Angleterre pendant l'interrègne, dont les dix dernières années avaient représenté une expérience de tolérance effective—sinon totale—riche de promesses à long terme pour la culture britannique. Mais, imprimés en anglais, ces textes sont restés inaccessibles pour Bayle. Dans le surgissement de sa conception de la tolérance, l'expérience personnelle et les événements semblent avoir été décisifs: ce qui l'a marqué, ce fut la Révocation de l'Edit de Nantes, la mort en prison de son frère Jacob et aussi la tolérance de fait qui règnait en Hollande, en vertu des lois et surtout de l'attitude libérale des magistrats, précisons-le, car les Synodes, "flamands" ou "wallons", se complaisaient volontiers aux anathèmes, bien que leurs victimes n'en aient pas subi de conséquences trop fâcheuses.

Idéologiquement, Bayle ne s'est pas reconnu de prédécesseur, en matière de doctrine de la tolérance: lui, si modeste en général, parle avec une surprenante condescendance de Castellion et de son idéal irénique, par exemple.

En effet, nous venons de le rappeler en faisant allusion aux Synodes, on ne saurait assez souligner combien parfaitement intolérantes étaient la théologie et l'ecclésiologie des Eglises Réformées. Le calvinisme avait conservé intacte la notion catholique d'église multitudiniste, couvrant tout un territoire et en embrassant toute la population grâce à un monopole exclusif. Seule la "Réforme radicale"–anabaptistes, sociniens, quakers, etc.–avait tiré les conséquences logiques de l'individualisme religieux implicite dans la crise de la Réforme, qui conduit si aisément au volontarisme de la Secte. Les grandes confessions réformées, en revanche, jusqu'au XVIIIe siècle, étaient restées très proches du catholicisme quant à leur dogmatisme ingénu et à leur conception du pouvoir civil comme "bras séculier" de l'Eglise. L'érastianisme et le Droit Divin des Princes, s'ils ne ralliaient pas tous les théoriciens–la théocratie conservait des partisans en Ecosse, par exemple–, représentaient l'idéologie rêvée partout où la Réforme avait triomphé, car, au XVIIe siècle, leur signification était avant tout anti-romaine. Le principe *hujus regio cujus religio* n'avait que des avantages là où le Prince se trouvait appartenir à la "bonne religion." Cependant il va de soi qu'en France, les Huguenots, ces minoritaires, devaient le modifier en hypergallicanisme, arme de choix à l'encontre des prétentions usurpatrices du Saint Siège, mais simultanément, épée à double tranchant, puisqu'au moment de la Révocation Louis XIV enjoignit à ses sujets réformés de passer au catholicisme, en vertu d'une conception de ses droits régaliens à peine plus exorbitante que celle qu'exposaient les théoriciens huguenots depuis plus d'un demi siècle. Exemple éclatant de l'emprise du Droit Divin, le Réfugié Pierre Jurieu caressa un temps l'espoir d'une conversion de Louis XIV (ou du Grand Dauphin) au protestantisme et en pareil cas, le théologien de Rotterdam aurait reconnu de bon coeur au roi de France le droit et, par conséquent, le devoir, d'imposer sa propre religion à ses sujets! Mieux que tout autre, cet exemple instructif révèle l'ascendant de l'érastianisme sur les auteurs protestants français.

C'est peut-être sous cette perspective qu'apparaît le mieux l'originalité de Bayle, qui retrouve par des voies propres les théories des Sectaires. Son système repose ici sur deux distinctions fondamentales qui contribuent l'une et l'autre à désolidariser l'Etat de l'Eglise (Ce qui est un axiome de départ chez Locke est une conclusion laborieusement acquise chez Bayle).

1) La première distinction est celle de la théorie et de la pratique, de la profession de dogmes ou de principes religieux ou métaphysiques et du comportement concret et effectif d'un individu donné. On a parfois su gré à Bayle d'avoir affirmé l'autonomie de la morale, en oubliant trop que la constatation qui l'y conduit est à ses yeux un fait déplorable et scandaleux. Les fautes, les vices, les péchés, les crimes des chrétiens "de bouche" sont pour lui une donnée d'expérience plus significative encore que ne saurait l'être la vertu admirable de certains athées (tel Spinoza); les observations de Bayle se présentent dans un contexte d'extrême pessimisme anthropologique. Comment ne pas déplorer que l'homme soit une créature inconsistante et déchirée, qu'il tire d'un Evangile d'amour l'injonction perverse de martyriser les minoritaires!

De ces constatations navrantes, il découle que le "civisme" du comportement (sa moralité, au sens superficiel du terme), explicable par le tempérament, l'amour propre, l'intérêt bien entendu et le sentiment de l'honneur de l'individu, ne doit rien aux dogmes que celui-ci professe croire. Un athée cesse donc d'être, en tant que tel, un danger social, en même temps qu'un chrétien convaincu a cessé d'être, *ipso facto*, un homme vertueux et un citoyen modèle; autrement dit, l'orthodoxie n'est plus une garantie d'orthopraxie. Or, le pouvoir civil—le Magistrat— ne s'intéresse, par vocation, qu'à cette dernière; dès lors que l'orthodoxie ne représente en rien le critère assuré d'un comportement socialement inoffensif, les autorités politiques perdent tout motif de choyer une Eglise d'Etat au point de maltraiter les hérétiques pour lui complaire. Il n'y a plus de délit d'opinion.

2) Bayle arrive à une conclusion identique en vertu d'une seconde distinction, qui le sépare des iréniques et des utopistes, ces "tolérants à outrance" qui prêchent si vainement une charité généralisée et pèchent, en somme, par angélisme. Il est assez informé, réaliste et anticlérical pour s'être convaincu que les théologiens professionnels, ces aigres boutefeux, ne tomberont jamais d'accord; les *adiaphora* des uns sont invariablement des "points fondamenteux" pour les autres, parce qu'en réalité, dans leurs débats, ils ne cherchent ni la vérité (puisque chacun croit déjà la posséder), ni l'entente fraternelle; l'orgueil, l'arrogance, la rancune, la volonté de puissance qui s'y déchaînent ne laissent aucune chance de succès au projet naïf de quelques "bonnes âmes." La seule issue consiste à distinguer tolérance civile et tolérance ecclésiastique et à ne préconiser que la première. L'intolérance ecclésiastique, telle que Bayle l'a vu règner en Hollande, perd le plus clair, sinon de son caractère odieux, du moins, de ses dangers pour ses victimes, une fois que le magistrat cesse de renforcer les verdicts des théologiens par la

sanction des lois civiles. Les irénistes qui cherchent à réunir les confessions chrétiennes ne se payent pas moins d'illusions que ceux qui sont en quête de la pierre philosophale! Bayle tranche le noeud gordien: il faut—mais *il suffit*—que le pouvoir civil comprenne enfin quels sont les intérêts réels de l'Etat, entité temporelle que la moralité effective des citoyens ou des sujets intéresse seule; si dans leur conduite, ils respectent les lois, leurs options spéculatives doivent être complètement indifférentes aux autorités. Puisque les convictions théoriques des hommes sont dépourvues de conséquences pratiques—elles ne déterminent pas leurs actions, tout au plus leur servent-elles de prétextes—le magistrat n'a qu'à laisser les théologiens fulminer leurs anathèmes et leurs excommunications en se gardant bien de les sanctionner par des conséquences civiles.

Donc, pour Bayle, le dogmatisme religieux se trouve cantonné dans la vie privée: s'il n'est pas d'un intérêt vital pour l'Etat de se soucier des Eglises, la religion devient inéluctablement une affaire individuelle. On trouve par conséquent, chez Bayle, l'essentiel des thèses que les hommes des Lumières adopteront en la matière. Cependant, c'est dédaigneusement que les auteurs du XVIIIe siècle (Rousseau est ici l'exception) concèdent une portée civilement nulle aux convictions religieuses, ces excentricités anodines. Souvenons-nous de l'ironie de Voltaire face à l'opiniâtreté ridicule des Huguenots! Le défenseur de Calas et de Sirven juge leur engagement religieux une sottise, s'il refuse passionnément qu'une sottise autorise à faire couler le sang de qui la professe. En revanche, chez Bayle, la théorie de la conscience est une explicitation fervente de l'individualisme religieux de la Réforme et du thème du sacerdoce universel, puisque la conscience de chacun est le lieu privilégié de ses rapports avec Dieu. Bayle universalise le caractère sacré de la conscience en s'attachant à la considération de sa forme seule, abstraction faite de son contenu; fût-elle errante, la conscience de chaque individu a droit au respect scrupuleux de tous. C'est ici Rousseau et Kant, bien plutôt que Voltaire, de qui Bayle est l'annonciateur.

Persécuter un homme à cause de ce qu'il croit est non seulement inefficace et superflu, c'est en outre un crime contre l'humanité et c'est pour comble un effroyable péché, une sanglante insulte à la divinité elle-même. Le poids relatif de ces divers arguments change très significativement de Bayle à ses admirateurs du XVIIIe siècle, parce que la société autour d'eux s'est de plus en plus éloignée du modèle médiéval. La sécularisation accélérée a fait d'un crime de "lèse-majesté divine" un anachronisme; l'affaire du chevalier de La Barre attestera un monstrueux décalage entre l'opinion et la législation. En revanche, le service de l'intérêt bien entendu de la société s'imposera de plus en plus comme un impératif essentiel.

La Peyrère, the Abbé Grégoire, and the Jewish Question in the Eighteenth Century

RICHARD H. POPKIN

The discussions of Jewish 'Emancipation' from the French Revolution up to Napoleon's decrees deal mostly with the social, political, and economic motives and problems involved, and with the Enlightenment ideology that furthered the extension of the rights of man to everyone, regardless of religious creed.[1] It is only to a lesser extent that religious issues have been treated, and that the forces pressing for Jewish 'Emancipation' have been placed in the context of either Christian or Jewish eschatology of the time.[2]

When Jews first became citizens of a modern Western state, in the newly formed United States of America in the beginning of 1789, no serious political or religious debate preceded the event, and no significant implications were seen in either the Jewish or Christian worlds.[3] However, a few months later, when at the outset of the French Revolution the abbé Grégoire proposed that French Jews should be made citizens, many voices anticipated all sorts of far-reaching consequences, both to Christian and Jewish theologies, and to political and social structures.[4]

As has been pointed out in studies of Grégoire, most recently in Ruth Necheles' biography of him, the good abbé's interest and concern with the Jewish problem arose principally from his Jansenist millenarianism. The

'Emancipation' of the Jews for Grégoire was a crucial step that had to be achieved before the commencement of the Messianic Age would or could begin.[5]

What I want to examine, in this paper is the role played by a special French Messianic theory, that of Isaac La Peyrère, in providing the rationale for Grégoire's views and actions, and later, for Napoleon's, with regard to the Jews. Grégoire's first, and basic statement of his views appeared in his contribution to the question posed by the Society of the Sciences and Arts of Metz, "How to make the Jews happy and useful in France? " Grégoire's *Essai sur la régéneration physique, morale et politique des Juifs* of 1787, presented his case. There, he sees the state of the Jews since the dispersion after the Fall of the Temple as deplorable. Most of the sad situation that had led to the present degenerate state of the Jews he believes to be the result of Christian actions—anti-semitic legislation, maltreatment of Jews, miserable living conditions in ghettoes, unworthy marginal occupations like money-lending forced upon them, precarious political existence, and so on. His solution is to make the Jews citizens and abolish anti-semitic regulations so as to give Jews the opportunity to live healthy, decent French lives and to bring about a regeneration of them in most respects. The Jews, Grégoire sees as slightly responsible for their own situation since they were keeping themselves in ignorance and superstition through their concentration or rabbinic fantasies and of false Messianic expectations. Enlightenment education would break the bonds of their self-imposed moral and intellectual degeneracy. Grégoire argues that the cases of the Dutch economist, Isaac de Pinto, and the German philosopher, Moses Mendelssohn, already had shown the creative Jewish genius that could emerge from the liberation of Jews from their ghetto mentality.[6]

What Grégoire saw as the outcome of Jewish emancipation was a crucial stage in the march towards the Messianic kingdom. Prior to the Revolution, Jansenist millenarians had written lots of works on the Recall or Return of the Jews as the crucial antecedent event to the Second Coming, and they were offering schemes for bringing the Jews back to the mainstream of European life through conversion by love, not force, to Christianity. The reunion of Jews and Christians was believed to be critical to the culmination of human history.[7] Grégoire appears to be on the extreme edge of this movement in wanting to prepare the ground for the end of the world by making the Jews citizens and by encouraging their self-liberation through Enlightenment education. The first two measures Grégoire pressed for in the Revolution were Jewish citizenship and state control of the Church. He was not in favor of an active conversionist program, because he felt that only God could decide when the Jews would become self-motivated to join the Christians and thus bring about the Millennium. In the meantime, the baleful effects of anti-semitism could be removed, and the Jews could be enlightened.[8]

In presenting his theory, Grégoire used a vast range of Jewish and Christian sources, including the views of the heretical Messianist, Isaac La Peyrère, 1596-1676.[9] La Peyrère's most famous work—indeed it was notorious—is *Prae-Adamitae, Men before Adam* (1655),[10] in which he advances the views that the Bible is not the history of all mankind, but only the history of the Jews, that Adam was not the first man, but only the first Jew; and that the existing text of the Bible is not accurate and was not written by Moses. To these he adds many other heresies. The immediate effects of La Peyrère's views was to launch the Higher Criticism of the Bible, and a polygenetic interpretation of human origins in which most if not all of mankind was seen as developing outside of any Providential framework.[11]

Grégoire saw that the upshot of La Peyrère's many heresies was to isolate Jewish history as Divine history, and to show that the culminating events in Jewish history were about to occur in France—the conversion of the Jews, the rebuilding of Palestine by the converts, and the establishment of the Messianic world, to be run by the Jewish Messiah, and his temporal aide, the King of France, with his court of Jewish Christians.[12] The enormous number of refutations of La Peyrère in the seventeenth and eighteenth centuries deal primarily with his pre-Adamite theory, and his denial of the Mosaic authorship of the Pentateuch.[13] Grégoire ignored these features, and just discussed what appears in La Peyrère's dedication of the work to all of the Synagogues of the world—the conversion of the Jews, the return of the Jew to Jerusalem, and the rebuilding of the Temple. In *Essai sur la régénération physique, morale et politique des juifs,* Grégoire quotes the text, and then summarizes the French nationalist Messianism that appeared in La Peyrère's *Du Rappel des Juifs.*[14] (At this point Grégoire had not seen the work, only a summary of it.) Regarding the role La Peyrère gave for France and its king in the Messianic Drama, Grégoire finds "Les preuves de l'auteur sont convaincantes." His argument includes the view that the King of France has the power of curing the inveterate maladies of the souls of the Jews, and that France will probably be the place where the Jews will be first invited to become Christians.[15]

It may be that Grégoire took La Peyrère's heretical French Messianism seriously prior to the Revolution; his actions at the outset of the Revolution can be seen as a secularized version of La Peyrère's grand scheme. Part of La Peyrère's program was to bring the Jews to France, because it is the land of "liberty" [*sic!* so written in 1641]; to eliminate anti-semitism, because it kept Jews from converting; to create a Jewish-Christian Church which would have no doctrines, dogmas, or practices offensive to Jews; and then to await the moment when the Recall of the Jews to France and to the Jewish-Christian Church would lead to God's ushering in the Messianic Age.[16] Grégoire from 1789 onward was fighting for a Jewish-Christian egalitarian republican state in France. The Church would be regenerated by being state controlled. The state would be regenerated by eliminating the king and all vestiges of privilege. And the Jews would be regenerated by living in such a state, as equal citizens with everybody else. The regeneration of the Church, the State, and the Jews, and their reunion in Revolutionary France would set the stage for God's further intervention in history, first by making the Jews want to join the Christians, and then by producing the Millennium. [17]

This is probably a fair assessment of Grégoire's vision at the beginning of the Revolution. If so, then it may be said that La Peyrère's scenario in secularized form began to unfold for the believers at this time. The Constitutional Church was established, the Jews were officially made citizens, the king was deposed, the Republic proclaimed. In addition, Grégoire kept pushing for a more thorough moral and spiritual housecleaning—the liberation of mulattoes and blacks, the abolition of slavery, the recognition of Haiti, and the creation of the pure Church in Haiti, for example.[18]

The events of the Terror, the fall of Robespierre, and so on may have made political and social observers see the course of events in purely secular terms, but for the eschatologist, signs were everywhere. The Young Bonaparte overthrew the Pope, who in Grégoire's view was the anti-Christ. In 1798, a proclamation was issued in Napoleon's name, right after he left for Egypt, to the Jews of Africa and Asia, urging them to join Napoleon in rebuilding the Temple in Jerusalem.[19] To understand the implications of this announcement, one must know that Jews have been praying since Titus destroyed Jerusalem in 70 A.D. for the rebuilding of the Temple. It is a major theme in Jewish services, an event that it is hoped God will bring about as a central episode in the Redemption of Israel. In traditional Judaism only God can bring about this crucial event, which is foreseen as the beginning of the Messianic Age.[20] Julian the Apostate had proposed rebuilding the Temple. Some visionaries in the seventeenth century, like La Peyrère, proposed either that the Jewish Christian do it or that the pure Christian do it. But in Orthodox Judaism it is still not conceivable that human beings can or should accomplish this feat. It is something that only the Holy One, blessed be He, can bring about when He sees fit. Yet Napoleon Bonaparte proposed undertaking this eschatological building project!

The importance of Napoleon's proposal was not lost on the visionaries of the time, though apparently they understood that he and France where instruments of God's will. The great Irish revolutionist, Wolfe Tone, who had been urging Napoleon to help the Irish rebellion of 1798, was thunderstruck when he read the proclamation.

> With regard to this last country, in which Palestine is included, I
> see today an article in the *Telegraph* which, has struck me very

much. It is a proposal to invite the Jews from all quarters of the world to return to their parent country and restore their ancient temple; it has not struck me so much in a political, as in a far different point of view. I remember Whitley Stokes, more than once, mentioned to me an opinion of his, founded on an attentive study and meditation of the Old and New Testament, that he did not despair, even in his own lifetime and mine, of seeing this great event take place; and I remember I laughed at him heartily for his opinion, which, however, seems this day far less visionary than it was at that time, in 1793. It is now not only possible, but highly probable, that the Jews may be once more collected and the temple restored. The French will naturally take care to stipulate for advantages in return, and there is a giant's stride made at once into Asia, the extent and consequences of which I am at this moment utterly unable to calculate or perhaps to comprehend. I see every day more and more, that after ten years of war and the defeat of all the despots of Europe united, the French Revolution is but yet begun; the Hercules is yet in swaddling bands. What a people! Combining this intended measure with the downfall of the Pope, already accomplished, I have no doubt but a person who had made the prophecies and revelations his study (Stokes for example), might build very extraordinary systems.[21]

Another Irish revolutionist, Thomas Corbet, submitted a plan to the Directory which proposed that the hopes of the Jews to be reestablished as a nation in Palestine, hopes based on "an abundance of prophecies," will be fulfilled by the French government. The Jews may "prefer France as their temporary home but, at the same time looking at themselves merely as wanderers, they would feel that they are not yet the Jewish people. It is for France to grant them a territory on which to lay the foundations of their restored Republic." To do this, Corbet suggested a union of the Jews, the French army under Napoleon, and the Irish revolutionaries. Using Jewish money, secret societies of Jews and Irish revolutionaries, and the French military might, the world would be transformed. The reestablishment of the Jews in Palestine would affect everybody: "Assuredly, even China would feel the influence of their return."[22]

Corbet's plan, which only became known to scholars when some of Napoleon's papers were sold in 1951, amounts to a conspiracy for taking over the world, with the Jewish goal of return to Israel as its core. Apparently the first version of the Protocols of the Elders of Zion was written to expose this.[23] Corbet's brother became a commander in Napoleon's army in Egypt, but nonetheless this Messianic scheme came to naught.[24]

Grégoire kept seeing signs of the unfolding of the events he so fervently hoped for, but Napoleon in many ways was frustrating them. The Concordat and the gutting of the Constitutional Church, the failure to enforce Jewish citizenship, the refusal to recognize Haiti led to a grim evaluation of Napoleon's role in Grégoire's scenario.[25] Then, in the great year of the Napoleonic reign, 1806, things took a new turn, and La Peyrère's vision seemed to be becoming reality. Napoleon had won a string of great victories, had deposed the kings of the earth (and replaced them with his relatives), and in the midst of all this, had suddenly announced that he was calling the Grand Sanhedrin into session. The Sanhedrin last met just before Titus conquered Jerusalem and destroyed the Temple. It is the only body that can change Jewish law, and it can only be reconstituted by the Messiah when He comes. The reconvening of the Sanhedrin is another of the great events anticipated by the Jews, but only when it pleases God to bring Jewish history to its culmination.[26]

The Napoleonic Sanhedrin is usually considered a joke by Jewish historians.[27] Its meeting is portrayed by French historians as a political ploy to gain Jewish support, to settle the problem of usury in Alsace, and to gain control of the Jewish population.[28] However, many contemporaries, reared in the religious interpretations of events, saw it differently. English and German millenarians saw it as the sign the Messiah had returned.[29] Catholic opponents of Napoleon saw it as an attempt by Napoleon to proclaim himself the Messiah of the Jews, when he was in fact the anti-Christ.[30] Martin Buber, in his novel *For the Sake of Heaven*, portrays a Hasidic group in Poland trying to figure out Napoleon's place in the Messianic scheme of things.[31]

Napoleon seems to have understood the significance of what he was doing (he may have gotten the idea from a proposal by one of Mendelssohn's disciples);[32] and he seems also to have understood the need to do it in convincing fashion. He first appointed an assembly of Jewish Notables and proposed twelve questions to them, which would determine whether Jews could be genuine French citizens and whether Jewish Law could be put in line with French law. Napoleon had decided the answers in advance. The Assembly was then to appoint the members of the Sanhedrin, according to the formula of ancient Judaism. Finally the Sanhedrin was to ratify and promulgate the revised Jewish Law throughout the world.[33]

Aside from the logistical details of the operation, Napoleon, Grégoire, and the Jewish leaders each had a different view of what was going on and what it all hoped to achieve, Napoleon observes, "Depuis la prise de Jérusalem par Titus, un aussi gran nombre d'hommes éclaires, appartenant à la religion de Moïse, n'avaient pu se réunir."[34]

At the gathering of the Sanhedrin itself, Napoleon was to offer a solemn assurance. "On n'exige des Juifs ni l'abandon de leur religion, ni aucune modification qui repugne à sa lettre ou à son espirit."[35] Then he was to blame what was wrong with Judaism on persecution, rabbinical reactions, and the

Talmud (practically the same diagnosis as Grégoire had offered). The Sanhedrin's decisions were to rank with the Talmud, and even replace it, if possible. The decisons were to form "une second législation des Juifs, qui, conservant la caractère essentiel de celle de Moïse, s'adapte à la situation présente des Juifs, à nos moeurs et à nos usages."[36] After presenting his questions, and the answers the Sanhedrin would have to give, Napoleon concludes that he would preserve Jewish rights—"je désire prendre tous les moyens pour que les droits qui ont été restitués au peuple juifs ne soient pas illusoires, et, enfin, pour leur faire trouver Jérusalem dans la France."[37]

Napoleon's vision in 1806 was that the Jews would be citizens and would become just like other Frenchmen, except for their religion. This would be the end of the Diaspora; the first crucial development in Jewish history since the Fall of Jerusalem. The Jews would belong to a country—France—and France would be the New Jerusalem. It would no longer be necessary, as planned in 1798, to rebuild the Temple, or to move the Jews back to Palestine.

To reinforce this new Messianic version of the culmination of Jewish history, it was arranged that certain events would take place during the meeting of the Assembly of Jewish Notables. Like Sabbatai Zevi before him, Napoleon changed religious holidays. He declared his birthday, August 15, to be no longer Assumption Day but the Festival of Napoleon.[38] He issued a coin showing himself giving the Ten Commandments to Moses.[39] He got the Jewish notables to celebrate his birthday in the Synagogue, with his name and Josephine's put up next to the name of God, *and* he had his Imperial Eagle placed over the Holy Ark.[40] (The revolt that led to the Fall of Jerusalem and the Diaspora was precipitated when the Roman Imperial Eagle was placed in the Temple. Jewish history had come full circle. The Jews accepted Napoleon's Eagle, and the Diaspora came to an end—they were French citizens.)

The Jewish version of the matter, as expressed in the speeches on Napoleon's birthday, is in some ways similar. The achievement of citizenship was portrayed as the redemption of Israel from the Diaspora, as *the* or *a* crucial turning point in Jewish history. Napoleon was portrayed as being above country, religion or time, God's agent who had made a new stage of Judaism possible.[41] As Jacob Katz in his new book, *Out of the Ghetto*, shows, prior to the late eighteenth century, the issue of Jewish citizenship was not pressed by the Jews. They wanted legal residency rights, but they considered themselves temporary residents of European countries while they were waiting for the Messiah to bring them back to Palestine. Under the impact of the Enlightenment, Messianism was transformed for many into a drive to end the Diaspora by becoming citizens of modern nations.[42] Napoleon's desire to make France the New Jerusalem coincided with many Jewish leaders' desire to become *French* Jews, *German* Jews or *Italian* Jews, and to become part of the Enlightenment world. In the speech by the president of the Sanhedrin, the leading Talmudist from Strassbourg, Rabbi David Zinzheim, began by saying "this day is a day of joy, for us such as our nation has never witnessed." He then traced the sad history of the Jews since the Fall of Jerusalem. It was his view that things had begun to get better with the dawn of enlightened philosophy in the Renaissance. And now with the Enlightenment, with Napoleon, and with citizenship a genuinely new era was beginning.[43] Rabbi Segre of Italy believed that the time had come when the Jews would become useful citizens, scientists, and so on. The degradation that started with the Fall of the Temple was over.[44]

Just as this orgy of appreciation for the new form of Jewish existence was taking place, the Paris newspapers announced the discovery of "un livre aussi rare que singulier," Isaac La Peyrère's *Du Rappel des Juifs*.[45] The *Gazette de France* for August 28, 1806, said that everyone was talking about the meeting of the Jewish Synod, and then gave a summary of La Peyrère's opus of 1643, that predicted the Jews and Christian would be reunited in France, forming the basis for the New Age which would be run politically by "un roi universel," the King of France. And here it was all happening, in a Jewish-Christian state, under the aegis of the universal monarch, Napoleon of France. The full text of La Peyrère gave a more monumental interpretation to the events, and apparently underwrote Napoleon's Messianic pretensions. (The French government was apparently the source for the newspaper accounts.)

Thanks to Professor Necheles and Madame Labrousse I have obtained a photocopy of the notes of Grégoire's secretary on this event.[46] Grégoire was involved in the Sanhedrin affair as an adviser and consultant to the Jewish leaders. He, of course, was delighted at the prospect of genuine citizenship for the Jews, and of the modification of Jewish law that would help assimilate the Jews into the Napoleonic Empire. The notes show that Grégoire obtained his own copy of La Peyrère on September 11, 1806, that he had his secretary research all the information available about it, copy the most Messianic portions about the significance of the reunion of Jews and Christians in France, and make a summary of the whole work.[47]

For some of those involved, La Peyrère's French Messianism provided the theological interpretation of the amazing events of 1806 and 1807 (when the official Sanhedrin met, and ratified the decisions of the Assembly of Jewish Notables). The Jews were now real citizens of France, Germany, Italy, and Holland. It was not just a political event, it was taken to be the Regeneration of the Jews. The Diaspora had ended. And for Napoleon, and some of the Jewish leaders, the Jewish-Christian Napoleonic Empire was the Enlightenment form of the Messianic Kingdom. Napoleon had said "that Jews ought to behave, in all places where they are citizens, as though they were in Jerusalem itself."[48]

The Sanhedrin only met in 1807, when it gave Napoleon the right to put Jewish political law in line with the Code Napoleon. He did this with a vengeance in 1808, in his so-called "Infamous Decrees," in which he put Grégoire's assimilationist policies into force by fiat, forcing the Jews of Alsace to give up illegal usury, to take up ordinary French occupations, and to allow political control of the rabbis. Though the lasting effect of French Jewish policy from the beginning of the Revolution until the time of Napoleon has indeed been the Emancipation of the Jews in Western Europe, that policy is also responsible for the creation of secular anti-semitism as a reaction to it.

In this paper I have tried to show how the problem of Jewish citizenship grew, at least in part, out of Messianic interpretations of what was going on by Grégoire and Napoleon, and how Jewish leaders saw citizenship as *a* or *the* redemptive stage of Jewish history, ending the Diaspora. Thus religious currents, spurred on by reinterpretations of La Peyrère's French Messianism helped bring forth some of the liberating policies of the Revolution. Grégoire could say, after the meeting of the Sanhedrin, that the vulgar will only find human and political events involved, "mais les hommes éclairés par la révélation rattachent cet evénément à des espérances d'un ordre surnaturel."[49] Without such an interpretation, based on La Peyrère's scenario, the Emancipation of the Jews might not have occurred in France, or might not have been seen as crucial to the whole upheaval taking place.

NOTES

1 See, for instance, Arthur Hertzberg, *The French Enlightenment and the Jews* (New York, 1968); and Zosa Szajkowski, *Jews and the French Revolutions of 1789, 1830 and 1848* (New York, 1970).

2 To some extent this is done in the recent work by Jacob Katz, *Out of the Ghetto, The Social Background of Jewish Emancipation 1770-1870* (Cambridge, Mass., 1973).

3 Jews became citizens of the United States with the ratification of the U.S. Constitution and of the Bill of Rights in the beginning of 1789. The constitutional debates do not indicate that the matter of Jewish citizenship raised any theological or political questions. However, there were cases where state constitutions prevented Jews from holding office, and these regulations had to be challenged and were declared unconstitutional.

4 For details of the debates on Jewish emancipation during the French Revolution, see Hertzberg, *op. cit.*, Chap. X.

5 Ruth Necheles, *The Abbé Grégoire 1787-1831, The Odyssey of an Egalitarian* (Westport, Conn., 1971), Chaps. 1 and 2. The benevolence of Grégoire's views was challenged by W. Rabi in his *Anatomie du Judaisme français* (Paris, 1962), Chap. 1. He was answered by Paul Grunebaum-Ballin in his "Grégoire convertisseur? ou la croyance au 'Retour d'Israel,' " *Revue de Études Juifs*, 121 (1962), 383-407.

6 Henri Grégoire, *Essai sur la régénération physique, morale et politique des juifs* (Metz, 1789). This work appeared in English at London in 1791.

7 There were a great number of works on the subject in the second half of the eighteenth century, such as Jules Deschamps, *Rappel futur des Juifs* (Paris, 1760); Laurent Etienne Rondet, *Dissertation sur le rappel des Juifs* (Paris, 1777); François Malot, *Dissertation sur l'epoque du rappel des Juifs* (Avignon [?], 1776); and Charles François Desfours de la Génetière, *Avis aux catholiques sur le caractère et les signes des temps ou nous vivions, ou De la conversion des Juifs, de l'avènement intermediare de Jesus-Christ et de son regne visible sur la terre* (Lyon, 1794).

8 Necheles, *op. cit.*, Chap. 1.

9 On La Peyrère see Don Cameron Allen, *The Legend of Noah* (Urbana, Ill., 1963), pp. 86-90 and 130-37; David R. McKee, "Isaac de la Peyrère, a Precursor of the Eighteenth-Century English Critical Deists," *PMLA*, 59 (1944), 355-61, 379, 399, 420-24 and 430; Hans Joachim Schoeps, *Philosemitismus im Barok* (Tubingen, 1952), pp. 3-18; Leo Strauss, *Spinoza's Critique of Religion*, trans. by E. M. Sinclair (New York, 1965), Chap. III; and R. H. Popkin, "The Marrano Theology of Isaac La Peyrère," *Studi internazionale di filosofia* (1973), pp. 97-125.

10 The work appeared in Latin in three editions published by Elzivier, one published in Basel, and one not identified; all in 1655. The next year the work appeared in an English translation, and in 1661 in Dutch. It was widely condemned and there were many, many refutations of it. The author was arrested and forced to recant.

11 On La Peyrère's role in the development of Bible criticism, see the works cited in note 9, as well as Adolphe Lods, "Astruc et la critique biblique de son temps," *Revue de'Histoire et de Philosophie religieuses* (1924), pp. 109-39 and 201-27; Klaus Scholder, *Ursprünge und Probleme der Bibelkritik im 17 Jahrhundert* (Munich, 1966); and R. H. Popkin, "Bible Criticism and Social Science," *Boston Studies in the Philosophy of Science*, XIV, 339-60.

La Peyrère's polygenetic theory played an important role in the development of anthropology, and of anthropological racism. On this see R. H. Popkin, "The Pre-Adamite Theory in the Renaissance," *Festschrift* for Paul Oskar Kristeller, forthcoming; "The Philosophical Basis of Eighteenth-Century Racism," *Studies in Eighteenth-Century Culture*, 3 (1973), 245-62; and "The Philosophical Bases of Modern Racism," *Essays in Honor of Herbert W. Schneider*, forthcoming.

12 Grégoire, *op. cit.*, pp. 228-29.

13 There were a very great number of refutations of La Peyrère in the seventeenth and eighteenth centuries. Not only were many books specifically written against his theories, but also his theories were discussed and answered in many theological and scholarly works.

14 Grégoire, *op. cit.*, pp. 228-29

15 *Ibid.*

16 Isaac La Peyrère, *Du Rappel des Juifs* (Paris, 1643).

17 Necheles, *op. cit.*, Chap. 2.

18 Grégoire's career, and his radical egalitarian reform projects, are treated in detail in Professor Necheles' study.

19 The proclamation was apparently published in Paris newspapers of the time. The great Irish revolutionist, Theobald Wolfe Tone, described it in his *Autobiography*, entry for April 21-24, 1798. *The Autobiography of Theobald Wolfe Tone 1763-1798*, ed. R. Barry O'Brien (London, 1893), II, 303-4. The proclamation is dated April 4, 1799.

20 For example, there are prayers saying, "May it be thy will, Lord our God and God of our fathers, to have mercy on us and pardon all our sins, iniquities and transgressions; and rebuild the Temple speedily in our days"; "May it be thy will, Lord our God, and God of our fathers, that the Temple be speedily rebuilt in our days"; "May the righteous rejoice over the rebuilding of thy city, the reconstruction of thy Temple, the flourishing dynasty of thy servant David and the continuance of the offspring of the anointed, the son of Jesse." *Daily Prayer Book,* translated and annotated by Philip Birnbaum (New York, 1949), pp. 28, 46, and 98. The context of these prayers, and many other similar or identical ones, is the hope that the worshipper will be alive when God chooses to rebuild the Temple, and to commence the culmination of Jewish history. It is always up to God to decide when this will happen. The same point is involved in the final wish and hope in the Passover Seder, "Next year in Jerusalem," i.e., next year we hope the *real* Passover celebration can occur, if God has chosen to rebuild Jerusalem, and bring us back to it.

21 Wolfe Tone, *Autobiography*, II, 303.

22 Letter of Thomas Corbet to Paul Barras, Lorient, the 29th Pluvoise, 7th year, printed in English translation in Louis Hyman, *The Jews of Ireland* (London and Jerusalem, 1972), pp. 237-40. Details about Corbet and the history of his letter (which was found in some of Napoleon's papers) appear in notes 15 and 16, p. 319.

23 Norman Cohn, in his *Warrant for Genocide, The Myth of the Jewish World Conspiracy and the Protocols of the Elders of Zion* (London, 1970), pp. 31-32, suggests the theory was put forth first in 1806 to oppose Napoleon's calling of the Sanhedrin. The content of the first proposal of the theory seems to fit the details of Corbet's plan.

24 Hyman, *op. cit.*, p. 319, n. 16, Thomas Corbet was killed in a duel in 1804. The Jewish governor of Turkish-controlled Jerusalem chose to oppose Napoleon and helped keep him from ever entering the city.

25 Grégoire's growing opposition to Napoleon is discussed in Necheles, *op. cit.*, Chap. 9.

26 There was a brief attempt to reconvene the Sanhedrin at Safed in Palestine in the early sixteenth century under the inspiration of some of the Kabbalists there. This came to nothing because it was not possible to determine who were the authorized members (the Messiah will decide). Last year the Askenazi Chief Rabbi of Israel, Rabbi Goren, proposed a world conference of Jewish religious leaders. This was rejected, partly, I believe, because it sounded too much like a proposal for a man-made Sanhedrin.

27 See, for instance, the recent discussions of the episode in Raphael Mahler, *A History of Modern Jewry, 1780-1815* (New York, 1971), pp. 59-72, and Norman Cohn's in *Warrant for Genocide*, p. 34; as well as the early one in Heinrich Graetz's *History of the Jews* (Philadelphia, 1895), V, 479-500; and in Simon Dubnow's *History of the Jews* (South Brunswick, 1971), IV 543-66.

28 The French literature on Napoleon is enormous. Most works ignore the calling of the Sanhedrin altogether, or have it as a surd in the midst of the great Napoleonic battles of 1806, resulting from Napoleon's having been apprized of the problem of Jewish usury when he was in Strassbourg, and quickly deciding to do something about it, between military campaigns. Given his power, Napoleon could have solved the usury problem without the rigamarole of the Assembly of Jewish Notables and the Sanhedrin, which consumed almost a year.

29 See Baruch Mevorah, "Napoleon Bonaparte," *Encyclopedia Judaica*, XII, 824-25.

30 See references given in Cohn, *op. cit.*, pp. 34-35. The French emigré journal in London, *L'Ambigu*, said, "Does he hope to form, from these children of Jacob, a legion of tyrannicides? . . . Time will show. It remains for us only to watch this Antichrist fight against the eternal decrees of God; that must be the last act of his diabolic existence." See also Louis Gabriel Ambroise Bonald, "Sur les Juifs," *Mercure de France*, 23 (1806), 249-67.

31 Martin Buber, *For the Sake of Heaven*, trans. by Ludwig Lewisohn, (Philadelphia, 1945).

32 See Katz, *op. cit.*, pp. 139-40; and the letter of Israel Jacobson printed in *Les Premiers pas de la nation vers son bonheur sous les auspices due grand monarque Napoléon* (Paris, [1806]), pp. 7-14.

33 Napoleon's letter to M. de Champagny, Rambouillet, 23 août 1806, in *Correspondance de Napoleon Ier* (Paris, 1863), XIII, No. 10686, 122-26.

34 *Ibid.*, p. 123.

35 *Ibid.*

36 *Ibid.*

37 *Ibid.*, p. 126

38 The President of the Assembly of Jewish Notables, Furtado, addressed Napoleon as follows, "Sir, Your French and Italian subjects, whatever

religion they profess, celebrate this day the anniversary of Your Majesty's birth-day; all implore the King of Kings in their respective temples that he may be pleased to pour his most signal favours on your sacred person, and on the august imperial family." *Transactions of the Parisian Sanhedrin*, translated from the original published by M. Diogene Tama, with a preface and illustrative notes by F. D. Kirwan (London, [1807]), p. 190.

The Messiah of the seventeenth century, Sabbatai Sevi, had made the changing of holidays, including changing his birthday, which was the fast day, Tisha b'Av, into a feast, a crucial part of his movement. On this, see the new work of Gershom S. Scholem, *Sabbatai Sevi: The Mystical Messiah* (Princeton, 1973), pp. 613-33.

39 This coin, of which I have a copy, was issued in 1806. The face shows a bust of Napoleon with the inscription, "Napoleon, Emp. et Roi." On the reverse side Napoleon, in Roman robes, is shown giving the tablets with the Ten Commandments to a kneeling Moses. The inscription is "Grand Sanhedrin XXX Mai MDCCCVI." The coin is still issued by the Paris mint from the original die. The only reproduction I have seen of the coin is in Ismar Elbogen, *History of the Jews after the Fall of the State of Jerusalem* (Cincinnati, 1926), facing p. 167. The reverse is described as "Napoleon receiving the Tablets of the Law," hardly what seems to be depicted.

40 The instructions for the celebration of the Festival of Napoleon in the Jewish Temple of Rue Sainte-Anne, prepared by a group of the Assembly of Jewish Notables headed by M. Rodrigues of La Gironde, appear in the *Transactions of the Paris Sanhedrin*, pp. 191-92. Besides including the music to be played (a Haydn symphony) and the hymns to be sung, there is an instruction 7, "The Temple shall be illuminated and ornamented with garlands and flowers; the Imperial Eagle shall be placed above the Altar." A description of the actual celebration appears in the *Transactions*, pp. 212-13, followed by the sermons that were given on the occasion. On p. 212 we are told, "The Temple was ornamented with taste. The name Jehovah, the cyphers, and the arms of *Napoleon* and of *Josephine* shone on every side." The editor of the English edition of the *Transactions*, F. D. Kirwan, complained "that the contagious infidelity of France had crept in among the Israelites" because "cyphers of *Napoleon* and of *Josephine* were profanely blended with the unutterable name of Jehovah, and the Imperial Eagle was placed over the Sacred Ark." Kirwan further reported many Jews were justly offended by this, pp. xiv-xv. The celebration was described without comment in Charles Malo, *Histoire de Juifs* (Paris, 1826), p. 440; but the Scottish Millenarian, James Huie, was outraged. In his *History of the Jews* (Andover, 1843), he said, "But the despicable and impious flattery of some of the really infidel Jews, whom Napoleon had gained over, effectually disgusted their conscientious brethren." After describing the placing of Napoleon's and Josephine's ciphers with the ineffable name of Jehovah, and the elevating of the imperial eagle over the Ark, he declaimed, "No Jew who really

adhered to the faith of his fathers, could for a moment tolerate such audacious adulation, which in effect placed the Creator and the creature on the same undistinguished level" (pp. 249-50).

41 See the sermons given on Napoleon's birthday, in *Transactions,* especially the one by Rabbi David Zinzheim, pp. 221-29, and the discourse by M. Avigdor (on Feb. 5, 1807), pp. 320-33.

42 Cf. Katz, *op. cit., passim.*

43 *Transactions,* pp. 222-26.

44 *Transactions,* pp. 217-21.

45 *Journal de Paris,* 29 août 1806; and *Gazette de France,* 28 août 1806. Two brief letters by "Christianus" in *Gentleman's Magazine,* 82 (1812), Part II, 432-34 and 83 (1813), Part I, 614-16, claimed that La Peyrère's *Rappel des Juifs* had never been printed until Napoleon called the Sanhedrin into session. There is no evidence that the book was reprinted in 1806, but there definitely seems to have been a revival of interest in its contents.

46 The notes by Rondeau are at the Bibliothèque de Port-Royal, and consist of two items, one "Recueil des Pieces sur Le Rappel des Juifs," which contains information from the Paris newspapers cited in n. 45, information from various biographical dictionaries and book catalogues about La Peyrère's *Rappel des Juifs,* the concluding "Advis au Lecteur" from the work, and the response of the Assembly of Jewish Notables to the twelve questions proposed to it by Napoleon (from the sessions of Aug. 4, 7, and 12, 1806); the other, "Analyse de L'Ouvrage intitulé Du Rappel des Juifs 1643 dont Isaac La Peyrère est Auteur, Faite en 1806."

I plan to reproduce and analyze these materials in a separate study in the near future.

47 "Recueil des Pieces sur Le Rappel des Juifs," p. 6 and following.

48 "Les Juifs doivent considérer, comme s'ils étaient à Jerusalem, tous les lieux où ils sont citoyens." Lettre à DeChampagny, 23 août 1806, p. 125.

49 Henri Grégoire, *Histoire des Sectes religieuses* (Paris, 1810 [1814]), I, 201. The English editor of the Sanhedrin *Transactions,* Kirwan, was sure there were some "dark purposes" behind what Napoleon was doing with regard to the Jewish nation, and decided it was part of Napoleon's conspiratorial plans to take over the Near East and to set up a wide-scale espionage system. *Preface,* esp. p. xii. A religious interpretation of Napoleon's activities of an opposite variety appears in George Stanley Faber, *A General and Connected View of the Prophecies, relative to the Conversion, Restoration, Union, and Future Glory of the Houses of Judah and Israel; The Progress, and Final Overthrow, of the Anti-Christian Confederacy in the Land of Palestine; and The Ultimate General Diffusion of Christianity* (London, 1809). Faber saw Napoleon as the head of the Anti-Christian Confederacy, who would be overcome by an English force that would bring about the conversion of the Jews and the Messianic Age, starting in Great Britain. See, for instance, I, 213-27.

The Third War
of the Musical Enlightenment

ROBERT M. ISHERWOOD

On March 31, 1780, the chevalier Christoph Willibald von Gluck wrote the following in a letter from Vienna to his friend Baron Tschudi in Paris: "But as to my going to Paris again, nothing will come of it, so long as the words 'Piccinnist' and 'Gluckist' remain current, for I am, thank God, in good health at present, and have no wish to spit bile again in Paris. . . . I shall hardly allow myself to be persuaded again to become the object of the criticism or the praise of the French nation, for they are as changeable as red cockerels. . . . I could wish that someone might come one day to take my place and to please the public with his music, so that I might be left in peace, for I am still unable to forget the tittle/tattle to which friends and foes made me listen concerning *Narcissus* and the pills I have had to swallow, for Messieurs the Frenchmen cannot yet see any difference between a musical eclogue and a 'poème épique'. . . .[1]"

The acknowledged king of European opera, Gluck had recently become the center of controversy in the third war over music of the French Enlightenment. Earlier, Gluck had conquered audiences throughout Italy and at the Viennese court with his operas in the Italian style. While still in Vienna, he had proclaimed a new philosophy of music drama to elucidate the principles behind his first great reform operas, *Orfeo* and *Alceste*. Basking in his triumphs, he had come to France to breathe new life into the declining Opéra. The reforms of Gluck and his librettist, Raniero Calzabigi, were more likely to succeed in France than in Italy because of the traditional French conception of opera as a lyric drama. Gluck's reforms were preeminently dramatic. The problem was that this was not the main direction that the *philosophes* wanted opera to follow. Their conception of reform was more musically oriented, which entailed the infusion into French opera of Italian melody. Although the socially powerful Gluckists prevailed over the heirs of the *philosophes* (Marmontel, La Harpe, Chastellux, and others) in the struggle over operatic reform, Gluck had become embittered by the war of words and had withdrawn to Vienna. Thus, in 1780 he was living in semi-retirement, refusing the appeals of his friends and the rich invitations from the Opéra to return to France. He had finished his career locked in a battle of opposing musical ideologies.

For some years historians have interpreted the musical war of the 1770's as a meaningless feud among journalists most of whom were musically ignorant. In his biography of Gluck, Martin Cooper dismisses the Gluck-Piccinni dispute as "a question of journalism."[2] More recently, Norbert Dufourcq, an outstanding musicologist, charges that the whole controversy among the *philosophes* over the merits of French and Italian opera is a "faux problème," of no importance to the music historian.[3]

A second popular view of the musical war is that Gluck was the answer to the *philosophes'* call for reform.[4] Alfred Richard Oliver, for example, cites Gluck's selection of the drama *Iphigénie en Aulide,* which Diderot commended as perfect for opera, as evidence of the concord between Gluck and the *philosophes.* Oliver finds Diderot's ideas echoed in Gluck's writings and operas, and he suggests that Diderot's refusal to take part in the Gluck-Piccinni quarrel is evidence that in the minds of the Encyclopedists the reform opera had been achieved.

Neither of these interpretations is satisfactory. In the first place the third musical war was not a brief skirmish confined to a few journalists. In fact it was only the latest battle in a continuous struggle to reform the French lyric theater. Originating in the reign of Louis XIV, musical controversy had erupted into open hostilities twice earlier in the eighteenth century: first, in the 1740's, when the combat was between the proponents of Jean-Baptiste Lully, whose works were still performed regularly at the Opéra years after his death in 1687, and the advocates of Jean-Philippe Rameau, whose works dominated the Opéra in the middle years of the century; second, in the Querelle des Bouffons of the 1750's, when the *philosophes* united in support of Italian comic opera and waged a vigorous assault on traditional French music. Although the Italian performers were expelled on the king's order in 1754 and the Querelle ended in an apparent victory for the French side, the conflicts over music were not abated. Gluck's appearance in Paris in 1773 was only a new escalation of the conflict, and the issues of the Gluck-Piccinni rivalry were in many cases variations on old themes.

Contrary to what many historians have maintained, some of the issues were very serious, at least in the minds of the writers, and they had far-ranging implications. The central issue was the dispute over the respective merits of French and Italian opera. The most partisan on both sides felt that either Italian or French opera must prevail as *the* musical style of the lyric theater. A few, more moderate spokesman argued for a fusion of styles incorporating the best of both, or for musical toleration in which both types of opera could coexist. In many ways the goal of the *philosophes* was either to press the Opéra to become more like the Opéra-comique or to force the Opéra to become more cosmopolitan, diverse, and tolerant. The debate focused on such issues as whether Italian music could be adapted to the French language and whether opera was primarily a melodic or a dramatic genre. But beneath these issues lay a deeper struggle between institutions and between conflicting social and aesthetic philosophies. It was a struggle between the Opéra (Académie royale de musique) on the one hand, an institution anchored deeply in the old regime, supported by the crown, catering to the taste of the aristocracy, yet crumbling under the weight of financial deficits (in 1762 the deficit was 186,000 livres) and a stale repertoire; and on the other hand the theater of the fairs, the Opéra-comique, an institution nearly suffocated by the special privileges accorded to the other theaters, an institution of popular origins, which through the freshness of its vaudevilles and parodies, infused with the music of Italian opera bouffa, was flourishing financially and artistically. The Opéra-comique answered the *philosophes'* demand for musical and dramatic simplicity. The Opéra did not.

In their battle to reform the Opéra, the *philosophes* attacked aristocratic taste and a prestigous institution of the old regime. This point has been made in recent articles on the Querelle des Bouffons by Servando Sacaluga and Edward Lowinsky.[5] Sacaluga argues that the real issue was "the abolition of an old order." In defending Italian opera, with its roots in popular culture, the *philosophes* discredited the government and the musical genre it patronized. The musical quarrel was an important part of the pre-revolutionary tradition. Lowinsky goes too far in seeing "overtones of a class struggle . . . in the bitter quarrel over Italian versus French opera," but he is quite correct to point out that "the great quarrel that divided Paris was not only a matter of taste and style but involved questions of social ideology as well."[6]

The aesthetic dimension of the musical conflicts centered on the accepted belief that music is, or should be, an imitation of nature. Both sides, of course, believed their favorite composers imitated nature. The dispute was over what this meant. Beginning with Rousseau, the *philosophes* took the position that natural music consisted of simple melody that appeals directly to the feelings of the individual.

Prior to Gluck's arrival in Paris, both the aesthetic and social issues remained alive within the larger framework of the continuing struggle between Italian and French opera. The *philosophes,* whose musical writings are too extensive to consider here, remained firm partisans of Italian opera. Grimm, for example, in his *Poème lyrique* defended Italian operatic procedures, especially the supremacy of melody, and attacked French opera as artificial, bizarre, and boring. He proposed making opera a more popular, less aristocratic entertainment. And D'Alembert in his essay *De la liberté de la musique* (1759) accused the Opéra and its royal defenders of prejudice and intolerance. It has reached the point, he declared, at which everything Italian "from the Bull Unigenitus to the music of the intermezzos" is considered a threat. "It is difficult to believe," he maintained, "but it is the exact truth that in the dictionary of certain persons, bouffonist, republican, frondeur, atheist, I would overlook materialist, are so many synonomous terms."[7] Diderot was the most vigorous advocate of Italian music. In his essay *Pantomime dramatique,* written in 1769, on the eve of the third musical war, he states flatly that the Italians are responsible for musical progress. Looking back at the Querelle des Bouffons, he writes: "Some miserable bouffons . . . enabled us to hear excellent music; and ours, poor, monotonous, timid, set itself free from its narrow confines: the presumption that the music of Lulli and Rameau was the only one to which the declamation and prosody of our language could be adapted, falls, and we have some opéras-comiques that are applauded in all the theaters of Europe."[8]

Diderot's reference to opéras-comiques is significant. This popular genre, incorporating traditional French vaudevilles and Italian songs or ariettes, enjoyed great popular success at the Parisian fairs in the 1760's and seemed to the *philosophes* and others to be the harbinger of musical reform and enlightenment. Several writers, including Nicolas Bricaire de La Dixmérie, André Contant d'Orville, and Pierre Jean Baptiste Nougaret, devoted books and brochures to the progress of the Opéra-comique and contrasted it with the decadence of the Opéra. When the Opéra-comique and the Théâtre Italien were unified in one theater in 1762, these writers hailed the achievement as a cultural renaissance and a victory over special privilege and intolerance. Contant declares that the union of the theaters is tantamount to conferring citizenship on the new comic genre. It is a "day to celebrate forever in the annals of the theater . . .";[9] and Bricaire observes that "it is not the first time that newcomers, scorned at first or little feared, have overthrown ancient and powerful monarchies."[10] The Opéra, he insists, must now yield to popular taste and descend from its dignity. It should learn from such works as Rousseau's *Le devin du village* and Monsigny's *Le roi et le fermier.*

Contant, however, perceived a major problem inherent in this approach to reform. It is simply that the public through "tacit convention" associates each theater with a certain type of production, so that it has difficulty accepting a transfer of genres from one theater to another. What is charming at the fairs seems out of place at the Théâtre Italien and "insufferable" at the Opéra. "Despite the public's predilection for the *pièces à ariette*, the connoisseurs felt that this new genre could be ennobled; but no author dared to make the leap. A common but pleasant intrigue, some characters forced . . . into the rank of the common people, an epigrammatic or equivocal style, such are the materials that should be used, it has been said, in these dramas in which the music comprises the principal or sole embellishment; whoever intends to do away with the interest, the nobility, the feelings will run the risk of an embarrassing failure." [11] But there are others, Contant declares, who believe that the new drama with its mixture of spoken and sung dialogue could be upgraded by talented artists so that it would "speak to the mind and to the heart."

Nougaret, in his two-volume study of the lyric theater, tries to solve the problem that Contant raised by emphasizing the long history, the thoroughly French character, and the edifying value of the opéras-comiques. Although the theater of the fairs developed in humble surroundings, he argues, its entertainments have moral value even for a man of noble birth, who can learn from fishermen and woodcutters. Indeed, it is a good thing for "rich people to cast their eyes on the poor . . . who open the earth's treasures and give us the commodities of life." [12] Moreover, if the taste for Italian music played at the Comique is degrading, why, Nougaret asks, are the most enlightened, reputable men of France its partisans? Why do members of the Académie Française compose pieces for it? Nougaret's point is that unlike the Comique, the Opéra is neither edifying nor endemically French. It survives only because it is protected by the powerful house of Orléans, the Secrétaire d'Etat, and the gentlemen of the king's chamber. Thus, it would be natural and beneficial for France to come home to the spirit of her earliest, most popular music dramas. Reforming the Opéra on the model of the Opéra-comique was, accordingly, the aim of the *philosophes* and other writers when Gluck appeared in Paris.

The third war of the musical Enlightenment was precipitated by a dispute over one of the most controversial and widely discussed problems of the age, the issue of whether the composer or the poet should dominate in the creation of an opera. In many ways the entire history of opera is a constant reform in the direction of balancing the scales between music and drama. Eighteenth-century Italian opera was at the mercy of singers and composers. People came to the theater to hear the arias; the drama was inconsequential. French opera had been conceived in the seventeenth century as a lyric tragedy embellished by visual spectacle. The role of music was to support the text, so that traditionally the recitative, that part of opera in which the action unfolds, was not always clearly distinguishable from the aria, in which a character expresses his feelings about the action. By contrast, in Italian opera, the distinction between recitative and aria was sharply drawn. The French conception of opera as classical or historical tragedy supported by music persisted in the eighteenth century, though the trend in Rameau's time was toward emphasizing the visual spectacle and the music of the ballets and choruses. In short, the drama *per se* was less important than it had been in Lully's time, but the contrast between the musical domination of Italian opera and the dramatic domination of French opera persisted.

The publication in 1765 of an *Essai sur l'union de la poésie et de la musique* by Jean-François Chastellux reopened the controversy over the relative importance of text and music. Chastellux, a disciple of the Encyclopedists, contended that since antiquity music had been the slave of poetry. His argument may be summarized in a few sentences. The Greeks forced music to drag along in servile fashion, following the metre of the text. The tyranny of Greece prevailed in Europe until the Italians created expressive melodies. France, however, resisted this innovation. The result was the contrast between the French air, "a series of distended notes which have no principle, no object," and the Italian air which has unity, proportion, and simplicity. The secret of the beauty of the Italian air is its periodic return to the principal theme or motif. Thus, in Italy music became the main ingredient in opera, and the poet Metastasio created a lyric verse with symmetrical, periodic phrases to correspond with the musical phrases. In contrast French operas plod along with painfully declaimed monologues; composers are ignorant of the musical phrase; they create for the mind, not the senses.

Chastellux' arguments for the supremacy of music formed the basis of the musical ideology of the Italian party. His *Essai* became the subject of a sharp dispute in the early 1770's, when Laurent Garcin, a poet and librettist, challenged Chastellux' contentions in his *Traité du Mélodrame* (1770). Garcin charged that Chastellux equated beauty with pleasure, music with sensation. Garcin attempted to prove that French was a musical language fit for dramatic expression in refutation of Jean-Jacques Rousseau's earlier insistence (*Lettre sur la musique françoise*, 1753) that the lack of accentuation in the French language makes it unsuitable for musical expression. The error of the Italian party, according to Garcin, is their shallow identification of musical expression with sensual sonority rather than with tragic effects. Garcin accepts Chastellux' distinction between the two musics, but he maintains that Italian melody and the prosodic character of the Italian language are suitable only for concert music, whereas the "accent oratoire" of the French language is more flexible and appropriate in expressing the varied emotions of lyric drama.[13] The result of these distinctions, Garcin contends, is that Italian music appeals only to the ear, whereas French music stimulates the mind.

Garcin joins an endorsement of the traditional French taste for musical drama, wherein the poem is supreme, with a reaffirmation of the ancient Greek idea that the perfect union of poetry and music produces powerful moral effects by imitating the movements of the soul. In an effort to give intellectual weight to his defense of French opera, Garcin resorts to the Platonic doctrine of the effects as the justification of the supremacy of text over music, of French music drama over sensual Italian melody. In a lengthy review of music history since antiquity, Garcin traces the decline of music from its lofty role under the Greek Republic as the primary ingredient in moral education to its debased place in Roman and modern times as a simple object of amusement. The invention of opera in the sixteenth century was a valiant effort to resurrect ancient Greek tragedy, but modern Italians have failed to restore the powerful effects of Greek drama because they have not realized that the secret of the power of music lies in its union with poetry and the other arts. The error of Chastellux, the *philosophes*, and the Italians is their emphasis on melody to the near exclusion of poetry, which perpetuates the musical theater as a frivolous amusement. Finally, Garcin charges that Chastellux has reopened the musical war of the 1750's; that he has taken up the cudgels of Rousseau and D'Alembert in advocating the "miserable farces" of the Italians. Chastellux equates beauty with pleasure rather than with edification; he links music with sensation rather than with the mind. He fails to understand that the true interest of opera lies in the drama. "If you place music on the throne of opera, you will destroy a noble and great spectacle in order to substitute for it one which has no purpose and whose puny effects are entirely mechanical; you will sacrifice the mind to the senses, you will cause the end of the theater, you will leave only the name of it."[14]

The controversy continued in the journals, as Chastellux' ideas were used to defend Italian opera, while Garcin's were upheld by the proponents of the French operatic tradition and the music drama of Gluck. It is important that Diderot upheld Chastellux' belief that the essence of music is periodic song and that lyric verse should be adapted to the pace and form of the song.[15] "I do not think that one could say anything more sensible," Diderot declared. He also thought Chastellux right to stress the sensual pleasure of music; music designed to appeal to the soul or mind would be tiresome. I hold, Diderot says, to the advice I once gave to a clavecinist: "Do you want to compose instrumental music so that your instrument always speaks to me; put Metastasio on your music stand; read one of his arias, and let your head go! "[16] Diderot concludes with the interesting observation that Marmontel, who once held the same views as Garcin, after reading Metastasio became convinced "that the poet is made for the musician." That Diderot welcomed Marmontel into the fold of the *philosophes* is significant, for Marmontel became the major spokesman of the Italian party against Gluck.

When Gluck arrived in Paris in 1773, the battle lines had already begun to form. The circumstances surrounding his arrival are important, however, because they indicate the identity he had in the minds of the reformers. Gluck himself had taken the initiative by ingratiating himself with Sévelinge, the president of the Concerts des amateurs. Gluck met Sévelinge in Vienna, at the home of François-Louis, Comte d'Escherny, who reported that Gluck praised the operas of Lully to Sévelinge. Gluck said that as a result of studying Lully's operas "he had perceived a real basis for pathetic and theatrical music, and the true genius of the opera, which only required to be developed and brought to perfection; and that if he should receive an invitation to work for the Opéra at Paris he would hope, by preserving the style of Lully and the French cantilena, to create in this manner the true lyrical tragedy."[17] D'Escherny added that on his return to Paris, he found that Sévelinge had acquainted many people with Gluck's views.

Although Gluck was obviously appealing to Sévelinge's national pride, his admiration for traditional French opera was probably sincere. Many scholars have made the point that Gluck's reforms were in the tradition of French opera. And it is worth noting that Charles Burney, who during a trip to Vienna in 1770 heard Gluck play passages from his new French opera and from his other reform operas, was impressed by the compatibility of Gluck and the French. Burney wrote that Gluck aimed "to satisfy the mind more than the ear. . . . If it is possible for the partisans of *old French music* to hear any other than that of Lully and Rameau with pleasure, it must be M. Gluck's *Iphigénie*, in which he has so far accommodated himself to the national taste, style and language, as frequently to imitate and adopt them."[18]

Gluck's librettist for *Iphigénie en Aulide*, François-Louis-Gand Le Bland Du Roullet, who was attached to the French embassy in Vienna, acted as his emissary to the Paris Opéra. Alfred Einstein has remarked that "the moves by which Gluck and Du Roullet set to work on the conquest of Paris were diplomatic in the highest degree."[19] On August 1, 1772, Du Roullet sent a letter to Antoine Dauvergne, the director of the Académie royale de musique, which was intended for publication and which appeared in the *Mercure de France* in October. The letter indicates that Du Roullet, doubtless with Gluck's compliance, wanted the chevalier to be identified with the anti-Italian, traditionalist side in the public mind. Du Roullet declared that Gluck had composed a French opera because he was convinced that "the Italians have deviated from the true path in their theatrical compositions; that the French style is the true musical-dramatic style; that if it had not attained perfection, it was not the fault of the French musicians, whose talents are truly estimable. . . . Gluck was shocked by the rash assertions of those among our famous writers who dared to slander the French language by contending that it was not capable of adaptation to great musical composition."[20] Everything in *Iphigénie*, according to Du Roullet, is in "our style; nothing in it seemed strange to French ears."

Thus, as Gluck had appealed to the national pride of Sévelinge, Du Roullet represented the knight of the Palatinate as an anti-Rousseauist who was coming to France to prove the worth of French music drama against the criticism of the *philosophes*.

Conscious of the influence of the *philosophes*, Gluck now moved to cover his other flank. He went all out to court the favor of Rousseau, whom he regarded as the spokesman of the Italian party. In February 1773, he sent a letter to the *Mercure*, explaining his operatic innovations and expressing his admiration for Rousseau. Referring to his new French opera, Gluck wrote: "I declare that I would have it produced with pleasure in Paris, because by its effect and with the help of the famous Rousseau of Geneva, whom I intend to consult, we may perhaps together, by looking for a noble, sensible, and natural melody with an exact declamation following the prosody of each language and the character of each people, be able to determine the means that I envisage to create a music appropriate for all nations and to make disappear the ridiculous distinction of national music. The study that I have made of the works of music of this great man . . . proves the sublimity of his knowledge and the reliability of his taste, and has filled me with admiration. I am inwardly persuaded that if he had wished to apply himself to the practice of this art, he would have been able to realize the prodigous effects that antiquity attributed to music. I am delighted to take this opportunity to render to him publicly this tribute of praise that I believe he deserves."[21]

After such a testimonial, how could Rousseau resist becoming a Gluckist? These published letters cleverly flattered Rousseau while at the same time fixing Gluck's image as an anti-Italian reformer working within French traditions. Gluck had the cunning to follow up on his unctuous letter by paying Rousseau a visit and later sending him the score of *Alceste* for his criticism. The chevalier's sincerity is doubtful. Rousseau later complained that Gluck withdrew the score before he had completed his analysis. Nevertheless, Gluck's flattery worked. Rousseau became his advocate. He praised Gluck's *Orfeo* as "one of the most sublime creations in this genre that I know."[22] He even conceded that he had been wrong to deny the musicality of the French language. In April 1774, he wrote: "You have realized what I held to be impossible up to this very day. Please accept my sincere congratulations."[23] The final stroke in the conquest of Rousseau was Gluck's intercession on his behalf with the directors of the Académie, who had banned him from the Opéra twenty years earlier for his attack in the *Lettre sur la musique* (1753).[24]

Other writers were not taken in, however. They perceived Gluck not only as a traditionalist, but also as a creature of the crown. Marie-Antoinette, the dauphine, who had studied music with Gluck in Vienna, intervened to overcome the final obstacles to Gluck's appointment at the Opéra.[25] Moreover, the dauphine was demonstratively enthusiastic at the first performance of Gluck's *Iphigénie* on April 19, 1774. There could be no mistake about where Gluck stood in the eyes of the court. Having ordered the lieutenant of police to suppress any hostile demonstrations, Marie-Antoinette arrived at the Opéra with a covy of courtiers. She vigorously applauded the performance and encouraged the audience to follow suit.[26] Gluck received the large sum of 20,000 livres for his opera from the Académie. Less than four months later, following the performance of Gluck's *Orfeo* (2 August 1774), Queen Marie-Antoinette secured a pension of 6000 livres for the chevalier and invited him to present an opera at Versailles. Even the king became an enthusiastic partisan. After attending a revival of *Iphigénie* at the Opéra in January 1775, Louis XVI wrote the following to the Duc de la Vrillière: "I was carried away yesterday by the opera *Iphigénie en Aulide* by the chevalier Gluck, which I heard in Paris....I demonstrated my satisfaction to the author after the spectacle; I want to send him a present to indicate my esteem for him personally and for his talent."[27]

Gluck's operas were also successful with the public. *Orfeo* took in 5,498 livres at the first performance and averaged 3,542 livres for the next seven performances. By contrast Jean-Joseph Mondonville's *Carnaval du Parnasse*, performed concurrently in the summer of 1774, drew less than 3000 livres a performance.[28] Gluck returned triumphantly to Vienna in the spring of 1775, armed with a commission from the Académie for two new operas, *Armide* and *Roland*, both based on texts by Lully's librettist, Philippe Quinault. He was also working on a French adaptation of *Alceste*.

Although Gluck had not silenced the Italian reform party for whom none of the old issues had been resolved, he had achieved a triple victory over the crown, Rousseau, and the public. Even before the public had seen *Iphigénie*, the *Gazette de politique* proclaimed Gluck's immanent triumph in Paris. The *Gazette* suggested disdainfully, however, that the Italian party would not be placated because of the chevalier's conviction that the form of Italian operas "was incompatible with a sustained interest, and that the music, by sacrificing everything to the ear, became more and more removed every day from the true purpose of all dramatic action."[29] Consequently, Gluck has chosen the French operatic form for his innovations in the belief that it is "more appropriate to produce great effects." In order to acquaint its readers with Gluck's reforms, the *Gazette* appended a translation of the composer's now famous letter of dedication (to the Grand Duke of Tuscany, later the Emperor Leopold II) that had accompanied the publication of the score of *Alceste* in 1769, and which explained his dramatic principles. The letter was actually written by Calzabigi, though signed by Gluck.

To all the writers who for years had proclaimed the virtues of Italian opera and the supremacy of music over text, the opening lines of Gluck's *Epître* could only have been regarded as a searing rebuke. The dedication begins, "When I undertook to write the music for *Alceste,* I resolved to divest it entirely of all those abuses . . . which have so long disfigured Italian opera and made of the most splendid and most beautiful of spectacles the most ridiculous and wearisome. I have striven to restrict music to its true office of serving poetry by means of expression and by following the situation of the story, without interrupting the action or stifling it with a useless superfluity of ornaments."[30]

In its next issue (19 April 1774), the *Gazette* published the first article of the war by one of its four major generals, the Abbé François Arnaud. In the 1740's, Arnaud taught himself music while working at the library of the Trappists in Carpentras; in 1760, he became co-editor, with Jean-Baptiste-Antoine Suard, of the *Journal étranger,* and in 1762, of the *Gazette de France.* Later published in the collection *Variétées littéraires,* their musical articles favored Rameau and criticized Italian opera.[31] Believing that the essence of opera is drama, Arnaud contended that music must conform to the prosody of the language and that Italian music can not be adapted to French words. Arnaud adopted the view held since Lully's time that French opera is distinguished from Italian in being a drama reinforced by music. He held that Gluck conformed to this conception; that *Iphigénie* was a lyric tragedy, not an operatic concert in the Italian manner.

Arnaud continued to give Gluck strong support when his opera *Alceste* was coolly received at the first performance on April 23, 1776. Arnaud defended Gluck in a satirical dialogue called *La soirée perdue à l'opéra.* Accosted during the fifth performance of *Alceste* by several of Gluck's enemies, Arnaud was obliged to demonstrate Gluck's genius. He does so by making Gluck's critics foolish advocates of the vocal convulsions of the Italian singers. Their inability to hear any song in *Alceste* is dismissed on the grounds that they confuse vandevilles and drinking airs with true dramatic arias. In the name of Apollo and the Muses, Arnaud says, leave to "the ultramontane music, the ornaments, the tinsel, the extravagances that for so long dishonored it; prevent yourself from envying corrupt and miserable wealth and do not invoke a style proscribed everywhere there are philosophers, intelligent people, and enlightened amateurs."[32]

Until 1777, Gluck and his supporters held the offensive in the musical war, *Alceste* increased in popularity, and *Iphigénie* and *Orfeo* were repeated successfully early in 1777. Gluck's new opera *Armide* was also acclaimed at the first performance on September 23, 1777. Marie-Antoinette continued to act as the chevalier's foremost promoter, and the journals published a steady flow of letters hailing Gluck as the musical messiah.[33] Signing his letters the

Anonyme de Vaugirard, Suard joined Arnaud in supporting Gluck. But a strong counterattack also began in 1777, led by the two generals of the Italian party, Jean-François de La Harpe and Jean-François Marmontel. [34]

Marmontel was the best known protagonist of the musical war and the one most directly involved with the lyric theater. He composed the texts of three of Piccinni's operas and seven of André Grétry's. Many of Marmontel's *Contes moraux* were fashioned into dramas and opéras-comiques. He contributed several articles to the *Encyclopédie,* including one on opera that foretold his position in the musical war. "The Italians," he declared, "are constantly telling us, and we must end by believing them, that the essence of music is song, and melody is the soul of song."[35] Marmontel's liberal social and political views, greatly influenced by Rousseau, appear to have had an important bearing on his musical and dramatic writing. The son of a poor artisan, he sympathized with the peasantry, whose values he sentimentalized in his moral tales. He attacked the luxury of the aristocracy and advocated equality of oportunity. These attitudes found their way into the texts of his opéras-comiques. The Marquise de Créquy comments angrily on his opera *Sylvain* (1770, music by Grétry): "The moral and political disorder was fomented not only by the big encyclopedic books and the filthy novels, the godless brochures and the five-act tragedies, but even by the almanacs of the muses and the low comic operas. Marmontel wrote one comedy mixed with ariettes in the Italian style, whose purpose and moral tone consisted in proving that it was good to marry one's servant and it was proper to let one's peasants poach. This opera, called *le Sylvain,* contained a thousand wild declamations against inequality among men and the prejudices of birth."[36]

The counterattack of the Italian party began in March 1777, when La Harpe announced the revival of *Iphigénie* in the *Journal de politique et de littérature.*[37] He charged that in comparison with Italian music, Gluck's airs were not melodious. He compared a duet in the opera to a vulgar quarrel, because both heroes speak simultaneously in menacing cries. Furthermore, the music is "anti-harmonic." La Harpe's brief report touched off a sequence of letters from the Anonyme de Vaugirard (Suard) to the *Journal de Paris,* which were countered by La Harpe in the *Journal de politique et de littérature.*[38] The major points of contention can be isolated.

The dominant issue was the matter of musical criticism itself. How should music be evaluated and who has the right to do it? In his first letter (*Journal de Paris,* March 8) Suard maintains that whereas La Harpe may be a good judge of poetry, his musical criticism is imprecise and amateurish, betraying an ignorance of music. The proof is his meaningless statement that Gluck's music is anti-harmonic. In his reply La Harpe explains that he had intended nothing more than an expression of his feelings. He insists on his right to comment on the effects of music, because there are two aspects of art: the first is "elementary and mechanical," known only to artists; the second pertains to "the operations of an art," which may be judged by anyone with "an honest intelligence and sensitive organs."[39] La Harpe finishes his defense by calling on the Anonyme to be less tyrannical about his enthusiasm for Gluck and to tolerate observations by those who sincerely admire genius.

In response, Suard maintains that although a man of letters has the right to speak about music, "the public is the natural judge of all the arts to the extent that a certain portion of the public, arriving at a spirit naturally more subtle, more just, more energetic than that of the common man, has perfected its natural faculties through use, reflection, analysis, and comparison of the different objects which pertain to taste, imagination and understanding."[40] Clearly Suard's notion of the public was sufficiently exclusive to remove La Harpe from the select body. In his fourth letter (April 1777) the Anonyme denies that he is tyrannical and points out that enthusiasm is the only way to promote the arts. Enthusiasm is fine, he explains, when it stems from intellectual judgments, not sense impressions.

The second major disagreement between La Harpe and Suard centered on the role and character of operatic music. Like the dispute over musical criticism, their exchange over the importance of melody had reverberating aesthetic and social overtones. For the Italian party, Gluck's failure to compose simple, natural melodies was the heart of the controversy, and they continued to drive the point home to the Gluckists. When the Anonyme tried to brush off La Harpe's charge that Gluck's music was unmelodic, La Harpe seized the issue. He insists that Gluck's weak airs are no match for the melodies of Jommelli, Piccinni, and Sacchini. Suard's reply simply refuses to consider La Harpe's questions, on the grounds that the public has already decided the issue by applauding Gluck's airs. But he makes the countercharge that La Harpe fails to perceive the distinction between the airs of opera bouffa and those of a tragedy.

And so it went. The exchange of letters became an acrimonious squabble over details that often obscured the deep, serious divisions between the combatants. The Gluckists still held the high ground in the battle when Marmontel's *Essai sur les révolutions de la musique en France* appeared in the spring and became the talk of Paris. It was the strongest, most effective statement of the Italian position that had yet appeared.

Marmontel's thesis is that the opportunity of a people to experience different kinds of music is the cause of musical progress and enlightenment. He presents the history of music in France as a battle between reformers attempting to give the public new musical experiences, and traditionalists, motivated by prejudice, intolerance, and fear, struggling to block innovation. Marmontel sees the battle reflected in the contrast between the Opéra, which is closed to innovation, and the Opéra-comique, which is open. Grétry, for example, "demonstrated to the most incredulous that our music was susceptible to all the nuances of musical expression."[41] To the great consternation of the traditionalists, the public, Marmontel declares, discovered a noble pathos in the simple airs of *Tom Jones* and *Sylvain* and demanded that the airs of Philidor and Grétry be brought to the Opéra.

As for Gluck's place in the struggle, Marmontel brushes off the German composer's alleged reforms by asking if the chevalier's music might not "be only our old French music reinforced by the accompaniments of the chant of the Italian Church? " Gluck's agitated operas are successful because the public, bored, inexperienced, unenlightened, welcomes the excitement of his noisy orchestra and the piercing squeals of his mutilated declamation, Marmontel argues. The Gluckists condemn Italian music out of fear that if the people become used to natural, melodious song, "to the accents which are not cries of physical pain, . . . to the elegant, pure designs of the musical phrase whose secret the Italians possess, then everything would be lost." But, maybe, Marmontel says, "the interests of glory are not the interests of our pleasures. . . . The aim of the arts that stir the soul is not just emotion, but the pleasure that accompanies it. It is not enough that the emotion be strong, it must also be agreeable." Marmontel appeals for musical freedom. Experience, not power, must decide the issue. "Liberty, the mother of competition, will rule the lyric stage."

Needless to say Marmontel's essay was greeted with a flurry of angry letters and brochures. One writer, in a letter printed in the *Journal de Paris*, even complained that Marmontel was prejudiced against the Germans and stirred up national hatreds.[42] But the main defense of the Gluckists was the popularity of Gluck's operas. A certain M. Urlubrelu contrasted the receipts for June of Gluck's *Iphigénie* with those of *Céphale et Procris* by Grétry and Marmontel. Gluck was the victor by over 2000 livres per performance.

The musical war entered its most violent period following the first performance of Gluck's new opera *Armide* in September 1777. In a letter written shortly thereafter, La Harpe renews the battle, calling *Armide* a "monotonous, tiresome brawl."[43] Again he raises the aesthetic issue, insisting that to mimic nature is not to imitate it; one imitates nature by composing music that penetrates the heart, he explains. La Harpe also returns to Suard's old charge that he is not a qualified judge of music. Referring the reader to Chastellux' *Essai* and Rousseau's *Dictionnaire de musique,* La Harpe tries to prove that their informed analyses correspond exactly to his sensations; that their musical science jibes with his instinct. Finally, he declares the lack of melody in Gluck's operas to be the fundamental issue in the war. "When I go to the opera, it is to hear music," La Harpe concludes.

La Harpe's article brought Gluck into the battle. The chevalier lashed out at his critic with bitter sarcasm: "You prove to me sir, that it is sufficient to be a man of letters in order to talk about everything. You convince me that the music of the Italian masters is the music; that to be entertaining, song must be regular and periodic. . . . I sincerely ask God's pardon for having *stunned* my listeners by my other operas; the number of their performances and the applause that the public desired to give them does not prevent me from seeing that they are pitiful."[44] Gluck promises to do over all his operas in order to give the characters such sweet songs that "the most vapid mistress" can listen to them without "the least nervous irritation."

In 1778, a new phase of the musical war began when Niccolo Piccinni, a fifty-year-old Italian musician, arrived in Paris. For the first time the Italian party had their own composer, so that they were able to take a more positive stand in the conflict.[45] Piccinni, the chapel master and organist of the king of Naples, had achieved considerable success in Italy for both his comic and his serious operas. Madame Du Barry, along with some other patrons, arranged for Piccinni to come to Paris at a salary of 6000 livres. If the queen could have her German knight, the king's mistress would have her Italian, whose music, the Neapolitan ambassador assured her, had triumphed over Gluck's at the court of Naples.[46]

The Opéra received Piccinni warmly, especially after Jacques Devisme du Valgay became its director in the fall of 1778. Taking advantage of the climate produced by the musical war, Devisme tried to free the Opéra from its traditional moorings by staging a greater variety of works. He produced, back to back, the operas of Lully, Rameau, Philidor, Gluck, Piccinni, and Grétry, and he brought in an Italian company, placed under Piccinni's supervision, to perform opera bouffa. But Devisme's experiment failed. The public appeared less eager for new musical experiences than either Devisme or Marmontel had anticipated. Reeling under heavy debts (Devisme had taken over the Opéra as a private enterprise) and confronted with near mutiny by the singers and dancers, most of whom were committed to Gluck, Devisme was forced to relinquish the Opéra to the city in 1779. In 1780 the crown reclaimed the Opéra and placed its administration under an appointed committee.[47]

In the meantime, Piccinni had settled into his quarters on the rue Saint-Thomas-du-Louvre, opposite Marmontel's house. While the war raged about him, the mild-mannered composer studied French under Marmontel's tutelage. Together they carefully prepared Piccinni's first French opera, *Roland,* based on a text by Quinault, for its initial performance in January 1778. Soon after, the musical war moved to the box office, where it became a contest of receipts. The first twelve performances of *Roland* brought in a total of 61,920 livres, an average of over 5000 livres a performance. It exceeded slightly the receipts of Gluck's first opera, *Iphigénie,* whose first dozen performances produced 61,835 livres.[48] La Harpe proclaimed that the success of *Roland* had terminated the war in favor of the Italian party. The Gluckists answered that the receipts for Gluck's operas increased after the first twelve performances, whereas those for *Roland* declined. They also held that arithmetic should not decide matters of aesthetics.

The most effective rejoinder of the Gluckists, however, was the brilliant success of the chevalier's best opera, *Iphigénie en Tauride*, performed in May, 1779. Led by Marie-Antoinette, to whom the opera was dedicated, the audience on opening night greeted Gluck with enthusiastic applause. He received the sum of 12,000 livres for *Iphigénie* from the Académie, plus an additional gratuity of 4000. Not even the lukewarm reception accorded to his last opera, *Echo et Narcisse,* produced in September, could shake Gluck's preeminence at the Opéra or the enthusiasm of his royal patron. Gluck was irritated, however, that *Echo* did not fare better at the box office. Irritation grew into anger when the exasperated Italian party resumed their attack. Although he had really won the contest with Piccinni, he left the field to his Italian rival and returned to Vienna for good. He was in poor health, anxious to rest on his laurels, and in no mood to endure yet another round of combat with the "red cockerels" of Paris. His operas continued to be performed successfully at the Académie, and the queen honored him with the title of music master of the children of France, but the chevalier could not be persuaded to leave his comfortable home in Vienna.

Although the worst fighting was over, in Gluck's absence the war of words erupted after each new Piccinni opera. Attempts to arrange a cease-fire failed. When the Abbé Maury tried to conciliate the parties, he was turned down for membership in the Académie française on the grounds that his position on the Gluck-Piccinni conflict was equivocal. Although D'Alembert and the *philosophes* held the upper hand in the Académie by 1780, the musical war had badly divided the membership. A showdown occurred in 1783, when Marmontel was elected over Suard to succeed D'Alembert as permanent secretary. His election was viewed as a victory for the Piccinnists,[49] but this success was not matched by conquest of the Opéra. The reform party was, of course, victorious at the Opéra-comique, which became the haven of young, talented composers whose productions, still enriched by Italian ariettes, packed the house and set the stage for the rich repertoire of the nineteenth century. But the Opéra, which they had waged the war to capture, remained hostile.

Friedrich Nietzsche has written that "unfortunately in the aesthetic wars, artists provoke by their works and apologias for their works, just as is the case in real war, it is might and not reason that decides. All the world now assumes as a historical fact that in his dispute with Piccinni, Gluck was in the right. At any rate, he was victorious, and had might on his side."[50] Power helped to secure victory for the traditionalists. The Gluckists never lost control of the Opéra except for Devisme's brief tenure. This control was strengthened in 1780, when Suard and François-Joseph Gossec, a close friend of Gluck, became members of the Comité of the Opéra. The Comité made life difficult for the Italian party. For example, the directors suddenly halted rehearsals of Sacchini's opera *Olympiade* and sent it to the Opéra-comique, where a failure was anticipated because *Olympiade* was a serious opera, not of the comique genre. Despite the drastic alterations required to convert the recitatives to spoken passages, *Olympiade* turned out to be an enormous popular success. The news spread that it was better than Gluck's *Armide*. The Comité now demanded that *Olympiade* be stopped on the grounds that the Opéra-comique was forbidden by law to produce pieces with seven singers on the stage. The Opéra's demand was enforced.[51] There is also evidence indicating that Piccinni's operas were subverted by the Opéra administration. Piccinni was often forced to use substitute singers, and on the opening night of his *Iphigénie en Tauride,* the soprano, Mademoiselle de La Guerre, showed up drunk and gave a staggering performance. The Gluckists labelled the opera "Iphigénie en Champagne." Piccinni's opera *Pénélope* with a text by Marmontel was cancelled by the Comité after nine performances, on the grounds that it was not making money. In fact, every performance took in over 2000 livres, while operas by other composers that brought in as little as 1000 livres were retained by the Comité. The Comité also refused to pay Piccinni the full pension of 3000 livres normally given to composers on completion of six operas, for the reason that two of his operas had failed. Piccinni's last years were desperate, and he died impoverished. Not long before his death in 1800, he wrote this pathetic appeal to one of the ministers: "Piccinni dies of hunger near the French government; Piccinni dies of hunger near the theaters that are rich only through his talents."[52]

The last phase of the war brought one important achievement for the Italian party: the crystallization of their aesthetic doctrine with its implicit suggestion of a social philosophy. During the war the aesthetic issue never emerged in clear relief because the Piccinnists kept trying to tie their defense of the primacy of music in lyric drama and of the supremacy of melody generally to the imitation of nature. Italian melody was the true imitation of nature, they argued, because it was simple, clear, not complicated by the artificial harmonic contrivances of composers bent on making music an intellectual exercise. Moreover, it was natural because it appealed directly to the human heart and gave pleasure. The Gluckists were no less committed to the proposition that music imitates nature, but they held that Italian melody had a superficial, sensual appeal. A truly imitative music depicts the movements of the soul and impresses the mind; and in their view, music achieves imitation by expressing the meaning and mood of the poet's text. The Greeks had discovered this truth, and Gluck's operas, they argued, were a return to the Greek practice of using music to project every nuance of the text. In their opinion the result was not only a perfect opera, but a music drama that could produce the powerful effects attributed by writers from Plato to Ficino to Greek music. One of the many examples of this argument in the third war was a poem based on Dryden's *Alexander's Feast*, the ode on the power of music, published in the *Almanach des muses* in 1780. The poem likened the power of Gluck's music to that of Timotheus and credited Gluck with defeating the "cold mechanism" of song.[53]

Late in the war the Italian party broke loose from the old doctrine that the effects of art determine its value; they also gave up the unproductive assumption that music imitates nature, a view that had dominated eighteenth-century musical thought. Two writers, Michel Paul Guy de Chabanon and Pascal Boyer, developed the philosophy that for years had been implicit in the musical writings of the *philosophes* and their successors. Boyer, a friend of Diderot and editor of the *Journal des spectacles* in the Revolutionary period, posed the question: Can music express the passions and paint the movements of man's soul? His answer was that it cannot. His *L'expression musicale mise au rang des chimères* (1779), argues that the soul manifests its inner movements in external gestures, sounds, and actions which are expressed forcefully, in painting, dancing, and other imitative arts which do not properly include music. Music can imitate the manifestations of the soul only imperfectly in song, according to Boyer. The voice alone without music can express cries, groans, laments, and laughter better than song, because a musical note is fixed and constant, whereas a purely vocal inflection, even in a simple word like "oui," is indeterminate and flexible, Boyer reasons. Operatic music with a text is comprised of fixed, determinate sounds which are utterly divorced from the soul and its natural manifestations. Gluck allegedly paints the passions and expresses all the movements of the soul; in reality, it is the poem and the actors' vocal intonations that generate whatever passion his operas arouse. Logically, music comes closest to imitating nature and expressing the soul in the declamatory passages of opera, that is, in the recitative; yet, ironically, according to Boyer, the recitative is musically the most boring part of any opera, and Gluck's operas are poor precisely because they are overburdened with cold, boring recitatives.

If music cannot express the external manifestations of the soul when joined to a text, it certainly cannot imitate anything when divorced from a text, Boyer points out. Music seen from this point of view is an "inexplicable hieroglyphe." Indeed, detached from the text, music lacks the power to express any specific emotions. Nor can it imitate the sounds of water and wind. Fast notes are fast notes, not the noise of battle or a babbling brook. An Italian melodic air, with or without a text, imitates nothing; its appeal is purely sensual and is unrelated to the text. Boyer concludes: "The principal object of music is to please us physically, without involving the mind in seeking useless comparisons. It should be regarded absolutely as a pleasure of the senses, not the intellect. In so far as one will strain to attribute the cause of the impressions that we are made to feel to a moral principle, one will only get lost in a labyrinth of extravagances; one will search for music in vain; it is hidden forever from the exertions of our reason."[54]

Boyer then draws out the social implications of his heretical aesthetics. He raises the old question of who is the real musical connoisseur and critic, and he concludes that "the shepherd with his flute, the Breton with his bagpipe, the Provencal with his tambourin have the right to vie with the greatest philosopher over the enjoyment of sounds." Boyer admits that musical knowledge provides the pleasure of understanding how well composers and performers use the elements of musical style. But this is the pleasure of detail; it is confined to the mind and it may have no relationship to the pleasure born of a genuine love of music. "Whoever is capable of sensing the charms of music," he concludes, "can feel the liveliest affections without the aid of analysis. . . . Perhaps the mortal most deeply moved by musical impressions is a wood pedlar."[55]

In several books and articles written in the 1780's, Michel de Chabanon, an outstanding violinist and a proponent of Chastellux' views in the early stages of the war, developed fully Boyer's philosophy of musical Sensationalism, with its egalitarian ramifications. Chabanon's works anticipate Romanticism in attributing artistic creativity to genius and to spontaneous, instinctive feelings, rather than to philosophical rules. According to this view, even artistic judgment stems from sensual pleasures, not from intellectual analysis. "One judges the arts better through instinct that through reason, Chabanon declares, "because their primary effect is a sensation."[56] It follows that everyman is a judge of music. Sensual airs are like open books to the multitude. "The entire essence of music is included in the single word *song* or *melody*,"[57] and songs, Chabanon maintains, are made for everyone; they are universal truths. Finally Chabanon insists that the true difference between Italian music and French music goes even beyond the issue of melody; it is a difference between a society that proscribes art within rules dictated by philosophers and enforced by a privileged, aristocratic institution, and a society that has allowed art to perfect itself freely.

Irrespective of who won, the third musical war was fought over serious issues of long-standing. This was not a petty squabble of ill-informed journalists. The parties were deeply divided on fundamental issues of musical, aesthetic, and social philosophy, which their partisan bickering often masked, but never completely concealed. Musically, the conflict was between those who believed reform should be based on the model of Italian opera and of the opéra-comique, which meant the supremacy of music over text and simple melody over dramatic declamation, and those who believed reform should conform to the traditional French idea of opera as a lyric drama embellished by music and visual spectacle. Aesthetically, the war was a battle between the widely accepted theory that art is an imitation of nature, combined with the antique doctrine of the effects, and the radical aesthetics of Sensationalism. The social issue of the war revolved around the belief of the Italian party that melodious music, Italian music, has a direct, popular appeal and that every sensitive individual is a competent judge of art and taste, versus the Gluckist view that the value of lyric drama lies in its appeal to the mind and soul and that artistic judgment is reserved to trained connoisseurs.

The long disputed issue of whether Gluck incorporated into his operas the musical reforms proposed by the *philosophes* is the real "faux probléme" of the musical war. For the historian the important matter is that the *philosophes,* both the old warriors (with the exception of Rousseau) and the younger writers, did not perceive Gluck's music as the answer to reform. From the outset Gluck was perceived as the creature of the conservative forces who controlled the Opéra and as the protégé of Marie-Antoinette and the court. His operas were judged to be unmelodious, anti-Italian, and out of step with the progressive, popular style of the opéras-comiques. And Nietzsche was probably right: if Gluck may be said to have won the war, his victory was determined as much by his power and prestige as by his musical talent.

NOTES

1 Quoted in Alfred Einstein, *Gluck,* tr. Eric Blom (New York: McGraw Hill, 1964), p. 176.

2 Martin Cooper, *Gluck* (New York: Oxford University Press, 1935), pp. xiii-xiv.

3 Norbert Dufourcq, "La musique française au XVIIIe siècle: Etat des questions," *Dix-huitième Siècle,* No. 2 (1970), pp. 313-19.

4 See, among others, Romain Rolland, *Some Musicians of Former Days,* tr. Mary Blaiklock, 4th ed. (London: Kegan Paul, Trench, Trubner, n.d.), 251-98; Jacques Gabriel Prod'homme, "Diderot et la musique," *Internationale Musik-Gesellschaft Zeitschrift,* 15 (March, 1914), 156-62 and (April, 1914), 177-82; Julien Tiersot, "Gluck and the Encyclopedists," *Musical Quarterly,* 16 (Oct., 1930), 336-57; Einstein, *op. cit.,* pp. 102-3.

5 Servando Sacaluga, "Diderot, Rousseau et la querelle musicale de 1752; Nouvelle mise au point," *Diderot Studies,* 10 (1968), 133-73; Edward Lowinsky, "Taste, Style and Ideology in Eighteenth-century Music," in *Aspects of the Eighteenth Century,* ed. Earl R. Wasserman (Baltimore: Johns Hopkins Press, 1965), pp. 163-205.

6 Lowinsky, *op. cit.,* p. 170.

7 Jean D'Alembert, *De la liberté de la musique*, in Vol. III of *Oeuvres philosophiques, historique et littéraires* (Paris: Bastien, 1805), pp. 337-409.

8 Denis Diderot, *Pantomime dramatique ou essai sur un nouveau genre de spectacle à Florence*, in Vol. VIII of *Oeuvres complètes*, ed. Assézat (Paris: Garnier, 1875), p. 458.

9 André Guillaume Contant d'Orville, *Histoire de l'opéra bouffon contenant les jugemens de toutes les pièces qui ont paru depuis sa naissance jusqu'à ce jour*, I (Amsterdam: Grange, 1768), 210.

10 Nicolas Bricaire de la Dixmérie, *Letters sur l'état présent de nos spectacles, avec des vues nouvelles sur chacun d'eux; particulièrement sur la Comédie françoise et l'opéra* (Amsterdam: n.p., 1765), p. 41.

11 Contant d'Orville, *op. cit.*, p. 251.

12 Pierre Jean Baptiste Nougaret, *De l'art du théâtre où il est parlé des différents genres de spectacles et de la musique adaptée au théâtre*, I (Paris: Cailleau, 1769), 112.

13 Laurent Garcin, *Traité du mélodrame ou réflexions sur la musique dramatique* (Paris: Vallat-La-Chapelle, 1772), pp. ix-xxxii.

14 *Ibid.*, p. 98.

15 Denis Diderot, *Lettre au sujet des observations du Chevalier de Chastellux sur le Traité du Mélodram*, in Vol. VIII of *Oeuvres complètes*, ed. Assézat (Paris: Garnier, 1875), pp. 506-10. This letter has survived in two nearly identical versions: one is the version published in Assézat's edition of Diderot's works. This version was apparently first published as a brochure in 1814. The other version is contained within a letter to Charles Burney, dated October 10, 1771. R. A. Leigh, who possesses the letter to Burney, suspects that Diderot's *Lettre* was intended for publication in the *Correspondance littéraire*, but that Grimm decided not to use it. See R. A. Leigh, "Les amitiés françaises du Dr. Burney; Burney et Rousseau," *Revue de littérature comparée*, 25 (April, 1951), pp. 183-89. It is Diderot's last statement on the musical conflicts and clearly reveals his fidelity to the Italian party. In this he was in perfect accord with Burney.

16 Diderot, *Lettre, op. cit.*, p. 508.

17 From D'Escherny, *Mélanges de littérature*, II (1811), 356-58, quoted in Ernest Newman, *Gluck and the Opera* (London: Dobell, 1895), p. 112. See also Gustave Desnoireterres, *La musique française au dix-huitième siècle; Gluck et Piccinni, 1774-1800* (2d ed.; Paris: Didier, 1875), pp. 77-78; Lionel de La Laurencie, *Orphée de Gluck: étude et analyse* (Paris: Mellottée, 1935), p. 79.

18 Quoted in Newman, *op. cit.*, p. 109.

19 Einstein, *op. cit.*, p. 135.

20 *Mercure de France*, October, 1771, In *Mémoires pour servir à l'histoire de la révolution opérée dans la musique par M. le Chevalier Gluck*, ed. Gaspard Michel Leblond (Naples and Paris: Bailly, 1781), pp. 1-2. Hereafter referred to as Leblond.

21 Leblond, p. 9.

22 Leblond, p. 22.
23 Quoted in Alfred Richard Oliver, *The Encyclopedists as Critics of Music* (New York: Columbia University Press, 1947), p. 120.
24 Edouard G. J. Grégoire, *Les gloires de l'opéra et de la musique à Paris*, 2 (1751-1768) (Bruxelles, 1878), 54. See also Adophe Jullien, *La ville et la cour au XVIIIè siècle* (Paris: Rouveyre, 1881), p. 133.
25 Louis Petit de Bachaumont, *Mémoires secrets pour servir à l'histoire de la république des lettres en France depuis MDCCLXII jusqu'à nos jours; ou, Journal d'un observateur*, 7 (London: Atkinson, 1780-1789), 110. See also Desnoireterres, *op. cit.*, pp. 83-84; Julien Tiersot, *Gluck* (4th ed. rev.; Paris: F. Alcan, 1919), p. 103.
26 Bachaumont, *op. cit.*, p. 163. See also Desnoireterres, *op. cit.*, pp. 97-100; Newman, *op. cit.*, p. 142.
27 Quoted in Desnoireterres, *op. cit.*, pp. 119-20.
28 La Laurencie, *Orphée, op. cit.*, pp. 84-85.
29 Leblond, p. 12.
30 Quoted in Einstein, *op. cit.*, p. 98.
31 See, for example, "Lettre sur un ouvrage Italien intitulé 'Il Teatro alla moda,' le Théâtre à la mode," in François Arnaud and Jean-Baptiste-Antoine Suard, *Variétées littéraires, ou recueil de pièces tant originales que traduites concernant la philosophie, la littérature, et les arts*, I (Paris: Lacombe, 1768-1769), 192-208; "Essai sur le Mélodrame ou drame lyrique," *ibid.*, III, 256-64.
32 Leblond, p. 51.
33 Leblond, pp. 102-12.
34 For pertinent biographical information see François-Joseph Fétis, *Biographie universelle des musiciens et bibliographie générale de la musique*, 5 (2d ed. aug.; Paris: Didot, 1863), 167-68, 460.
35 Quoted in Oliver, *op. cit.*, p. 42.
36 Quoted in Michael Cardy, "Rousseau's 'irréconciliable ennemi,' Marmontel," *Studies on Voltaire and the Eighteenth Century*, 87 (1972), 231.
37 Leblond, pp. 113-14.
38 Leblond, pp. 115-52.
39 *Journal de politique et de littérature*, 25 March 1777, in Leblond, p. 120.
40 *Journal de Paris*, 25 March 1777, in Leblond, p. 127.
41 Leblond, p. 158.
42 "Lettre d'un gentilhomme allemand," in Leblond, pp. 197-200.
43 *Journal de politique et de littérature*, 5 October 1777, in Leblond, p. 261. See also his reply to the Anonyme, 5 November 1777, Leblond, pp. 323-24.
44 "Lettre de M. le chevalier Gluck à M. de la Harpe," *Journal de Paris*, 12 October 1777, in Leblond, pp. 272-73.
45 Many historians believe that Piccinni was no match for Gluck. Although I am not ready to concede that, it does raise the question why Piccinni rather than some other Italian composer was brought to Paris. The answer may be that he was the only one available. Jommelli, one of Italy's best

composers, had just died; Traetta was in poor health; Sarti was committed to the Viennese court; Paisiello was about to succeed Traetta in St. Petersburg; Sacchini, it was believed, was dissolute. See W. H. Hadow, *The Viennese Period,* Vol. 5 of *The Oxford History of Music* (2d ed.; London: Humphrey Milford, 1931), p. 97.

46 For biography, see Fétis, *op. cit.,* 7 (1864), 44-48. See also Desnoireterres, *op. cit.,* pp. 167-70.

47 Fétis, *op. cit.,* 3 (1862), 11.

48 Desnoireterres, *op. cit.,* pp. 233-34.

49 Lucien Brunel, *Les philosophes et l'Académie française au dix-huitième siècle* (Geneva: Skatkine Reprints, 1967), pp. 271-94.

50 Friedrich Nietzsche, *Human, All-Too Human,* Vol. 7 of *The Complete Works of Friedrich Nietzsche,* ed. Oscar Levy (New York: Russell and Russell, 1964), p. 272.

51 Desnoireterres, *op. cit.,* pp. 218-19.

52 Quoted, *ibid.,* pp. 406.

53 "A M. Gluck, en lui envoyant une imitation en vers de l'ode de Dryden, sur le pouvoir de la musique," *Almanach des muses,* 1780, in Leblond, pp. 484-85.

54 Pascal Boyer, *L'expression musicale mise au rang des chimères* (Paris: Esprit, 1779), pp. 23-24.

55 *Ibid.,* pp. 41, 42-43.

56 Michel Paul Guy de Chabanon, *Observations sur la musique et principalement sur la métaphysique de l'art* (Paris: Pissot, 1779), p. 15.

57 *Ibid.,* p. 15.

Pictorial Sources of the Neo-classical Style: London or Rome?

DAVID GOODREAU

It is my hope that this essay will begin to answer the question posed by its title. The title itself is at best no more than a device to draw attention to one area of a much larger problem, namely, what are the sources of the neo-classical style and its subject matter, which appear in late eighteenth-century history painting? Because this is a question which favors open-ended answers, a few words about the state of the relevant scholarship may be in order.

Until only a few years ago, most scholars agreed that the *Parnassus* (Fig. 1), painted at Rome early in 1761 by Anton Raphael Mengs, was the first work executed in the neo-classical style. Because of the influence of Mengs and his *Parnassus*, the neo-classical style in history painting was believed to have developed at Rome. Foreign artists, it was thought, went to Rome to study, were attracted to Mengs's new style, and in effect brought about a "School of Mengs" in the painting of historical subject matter.[1]

This account of the expansion of the neo-classical style in history painting was exploded in 1954 by Professor Ellis K. Waterhouse.[2] Professor Waterhouse pointed out that within three months after completing the *Parnassus*, Mengs left Rome to become Court Painter in Madrid, where he stayed until the end of 1769. Because of his absence from Rome during most of the

247

Figure 1: Anton Raphael Mengs, *Parnassus*. Villa Albani, Rome. (Photo: Anderson)

248

critical decade of the 1760's, Mengs's influence on those young artists who are associated with early developments in the neo-classical style of history painting was, of course, necessarily limited. Furthermore, the style and the allegorical subject matter of Mengs's *Parnassus* are very different from the neo-classical ideal as it appears in Jacques-Louis David's *Oath of the Horatii* (Fig. 2). David's *Horatii*, the most famous neo-classical history painting, was completed in 1784, less than twenty-five years after Mengs's work.

Professor Waterhouse proposed that the work of Gavin Hamilton was more important than that of Mengs in the development of the neo-classical style and its subject matter. Figure 3 reproduces an engraving after Hamilton's *Andromache Weeping over the Body of Hector.* Hamilton's painting—like Mengs's fresco—was completed in 1761. Hamilton was a Scottish history and portrait painter who established permanent residence at Rome about 1755. Unlike Mengs, Hamilton was at Rome at the moment when many young artists began to arrive there to study, and, therefore, he could have influenced them to adopt the neo-classical style. After completing their studies at Rome, most students returned to their native countries, committed to some version of the neo-classical style in history painting. Moreover, there is another way in which Hamilton could have put the neo-classical style on the map. He had his paintings engraved, and prints after his works flooded Europe.

Since the publication of Professor Waterhouse's article in 1954, British priority in the development of the neo-classical style and its iconography in history painting at Rome has rightly been well-accepted by scholars. But because modern scholarship classically begins its examination of the neo-classical phenomenon with the study of British artists, most notably Gavin Hamilton, already living at Rome, there has been little recognition of the possibility that some elements which were important to the beginning of the neo-classical activity at Rome may have been brought to Italy from England. It is my purpose here to investigate and, I hope, to discredit the assumption that the young British artist forgot or abandoned the training acquired in his native country when he came into contact with the artistic scene at Rome. To do so, I shall discuss the *Death of Virginia*, a work executed at Rome by a young English artist, Nathaniel Dance, and in the process try to show that the source of inspiration for Dance's early neo-classical painting lies in the artist's experience in England, not in Italy.

In 1959, Basil Skinner published in the *Burlington Magazine* a print (Fig. 4) after Dance's *Death of Virginia.* Dance's painting was exhibited at London in 1761, it was engraved in 1767, but the painting itself has since disappeared.[3] The year 1761 marks, of course, the completion of Mengs's fresco as well as Hamilton's earliest surviving history painting, *Andromache Weeping over the Body of Hector.* So Dance's *Virginia* is potentially an important document in the history of the development of the neo-classical style and its iconography.

Figure 2: Jacques-Louis David, *Oath of the Horatii*, Louvre, **Paris.**
(Photo: Archives Photographiques—Paris)

250

Figure 3: Gavin Hamilton, *Andromache Weeping over the Body of Hector*, engraving.

Figure 4: Nathaniel Dance, *Death of Virginia*, engraving. British Museum, London.

In his *Transformations in Late Eighteenth Century Art,* published in 1967, Robert Rosenblum correctly observes that in the severity of its style and content Dance's *Death of Virginia* prophesies the standards of David's art.[4] Rosenblum goes on to say that Dance's painting depended on Hubert Gravelot's interpretation of the same scene (Fig. 5), which served as an illustration to Charles Rollin's *Roman History.*[5] In this instance, Rosenblum followed his student, Peter Walch, who, also in 1967, published in the *Art Bulletin* his work on Gravelot's illustrations.[6] In his important article, "Charles Rollin and Early Neoclassicism," Walch pointed the way toward the present discussion about the possibility that the place of origin of some of the neo-classical developments at Rome may be Britain. But he broached the subject only indirectly, in a limited way, in that he concerned himself mainly with looking for the influence of one early source—that is, Gravelot's illustrations—on later art. Given Walch's purposes, his treatment of the subject quite properly did not include his first looking at the early neo-classical works painted at Rome, and then seeking sources in the artist's immediate pre-Roman experience. But for reasons that must already be apparent, I have adopted just this methodology in my examination of Nathaniel Dance's *Death of Virginia.*

Nathaniel Dance's surviving neo-classical pictures are far less numerous than contemporary works by Gavin Hamilton. Partly because of this, Hamilton's history paintings are more familiar to scholars than are Dance's works, including the *Death of Virginia.* It is useful, therefore, first of all to discuss the importance of Dance's *Virginia* in terms of Hamilton's work of the early 1760's.

Dance's *Death of Virginia* was shown in London at the first exhibition of the Society of Artists in 1761. This was one year before the appearance in London of Hamilton's *Andromache Weeping over the Body of Hector.* The artists, aristocrats, and connoisseurs in London saw for the first time in Dance's *Virginia* an example of the new style in history painting in its first stage of development at Rome.

Moreover, Nathaniel Dance's painting can be dated earlier than 1761. What spurred my interest in Dance's *Death of Virginia* is the pen, ink, and grey wash drawing (Fig. 6) which Dance executed on a letter to his father in answer to a request for more information about the painting on which he was then working.[7] Nathaniel's letter is dated Rome, July 28, 1759, so this drawing is really very early in relation to the works by other artists that we have just looked at. The drawing is in fact the earliest firmly dated visual record, presently known, of a history painting, based on classical subject matter, executed by a British artist at Rome. Dance makes clear in his letter that Gavin Hamilton was already established at Rome as a history painter, but the earliest date we can attach to a history painting by Hamilton is 1761. The source of our information is a letter dated January of that year, in which

Figure 5: Hubert Gravelot, *Death of Virginia*, engraving.

Figure 6: Nathaniel Dance, *Death of Virginia*, pen, ink, and grey wash. Sir John Soane's Museum, London.

Figure 7: Gavin Hamilton, *Oath of Brutus on the Death of Lucretia.*
Theatre Royal, Drury Lane, London.

Johann Joachim Winckelmann describes Hamilton's recently completed painting of *Andromache Weeping over the Body of Hector.*[8] Although Hamilton's *Andromache* has served as a point of departure for many discussions about the first efforts in neo-classical history painting by British artists at Rome, Dance's letter and his drawing on it precedes Winckelmann's letter by one year and a half.

Dance's *Death of Virginia* is important also because it had an almost immediate impact on Gavin Hamilton, a conclusion that may be inferred from one of Hamilton's most significant works, the *Oath of Brutus on the Death of Lucretia* (Fig. 7). The version here represented is only one of several which the artist painted on the subject between 1763 and 1766, but it may well be the version which Hamilton had engraved in 1768. In his article on Gravelot's illustrations, Peter Walch noted the influence of Dance's painting on Hamilton's.[9] Walch saw that Hamilton had reversed several of the principal figures in Dance's composition; the influence of Dance's *Virginia* on Hamilton's *Brutus* is quickly seen in the collapsing body of the stabbed woman, her supporter with a cloak drawn up to his face, and the powerful torsion in the body of the central oath-taking male.

But the iconography of the oath-taking scene as it appears in neo-classical history painting is yet another point of contact between Dance's *Death of Virginia* and Hamilton's *Oath of Brutus on the Death of Lucretia.* The source of the death of Virginia story is a classical text, Livy's account of the history of Rome. In his interpretation of Livy's story, Dance depicts the moment immediately after the murder of Virginia by her father, Virginius. Virginius is shown turning violently toward the corrupt Roman decemvir, Appius Claudius, and crying out to him, "With this innocent blood, Appius, I devote your head to the infernal gods." Although the title of Dance's painting suggests merely a scene of death preferred to dishonor, the actual moment of Livy's story portrayed by Dance indicates that the subject matter of the painting is, iconographically speaking, on oath-taking scene. It now appears quite likely that Dance also influenced Hamilton in his very choice of an oath-taking scene for the subject matter of his painting. Furthermore, the story depicted in Hamilton's painting is also found in Livy.

The significance of Dance's *Death of Virginia* did not go unrecognized by late eighteenth-century artists other than Hamilton. Dance's painting was engraved in 1767, and, like Hamilton's, became available to artists throughout Europe. I shall now venture the proposition that Dance's *Virginia* appears to have been important to the development of neo-classical history painting in France.

In an important article, Robert Rosenblum recently published his discovery of Jacques-Antoine Beaufort's *Brutus* (Fig. 8), which was exhibited at the Salon of 1771.[10] It had been proposed for a long time that Beaufort's *Brutus*

Figure 8: Jacques-Antoine Beaufort, *Brutus*. Musée Municipal, Nevers.

was the missing link between Hamilton's *Brutus* and David's *Horatii*, and Rosenblum demonstrated this fact beyond the shadow of a doubt. However, Rosenblum's discovery of Beaufort's painting proved valuable in another way. The publication of Beaufort's *Brutus* made possible the identification of an oil study (Fig. 9) by Beaufort for his finished work. This study is now in a private collection in Rouen. The painting technique and dimensions of the study then led to the positive attribution to Beaufort of an oil sketch (Fig. 10), which was painted before the study, and which is now in a private collection in London.[11]

In his interpretation of the Brutus and Lucretia story, Beaufort undoubtedly used the 1768 engraving after Gavin Hamilton's *Brutus*. However, the use of multiple sources was a common academic method of working in history painting during the eighteenth century, and the 1767 engraving after Dance's *Virginia* also was available to him. Because we have not only Beaufort's finished painting but also two preparatory works for it, the role of Dance's *Virginia* in the development of Beaufort's *Brutus* can be clearly and precisely traced.

It has been noted already that the poses of several principal figures in Hamilton's *Brutus* are largely mirror images of figures in Dance's *Virginia*. Beaufort's individual figures and the composition of his work are also conventionally derived from models. For example, Beaufort's figure of Lucretia is composed of elements drawn from both Hamilton's Lucretia and Dance's Virginia. Although Beaufort retained the partial nudity of Hamilton's figure, the upper torso of his Lucretia is much closer to Dance's figure than to Hamilton's. But it is much more important that Beaufort's Lucretia, like Dance's Virginia, is already dead, and not in the process of dying, as she is in Hamilton's version. Beaufort's decision to follow Dance's example in this detail permitted him to emphasize the oath-taking scene, thereby increasing its emotional impact. Furthermore, in Beaufort's composition the spatial relationship between the dead body of Lucretia and the figure of her enraged husband, Collatinus, shown with the dagger, is similar to that between Virginia's body and the figure of her maddened father. Because the final composition of Beaufort's *Brutus* is related in this way to Dance's *Virginia*, instead of to Hamilton's work, Beaufort took a long step toward the dramatic isolation of the oath-taking scene in David's *Horatii*. The comparative diffusion of emotional energy in Gavin Hamilton's closely packed group makes this point clear enough.

Although the role played by Dance's *Virginia* in the development of Beaufort's *Brutus* can be traced in great detail, I have selected only three specific points to examine here. The first is the figure of Collatinus. In the sketch now at London, which shows Beaufort's first ideas, the figure of Collatinus strongly reflects Dance's figure of Virginius in the handling of the drapery, and in

Figure 9: Jacques-Antoine Beaufort, *Brutus*. Private Collection, Rouen.

Figure 10: Jacques-Antoine Beaufort, *Brutus*. Private Collection, London.

the position of the left arm and the twist of the head. After completing this sketch, Beaufort took a harder look at the figure of Hamilton's Brutus, and the tortured pose of the figure of Collatinus in the London sketch then gave way in the Rouen study to a figure more nearly approximating that of Hamilton's Brutus.

Second, the architectural background in Beaufort's composition is characterized by an increasing severity, as Beaufort methodically and rigorously simplified this area of his painting. In the London sketch the background consists mainly of the generalized curtains and columns seen in Hamilton's *Brutus*. However, the background wall in Beaufort's finished painting is articulated by means of Doric pilasters and is also parallel with the picture plane; it is in fact identical with the exterior wall of the building in the extreme lower background of Dance's work.

The last motive I shall examine also shows an increasing clarity in the spatial structure of the composition. The floor pattern in all three paintings by Beaufort shows a checkerboard pattern of alternating light and dark colored paving blocks. However, the floor in the preparatory works consists of paving blocks, all of the same size, like those in Hamilton's painting. But in Beaufort's final composition, the paving blocks of different sizes and their arrangement are identical to those in Dance's work. Because Beaufort increased the number of geometric units in the same amount of pictorial space, he created a floor plane which functions, like Dance's, as an obvious spatial grid for the principal figures in the foreground of the composition. In conclusion, it should now be apparent that through Hamilton's and Beaufort's interpretation of the Brutus story, David's *Oath of the Horatii* received decisive impulses from Dance's *Death of Virginia*.

This brief examination of the impact which Nathaniel Dance's *Death of Virginia* had on the course of late eighteenth-century history painting points out that his painting generally is important and is worthy of our study. Furthermore, Dance's *Virginia* promises to be significant to our understanding of the origins of neo-classical history painting as it developed at Rome. In the expectation that it will prove to be so, I shall attempt to trace the pictorial sources of this work.

When Peter Walch showed how Hubert Gravelot's frontispiece illustrations to Charles Rollin's *Roman History* influenced several early neo-classical artists, he demonstrated that Nathaniel Dance was aware of Gravelot's engraving of the *Death of Virginia*.[12] Walch noted that Dance followed Gravelot in depicting the moment immediately after Virginius had stabbed his daughter, a scene rarely portrayed in earlier representations of the Virginia story. However, I believe that the influence of Gravelot's illustration on Dance's *Virginia* ends here. For example, Gravelot's graceful rococo figures do not bear close comparison with the main protagonists in Dance's work. Besides, Gravelot's rococo composition is based on intersecting diagonals; it contrasts sharply with the static compositional balance of Dance's figures, which are parallel with and close to the surface of the picture plane.

A much closer source of inspiration for Dance's composition exists in the work of his teacher in England, Francis Hayman. Hayman's pen, ink, and grey wash drawing of *Caractacus* (Fig. 11) is a work after which a print was made, one of an immensely popular series depicting scenes from English history, first published in 1751 and 1752. Hayman's drawing shows Caractacus, a British king famous for his battles against the Romans, appearing as a captive before the Emperor Claudius in Rome. Dance must have been familiar with this particular composition by Hayman; he may even have been in Hayman's studio when the print after this drawing was published. The figures in Hayman's composition are parallel with the picture plane and are strung out across a grid-like floor. The row of columns immediately behind and parallel with the figures further emphasizes an inherent planar quality. In short, Hayman's composition is balanced and planar, and is much closer to that of Dance's *Virginia* than is Gravelot's illustration.

It should not be surprising that in his letter to his father, Nathaniel Dance explained his *Death of Virginia* by comparing it with the work of Francis Hayman. Dance's father certainly would have known Hayman's work because Nathaniel had spent at least two years as Hayman's student before he left England for Italy. But, more important, during the early 1750's, when Dance was in Hayman's studio, Francis Hayman was recognized by his contemporaries as the best history painter in England. Dance's interest in history painting probably began there; moreover, Dance's letter shows that at Rome he continued to hold Hayman in high regard.[13]

Because of Dance's opinion of Hayman's work and because of the apparent similarity of compositional principles between the *Death of Virginia* and the *Caractacus*, I would like to examine briefly another genre with which both artists were intimately involved, namely, the conversation group portrait. The conversation piece containing pictorial references to classical antiquity and to Rome began to flourish in Rome at the beginning of the 1760's, and this fashion appears to have been initiated largely by Nathaniel Dance.[14] In Dance's conversation piece of 1760, depicting four Englishmen in Rome (Fig. 12), this mode of portraiture appears fully developed.[15] The source of the classical motives in Dance's conversation pictures painted at Rome is a problem directly related to that of the sources of the *Death of Virginia*.

Brinsley Ford has best expressed current scholarly thought on this subject when he attributed the inspiration for this fashion to the growing interest in antiquities, the influence of Winckelmann and of English antiquarians, and the popularity of such publications as Piranesi's the *Antiquities of Rome*.[16] These events undoubtedly helped to create the climate in Rome that enabled

Figure 11: Francis Hayman, *Caractacus*, pen, ink, and grey wash.
Mrs. H. A. Hammelman, Lucca.

Figure 12: Nathaniel Dance, *A Conversation Piece—James Grant of Grant,*
Mr. Mytton, Hon. Thomas Robinson and Mr. Wynne. Philadelphia
Museum of Art: Given by John H. McFadden, Jr.

Dance to establish the conversation group portrait there, but they did not
provide the artist with pictorial precedents. As in the case of his history
painting, the artistic ideas which Dance brought with him from England were
the principal factor in his development of the conversation piece at Rome.

Of all the artists working in London immediately before Dance left for
Italy, Francis Hayman was the most important painter of the conversation
piece type of portrait. Moreover, Hayman, like Arthur Devis and the young
Gainsborough, occasionally used classical motives to enhance the sitters in his
conversation portraits. The sitters in Figure 13, which represents a conversation piece done by Hayman before Dance left his studio, have been tenta-
tively identified as Margaret Tyers and her husband. From Hayman's conversation portrait, Dance borrowed, probably from memory, the composition for the whole right half of his conversation piece. The slanting tree, the
poses of the two figures at the right, and the pedestal with an antique urn are
straight out of Hayman's painting.

The source of the classical motives which appear in Dance's conversation
pieces painted at Rome lies well within the tradition of English conversation
portraiture of the period, as seen here in Hayman's work. Moreover, Dance's

Figure 13: Francis Hayman, *Margaret Tyers and her Husband (?)*.
From the Collection of Mr. and Mrs. Paul Mellon.

approach to pictorial models for his history painting at Rome also derives from his training under Hayman. According to a contemporary, Francis Hayman "uniformly paid the highest compliments to the merits of Michael Angelo, Raphael, and the rest of that illustrious group . . . ."[17] Hayman's consistently favorable atitude toward the Italian Old Masters was typical of his day and was shared by his pupil, Nathaniel Dance.

When Nathaniel Dance left England to study in Italy, English taste in history painting still centered primarily on the Italian Old Masters, and the closer that a history painting could be associated with one of the few well known giants of Italian art, the more readily would aristocrats and connoisseurs purchase it. Of course, after 1763, when the Seven Years' War ended, pictorial sophistication in England increased rapidly with the flood of English visitors to the Continent on the Grand Tour. But English artists of the 1750's shared with their contemporaries the earlier cultural values, and they had a range of appreciation of Italian art which was rather narrow when compared with artists later in the eighteenth century. The tendency among older artists to gravitate toward a few big names in Italian painting can be noted in the most serious work of Hayman's friend, William Hogarth.

In 1759, the year in which Dance painted his *Death of Virginia* at Rome, Hogarth painted the *Sigismunda*, his last attempt—it was abortive—to gain acceptance in England as a classical history painter. With his *Sigismunda,* Hogarth competed directly with a painting of the same subject which had recently attained a high price at auction as by Correggio. This work was in fact by a minor early seventeenth-century Florentine artist, Francesco Furini. The Italian Old Master current of Hogarth's eclecticism is seen in another history painting which was of great importance to him. His *Paul Before Felix* of 1748 has as its model one of Raphael's cartoons, the *Paul and Elymas Before Sergius Paulus.*[18] Raphael's famous cartoons were then in the Royal Collection at Hampton Court and were well known to English artists.

By now it should come as no surprise that for the composition of the *Death of Virginia* Nathaniel Dance took a hard look at works by the Italian Old Masters. Indeed, Dance developed his composition directly out of another of Raphael's cartoons, the *Sacrifice at Lystra* (Fig. 14). The grouping of the figures, their relationship to the architecture, and the arrangement of the architecture itself function identically in the two compositions. Even specific features common to both works may be pointed to. A circular temple is at the right in both compositions; the pose of the old man at the left in Dance's work is similar to the stooped figure near St. Paul in Raphael's cartoon; and the shrinking movement and the position of the left arm of Appius Claudius, as seen in Dance's drawing, are derived from Raphael's figure of St. Paul. Finally, the internal torque of the body of Virginius owes much to Raphael's man wielding the sacrificial axe. That the composition and details of

Figure 14: Raphael, *Sacrifice at Lystra*. On loan from Her Majesty The Queen. Victoria & Albert Museum, London. (Photo: Crown Copyright)

Nathaniel Dance's neo-classical painting is heavily dependent on one of Raphael's cartoons links the artist with the artistic values of England in the 1750's and earlier decades.

Finally, it is significant that Dance's decision to paint the death of Virginia also originated from his English background; it did not result from his stay in Italy. The story of Virginia was very much in the public imagination at the time of Dance's departure from England. Early in 1754, Samuel Crisp brought out *The Story on which the New Tragedy, called Virginia, now in rehearsal at the Theatre Royal in Drury Lane, is founded*. David Garrick played Virginius, and Crisp's play ran for a few nights in February, 1754. The story of Virginia continued to be a part of the London literary scene in the mid-1750's. Toward the end of 1754, Crisp published the text of his play, and in March, 1755, *Appius, a Tragedy*, written by John Moncreiff, was acted at Covent Garden. Then, in the following year, 1756, Mrs. Frances Brooke published *Virginia, a Tragedy, with Odes, Pastorals, and Translations*.[19] When Nathaniel Dance's *Death of Virginia* was exhibited in London, in 1761, the story shown in the painting was undoubtedly a familiar dramatic theme because of the recent literary vogue there.

Up to now, scholars have examined neo-classical history paintings by British artists in Rome almost exclusively within a Roman context, and in so doing they have, perhaps unconsciously, made use of a residual form of the discredited theory that the neo-classical style radiated from a "School of Mengs" at Rome. My aim has been to show that Nathaniel Dance's work in Rome reflects artistic, cultural, and literary currents in England instead of Italy. Dance's conversation pieces containing classical motives derive from a tradition well established in England; and the *Death of Virginia*, though executed in Rome, also has its origins in England.

NOTES

1 This theory continues to enjoy a surprisingly long life. For example, Levey feels that Mengs "remains central to the whole [neo-classical] movement." Michael Levey, *Rococo to Revolution: Major Trends in Eighteenth-Century Painting* (New York, 1966), p. 176. For a recent discussion of the *Parnassus* which credits this painting with inaugurating the neo-classical movement, see Gert Schiff, "Teutons in Togas" in *The Academy*, ed. by Thomas B. Hess and John Ashbery, *Art News Annual*, 33 (1967), 47-58.

2 Ellis K. Waterhouse, "The British Contribution to the Neo-Classical Style in Painting," *Proceedings of the British Academy*, 40 (1954), 57-74.

3 Basil C. Skinner, "Some Aspects of the Work of Nathaniel Dance in Rome." *Burlington Magazine*, 101 (Sept./Oct. 1959), 346-49. Skinner stated incorrectly that John Gottfried Haid's engraving after Dance's

painting was published in 1760, but Robert Rosenblum provided the correct date of publication, August 2, 1767. See Robert Rosenblum, *Transformations in Late Eighteenth Century Art* (Princeton, 1967), p. 65 n. 56.

4 Rosenblum, pp. 65-66.

5 Gravelot's 1739 engraving served as the frontispiece to Volume II of the second edition of Rollin's *Roman History*, which was published in London in 1754. See Rosenblum, p. 66 n. 58.

6 Peter S. Walch, "Charles Rollin and Early Neoclassicism," *Art Bulletin*, 49 (June 1967), 123-26.

7 For Dance's letter, see David Goodreau, "Nathaniel Dance: An Unpublished Letter," *Burlington Magazine*, 115 (Oct. 1972), 712-15. I wish to thank the Trustees of Sir John Soane's Museum for permission to reproduce the drawing.

8 David Irwin, "Gavin Hamilton: Archaeologist, Painter, and Dealer," *Art Bulletin*, 44 (June 1962), 93.

9 Walch, p. 124.

10 Robert Rosenblum, "A Source for David's 'Horatii'," *Burlington Magazine*, 112 (May 1970), 269-73.

11 Pierre Rosenberg and Antoine Schnapper, "Beaufort's 'Brutus'," *Burlington Magazine*, 112 (Nov. 1970), 760.

12 Walch, pp. 123-24.

13 Dance writes of Hayman, "Though he is very deficient in point of colouring and correctness of drawing, yet he certainly has genius and a great facility of invention." Comparison of Dance's and Hayman's drawings reveals that Dance's academic life study at Rome enabled him to construct his principal figures with a minimum of the broken outlines which is characteristic of Hayman and his rococo idiom. By the end of the 1750's, Hayman's work as a history painter had fallen out of favor in England. See Goodreau, p. 715.

14 I am now preparing an article on this topic.

15 In Dance's conversation piece are represented (from left to right) Sir James Grant of Grant, Mr. Mytton, Thomas Robinson, and Mr. Wynne.

16 Brinsley Ford, "A Portrait Group by Gavin Hamilton: with some Notes on Portraits of Englishmen in Rome," *Burlington Magazine*, 97 (Dec. 1955), 376.

17 Anthony Pasquin (pseud. for John Williams), *Memoirs of the Royal Academicians: Being an Attempt to Improve the National Taste* (London, 1796), p. 139.

18 For Hogarth's *Sigismunda* and *Paul Before Felix*, see Ronald Paulson, *Hogarth: His Life, Art, and Times* (New Haven and London, 1971), II, 270-78 and 50-55.

19 For the literary interpretations in London of the death of Virginia story, see Percy Fitzgerald, *The Life of David Garrick* (London, 1899), p. 153, and John Nichols, *Literary Anecdotes of the Eighteenth Century*, II (London, 1812), 346.

The Informing Word:
Verbal Strategies in
Visual Satire*

KATHRYN HUNTER

Just as the act of reading is not entirely verbal, our perception of art is not wholly a visual experience. Every work of art requires of its audience some knowledge of the context and conventions. As E. H. Gombrich has taught us, the naked eye—could there be such a thing—is not enough: to see even an apparently "culture-free," "natural" painting like a still life or a landscape is to be guided by perceptual and representational conventions.[1] The importance of these conventions is so great that Morse Peckham has argued that the value of all art lies in its capacity to disturb us by its unexpected variation, its departure from the conventions we know.[2]

Because representational conventions exist, most art theorists grant the resemblance of art to language, but whether the relation between them is analogue or metaphor or identity is a matter of dispute.[3] An interesting description is given by the semioticist C. W. Morris: painting and music, though they signify iconically and thus operate as languages themselves, are " 'post-linguistic' in that they are dependent upon language for their appearance."[4]

Satiric art shares the language-like qualities of all art, but it is verbal in a further sense. By its nature satire must do more than speak itself. It must go beyond the iconic sign to refer to the world outside; it must designate its

*I should like to express my gratitude to the American Philosophical Society for a summer grant in support of the research that led to this essay.

extra-artistic context; it must mean. Such allusions are almost always verbalized conceptions, and therefore, a satiric work must either use words themselves or word substitutes: the verbal constructions of emblem and symbolic allegory or the referential signs of caricature. To understand visual satire, the viewer needs to perceive it verbally. It is especially true that the naked eye is not enough in looking at a satiric print. We must recognize allusion, see metaphor, apprehend clues to the context; and this experience is primarily a verbal one. Looking at satire requires an educated eye, one that is aware of satiric modes and the issues of the day. And to see the work truly, that eye probably must be slightly jaundiced in the same political or philosophical way as the artist's. It is not that satirical prints are not visual, it is that they are essentially verbal. If you have ever tried to explain an editorial cartoon to a five-year-old, you have faced this essential verbalness: "That donkey riding a bicycle backwards is Lester Maddox, who once rode a bicycle backwards, and who for four years was a backwards governor, and he looks like a donkey because he is a Democrat for one thing, and . . . ."[5]

Though this verbalness characterizes visual satire in every age, eighteenth-century English prints provide a particularly good illustration of visual satire's dependence on language. In this as in so many other ways the age was one of variety and change, and it offers us a sampling of almost all the strategies of visual satire in other times and places. Some of these are represented in emblematic prints and political allegories like Hogarth's *The South Sea Scheme* (Fig. 1), a work which would not have seemed strange to a sixteenth- or a seventeenth-century viewer; after the mid century there is also caricature, which was to become the mainstay of nineteenth- and twentieth-century graphic satire. We can even find in the eighteenth century some generalized satire of social types, although except for brief vogues like the one of macaroni prints and the foretaste that Rowlandson provides, type satire does not predominate, as it does in medieval admonitory prints and in nineteenth-century social comedy drawings. Even where we suspect a satire of manners or social types—as in Hogarth's pompous doctors in the fifth plate of *A Harlot's Progress*—when we look closer, and, above all, when we know more, we find a pointed, particular satire. Hogarth's doctors are identifiable contemporaries, a French quack and the well known Dr. Missubin, both famous for their unavailing remedies for the pox. When it appeared, caricature did not replace words, emblems, and symbolic imagery, it combined with these verbal strategies. It is this combination we have inherited in the twentieth-century editorial cartoons, in the deceptively wordless caricatures of Gerald Scarfe and David Levine, and in the satiric drawings of George Grosz, Ben Shahn, and Saul Steinberg.

Words themselves abound in eighteenth-century English satirical prints. There are titles and captions, keys and accompanying verses outside the print.

Figure 1: Hogarth, *The South Sea Scheme*, 1721. Courtesy of
Professor Ronald Paulson.

Inside are balloons of dialogue, title plates on paintings, covers of books and
sermons, and broadsides and playbills left lying conspicuously about. When
we look at Hogarth's paired prints, *Before* and *After*, if the occasion of their
contrasted pleas is not immediately clear, each print provides a number of
verbal clues. The title of each print is echoed in the title plate on the emblematic paintings of Cupid and his rocket. In *Before* we see the contrast of
Rochester's licentious poems on top of the table and *The Practice of Piety*
stuffed in the drawer; in *After*, lying near the fallen table and its broken
mirror is a book marked with Aristotle's observation, "omne animal post
coitum triste."

More important than actual words are the verbal constructions which are
the basis of many satires. In 1752 Mary and Matthew Darly printed a satirical
card, *Guy Vaux the Second* (Fig. 2), a visual-verbal pun on the name of
political character of Henry Fox, which alludes to *The Double Deliverance*,
an early cartoon concerned in part with Guy Fawkes's attempt to blow up the
Houses of Parliament. Thirty years later, James Gillray borrowed the pun,
without the visual allusion, for Henry's son, Charles James Fox (Fig. 3). In

Figure 2: Mary and Matthew Darly, *Guy Vaux the 2d,* 1756.
Courtesy of the Trustees of the British Museum.

satires of the 1760's, the prime minister, John Stuart, Third Earl of Bute, was represented and his Scottish accent ridiculed by a punning jack boot (Fig. 4). A favorite strategy then as now was to literalize clichés and revive dead metaphors. Early in the century a cartoon represented religious turncoats wearing clerical gowns lined with Geneva cloaks "to turn at pleasure" (B.M. 1507), and there is a 1774 print which suggests that several members of Parliament have literally "lost their heads" (B.M. 5224). M. Dorothy George in her study *English Political Caricature* reprints a cartoon commemorating Admiral Keppel's acquittal of responsibility for his disastrous naval defeat.[6] The print reveals the villain: NOBODY (Fig. 5). At the end of the century Gillray unfailingly represented the French Revolutionary sans culottes—and occasionally some of their English sympathizers (Fig. 6)—literally *sans culottes.* This strategy of re-rooting dead metaphors might have been learned from

Figure 3: Gillray, *Guy Vaux*, ca. 1782. Courtesy of the Trustees
of the British Museum.

Bosh or Breughel—or from Swift. It is a visual satire upon our misuse or
habitual ignorance of metaphor.

Satire's verbalness is a consequence of its reliance upon metaphor—either in
its mockery of metaphor's misuse or in its construction of new and absurd,
ironic vehicles for the objects of its attack. Jean Hagstrum has noted that
imagery is the point at which poetry most resembles painting;[7] the converse
is also true. Imagery, the iconic sign, is art's most language-like element. In
satiric art this image, whether emblem or allegory or caricature, must allude.
Like the imported term of a metaphor, it must signify something beyond
itself.

Emblems perform this verbal function readily. Drawn from medieval iconography and Renaissance emblem books, they had been the major resource of
seventeenth-century English and Dutch political satire, and they continued to
predominate for another fifty years. Emblems may function as signs; early
eighteenth-century satirical prints making such use of emblem often were
called hieroglyphics. Early and late Hogarth relied on the emblematic mode.[8]
In his first satiric venture, *The South Sea Scheme* (1721) (Fig. 1), horns
crown the building where newly rich men are raffled to willing women, and
wolves snarl about the monument to greed and folly, while near the merry-
go-round the mob clamors to be taken for a ride. The satiric objects of
Royalty, Episcopacy and the Law (Fig. 7), done four years later, are truly

Figure 4: Anonymous, *The Loaded Boot*, 1762. Courtesy of the Trustees of the British Museum.

Figure 5: Anonymous, *Who's in Fault? NOBODY,* 1779. Courtesy of the Trustees of the British Museum.

objects: a crown and coin, a miter and jew's harp, a wig and gavel form the heads of the established order, and they are surrounded by courtiers whose substances are variously fans and teapots, sconces and mirrors.

Hogarth's emblematic habit in part accounts for Charles Lamb's description of him as second only to Shakespeare, an artist who must be read. "His graphic representations are indeed books," wrote Lamb, "they have the teeming, fruitful, suggestive meaning of words. Other prints we look at,—his prints we read."[9] It could be argued that Hogarth's abundant use of detail in his major works, particularly in the comic histories, is in an extended, typological sense, emblematic. Certainly Georg Christoph Lichtenberg, the German physics professor, son of a protestant minister, who wrote the detailed and perceptive *Commentaries* upon Hogarth's works, found them an adequate field for what he described as "one of the most remarkable traits of my character," "a curious superstition which makes everything into an omen and interprets hundreds of things every day as oracles . . . ."[10] Late in Hogarth's career he used not only traditional emblems as in the *Industry and Idleness* series but many he had himself created. Occultism and dissent are mocked in

Figure 6: Gillray, *A Democrat, or Reason & Philosophy*, 1793. Courtesy of the Trustees of the British Museum.

Some of the Principal Inhabitants of y.e Moon, as they Were Perfectly Discoverd by a Telescope brought to y.e Greatest Perfection since y.e last Eclipse; Exactly Engraved from the Objects, whereby y.e Curious may Guess at their Religion, Manners, &c.

1725: Price Six Pence

Figure 7: Hogarth, *Royalty, Episcopacy, and the Law*, 1725. Courtesy of Professor Ronald Paulson.

Figure 8: Hogarth, *Credulity, Superstition, and Fanaticism*, 1762. Courtesy of Professor Ronald Paulson.

Figure 9: Hogarth, *The Times, plate 1*, 1762. Courtesy of
Professor Ronald Paulson.

Credulity, Superstition and Fanaticism (Fig. 8), the castle is crumbling and
the world is in flames in *The Times* (Fig. 9), and *Tailpiece or the Bathos*
(Fig. 10) is a chaos of guttering candles, crumbling buildings, broken time-
pieces—emblems that proclaim the end of creation.

Hogarth's were of course not the only emblematic prints. In 1729, the
"Caleb D'Anvers" frontispieces to *The Craftsman* were published separately,
with a lengthy explication. Also in 1729, the Opposition party attacked
Walpole in *Robin's Reign, or Seven's the Main, being an explanation of
Caleb Danver's Seven Egyptian Hieroglyphics prefixed to the Craftsman*. In
1736 the Gin Act provoked a number of prints commemorating the untimely
death of Madame Geneva, one of which is a monument constructed, like the
portraits of Arcimboldo two centuries earlier, of the tools of her trade (Fig.
11).

Symbolic allegory, too, is a venerable means of conveying verbal meaning.
The satiric metaphor is extended into a situation, frequently a political one,
and this allegory must be read precisely. Despite the demands it makes upon
its audience and the ease with which it becomes dated and inaccessible,
symbolic allegory has been the fundamental strategy of political cartooning

Figure 10: Hogarth, *Tailpiece, or the Bathos,* 1764. Courtesy of
Professor Ronald Paulson.

since the sixteenth century. W. A. Coupe has found the mock funeral, used obliquely for the Gin Act above, in a number of broadcasts from the *Thirty Years' War.*[11] Goya uses the motif in the next-to-last etching of *The Disasters of War* (Fig. 12); Daumier in the 1870's hopefully inters an old hag labeled Monarchy (Fig. 13); and recently in their local newspapers Americans have seen with less hope the social programs of the 1960's laid to rest.

An equally durable motif has been the game as a metaphor for diplomacy. What is probably the earliest political cartoon,[12] *The Reversal of the Swiss's Game*, pictures various heads of state around a card table, bluffing and cheating and double-dealing. Eighteenth-century England widened the allegorical possibilities to include chess, cricket, and games of chance. And again and again the balance of international or party power has been represented, as in Rowlandson's *The Poll* (Fig. 14), by symbolic figures on a see-saw.

Many of the earlier political allegories require keys, but by Rowlandson's

To the Mortal *Memory of*
Madam Geneva,
Who died Sep. 29. 1736;
Her Weeping Servants &
loving Friends consecrate
This Tomb.

cease to drop distill no more

To thee, kind comfort of the starving Poor!
To thee Geneva, that art now no more!
This sad but gratefull monument we raise;
Our Arms we yield no more our Sun shall blaze.
So, where Supine her mournful Genius lies,
And hollow barrels eccho to her cries;
On casks, around her Sad Attendants stand;
The Bunter Weeps with basket in her hand.

The Boy with heavy heart for Succour Sues;
What gave her birth now helps her Tomb to build.
The Tub a Spire, A Globe the Can unfill'd.
High in the Air the Still its head doth rear,
And on its Top a Mournfull Granadeer
The Clean white Apron as a Label shown
The dreadfull cause of all our Grief makes known.
Hither repair All ye that for her Mourn.
And Drink a Requiem to her Peacefull Urn.

Published according to Act of Parliament Oct. 18. 1736. Sold by ye Printsellers of London and Westminster.   For Bill- see Genl. Mag. Ab. 1736   *price 6ᵈ*
Sept. 21. 1736.

Figure 11: Vandermijn, *To the Mortal Memory of Madam Geneva*, 1736.
Courtesy of the Trustees of the British Museum.

Figure 12: Goya, *Truth is dead, The Disasters of War,* ca. 1810.
Courtesy of the Museum of Fine Arts, Boston.

time caricature conveys the information needed for a contemporary to identify Fox and his canvasser, the Duchess of Devonshire, on the right, who is
outweighed by "Madame Blubber," on the left, a rival canvasser for Pitt.[13]
This capacity to substitute for words confirms caricature's referential, language-like function. Caricature is, as Dryden described all satire, both truth
and wit, both iconic sign and outrageous but recognizable distortion. There is
a story about Sarah, Duchess of Marlborough, who, out of favor with Queen
Anne, is said to have requested of Bubb Doddington, newly returned from
Italy, "a caricatura of Lady Masham, describing her covered with running
sores and ulcers, that I may send to the Queen to give her a slight idea of her
favorite."[14] Caricature is, as this story suggests, a metaphor in itself. Hogarth
despised it as a trick, and his portrait of Simon Lord Lovat (Fig. 15) shows he
had little need of it. He could achieve its outward revelation of inward truth
without its distortion. Not until George Townshend returned from Italy in
the 1750's did he and Mary Darly, teacher of caricature, along with her
husband Matthew, an engraver who published their first satirical cards,
establish caricature as a part of the English satirical mode.[15]
    Caricature, especially from the hands of James Gillray, combined well with

Et pendant ce temps-là ils continuent à affirmer qu'elle ne s'est jamais mieux portée !

Figure 13: Daumier, *And during that time* . . . , 1872. Courtesy of the
Museum of Fine Arts, Boston.

the older satiric strategies. It was used as simple metaphor—as in the anonymous representation of Dr. Johnson as an owl (Fig. 16) and in Gillray's vision
of William Pitt as a "vile fungus" upon the dunghill of the crown (Fig. 17). It
could be a part of situational allegory: Voltaire, Rousseau, Godwin, and
Wollstonecraft are recognizable in the chaotic, godless throng of Gillray's
New Morality (Fig. 18). Caricature gives political point to what might otherwise be a realistic social scene in his *Temperance Enjoying a Frugal Meal* (Fig.
19), a satire on the miserly habits of George III and his queen. Caricature is
essential to parodic attack—whether in travesties like Gillray's representation
of Lady Hamilton as a fat Dido weeping as Lord Nelson abandons her to her

Figure 14: Rowlandson, *The Poll*, 1784. Courtesy of the Trustees of the British Museum.

Figure 15: Hogarth, *Simon Lord Lovat*, 1746. Courtesy of Professor Ronald Paulson.

Figure 16: Anonymous, *Old Wisdom Blinking at the Stars*, 1782. Courtesy of the Trustees of the British Museum.

numerous emblematic devices (Fig. 20) or in pure parody such as Paul Sandby's satiric version (Fig. 21) of Hogarth's *March to Finchley,* which substitutes a fat harried painter besieged by creditors for the handsome young soldier, a Hercules importuned by rival ballad-sellers. So little does caricature supplant these older modes that in fact they prove to be essential to caricature's success as satire. Where they are missing or insufficient, as in Thomas

An Excrescence;– a Fungus;– alias – a Toadstool upon a Dunghill.
– Pub.^d Decr 20.^t 1791. by H. Humphry N.º 18. Old Bond Street –

Figure 17: Gillray, . . . *A Toadstool upon a Dunghill*, 1791. Courtesy of the
Trustees of the British Museum.

Patch's caricature of Lawrence Sterne meeting Death (Fig. 22), we have difficulty understanding the work. The situation, borrowed from the medieval *danse macabre*, is ambiguous. The caller traditionally marks the end of earthly vanity, yet the inscription below, taken from Sterne's *A Sentimental Journey*, is inconclusive, almost welcoming: "And when Death himself knocked at my door ye bad him come again; and in so gay a tone of careless indifference, did ye do it that he doubted of his Commision. . ." The machine behind the door, a paper shredder with several old books in its

290

Figure 18: Gillray, *New Morality*, 1798. Courtesy of the Trustees of the British Museum.

Figure 19: Gillray, *Temperance Enjoying a Frugal Meal,* 1792. Courtesy of the
Trustees of the British Museum.

hopper, may simply allude to Sterne's allusiveness, or be yet another charge
of plagiarism. But the glass in Death's hand has yet to run, and perhaps the
print simply concerns Sterne's customary themes and strategies. Despite the
fairly harsh caricature, the work includes little allusion, few tonal clues, too
little of the reference that satire requires.

   All visual satire is verbally conceived; it communicates itself in images that

Figure 20: Gillray, *Dido in Despair*, 1801. Courtesy of the Trustees of the British Museum.

Figure 21: Paul Sandby, *The Painter's March from Finchley*, 1754. Courtesy of the Trustees of the British Museum.

are or can be verbalized. The satiric print figures forth its verbal conception, locating it in time and place, and we who would "see" that print must grasp the word that informs it. It was not idly that Hogarth described himself as the "author" of his prints.[16] The satiric works of eighteenth-century England exist alongside the richest literary satire since Augustan Rome. Parallel often in theme and always in their allusive, metaphoric method, these satirical prints illuminate satire's method as well as the human condition.

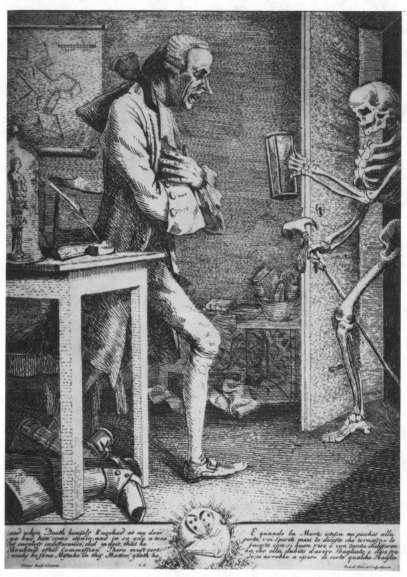

Figure 22: Thomas Patch, *Sterne and Death,* ca. 1768. Courtesy of the
Trustees of the British Museum.

NOTES

1 That art's history is an account of the continuity and change of these visual conventions has been a major theme of Gombrich's work. In *Art and Illusion: A Study in the Psychology of Pictorial Representation*, Bollingen Series 35, 5 (New York: Pantheon, 1960), he contrasts the conventions of Chinese and Western landscape art (pp. 84-86) and discusses Ruskin's notion of the "innocence of the eye" (pp. 296-97). See also his "Tradition and Expression in Western Still Life," *Meditations on a Hobby Horse and Other Essays in the Theory of Art* (London: Phaidon, 1963), pp. 195-205.

2 Peckham, *Man's Rage for Chaos: Biology, Behavior, and the Arts* (Philadelphia: Chilton, 1965). See especially "Order and Disorder," pp. 25-40.

3 Since the advent of linguistics and the structuralism modelled upon it, art is often described as language. Ernst Cassirer has discussed art and language as analogous symbolic formations by which and through which we perceive reality in *The Philosophy of Symbolic Forms, vol. 3: The Phenomenology of Knowledge*, tr. Ralph Manheim (New Haven: Yale Univ. Press, 1957), and structural anthropologists, accustomed to regarding every cultural form as a "language," would extend the description to all art, not excepting abstract expressionism. The idea of art as language has been reinforced by Professor Gombrich's account of the history of traditional Western art as not the increasingly closer observation of nature but the development of a conventional "vocabulary" for representing the phenomenal world (see especially chapter 5 of *Art and Illusion*). The practitioners of "concept art" and their critics assume the identity of verbal concepts and visual imagery; see for example Amy Goldin, "Words in Pictures," *Art News Annual*, ed. Thomas B. Hess and John Ashbery, 36 (1970), 60-71. Recently, however, Claude Lévi-Strauss's own use of linguistics has been described as metaphoric rather than the more radical epistemological model structuralists have supposed it to be; see "The Space Between—1971," *The Structuralist Controversy: The Languages of Criticism and the Science of Man*, ed. Richard Macksey and Eugenio Donato (Baltimore: Johns Hopkins Univ. Press, 1972), p. xi.

4 Morris, *Signs, Language, and Behavior* (New York: Prentice-Hall, 1946), pp. 192-96.

5 Clifford (Baldy) Baldowski's cartoons of Maddox in the Atlanta *Constitution* have renewed the metaphorical life of Thomas Nast's Democratic donkey, a cartoon figure which has come to operate in most contexts as a simple sign.

6 George, *English Political Caricature, vol. 1: To 1792* (Oxford: Clarendon, 1959), plate 58. Mrs. George traces the persistence of the Guy Fawkes motif in English graphic satire from *The Double Deliverance* of 1621 through the two Fox cartoons discussed above (pp. 15-16, 88, 105, and 165). She also explicates "The Loaded Boot" (p. 33), though not the

origin of the boot-bute homonym in Scottish speech, and discusses Vandermijn's *Monument to Gin* (p. 85) and Rowlandson's *The Poll* (p. 71).

7 Hagstrum, *The Sister Arts: The Tradition of Literary Pictorialism in English Poetry from Dryden to Gray* (Chicago: Univ. of Chicago Press, 1958), p. xv.

8 Ronald Paulson discusses the influence of the Anglo-Dutch emblematic satire in *Hogarth's Graphic Works, vol. 1: Catalogue,* rev. ed. (New Haven: Yale Univ. Press, 1970), pp. 28-29.

9 Lamb, "On the Genius and Character of Hogarth" (1811), *The Works of Charles and Mary Lamb, vol I: Miscellaneous Prose,* ed. E. V. Lucas (London: Methuen, 1903), p. 71.

10 Lichtenberg, *The World of Hogarth: Lichtenberg's Commentaries on his Engravings,* tr. and intro. Innes and Gustav Herdan (Boston: Houghton Mifflin, 1966), p. xviii. On the relation between realism and the emblematic vision see J. Paul Hunter, *The Reluctant Pilgrim: Defoe's Emblematic Method and Quest for Form in* Robinson Crusoe (Baltimore: Johns Hopkins Univ. Press, 1966).

11 Coupe, "Political and Religious Cartoons of the Thirty Years' War," *Journal of the Warburg and Courtauld Institutes,* 25 (1962), 79.

12 This assertion by Thomas Wright, an early student of graphic satire, has gone unquestioned by subsequent historians. Wright explicates the cartoon in *A History of Caricature and the Grotesque in Literature and Art* (London, 1865), pp. 347-49.

13 E. H. Gombrich observes that in seventeenth-century political drawings keys were used rather than caricature ("The Cartoonist's Armoury," *Meditations on a Hobby Horse,* pp. 133-34).

14 This story is often retold but is unsupported by contemporary evidence. Bohun Lynch is the modern source; *A History of Caricature* (Boston: Little, Brown, 1927), p. 46.

15 See George, pp. 115-17.

16 Hogarth customarily used the word "author" in his newspaper announcements of forthcoming prints, and he assumes the literary nature of his progresses in the *Autobiographical Notes*: "Subjects I considered as authors do." Paulson rightly cautions against taking "author" too literally since the first definition in Johnson's dictionary is "the first beginner or mover of any thing" while our sense is third; see *Hogarth: His Life, His Art, and His Times* (New Haven: Yale Univ. Press, 1972), I, 563, note 9. But the analogy of the "sister arts" is evident not only in Hogarth's works, but in his appeal to Parliament to extend to engravers the protection from piracy that writers enjoyed. I have been concerned here not with the literary or dramatic analogues which are useful for describing the narrative quality of Hogarth's works, but the allusive and metaphorical nature of all satiric art.

Innovation and Variation:
A Problem of Literary History*

RALPH COHEN

The study of literary history inevitably involves the study of literary change, and there can be no analysis of change without some theory of a norm and its transformation. The problem I have set myself is to determine "How can we distinguish between a change of genre or form that results in new poetic functions and a change that merely results in variations of commonly practiced functions? " I assume that we come to understand literary history by dividing it into some kind of segments that are differentiated by innovations that become accepted, improved upon, extended and varied, and finally, overturned by techniques that imply new concepts and functions. In this sense, periods, schools, movements are identified by innovations that become accepted. The principle of innovation, therefore, is dependent upon the hypothesis that there exists a prior group of conventions or functions of poetic features that no longer express the kind of experience the poems deal with. A new function of rhetorical features, therefore, replaces the old as does a new hierarchy of forms.

My discussion of innovation and variation is limited to the analysis of the eclogue and the georgic in the mid-seventeenth century, and I wish to argue that at this time there took place an innovative change in the writing of georgic poetry. The fact that I use georgic poetry as a model, especially John

*An expanded version of this essay entitled "Innovation and Variation: Literary Change and Georgic Poetry" is to be published in the William Andrews Clark Memorial Library Seminar Papers, 1975.

Denham's *Coopers Hill,* should be taken as just that—I use it as a model. The argument, if it is valid, ought to have applicability to other genres as well.

I

When Samuel Johnson wrote the life of Sir John Denham, he declared that *Coopers Hill* was a new "species of composition" in English literature:

> *Coopers Hill* is the work that confers upon him the rank and dignity of an original author. He seems to have been, at least among us, the author of a species of composition that may be denominated *local poetry,* of which the fundamental subject is some particular landscape to be poetically described, with the addition of such embellishments as may be supplied by historical retrospection or incidental meditation.
> To trace a new scheme of poetry has in itself a very high claim to praise, and its praise is yet more when it is apparently copied by Garth and Pope; after whose names little will be gained by an enumeration of smaller poets, that have left scarce a corner of the island not dignified either by rhyme or blank verse.[1]

The poem gave Denham the rank of an "original author," the "author of a species of composition." To the extent that one literary work is different from any other, it is unique, yet works can be and need to be grouped together. When this is done, some works introduce new ways of organizing and expressing thoughts in poetry, initiate new groupings. Johnson identified *Coopers Hill* as such a poem and selected as its novel literary features the description of a landscape "with the addition" of two kinds of "embellishments": "historical retrospection or incidental meditation."

The selection of these features proved, for Johnson, the basis for a "new scheme of poetry." They were, for him, new features. But Denham himself saw the poem as a georgic, as an innovation within the received form. And this view was shared by Pope and John Dennis. The latter identified the purpose of *Coopers Hill* as a form of persuasion or instruction:

> And as the Admirable Poet took Occasion before, from the View of St. *Anne's* Hill, to give the most important Instruction that can be given to this Island, upon a Religious Account; *viz.* That we should banish Persecution, and an ill-grounded Zeal, from among us; he takes an Opportunity now, from showing the Prince and the People assembled upon that memorable Occasion, to conclude this Poem, with the most important Instruction, that, upon a Civil Account, can be given, either to Prince or People, *viz.* That

the Prince should avoid intrenching upon Liberty, and the People
upon Prerogative; and thus he has in this short, but admirable
Poem, given those Instructions, both to the Prince, the Church,
and the People, which, being observ'd, must make the Prince
Powerful and Glorious, the Church Great and Venerable, and the
People a Flourishing and a Happy People; and which, being neglected, must bring universal Misery upon the Nation.[2]

There can be no doubt that Dennis saw the poem as a georgic, a poem for
which Virgil's *Georgics* was the model.

But the kind to which *Coopers Hill* belongs has also been identified as a
topographical poem for which "To Penshurst" was the model, as an antecedent of the "greater romantic lyric," as a pastoral as well as a georgic
poem.[3] The solution to this problem of classification is not a matter of
pluralistic choice; it is rather dependent upon a theory of change and innovation. Without an explanation that accounts for the difference between
changes that are variants of a type (norm) and those that alter the type
(norm), no resolution can be made between classifications that select descriptions and historical retrospection as governing features in contrast to those
that prefer references to a home or structure as primary.

And the issue cannot be resolved by proposing an analysis of *Coopers Hill,*
for such analysis presupposes a decision about the innovation or variational
category into which it is to be fitted. It begins as a perceptual poem: the
speaker mounts Cooper's Hill and from it surveys distant St. Paul's as well as
the nearby hills and dales, relating acts and events pertinent to these places.
Concluding his reflections on Windsor Castle, he turns to St. Anne's Hill:

> Here should my wonder dwell, & here my praise,
> But my fixt thoughts my wandring eye betrays,
> Viewing a neighbouring hill, whose top of late
> A Chappel crown'd, till in the Common Fate,
> The adjoyning Abby fell: (may no such storm
> Fall on our times, where ruin must reform.)[4]

To decide whether this practice of a survey leading to historical reflections
is a Virgilian technique being adapted to Denham's purpose, or some new
implication of the poet's view of his environment, cannot be answered by a
reading which does not interpret the technique as a response to or departure
from preceding poetry. The way the speaker proceeds in his transitions, re-
petitively organizing responses to hills which contrast with each other—the
great heritage of Windsor Castle and the destruction of Chertsey Abbey by
Henry VIII—cannot in itself explain whether the poem is suggesting a new
approach to the encomiastic procedures of "To Penshurst" or is using these as
features for a quite different end.

The basis for such a decision rests upon understanding whether repetition in preceding georgic poems functioned to establish God's harmony by contrast and spatial extent or whether repetition and survey functioned to make nature an emblem for man-made works.

Coopers Hill alludes to Edmund Waller's poem, "Upon His Majesties reparing of Pauls":

> *Pauls,* the late Theme of such a Muse, whose flight
> Hath bravely reacht and soar'd above thy height:
> (19-20)

But Denham's perceptual use of St. Paul's introduces a spatial concept foreign to Waller's poem. It also alludes to Virgil's first *Georgic,* in which the crops are described as overwhelmed by storms and floods of uncontrolled nature.

> Often, too, there appears in the sky a mighty column of waters, and clouds mustered from on high roll up a murky tempest of black showers: down falls the lofty heaven, and with its deluge of rain washes away the gladsome crops and the labours of oxen. The dykes fill, the deep-channelled rivers swell and roar, and the sea steams in its heaving friths.[5]

Coopers Hill incorporates this allusion in a political comparison:

> When a calme River rais'd with sudden raines,
> Or Snowes dissolv'd o'reflowes th'adjoyning Plaines,
> The Husbandmen with high rais'd bankes secure
> Their greedy hopes, and this he can endure.
> But if with Bays, and Dammes they strive to force,
> His channell to a new, or narrow course,
> No longer then within his bankes he dwels,
> First to a Torrent, then a Deluge swels;
> Stronger, and Fiercer by restraint, he roares,
> And knowes no bound, but makes his powers his shores:
> Thus Kings by grasping more then they can hold,
> First made their Subjects by oppressions bold,
> And popular sway by forcing Kings to give
> More, then was fit for Subjects to receive,
> Ranne to the same extreame; and one excesse
> Made both, by stirring to be greater, lesse.
> (1642)
> (333-48)

The manner in which these allusions are to be interpreted depends upon the relation the critic makes between them and the poems to which they refer. But this relation can only be defined in terms of the poet's concept of imitation, of relating past to present—in general, some form of variation of a past work or some attempt to innovate, using it as a point of departure. The most perplexing problems about the use of classical allusions in seventeenth- and eighteenth-century poems stem from the failure on the part of critics to recognize that the difficulty is not a matter of interpreting the poem but rather of assuming a theory that distinguishes conventional uses of allusion from others that are innovative, thus identifying allusive procedures as belonging to one group of poems rather than another.

I have deliberately used the term "conventional" in order to point up the historical assumptions that inevitably exist in interpretative criticism, even among the most able critics. In a valuable article on the eclogue tradition, Paul Alpers remarks in a discussion of Spenser's April eclogue that though "the tone is elevated, Spenser, like Virgil, extends rather than transforms the mode: throughout the eclogue he stays in touch with homely expressions and pretty descriptions." This implies that an extension of a mode can be achieved by varying but not transforming a feature like diction. Yet in a discussion of the December eclogue he remarks upon a fundamental transformation of the Virgilian eclogue: "The idea that there is a proportion between man and nature is basic to Renaissance pastoral and represents a fundamental point of difference between it and ancient pastoral, where life in nature is an ethical alternative, one possibility for the good life. In Renaissance pastoral, with its Christian perspective, man's life has an inherent relation to nature."[6] Unless I mistake these remarks, there is a fundamental difference between Renaissance and Virgilian pastoral in man's relation to nature, yet this fundamental difference does not lead to a transformation of mode, merely to extension of it. The question about analysis of a form that has a history requires distinctions between changes that are "extensions" and changes that are "transformations."

The concept of a "convention," for example, requires an understanding of the manner in which it functions in earlier poems in order for it to be assessed as "extending" rather than "innovating" a procedure. It will not do to explain, for example, as Earl Wasserman does—and he is our best critic of this poem—that the "ambience of this doctrine of *Concordia discors*" is drawn from Cicero and St. Augustine as well as Davenant, because it is the innovation or variant use that is necessary to be established if the interpretation is to be supported. To see all uses as variants of an "ambience" is to reduce literary study to no more than individual examples. Poetic conventions exist only in poems; they must, therefore, always be identified with a particular use or function. Consider the description of Penshurst in "To Penshurst" and that of Windsor Castle in *Coopers Hill:*

> Thou art not, *Penshurst,* built to envious show,
> Of touch, or marble; nor canst boast a row
> Of polish'd pillars, or a roofe of gold:
> Thou hast no lantherne, whereof tales are told;
> Or stayre, or courts; but stand'st an ancient pile,
> And these grudg'd at, art reverenc'd the while.[7]
>
> (1-6)

and

> So *Windsor,* humble in it selfe, seemes proud
> To be the Base of that Majesticke load.
> Than which no hill a nobler burthen beares,
> But Atlas onely, that supports the spheres.
> Nature this mount so fitly did advance,
> We might conclude, that nothing is by chance,
> So plac't, as if she did on purpose raise
> The Hill, to rob the builder of his praise.
>
> (1642)
> (65-72)

Both structures are harmoniously related to the place in which they stand; both are objects of reverence. In "To Penshurst" the structure becomes an emblem of the natural harmony of the grounds and the Sidney family. In *Coopers Hill* Windsor Castle is but one part of a contrasting relationship with Chertsey Abbey, a structure ruined by Henry VIII. It is, moreover, seen as a response to nature's creation of Windsor Hill on which it stands so that the hidden force in nature becomes the dominant feature in this use of the convention.

The failure to distinguish between variants and innovation in a convention, in allusions, in the manner of proceeding, in the classifying of a poem in a genre—and, I would add, in such matters as the semantic and rhetorical dimensions of a poem—results in interpretative difficulties. All these features have a history, but it is a history that exists only in poems. The use of a convention or an allusion or a way of proceeding must be understood, therefore, as interacting with other works. Whether it is a variant or an innovation of a convention, cluster of ideas or genre, the nature of this interaction forms the basis for divisions in literary study.

The only interaction leading to change that has been studied to any extent is that of the writer with himself: the study of drafts or revisions. These second thoughts or second "sights" are among the simplest of changes because they take place while other unrevised features remain constant. Such studies become the basis for our knowledge of a writer's range of choices as they affect his and our version of his stability and change. They provide an interpretative guide to his grammar and vocabulary, and they make it possible for us to distinguish procedures which are consistent with and thus variants of his earlier practices from those which are innovative, introducing conceptual changes through poetic transformations.

Denham's revisions of the 1642 *Coopers Hill* were published in 1655 and 1668. These sophisticated variations function consistently with the unchanged portions. They do not alter the structure of the poem, but they do extend some scenes and provide a model for the couplet. In 1642 Denham wrote, comparing his verse to the Thames,

> O could my verse freely and smoothly flow,
> As thy pure flood, heav'n should no longer know
> Her old *Eridanus,* thy purer streame
> Should bathe the gods, and be the Poëts Theame.
> (219-22)

He revised this in 1655:

> O could I flow like thee, and make thy stream
> My great example, as it is my theme!
> Though deep, yet clear, though gentle, yet not dull.
> Strong without rage, without ore-flowing full.
> (189-92)

The bold metonomy of the revision—"O could I flow like thee" for "O could my verse freely and smoothly flow"—referring to his inspiration as well as his verse, becomes an image of man naturalized, the moving stream being that to which the poet is compared. The unfolding of the image proceeds by indication of harmonious features that mingle natural with personified terms. This interrelationship by its repetitive patter—"Though ... yet, though ... yet not"—establishes those concessions which make for harmony; that is, harmony conceived of as a balance between opposite or contrasting qualities, and in the following line—"... without ... , without ..."—instead of concessions there are rejections by which strength and completion can still be seen as harmonious norms.

Denham's revisions run from 1642 (there were drafts that preceded the initial publication) to 1668, and the later revisions are improvements in the handling of the couplet. We can conceive of the revisions as helping Denham to fulfill more successfully the innovative concept that *Coopers Hill* represented. The "Thames couplets" did effect what the earlier ones did not quite achieve: the revelation of the reciprocal relation between man and nature governed by a harmony based on contraries the source of which was an underlying power. To have fashioned the couplet that expressed these ideas in its structure was a significant achievement, as Dryden and Johnson noted.[8]

To make this point more general, the innovation of the first "Thames couplets" was consistent with the retrospective and spatial features; what the revised couplets provided was an original way of phrasing the same experience. It should, therefore, be apparent that "innovation" in no way implies a value term, as I use it. I wish to reserve "originality" for such a term, indicating the qualitative response, a response that can sometimes occur in innovation poems, but is more likely to occur in those that provide variations of received conceptual views. The revised "Thames" lines provided a model for poets who exploited in variant ways the possibilities both of the couplet and of that new georgic scheme that Denham created. So much so, in fact, that Swift declared:

> Nor let my Votaries show their Skill
> In apeing Lines from *Coopers Hill;*
> For know I cannot bear to hear
> The Mimicry of *deep yet clear.*[9]

II

Johnson was right about *Coopers Hill;* it was a "new scheme of poetry," even though he neglected to see it in terms of its antecedents—its innovative use of the georgic didactic poem. His comments were, of course, retrospective. Writing more than a hundred years after Denham's final publication of the poem, he knew the frequency of variants or imitations that had been nourished by it. For him, therefore, the innovative quality was identifiable by the poems that came after it, thus constituting the group as a special class. If the first criterion for innovation is the conceptual change implied in the altered function of poetic features, agreement upon a new class by contemporary critics—Pope, Dennis, and Johnson, for example—is a second criterion.

But just as variants constitute a class, so too, innovation is not—with rare exceptions—a single phenomenon. Just as scientific discoveries tend to occur in the work of more than one scientist simultaneously—whether these are Leibniz and Newton, Darwin and Wallace, Salk and Sabin—so, too, innovative procedures begin to be noticed in the work of more than one poet. Thus the model of this paper could have been Marvell's "Upon Appleton House" or even Milton's "Lycidas."

Innovation is marked by the attempt to alter the poetic techniques characteristic of a form, to suggest that the manner of conceiving a poetic relationship is no longer tenable. To put the issue in terms of the language of problem solving, the poet finds that the problems exploited by the form need reordering. This is what takes place at the opening of *Coopers Hill:*

Sure there are Poets which did never dream
Upon *Parnassus*, nor did tast the stream
Of *Helicon*, we therefore may suppose
Those made not Poets, but the Poets those,
And as Courts make not Kings, but Kings the Court,
So where the Muses & their train resort,
Parnassus stands; if I can be to thee
A Poet, thou *Parnassus* are to me.
Nor wonder, if (advantag'd in my flight,
By taking wing from thy auspicious height)
Through untrac't ways, and aery paths I fly,
More boundless in my Fancy than my eie.

(1-12)

   This literalizing of Parnassus and Helicon by converting them to the actualities of the writing of poetry—where poetry is written there Parnassus is—reveals the demythologizing procedure of the poem. It plunges at once into the denial of the conventional place of the muses and the river Helicon, by making these imaginative places in the environment of the writing of poetry. Now this alteration of a mythological to an actual place, Cooper's Hill, near Denham's childhood home, is based on a perceptual rather than an allegorical or emblematic scheme. The eye is related to the "Fancy" as the hill is related to the body. To see the prospect from Cooper's Hill, the body must climb it; the imagination is dependent upon the actual height from which it can see. The relation of Windsor Hill to Windsor Castle, of Runnymede to the Magna Charta, of the river to its banks—of the literal place to its possibilities—is defined by the kind of acts associated with it.

   This perceptual procedure is expressed in poetic techniques that are innovative in dealing with man's relation to nature in the georgic poem. For example, the introduction of the prospect view, the technique by which distance is measured by reference to selected places, becomes a way of "contracting" or diminishing space, and in doing so, provides a basis for contracting time.

My eye, which swift as thought contracts the space
That lies between, and first salutes the place
Crown'd with that sacred pile, so vast, so high,
That whether 'tis a part of Earth, or sky,
Uncertain seems, and may be thought a proud
Aspiring mountain, or descending cloud,
Pauls, the late theme of such a Muse whose flight
Has bravely reach't and soar'd above thy hight.

(13-20)

The prospect view, as it attends to a specific place, leads to meditation or historical retrospection. The poetic feature of moving from place to time takes several variant expressions. The feature can be followed by moral reflections so that place is identified with events and these are seen in eternal time. Or they can be followed by historical retrospection in which past events are seen to offer to present spectators the possibilities of the future.

The observation of external details followed by reflection formed the basis for a new kind of poetic responsiveness. Early in the eighteenth century William Wollaston wrote that reflection and thinking were the two principal methods of perception. "The more frequent or intense the acts of advertence or reflection are, the more consciousness thre is, and the stronger is the *perception.*" And he went on to relate advertence or attention to sights and events in their temporal procedures.

> ... all perceptions are produced in time: time passes by moments: there can be but one moment present at once: and therefore all present perception considerd [sic] without any relation to what is past, or future, may be lookd [sic] upon as momentaneous only. ... But in reflexion there is a repetition of what is past, and an anticipation of that which is apprehended as yet to come: there is a *connexion* of past and future, which by this are brought into the sum, and superadded to the present or momentaneous perceptions.[10]

In quoting Wollaston, I mean to suggest a third criterion for the recognition of innovation: the manner in which philosophers and critics draw attention to a new kind of consciousness analogous to that which the reading of the poem evokes. The organizing techniques of prospect view, specific place, and historical or moral reflection, operate in the poem like a survey, moving from one scene to the other, the transition being associative rather than logical. When, for example, Denham concludes the London description with an exclamation of hope for peace and contentment, he continues his survey with Windsor Hill:

> Oh happiness of sweet retir'd content!
> To be at once secure and innocent.
> *Windsor* the next (where *Mars* with *Venus* dwells,
> Beauty with strength) above the Valley swells
> Into my eye, and doth it self present
> With an easie and unforc't ascent,
> That no stupendious precipice denies
> Access, no horror turns away our eyes:

> But such a Rise, as doth at once invite
> A pleasure, and a reverence from the sight.
>   (37-46)

On the most obvious level the survey technique insists on the visible variety, but this variety is distinguishable not only through hills and plains, but also through a series of repttitions of hills: Cooper's Hill, Windsor Hill, St. Anne's Hill. The latter become a basis for the contradictory possibilities of man's use of nature, the physical variety being analogically seen in terms of regal possibilities. The function of repetitive similarity and contrasting variety is to insist on a perceptual relationship which didactically forces the reader to choose among the possibilities. The manner in which this persuasion operates is to suggest an underlying absolute which is the true binding power of God.

The perceptual survey presupposes a journey—visual and imaginative. It is a journey which the poet announces as innovative: "Through untrac't ways, and aery paths I fly, / More boundless in my Fancy than my eie" (11-12). This relation between the speaker's eye and his imagination, in which the latter is "more boundless" than the former, nevertheless is tied to the bounds of Cooper's Hill. When his fixed thoughts settle on the heroic kings of Windsor Castle, his "wandring eye" betrays his thoughts, and he observes the ruins caused by Henry VIII's tyrannical behavior. The desire to rest on moral wonder and praise in counteracted by the need to examine the contrary actualities that have also left their visible traces. The contrary forces that have tugged at the speaker, the need for memory to be stimulated, not lulled, demand the continuity and variety of the journey. As Denham wrote in *The Progress of Learning*, the expulsion of Adam had to be remembered, if the offense was not to be forgotten. Memory arose out of disobedience:

> Had Memory been lost with Innocence,
> We had not known the Sentence nor th' Offence:
> 'Twas his chief Punishment to keep in store
> The sad remembrance what he was before.
>   (7-10)

The journey remains, in Denham, unfinished, and it is a reflection of the kind of anxieties that confront the reader. The innovative quality is not the journey, but the perceptual features of the journey which thrust political and moral implications upon the reader. If one compares the ending of the 1642 version with those of the 1655-1668 versions, the dependence upon the reader as participant becomes clear.

The first version insists on the need for restraint on the part of king and subject and urges the need to submit to restraint or law. But after the death of Charles I, this inner law was no longer an injunction that could persuade subjects or king to act with control, and the conclusion is the image of a river rampant. This image which was originally followed by an injunction for king and subjects to restrain themselves, now concludes the poem.

> No longer then within his banks he dwells,
> First to a Torrent, then a Deluge swells:
> Stronger, and fiercer by restraint he roars,
> And knows no bound, but makes his power his shores.
>
> (see p. 300, above)

Thus the revised poem concludes more anxiously open-ended than the earlier version, the didactic persuasion being superseded by the frightening deluge and its moral implications.

These innovative strategies of poetical organization have their sources in the naturalizing of mythology and allegory, and, in doing so, they suggest the secret power, the "law," the underlying but unknown force that God exercises in governing the world. That "nature" which makes possible the order in variety, which man must seek in himself if the is not to be governed by excess, is a concept that Denham introduced in other works as well. In *The Progress of Learning* (1688) Denham wrote that the necessary purpose of knowledge is to flow back to God, for then it is always under proper control.

> To Learning which from Reasons Fountain springs,
> Back to the sourse, some secret Channel brings.
> 'Tis happy when our Streams of Knowledge flow
> To fill their banks, but not to overthrow.
>
> (221-24)

The river image had occurred not merely at the conclusion of *Coopers Hill* but in the London section where the "secret vein" led only to continued loss:

> While luxury, and wealth, like war and peace,
> Are each the others ruine, and increase;
> As Rivers lost in Seas some secret vein
> Thence reconveighs, there to be lost again.
>
> (33-36)

The contrast between secret veins or channels that lead to God and those that lead to chaos reinforces the technique of alternatives. The surface scenes that reveal contradictions can be reconciled by underlying beliefs, for the variety and contrast have their source in and a commitment to God whose work they are.

These innovative features are reworkings of procedures found in Virgil's *Georgics* and in the poetry of Denham's predecessors and contemporaries. Since I have already mentioned Jonson and Waller, I wish to turn to Denham's use of the *Georgics,* the four model didactic poems in which political sentiments are either directly expressed or expounded in myths or allegories. In them political or moral sentiments do not arise from the perception or survey of nature. They arise, rather, in man's attempt to work with nature—to plant, to grow vines, tend crops, keep bees: acts of living that require man to manage nature; and although he succeeds at times as he performs these acts, he also fails when nature resists his control or his management. Thus in the *Georgics* the husbandmen seek to fulfill nature's possibilities; Denham's speaker recognizes that nature's contraries are reconciliable by God's unknown law. The perceptual pattern of the contraries involves the imaginative journey—a journey that in its variants can become the pilgrim's progress, spiritual journey, or the experiential journey—but no such journey defines the *Georgics.*

The speaker's perception of place in *Coopers Hill* provided a moving version of the environment; the river and the secret channels are part of the conception of a world in motion. Places call forth the events associated with them because the present is confronted with alternatives met previously in the past. Virgil dealt with the contrary forces of nature by seeing them in the present or by offering them as myths. His view is based on beliefs or myths as teaching: Denham's on the substitution of history for myths, or remembered knowledge. For Virgil, moreover, the *Georgics* was the second venture in treating man and nature. The first, his *Eclogues,* dealt with nature as the environment for celebration, mourning, competitive play, self-derision, and misfortune.

Virgil, therefore, has a range of relations that are missing from Denham's poem; his eclogues are to his georgics as play or ceremony is to work and effort. But at the time of Denham's innovative experimentation, this Virgilian order no longer existed. The two forms have a different kinship to one another. I have indicated some of the transformations in the georgic renewal —the perceptual view contracting space and time, the naturalizing of man as an aspect of nature, the extension of consciousness through reflection, the identification of place with the function of historical memory as a moral guide, the recognition of variety within repetitive features of nature, and the underlying force of God's creativity by which contraries move to resolution by restraint. These become aspects of a transformed didacticism; their innovative direction alters the conventions and techniques of the songs and poems that are part of the eclogue or pastoral tradition.

Contemporary critics have not alway been attentive to the fact that pastoral and georgic were different in their ends—the first a lyric and the second a didactic form. The reason for this has been the neglect of the interrelation of forms. But innovation cannot be understood by application merely to a single literary form like the georgic because forms themselves are interrelated in dealing with the varied possibilities of experience in poetry. The georgic becomes for the eighteenth century, a more important and more practiced form than the pastoral, and the manner in which this occurs reveals itself in the altered use of traditional features during the innovative period. R. S. Crane was one of the few critics who recognized the theoretical problems of such interrelations:

> From a historical point of view, the most significant shifts in literary ends are clearly those to which the historian can refer—as their necessary or probable consequences—the greatest number or variety of other changes in the kinds of materials writers chose to exploit and in the kinds of devices of construction, characterization, thought, imagery, diction, prosody, or representation they invented or revived for the purpose. Generally speaking, it may be assumed—again not as a dogma but a rough guide in interpretation—that a widespread shift on tthe part of the ablest writers from the cultivation of mimetic to the cultivation of didactic forms (such as occurred after the middle of the seventeenth century) is likely to have more far-reaching results of the kinds mentioned than a shift from serious forms to comic in drama or fiction, and that a shift of the latter sort is likely to be considerably more consequential than one involving only such formal differences. . . . [11]

Crane saw innovative changes as "more consequential" than variations. And he was correct. But he needed criteria to distinguish innovation from variations, the innovations of a Denham or Milton or Marvell from the variations of a Pope or Thomson. As part of the innovative procedures, what Crane called the change from imitative to didactic forms, the traditional pastoral form underwent alteration and finally became extremely limited in its possibilities. The innovative techniques to express the new perceptual and religious dilemmas are found not only in Denham but also in Milton's *A Masque presented in Ludlow Castle* (1634) and *Lycidas* published in 1638, four years before the initial publication of *Coopers Hill.*

Among the most important of these challenges is Milton's handling of the relation of place and figure to perception in the traditional disguise character. The Attendant Spirit and Comus both become shepherds: the problem is to distinguish virtue from vice through the disguise. The *Masque* is a journey like the perceptual journey in *Coopers Hill,* but one in which the secret forces of good both of the upper world (the Attendant Spirit) and the underworld (Sabrina) arrive to support young virtue. Both Milton and Denham turn to individual restraint and virtue as traits that help master the contrary possibilites offered by nature.

Milton's management of *Lycidas* also reveals an innovative effort to resist or transform the received conventions. His remarkable handling of gentle nature and of such destructive forces as occasioned the drowning of Edward King reveals the technique that reverberated through eighteenth-century georgic poems. The lowest of forms became capable of articulating the highest insights; it led to the abandonment of the pastoral as a form of play describing actual situations. Instead, it was reserved for the idealized play of the Golden Age or for satiric treatment of shepherds and their pursuits. The actualities of pastoral became part of the reformed georgic.

III

To summarize, I have been arguing that the study of literature inevitably involves the study of literary change, and that there can be no analysis of change without some theory of a type or norm and its transformation. The changes within a norm I have identified as variations, changes of a norm as innovations.

Innovations have as their criteria (1) the altered functions of literary conventions, themes, characters, language, and imagery to express new conceptions; (2) the retrospective grouping of poems in a single class by subsequent critics; (3) the analogous exploration by philosophers and critics of the kind of consciousness the new poetry is expressing; and, finally, the altered relation of other forms to the innovative ones. This last criterion is a result of the reshifted interrelation of forms. For example, the pastoral is accepted as a traditional lyric form in the Renaissance whereas the georgic has a very uncertain status. But by the end of the eighteenth century, critics provide an interpretation of pastoral that reduces its classical importance to idealized emptiness. The georgic becomes the more practiced form, the one for which important themes and subjects are reserved.

Having presented the arguments for innovative techniques and how they function, having followed these by examples of the altered hierarchies of forms, I wish to conclude by exploring the extra-literary areas in which poetic innovation takes place. In the seventeenth century, innovative changes in the political, religious, and scientific structure of existing institutions were taking place simultaneously with those in poetry. Thomas Kuhn in his discussion of the changes in science at this time points out that there are norms for scientific problem-solving and that the norms or paradigms change as a result of "the persistent failures of the puzzles of normal science to come out as they should."[12] Such failures result in anxiety and insecurity among scientists and lead to periods of "crisis." Robert Nisbet, in discussing sociological change, writes:

> A given way of behaving tends to persist as long as circumstances permit. Then, as [W. I.] Thomas points out, the way of behaving ceases to be possible, as the result of some intrusion, some difficulty which is the consequence of event or impact, and a period of crises ensues . . . .
>
> It is impossible for me to think of any empirical study of change in contemporary social science—change of political, economic, ethnic, rural, urban, or other type of social behavior—in which the element that Thomas called crisis is not clearly present . . . .[13]

The innovative poems I have been discussing have as one of their major themes the resolution of anxiety. The voyage in the *Masque* is fraught with danger, the Lady is subject to temptations, and the brothers almost neglect to free their sister. *Lycidas* develops its theme by the shepherd-singer referring to himself as plucking the unripe berries, as being compelled to an act that analogically is like the untimely drowning of Edward King. And the shepherd's lament is a series of questions about responsibility for death, about the aim of life or the role of poetry in life, about man's faith and its rewards—questions that suggest the immensity of the anxiety and crisis that the singer is himself undergoing. The anxiety characteristic of *Coopers Hill* is locatable in the imagery of contraries and in the recognition that man's relation to nature depends on his exercise of restraint and his willingness to fulfill its possibilities.

The sense of crisis is apparent in the organization of these poems as well as in some of their rhetorical features. Consider the use of the fictive narrative of the stag hunt and its contrast with the perceptual and didactic responses to the surrounding environment in *Coopers Hill.*

There is a shift in the poem from an observing and commenting speaker addressing the reader to a speaker who sympathizes with and tells a story from the point of view of the hunted stag.

> And as a Hero, whom his baser foes
> In troops surround, now these assails, now those,
> Though prodigal of life, disdains to die
> By common hands; but if he can descry
> Some nobler foes approach, to him he calls,
> And begs his Fate, and then contented falls.
> (313-18)

The narrative heightens the didactic statements by creating the example of the animal willing to submit to his killing by the king. The procedure is that of a moralized tale and it becomes a model for the sentimentalizing of situations, even though in later eighteenth-century writers the sentimentalizing of animals is achieved by opposing killing rather than by showing the animals' readiness to die.

The mixture of narrative and precepts serves, also, to point up the distinction between an imitated action and one spoken in the poet's voice. The precepts and the historical references to persons, places and events function in terms of statement and example. The poems for which *Coopers Hill* becomes a model have, therefore, two related kinds of truth value which support or undermine one another. The crisis situation becomes, in the variants, a subordinate element. The crisis arose from the clash between the possibilities and the actualities of nature, from the relation between the possibilities and the actualities of perception. The variants pursue this by presenting the conflict as burlesque or grotesque, as sentimental or pietistic.

The religious controversies do not need to be documented by me; they are well known to you. But it is, perhaps, useful to draw attention to the literary techniques derivable from the new merger of religion and science.

Using the 1646 essay by John Wilkins, "A Discourse concerning the Beauty of Providence," as a representative text, we can see that certain poetic features are consistent with and, indeed, can be derived from religious arguments. Wilkins declared that God's presence was available not merely through revelation, but through man's contemplation of the objects in nature. He pointed out that "in the works of *Nature*, where there are many common things of excellent beauty, which for their *littlenesse* do not fall under our sence: they that have experimented the use of *Microscopes*, can tell, how in the parts of the most minute creatures, there may be discerned such gildings and embroideries, and such curious varietie as another would scarce beleive [*sic*]."[14] This argument finds poetic expression in the techniques that point to the different aspects of the same objects—variation in repetition—and similar aspects of different objects. This procedure becomes, in poems that do not deal with nature, an example of Augustan wit and subtle discrimination. The observations of Wilkins provide an explanation for the gradual inclusion, in subsequent variations of georgic poems, of ordinary domestic objects that come to be part of the catalogs and the inclusive harmonies.

His argument, indeed, urged a scientific basis for classifying objects in nature, and it helps to explain the use of scientific terminology and classification in this poetry. It indicated, too, the evident limitation of man's ability to see all of nature's possibilities, thus reinforcing the techniques of limitation which form one of the key themes of this poetry. It insisted on the pattern of contemplation following upon observation, emphasizing that opposites such as insects smaller than the eye could see and the "aweful" heavens above revealed the immensity of God's variety and his bounty, benevolence and power. And because God's power operated in such diverse objects, there was present the justification of a metonymic language in which references to the whole, like nature, could refer to particular objects and situations.

Since I have been arguing that the crises that cause innovative procedures in poetry have parallels in the crises in society, the attempt to establish priority or to argue in terms of causality from one to the other is inappropriate. Rather, my argument is that the crises in poetry and society reinforce one another.

Thus the crisis in poetry leads poets like Denham and Milton to express contemporary experience in innovations that go beyond the received conventions: new problems call forth new techniques. Denham sought to convert direct praise of political action into indirect persuasion. His resolution involved the perception of nature as necessarily political and moral. Milton sought to convert pagan conventions by transforming them into preludes of Christian resurrection. Both poets in rejecting the classical solutions for pastoral and georgic were seeking to extend the bounds of poetical experience. The perceptual view of nature, and all the techniques this entailed, provided a basis for resolving this problem by offering God's nature as a model for resolving opposites.

The techniques and methods I have discussed must be seen as returning to the classics—especially Virgil and Horace—to select such features as the retreat passages, the fortunate husbandman, and the raging river in order to support views reinterpreting these phenomena. For instead of showing the contrasting forces as examples of nature's or of fate's action, they suggest that the opposites were part of God's larger harmony, thus making possible the excusing or transmuting of what appeared like unresolvable contrarieties.

In this respect, therefore, the literary historians of the late seventeenth and eighteenth centuries have failed to understand what the return to the classics meant for these poets, assuming that they were seeking to identify themselves with the classical writers. But the nature of their poetry was to break with the variant procedures and seek innovative explanations. The turn to certain aspects of classical poetry was to provide a norm against which to innovate. Literary historians who wish to place the classical tradition in "context" require a theory of change, of variation and innovation if "context" is to have validity as an interpretative principle.

I have undertaken in this essay to explore some of the problems of change in terms of variation and innovation. I have argued that to distinguish between the norm of variation and the rejection of this norm is to provide a basis for divisions in literary history. Such divisions are not only necessary for giving order to history, but for interpreting individual poems within this order. If my aim has been achieved, then I have succeeded in proposing more adequate ways of writing literary history and the interpretations that help define it.

NOTES

1 *Lives of the English Poets*, ed. G. B. Hill (London, 1905), I, 77.
2 "Remarks upon Mr. Pope's Translation of Homer" (1717), *The Critical Works of John Dennis*, ed. E. N. Hooker (Baltimore, 1945), II, 137.
3 See "Introduction to *The Forrest*," *The Complete Poetry of Ben Jon-son*, ed. W. B. Hunter, Jr. (New York, 1963), p. 75; M. H. Abrams, "Structure and Style in the Greater Romantic Lyric," *Romanticism and Consciousness*, ed. H. Bloom (New York, 1970), pp. 207-13; H. E. Toliver, *Pastoral Forms and Attitudes* (Berkeley, 1971), p. 212.
4 All quotations from *Coopers Hill* are from the 1668 edition of the poem (unless otherwise specified) in *Expans'd Hieroglyphicks*, ed. Brendan O'Hehir (Berkeley, 1969). Other poems by Denham are quoted from *The Poetical Works of Sir John Denham*, ed. T. H. Banks (New Haven, 1928).
5 *Virgil*, trans. H. Rushton Fairclough (London, 1932), p. 103.
6 "The Eclogue Tradition and the Nature of Pastoral," *College English* 34 (1972), 352-71.
7 Hunter, ed., *Jonson*, pp. 77-78.
8 Dryden is quoted in Banks, p. 29; for Johnson see *Lives*, I, 78-79.
9 "Apollo's Edict," *The Poems of Jonathan Swift*, ed. H. Williams (Oxford, 1958), I, 271.
10 *The Religion of Nature Delineated* (London, 1726), p. 32.
11 *Critical and Historical Principles of Literary History* (Chicago, 1971), p. 41.
12 *The Structure of Scientific Revolutions* (Chicago, 1970), p. 68.
13 *Social Change and History* (New York, 1969), pp. 282-83.
14 London, 1649, pp. 49-50.

Executive Board, 1974-1975

Institutional Members

of the American Society

for Eighteenth-Century Studies

Alfred University
Bryn Mawr College
Butler University
University of California, Berkeley
University of California, Davis
University of California, Irvine
University of California, Los Angeles
University of California, Riverside
Case Western Reserve University
Catholic University of America
University of Cincinnati
City College, CUNY
Claremont Graduate School
Cleveland State University
University of Colorado, Denver Center
University of Connecticut
University of Delaware
University of Denver
Detroit Institute of Arts, Founders' Society
Emory University
Fordham University
University of Georgia
Georgia Institute of Technology
Georgia State University
University of Hawaii
University of Illinois, Chicago Circle
University of Illinois, Urbana
University of Iowa
The John Hopkins University
Kent State University
University of Kentucky
Lehigh University

Lehman College, CUNY
The Lewis Walpole Library
University of Maryland
University of Massachusetts, Boston
McMaster University/ Association for
    18th Century Studies
University of Michigan, Ann Arbor
Michigan State University
Middle Tennessee State University
The Minneapolis Institute of Fine Arts
University of Minnesota
State University of New York, Binghamton
State University of New York, Fredonia
State University of New York, Oswego
University of North Carolina, Chapel
    Hill
North Georgia College
Northern Illinois University
Northwestern University
Ohio State University
University of Pennsylvania
University of Pittsburgh
Princeton University
Purdue University
Rice University
Rockford College
Rollins College
Smith College
University of South Carolina
University of Southern California
Southern Illinois University
Stanford University

Swarthmore College
Sweet Briar College
Temple University
Tulane University
University of Victoria
University of Virginia
Virginia Commonwealth University
Washington University
Washington and Lee University
Washington State University

Wayne State University
West Chester State College,
    Pennsylvania
University of Western Ontario
The Henry Francis du Pont
    Winterthur Museum
University of Wisconsin, Madison
The Yale Center for British Art and
    British Studies
Yale University

Index